FACING INVASION:
PROCEEDINGS UNDER THE DEFENCE ACTS 1801-1805

Charles Lennox 3rd Duke of Lennox and Richmond
Lord Lieutenant of Sussex 1763-1806

FACING INVASION:
PROCEEDINGS UNDER THE DEFENCE
ACTS 1801-1805

EDITED BY ROGER PEARCE

SUSSEX RECORD SOCIETY
VOLUME 99

Issued to members of the Society for the year 2017

Published 2019 by
Sussex Record Society
Barbican House
High Street
Lewes
East Sussex BN7 1YE

© Sussex Record Society, Roger Pearce
ISBN 978 0 85445 081 7

Printed by Hobbs the Printers Ltd., Totton, Hampshire

VOLUMES ISSUED BY THE SUSSEX RECORD SOCIETY

Vol. 1	Marriage Licences at Lewes, 1586-1642
Vol. 2	Sussex Fines, 1190-1248
Vol. 3	Post Mortem Inquisitions, 1558-1583
Vol. 4	Ecclesiastical Returns for East Sussex, 1603; Sussex Poll Book, 1705; Sussex MSS in the Harleian MSS; Bishop Praty's Register, 1438-1445.
Vol. 5	West Sussex Protestation Returns, 1641-1642
Vol. 6	Marriage Licences at Lewes, 1670-1732
Vol. 7	Sussex Fines, 1249-1307
Vol. 8	Bishop Rede's Register, 1397-1415 (Pt. 1)
Vol. 9	Marriage Licences at Chichester 1575-1730
Vol. 10	Subsidy Rolls, 1296, 1327 and 1332
Vol. 11	Bishop Rede's Register, 1397-1415 (Pt. 2)
Vol. 12	Marriage Licences at Chichester (peculiars), 1579-1730
Vol. 13	Cuckfield Parish Register, 1598-1699
Vol. 14	Post Mortem Inquisitions, 1485-1649
Vol. 15	Bolney Parish Register, 1541-1812
Vol. 16	Star Chamber Proceedings, 1500-1558
* Vol. 17	Ardingly Parish Register, 1558-1812
* Vol. 18	Angmering Parish Register, 1562-1687
Vol. 19	Sussex Manors and Advowsons, etc., 1509-1833, A-L
Vol. 20	Sussex Manors and Advowsons, etc., 1509-1833, M-Z
Vol. 21	Horsham Parish Register, 1541-1635
Vol. 22	Cowfold Parish Register, 1558-1812
* Vol. 23	Sussex Fines, 1308-1509
Vol. 24	East Grinstead Parish Register, 1558-1661
Vol. 25	Marriage Licences at Lewes, 1771-1837, A-L
Vol. 26	Marriage Licences at Lewes, 1772-1837, M-Z
Vol. 27	Preston Manor Court Rolls, 1562-1702
Vol. 28	Sussex Apprentices and Masters, 1710-1752
Vol. 29	Abstracts of Documents relating to the Dobell family, 16th-18th cents.
Vol. 30	Glynde Parish Register, 1558-1812
Vol. 31	Custumals of the Sussex Manors of the Bishop of Chichester, c.1256-1374
Vol. 32	Sussex Marriage Licences at Chichester, 1731-1774
Vol. 33	Sussex Inquisitions (from Bodleian Library), 1541-1616
Vol. 34	The Book of John Rowe, Steward to Lord Bergavenny, 1622
Vol. 35	Marriage Licences at Chichester, 1775-1800, with Index 1731-1800
Vol. 36	Sussex Chantry Records, 1535-1652
Vol. 37	Hastings Rape Records, 1387-1474
Vol. 38	Chartulary of Lewes Priory (Pt. I), 11th-14th cents.
* Vol. 39	The Buckhurst Terrier, 1597-1598

Vol. 40   *Chartulary of Lewes Priory (Pt. II), 12th-14th cents.*
Vol. 41   *Transcripts of Sussex Wills up to 1560 Vol.1 Albourne - Chichester*
Vol. 42   *Transcripts of Sussex Wills up to 1560 Vol.2 Chiddingly - Horsham*
Vol. 43   *Transcripts of Sussex Wills up to 1560 Vol.3 Horsted Keynes - Pyecombe*
Vol. 44   *Records of the Barony and Honour of the Rape of Lewes, 1265-1466*
Vol. 45   *Transcripts of Sussex Wills up to 1560 Vol.4 Racton - Yapton*
Vol. 46   *Chichester Cathedral Chartulary, 13th-16th cents.*
Vol. 47   *Survey of Robertsbridge Manor, 1567-1570*
Vol. 48   *The Town Book of Lewes, 1542-1701*
Vol. 49   *Churchwardens' Presentments, (Pt. I), Archdeaconry of Chichester, 1621-28, 1664-70*
Vol. 50   *Churchwardens' Presentments, (Pt. II), Archdeaconry of Lewes, 1674-1677*
Vol. 51   *Record of Deputations of Gamekeepers, 1781-1928*

Jubilee Volume *Sussex Views from the Burrell Collection*

Vol. 52   *Chapter Acts, Chichester, 1472-1544 (The White Act Book)*
Vol. 53   *The Manor of Etchingham cum Salehurst, 1597-1865*
Vol. 54   *Quarter Sessions Order Book, 1642-1649*
Vol. 55   *Ministers' Accounts of the Manor of Petworth, 1347-1353*
Vol. 56   *Lay Subsidy Rolls, 1524-1525*
Vol. 57   *Custumals of Sussex Manors of the Archbishop of Canterbury, 1285-1330*
Vol. 58   *Chapter Acts, Chichester, 1545-1642*
Vol. 59   *Chartulary of Boxgrove Priory, 12th-14th cents.*
Vol. 60   *Custumals of the Manors of Laughton, Willingdon and Goring, 1292-1338*
Vol. 61   *A Catalogue of Sussex Estate and Tithe Award Maps (Pt. l), 1606-1884*
Vol. 62   *Minutes of the Common Council of the City of Chichester, 1783-1826*
Vol. 63   *The Book of Bartholomew Bolney, 15th cent.*
Vol. 64   *Rye Shipping Records, 1566-1590*
Vol. 65   *Cellarers' Rolls of Battle Abbey, 1275-1513*
Vol. 66   *A Catalogue of Sussex Maps, (Pt. II) 1597-1958*
Vol. 67   *Estate Surveys of the Fitzalan Earls of Arundel, 14th cent.*
Vol. 68   *The Journal of Giles Moore of Horsted Keynes, 1655-1679*
Vol. 69   *The Town Book of Lewes, 1702-1837*
Vol. 70   *The Town Book of Lewes, 1837-1901*
* Vol. 71 *Accounts of the Roberts Family of Boarzell, 1568-1582*
Vol. 72   *Printed Maps of Sussex, 1575-1900*
* Vol. 73 *Correspondence of the Dukes of Richmond and Newcastle, 1724-1750*
Vol. 74   *Sussex Coroners' Inquests, 1485-1558*
* Vol. 75 *The Religious Census of Sussex, 1851*
Vol. 76   *The Fuller Letters, 1728-1755*
Vol. 77   *East Sussex Land Tax, 1785*

* Vol. 78   *Chichester Diocesan Surveys, 1686 and 1724*
* Vol. 79   *Saint Richard of Chichester*
  Vol. 80   *The Ashdown Forest Dispute, 1876-1882*
  Vol. 81   *Sussex Schools in the 18th century*
* Vol. 82   *West Sussex Land Tax, 1785*
  Vol. 83   *Mid Sussex Poor Law Records, 1601-1835*
* Vol. 84   *Sussex in the First World War*
  Vol. 85   *Sussex Depicted: Views and Descriptions 1600-1800*
* Vol. 86   *Sussex Shore to Flanders Fields: Edward Heron–Allen's Journal of the Great War*
* Vol. 87   *East Sussex Parliamentary Deposited Plans, 1799-1970*
  Vol. 88   *Sussex Cricket in the 18th century*
* Vol. 89   *East Sussex Coroners' Records, 1688-1838*
* Vol. 90   *The Durford Cartulary*
* Vol. 91   *Sussex Clergy Inventories, 1600-1750*
* Vol. 92   *Accounts and Records of the Manor of Mote in Iden, 1461-1551, 1673*
* Vol. 93   *East Sussex Church Monuments, 1530-1830*
* Vol. 94   *Winchelsea Poor Law Records, 1790-1841*
* Vol. 95   *Littlehampton School Logbook, 1871-1911*
* Vol. 96   *Letters of John Collier of Hastings, 1731-1746*
* Vol. 97   *Chichester Archdeaconry Depositions, 1603-1608*
* Vol. 98   *Church Surveys of Chichester Archdeaconry, 1602, 1610 & 1636*
* Vol. 99   *Facing Invasion: Proceedings Under the Defence Acts 1801-05*

In print volumes marked with an asterisk can be obtained from the Sussex Record Society, Barbican House, Lewes, East Sussex, BN7 1YE or through the Society's website: www.sussexrecordsociety.org

CONTENTS

Acknowledgements xi
List of Illustrations xiii
Prologue xv
Introduction xvii
    Revolution xvii
    Sources and returns xix
    Civil Defence and the Armed Forces xxi
    The Defence Acts 1798 and 1803 xxviii
    Census and Surveys xxxi
    Feeding the People xxxii
    The 3rd Duke of Richmond, Lord Lieutenant xxxvi
    Driving the Country xxxix
    Deliberations xl
    Conclusions xliv
Biographical Notes xlix
Bibliography lxi
Editorial Policies lxvii

PROCEEDINGS UNDER THE DEFENCE ACTS 1

Appendix 1: Bibliographic Analysis of the Sources 351
Appendix 2: A Nation under Arms: Selected Acts of Parliament 1798-1806 355
Appendix 3: 38 George III Cap 27 5 April 1798 [The Defence Act 1798] 361
Appendix 4: 43 George III Cap 55 11 June 1803 [The Defence Act 1803] 371
Appendix 5: Extracts from correspondence between the Duke of Richmond, William
    Ellis and Lt Col Powlett, Inspecting Field Officer 381
Appendix 6: Extract from a Letter from the Duke of Richmond to Lord Hobart,
    Secretary of State for War and the Colonies, 14 August 1801 385
Appendix 7: Letter from the Duke of Richmond to Lord Bolton, Lord Lieutenant
    of Hampshire, 29 August 1801 387
Appendix 8: Circular Letter from Lord Hawkesbury to Lords Lieutenant
    31 December 1805 389
Index of Persons 391
Index of Parishes and Places 407

ACKNOWLEDGEMENTS

My thanks are due initially to Wendy Walker and Peter Wilkinson, Chairman and Vice-President of the Sussex Record Society (SRS); and respectively County Archivist and former Deputy County Archivist of West Sussex. Wendy and Peter first responded to my interest in contributing to the work of the Society. Wendy steered me towards taking a greater role, and Peter encouraged my involvement in a number of Society volumes, including his own Volume 97 of Chichester Archdeaconry Depositions. Most important, Peter guided me towards editing this volume of Proceedings under the Defence Acts, with the aid of a rather tired photocopy of one of its pages.

Other colleagues on the Council of the Society have lent encouragement in different ways, in particular Andrew Foster and Danae Tankard, who have each very helpfully read and commented on earlier drafts; Andrew also drew my attention to the form of daily prayer introduced in 1803 in the face of imminent invasion. Professor Brian Short, President of the Society, made a number of helpful suggestions, particularly in relation to agricultural returns.

The records edited here are contained in two volumes in the custody of the East Sussex Record Office (ESRO) at The Keep. Christopher Whittick, former County Archivist of East Sussex, has been very supportive of this venture, and gave formal permission for publication; he also read an earlier draft and made a number of helpful suggestions and corrections. Chris also arranged for the second of the two volumes to be paginated and digitised. The SRS made a financial contribution to this, which I am also pleased to acknowledge.

I am grateful to the staff of ESRO, the West Sussex Record Office and the Hampshire Record Office for their help. Hampshire Library Services in Aldershot arranged for a volume to be transferred to Winchester, so that I could review it there while Aldershot Library was being refurbished. The University of Sussex library allowed me temporary access to their online resources; and the University of Reading library allowed me to visit and review a particularly elusive volume.

Copyright acknowledgements for the illustrations are given in the list of illustrations. Every effort has been made to trace and credit copyright. On the rare occasions where images are believed to be in the public domain, this has been noted; but corrections will be willingly received and, where appropriate, will be noted on the Society's website.

LIST OF ILLUSTRATIONS

Frontispiece

Charles Lennox, 3rd Duke of Richmond and Lennox, by George Romney; oil on canvas, 1776-1777; NPG 4877.

Plates

1 Storming of the Bastille, 14 July 1789, unknown artist; Musee Carnavalet, Paris, P248.
2 Charles Philip Yorke, Wimpole Hall, The Bambridge Collection; © National Trust, Image reference 1013014.
3 Francis Newbery, style of Thomas Gainsborough; Bradley Manor, The Woolner Collection, © National Trust, Image reference 986611.
4 Thomas Malthus by John Linnell, mezzotint, published 1 January 1834 (1833); NPG D38173.
5 Edmund Burke, studio of Sir Joshua Reynolds, oil on canvas, circa 1769 or after; NPG 655.
6 John Rickman by Samuel Bellin, after Samuel Lane (circa 1831), mezzotint, published 4 December 1843; NPG D19805.
7 Arthur Young by John Russell, pastel, 1794; NPG 6253.
8 Charles Goring, J.S.C. Schaak's depiction of Charles Goring of Wiston, circa 1765; reproduced by permission of the Goring family.
9 Charles Lennox, 4th Duke of Richmond and Lennox KG, 1823, by Henry Collen (1797-1879), after Henry Hoppner Meyer; (public domain).
10 Sir Charles Merrik Burrell by Joseph John Jenkins, after Ramsay Richard Reinagle, stipple engraving, 1810; NPG D32448.
11 George O'Brien Wyndham, 3rd Earl of Egremont, by John Samuel Agar, published by T. Cadell & W. Davies, after John Wright, after Thomas Phillips, stipple engraving, published 16 April 1810; NPG D36129.

Bramber Rape Schedule No 1 1801 cf. pp. 90-91.
Bramber Rape Schedule No 2 1801 cf. pp. 94-95.

12 Inigo Freeman Thomas by Thomas Goff Lupton, after Henry Perronet Briggs, mezzotint, 1840; NPG D4040.
13 Gen. Sir James Murray Pulteney, National Galleries of Scotland PG 638; unknown artist; licensed Creative Commons - CC by NC.
14 John Baker Holroyd, Earl of Sheffield, by and published by John Jones, after Sir Joshua Reynolds, stipple engraving, published 6 April 1789 (1788); NPG D19889.
15 John ('Mad Jack') Fuller, by and published by Charles Turner, after Henry Singleton, mezzotint, published 18 July 1808; NPG D14588.

16 Sir George Shiffner: *www.shiffner.net*.
17 Sir Timothy Shelley, by George Romney; from Roger Ingpen, *Shelley in England: New Facts and Letters*, from the Shelley-Whitton Press, 1917, public domain.
18 Thomas Davis Lamb, Oil on canvas, by Arthur William Devis 1797; National Army Museum Study Collection,
NAM Accession Number 2002-06-81-1,
Courtesy of the Council of the National Army Museum.
19 Thomas Pelham, Earl of Chichester, by and published by Samuel William Reynolds, after John Hoppner, mezzotint, published 17 June 1802; NPG D1409.
20 William Stephen Poyntz, by William Egley, after Legay; by permission the Burghley House Collection, Ref: MIN0097.
21 Gen. Sir David Dundas, coloured etching by and after Robert Dighton Snr, published by Robert Dighton Snr, London, April 1810; National Army Museum, NAM Accession Number 1964-12-139-14-1,
Courtesy of the Council of the National Army Museum.
22 Charles James Fox, by Karl Anton Hickel, oil on canvas 1794; NPG 743.
23 William Pitt the Younger, by Gainsborough Dupont, c1787, oil on canvas; public domain.
24 Charles Abbot, Baron Colchester, by John Hoppner, oil on canvas c1802; NPG 1416.
25 Sir John Leach, by Henry Edward Dawe, after Charles Penny, mezzotint, published 1825; NPG D3548.
26 Thomas Partington, by James Henry Hurdis, line engraving 1841; NPG D39559.
27 William Frankland, by Mather Brown, 1788-90; public domain.
28 Sir Henry Dundas, replica by Sir Thomas Lawrence, oil on canvas, c 1810; NPG 746.
29 Henry Addington, by Sir William Beechey, oil on canvas, engraved 1803; NPG 5774.
30 Armed Heroes, (Gillray 1803): Hawkesbury and Addington confronting Napoleon; NPG D12810.

Images © National Portrait Gallery (NPG) are licensed under Creative Commons Licenses.

Additional illustrations

Images of pages from the source documents on pp. 102, 153, 231 and 247 are used by permission of the East Sussex Record Office.

PROLOGUE

1797

'Our navy may become the sport of tempests, our regular troops may be defeated, but England can never be overrun; for every man that has a horse is in a corps of cavalry, and her infantry is as numerous as her property is diffused.'[1]

1803

'You must immediately choose which you would have: a Corsican master, with rapes, pillage, confiscations, imprisonments, tortures and scornful slavery, or George III with Old England, proud Freedom and Prosperity.'[2]

1803

His Majesty [George III] was ... pleased to deliver the following most gracious speech from the throne:

'My Lords and Gentlemen,
Since I last met you in Parliament, it has been my chief object to carry into effect those measures which your wisdom had adopted for the defence of the United Kingdom, and for the vigorous prosecution of the war. In these preparations I have been seconded by the voluntary exertions of all ranks of my people, in a manner that, has, if possible, strengthened their claims to my confidence and affection: they have proved that the menaces of the enemy have only served to rouse their native and hereditary spirit; and that all other considerations are lost in a general disposition to make those efforts and sacrifices which the honour and safety of the Kingdom demand at this important and critical conjuncture.'[3]

---

[1] Young (1797); Aspinall and Smith (1959): 887.
[2] *Strike or Die: Alfred's First Letter to the Good People of England,* Davey (2017): 47.
[3] House of Lords Hansard, 22 November 1803.

INTRODUCTION:
PROCEEDINGS UNDER THE DEFENCE ACTS

Revolution

14 July 1789 dawned cloudy and overcast in Paris. It was warm – about 61°F (16°C) at 7.00 am – but there was rain in the air.[4] It was a Tuesday, theoretically a normal working day, but the city was in a state of suppressed uproar, and angry groups of people were crowding the narrow streets.

At that time, the city was perhaps a twentieth of its present size, with a population of around 650,000. Many of them were hungry, and chronically malnourished. A poor harvest the previous autumn had led to famine conditions across France. The winter of 1788 to 1789 had been one of the harshest on record. Food riots broke out across the country in the spring.[5] By mid-July, Paris was in a state of virtual insurrection.

On the morning of the 14th, a mob broke into the Hôtel des Invalides to seize the stock of muskets and cannon stored there. But there was no ammunition: the commandant had earlier removed some 250 barrels of gunpowder for safety to the fortress of the Bastille prison on the opposite bank of the Seine. In the afternoon, the crowd gathered outside the prison, demanding the surrender of the command and the release of the powder and weapons. Shots were fired and fierce fighting broke out. Faced with overwhelming odds, and with limited food and water, the Governor concluded – perhaps prematurely – that he could not defend the fortress. The gates to the Bastille were thrown open to the insurgents a little after 17.00.[6]

In practical terms, the immediate consequences of the storming of the Bastille were limited. The prison reportedly contained only seven inmates: 'four forgers, two lunatics, and a dissipated young noble'.[7] 'The episode was a striking one, but the actual events have been greatly exaggerated by the romantic historians of the nineteenth century'.[8] But it was the symbolic trigger for a disaster which plunged much of Europe into war and bloodshed which lasted for a generation.

---

[4] Ludlum (1989): 141-42.
[5] Neumann and Dettwiller (1990): 37.
[6] Schama (1989): 403.
[7] Cobban (1957): 150.
[8] Ibid.

Initial reaction in Britain to the French Revolution was largely favourable. Charles James Fox saw the events as comparable to the Glorious Revolution of 1688, and famously exclaimed: 'How much the greatest event it is that ever happened in the world! and how much the best!' Fox's supporter Charles Grey, the future Prime Minister, claimed that the Revolution 'would tend to the diffusion of liberty and rational knowledge all over the world'.[9] A rare dissenting voice was that of Edmund Burke, whose celebrated *Reflections on the Revolution in France* very early, and with remarkable prescience, forecast the tragedy which was to unfold over the coming years:

> France has bought undisguised calamities ... Laws overturned; tribunals subverted; industry without vigour; commerce expiring; the revenue unpaid, yet the people impoverished; a church pillaged, and a state not relieved; civil and military anarchy made the constitution of the kingdom ... treasons, robberies, rapes, assassination, slaughters, and burnings, throughout their harassed land.[10]

The destruction of civil society wrought by the Revolution has echoes in France to the present day, for example in the legal framework which still regulates freedom of association.

As the Revolution progressed, the French armies proceeded to cause chaos and destruction across Europe. In Britain, the mood steadily darkened, and Burke's forebodings were progressively vindicated. In 1792 the British government, increasingly alarmed by events on the continent, joined forces with Prussia and Austria, Spain and the Netherlands in the First Coalition against France. But in 1797, the French armies under the command of Napoleon Bonaparte swept across the Habsburg Empire into Italy, and the First Coalition collapsed.

The peace formally created by the Treaty of Campo Formio in 1797 was clearly only going to be temporary. As hostilities recommenced in 1798, Britain began seriously to fear invasion by France. Owing to its geographical position, Sussex was in the front line in preparing to defend the nation.[11] The circumstances and nature of that defence have been studied in depth by a number of scholars, who have explored the development of the 'armed nation' in Britain;[12] the impact on politics, society and national identity;[13] the organisation of British

---

[9] Watson (1960): 362.
[10] Burke (1790); Norman (2015): 456-58.
[11] Cf. Goodwin (1985); Kitchen (1991); Leslie and Short (1999) contains maps of fortifications and defensive works along the Sussex coast.
[12] Cookson (1997).
[13] Emsley (1979).

defence, the navy and coastal fortifications;[14] the organisation and administration of the Revolutionary and Napoleonic Wars;[15] and mobilisation, defence and fortification after 1803.[16]

The focus of this edition is both more limited and more specific. Its core is a transcript of the proceedings of the Sussex Lieutenancy meetings held between 1801 and 1806 in response to government demands set out in a series of Acts of Parliament, their deliberations and – especially – the detailed information collected on the defensive capabilities of the county and its potential response in the event of invasion.

Sources and Returns

The surviving records of the Lieutenancy proceedings, together with the extensive schedules of information collected, are contained in two volumes in the East Sussex Record Office at The Keep, catalogued as
- L/C/G/3/1 : Proceedings under the Defence Acts: volume 2 or D (1801-1803)
- L/C/G/3/2 : Proceedings under the Defence Acts: volume 3 or E (1803-1806)[17]

Kenyon was clear that Volume 1 in this series was that labelled *On Lieutenancy General Defence* covering the period from 1 May 1794 to 4 August 1797, dealing with the formation and maintenance of the County Yeomanry.[18] This is now catalogued as L/C/V/1/2 in the East Sussex Record Office as: 'This volume (a thick gathering in limp covers) is numbered '1', may have been regarded at one time [sic] as preceding the two volumes of Proceedings on Internal Defence Acts which are numbered 2 and 3 (L/C/G/3/1-2)'.

The two subsequent volumes edited here record the Lieutenancy's response to two Acts of Parliament (the 'Defence Acts' of 1798 and 1803) and associated measures. They cover the period from mid-1801, beyond the 1803 Act, to early 1806. We know that there were returns collected in 1798 in response to the Defence Act of that year because the Lieutenancy Meeting of 13 August 1801 was presented with a summary of their statistics.[19]

The original 1803 returns by parish, from which the summary schedules were assembled, seem largely to have been lost. The exception is the Rape of Lewes,

---

[14] Glover (1973).
[15] Knight (2013).
[16] Philp (2006).
[17] Appendix 1 provides a detailed bibliographical description and analysis of these sources.
[18] Kenyon (1950): 57.
[19] see pp. 4 ff. below.

where it appears that the original parish returns survive, catalogued in the series L/L/D in the East Sussex Record Office. A provisional review suggests that there are valuable additional details in these records, but also some interesting inconsistencies: it appears that some details and statistics may have been 'rationalized' between collection and submission, perhaps for example to correct initial inaccuracies. These returns have never been edited, and constitute an important data source for Lewes Rape, well worthy of further study. Unfortunately, there has been no room in the present volume for a treatment of this substantial volume of records.

Nationally, the returns under the Defence Acts, and their collation into detailed schedules, are comparatively neglected and overlooked records: they have been overshadowed by the 1801 census. Colley states:

> Much less well-known [than the first census] are the detailed returns that the Defence of the Realm Act[20] of April 1798 demanded from each county: details of the number of able-bodied men in each parish, details of what service, if any, each man was prepared to offer to the state, details of what weapons he possessed, details of the amount of live-stock, carts, mills, boats, barges and grain available, details of how many elderly people there were, how many alien and infirm ... these returns supplied the British state with the most ambitious and precise taxonomy of its people compiled since the Domesday Book. These same documents, singularly neglected by historians and demographers, allow us to get behind the administrative details of civil defence, to reach the men themselves, the 'living beings in action'.[21]

How many of these records survive nationally is unknown, since there appears never to have been a systematic survey of them. An appendix in Ian Beckett's study of the Buckinghamshire *posse comitatus* of 1798 has a partial list of partial returns; but fails to include the records in the ESRO.[22] Kenyon extracted some details of crops and livestock from the ESRO returns;[23] otherwise they seem never to have been edited or studied. In a sense they represent the beginnings of modern bureaucracy, with the pressure of war driving the rapid expansion of the machinery of the state.

---

[20] The terms Defence Act and Defence of the Realm Act are used interchangeably as the short titles for these enactments.
[21] Colley (2009): 289.
[22] Beckett (1985).
[23] Kenyon (1950, 1954).

The details surveyed and recorded in the extensive schedules, parish by parish, offer close-grained insight into the condition of the county and its inhabitants in the very early 19th century. At the time, there was significant official ignorance of the numbers and distribution of the British population. The same period saw the birth of the national census, and as we shall see, there were interesting links between the proceedings recorded here and the first census in 1801. It was also a time of great concern about agricultural productivity and the nation's ability to feed itself. Against this background, developing an effective policy of defence, integrating militias, volunteers and yeomanry, was a major challenge, and one with which successive governments struggled. There was also significant political opposition to some aspects of government policy, which has important echoes in the deliberations of the Sussex Lieutenancy below.

The material presented in the returns edited here is unique in relation to Sussex: nowhere else is there equivalent information for the period. Owing to the county's crucial strategic position, the returns collected under the Defence Acts were no doubt seen as particularly important to the development of defence policy. Elsewhere, it appears that in many cases the equivalent records were not collected as assiduously or preserved as thoroughly; it seems that this edition is the first to offer a complete transcript of such material.

To understand its significance in the context of a nation fearing invasion, and engaged in wars which would last a generation, it is necessary to explore the organisation of national defence and the role played in it by the Lord Lieutenant, and the undercurrent of looming agricultural crisis which persisted throughout the period.

Civil defence and the armed forces: militias and volunteers

Responsibility for civil defence, and for raising militia, yeomanry and volunteers, historically fell to the Lords Lieutenant of counties. Today the office is almost entirely symbolic and honorary. But in the late eighteenth century the Lord Lieutenant had a vital role to play in organizing the defence of the realm. The office was originally created by Henry VIII; subsequently, the Lieutenants played a significant role under Elizabeth in the 1580s in planning to resist invasion by the Spanish Armada. After the Restoration in 1660, the role became more formalised. Lords Lieutenant were typically not simply peers of the realm, but men of extensive military experience, with wide powers of command, and with responsibility for appointment of deputies and officers. They were the prime focus of defence preparations when the country was facing invasion.

A century and a half later, the militarisation of British society during the Revolutionary and Napoleonic Wars raised a number of key issues: of organization, of command and of integration with existing militias and the regular army. But these were not novel issues. The obligation of armed service in civil defence had rested for many centuries on local militia, whose roots appear to extend far beyond the feudal period back into Anglo-Saxon times. The creation of Lords Lieutenant offered a more efficient and systematic mechanism for the recruitment of civilians to armed service; but the English Civil War destroyed the assumptions underpinning the distinction between a royal army – focused on foreign action – and militias devoted to domestic peace-keeping and security. Over the next two centuries, the fortunes of both the army and the militia fluctuated.

With the disbanding of Cromwell's New Model Army, the maintenance of a national standing army became politically unacceptable. The Bill of Rights in theory outlawed the establishment of a standing army, while permitting citizens to bear arms in their own defence. New regiments were raised individually to protect the coast and to ensure the safety of the king. The militia were brought under the formal control of the Lieutenancy as the primary guarantor of civil order. Nevertheless from the early eighteenth century it was the army, better organised and more responsive in the event of a crisis, which eventually became the primary military force, especially in action overseas;[24] by contrast, the militia faded in significance as the eighteenth century progressed.

The fortunes of the militia were revived by the threat of invasion from France during the Seven Years War (1756-63). Government financing reinforced the responsibilities of the Lords Lieutenant and their fellow peers of the realm; the Militia Acts of 1757-62 provided that officers were to be appointed by the Lieutenancy from among major landowners, and that ballots of men capable of active service, aged between 18 and 50, would be held to embody the forces under arms believed to be necessary; it was intended that the whole able-bodied male population should serve in the militia over a three-year cycle.

But the militia system had become poorly managed, and had fallen into disrepute. Balloted men were allowed to pay for substitutes to serve in their place, and a widespread trade grew up in furnishing substitutes, with the

---

[24] Although the focus remained very much on an assembly of individual regiments and companies, the term 'British Army' was formally recognised in 1707, after the union between England and Scotland; cf. Walton (1894): 16; Williams (1994): 1-2. For simplicity, the terms 'army' and 'regular army' are used here

result that only the poorest could avoid service. Nevertheless, by the time the Revolutionary Wars broke out, Sussex had joined other English (and Welsh) counties in fielding a reasonably effective and well-trained militia: the Royal Sussex Light Infantry Militia had already been raised by the Duke of Richmond in 1778 (and served until 1881); and Lord Sheffield had raised his own regiment of yeomanry cavalry, the 22nd Regiment of Light Dragoons.

Nationally, the militia were brought up to strength in the face of potential invasion. In 1795 the Quota Acts required counties to raise men both for the army and the navy.[25] The Supplementary Militia Act of 1796 called for 60,000 more men. The 1798 Militia Acts (there were nine in all)[26] aimed for 10,000 men to enlist in the militias for a £10 bounty per head. By the end of 1798, there were some 82,000 men enlisted in militias,[27] although subsequent years saw efforts to peel off militiamen to strengthen the regular army.

In parallel, the growing threat from revolutionary France fed a grass-roots movement for the formation of volunteer units to protect the nation. The Volunteer Act 1794 authorised Lords Lieutenant to raise local volunteer companies which could supplement the militia and man coastal defences. Sir Henry Dundas (later Viscount Melville), Pitt's Secretary of State for War (and the first man to hold that office), invited 'gentlemen of Weight or Property' to raise volunteer infantry and yeomanry cavalry for service locally; these were to be funded by public subscription in each county. Volunteers from the gentry typically joined the mounted units, the cavalry.

This was not only a military and defence initiative: as a political manoeuvre it 'effectively turned involvement in the measure into a public declaration of support for Pitt's ministry and its war policies.'[28] As the war developed, it became a steadily more divisive political issue:

> By the middle of the 1790s, [Britain] had become increasingly polarized between supporters of reform who sought to capitalize on popular discontent arising from the exactions and shortages caused by the war and by a series of poor harvests by mobilizing mass meetings to demand annual parliaments and universal manhood suffrage, and loyalists who used similar tactics of mobilization to secure the

---

[25] There is no evidence that the Sussex Lieutenancy gave any thought to the Navy. Pitt himself was Lord Warden of the Cinque Ports throughout this period.
[26] In total, depending on definition, more than 170 separate Acts of Parliament were passed between 1798 and 1806 concerning the conduct of war and the armed forces; see Appendix 2.
[27] Western (1965)
[28] Gee (1989): 48.

commitment to King and Constitution among the middling orders and political elite of the country.[29]

In May 1794 a meeting was held in Lewes to discuss raising volunteers; and during the next year, nine troops of Sussex Gentlemen and Yeomanry Cavalry were raised.[30] However, raising volunteers drained the pool of men available for recruitment to the regular army and the militias: volunteers served locally, and part-time; they were paid more; it was a much more attractive option than service in the militia or regular army. Service as a volunteer also granted exemption from the militia ballot. The confusion around the militia also had an adverse impact on recruitment into the regular army.

Pitt appealed again for volunteers in 1798; Dundas wrote a circular letter to Lords Lieutenant on 6 April 1798 to this effect. This was massively successful, yielding so many volunteers that managing the flow was a severe headache to the authorities: at one point Dundas attempted to restrict the acceptance of volunteers to 'respectable people'. This, and pressure of the war generally, drove efforts to refine and regularise the volunteer movement, and improve coordination of home defence policy with the militias and regular army. Eventually more than 300,000 men had been recruited to the volunteers.[31] By 1800, there were more than 200 Yeomanry troops.[32] National membership of volunteer corps reached a high point in 1804 with 380,258 men under arms.[33] However, 'the government soon resented the renewed growth of volunteering as a less than useful addition to the country's defence … The sheer size of the volunteer mass seems to have astonished all beholders'.[34]

Earlier, in May 1797, an initiative which later had far-reaching consequences saw the High Sheriff of Dorset, William Clavell, proposing to raise the *posse comitatus* in the county; this was the term given to the general mobilisation of the people for public defence or to impose civil order. As part of the preparations, returns were required of all males aged from fifteen to sixty, who were asked to provide voluntary service if they were not already engaged in a military capacity. This initiative was widely publicised. The threat of invasion dramatically enhanced the need for more accurate information, and when the

---

[29] Philp (2006): loc. 283.
[30] A troop was of indeterminate size, typically containing some dozens of men under the command of a Captain or Lieutenant.
[31] Cookson (1985, 1997).
[32] Becket (2011).
[33] Tamplin (n.d.).
[34] Cookson (1997): 69-71.

Defence Act was passed in 1798 (see below), it mandated the preparation of returns based on the Dorset format.

On 14 March 1801, Pitt resigned: he disagreed strongly with the King's opposition to Catholic emancipation following the Union with Ireland. The next three years of the war, including the initial confrontation with Napoleon, were overseen by Pitt's colleague Henry Addington (later Viscount Sidmouth), who succeeded him as Prime Minister: it is this period which provides the immediate context for the proceedings published in this volume. Addington negotiated the (temporary) peace provided by the Treaty of Amiens in 1802, and strengthened Britain's military defences with the construction of Martello Towers. But his strategic objectives remained broadly continuous with those of Pitt.

In the summer of 1801 Lord Hobart, Addington's Secretary of State for War and the Colonies, circulated the Lords Lieutenant requesting that they assemble and train the volunteer corps. On 25 July, Admiral Nelson wrote to the Admiralty stressing the importance of protecting the Sussex coast:[35] 'Whatever plans may be adopted the moment the Enemy touch our coast, be it where it may, they are to be attacked by every man afloat and on shore: this must be perfectly understood. Never fear the event.'[36]

The counties were generally reluctant to muster the volunteers. These were increasingly seen by those in authority as an inefficient means of meeting the overall military defence requirement; they were outside regular military control; and as volunteers they could withdraw from service at any time. The massive surge in volunteering since 1798 had created an almost uncontrollable and unmanageable situation. Nevertheless, on 7 September orders were issued to update and resubmit the returns which had been made under the 1798 Defence Act. The Sussex Lieutenancy meeting complied.

On 30 September 1801, peace preliminaries were signed in London, and on 25 March 1802 the Treaty of Amiens brought an end to hostilities, ushering in a 14-month long period of peace – the longest, albeit uneasy, truce in the whole period from 1792-1815. It was hardly a genuinely peaceful interlude: 'The Treaty of Amiens was admittedly only an experiment, and an experiment so doubtful that it could deserve no higher title than a suspension of arms.'[37]

---

[35] Although the emphasis was inevitably on defending the coast, it is important to remember that the response to the invasion threat covered the entire county.
[36] quoted in Goodwin (1985): 68.
[37] Fortescue (1909): 6.

Sheridan described it as 'a peace which all men are glad of, but no man can be proud of'.[38]

It was clear from the start that the peace could not hold, and that Napoleon's continued belligerence across the continent would force renewed confrontation. The Addington ministry took the opportunity to enact a number of measures during the remainder of 1802 in an attempt to rationalise control of the yeomanry, volunteers and militias (cf. Appendix 2). In the spring of 1803, the militias were re-embodied, and further volunteers were sought.

The British government issued a new declaration of war on France on 17 May 1803. The pace and complexity of legislation accelerated. There was 'an almost bewildering variety of other enactments eventually contributing to a total of no fewer than 21 separate acts passed in 1802 or 1803 to raise men either voluntarily or compulsorily for the defence of the country against invasion'.[39] On 28 May, Lords Lieutenant were directed to enrol the supplementary militia. In June the 1798 Defence Act was updated as the 1803 Act (see below) and the Additional Forces Acts, also known as Army of Reserve Acts, were passed.

At the end of July, the Levy en Masse Act 1803 was passed, actually intended to encourage additional volunteering to avoid the threat of the militia levy. This revived the notion of the *posse comitatus*, and called for a further round of returns. The drive for more volunteers produced a massive patriotic response. 'It was indeed so great that the government had no idea how to manage it: they had no arms to equip the companies nor instructors to teach them military discipline'.[40] Further legislation in 1804 attempted to regularize the volunteer process.[41]

One of the major anxieties about military service throughout this period was whether men could serve locally, or would be posted away or overseas: 'The evidence suggests a deep localism to the volunteer movement: people were willing to defend their localities, but had no desire to serve outside them – and were not reluctant to say so … volunteering was often a canny, pragmatic response to the crisis, a systematic avoidance of more authoritarian forms of military service, and a reluctance to put the nation before family and locality.'[42]

---

[38] *Annual Register* 1802: 40 (London 1803).
[39] Becket (2011): 92.
[40] Watson (1960): 416.
[41] 44 George III Cap LIV, Yeomanry 1804.
[42] Philp (2006): loc. 372.

Nevertheless: 'As the invasion cloud darkened the land, Britons did not funk their duty. But they did it on their own terms, as civilians in arms'.[43]

Colley notes that many more men joined the volunteers from the towns than from the countryside.[44] One of the main drivers of recruitment was widespread unemployment, which was much more prevalent in urban areas: in rural areas, there was usually enough agricultural work to go round, at least in summertime.[45] So as the war disrupted the economy of the towns, increasing numbers of men came forward as volunteers. However, the existing structures were unable to cope with the growing enthusiasm to serve, and once the immediate threat of invasion had passed, subsequent government action sought to *discourage* the volunteer units and channel potential recruits into the militia and then into the regular army.[46]

It should be apparent that by this time Britain – particularly England – was a heavily militarised society, with permanent and temporary armed forces brigaded variously in the regular army, county militias, volunteer units and yeomanry, and which was under virtual martial law. 'War became, for the first time, a national endeavour touching practically every family in the land'.[47]

> Every town was … a sort of garrison – in one place you might hear the 'tattoo' of some youth learning to beat the drum, at another place some march or national air being practised upon the fife, and every morning [at] five o'clock the bugle horn was sounded through the streets, to call the volunteers to a two hours' drill.[48]

The Church, too, played its part, alerting its congregations to the danger of invasion and stiffening the will to resist if it came. A prayer to be used in daily service was issued in early July 1803:

> Oh Almighty God …We are exposed to the dangers and calamities of War, and threatened with Invasion by a fierce and haughty foe, who would swallow us up quick, so wrathfully is he displeased with us. Vouchsafe we beseech Thee thine especial Blessing and Protection to

---

[43] Lloyd (1991): 128.
[44] Colley (2009): 300.
[45] Nevertheless, the *general* trend throughout the Industrial Revolution was that rural unemployment consistently drove people into the towns and cities.
[46] For a detailed account of the militias and volunteers during this period, see Fortescue (1909), especially Chapter II.
[47] Philp (2011).
[48] Wheeler and Broadley (1908) vol II: 104, quoting Cruikshank (1803): 11.

> our most Sovereign Lord, King George. Go forth with his fleets and armies; and let thy mighty arm be with his Chiefs and Captains …[49]

Nevertheless, the contrast with France was clear. On the continent, Napoleon led a more coherent and disciplined national army, rather than an uncoordinated collection of militia and volunteer forces. France was both militarised and on an effective war footing. Peter Hicks describes the situation in the UK up to 1804 as illogical and incoherent:

> In 1796, Dundas had reacted to the changes in the strategic system by enlarging the militia. In 1798 the same minister had encouraged the volunteer formation, thus starving the militia of men. In 1799, the militia had then been further weakened as men were taken from it to be used as a regular army for offensive operations. In 1803 Addington and his party returned to the militia as the bed-rock of home defence … but at the same time encouraged the volunteer movement.[50]

Cookson concluded:

> Pitt's second adminstration continued [the] illogical and incoherent system whereby the volunteers starved the militia system, the militia starved the army and the army had negligible authority over the country's fighting men.[51]

The Defence Acts 1798 and 1803

The first of the Acts which provide the framework for this volume – informally known as the Defence Act 1798 – was passed by Parliament on 2 April 1798.[52] It extended to volunteers the existing powers available to Lords Lieutenant in relation to the militia, so that they could act 'in such and the same Manner, and with the same Powers and Authorities, as by the several Acts now in Force, concerning the Militia Forces of this Kingdom'.

Introducing the measure, Sir Henry Dundas explained that its purpose was to 'enable his Majesty more effectually to provide for the defence and security of the realm, and for indemnifying persons who may suffer in their property by such measures as may be necessary for that purpose'. He went on:

---

[49] Williamson et al (2017): 698. This prayer was used daily until March 1805, when it was replaced by one in similar terms.
[50] Hicks (2008): 6.
[51] Cookson (1997): 82.
[52] 38 George III Cap XXVII: see Appendix 3.

> The object of the bill, is to have the power of knowing, in case of emergency, who are ready to appear in arms, in order to co-operate with the existing power of the country ... It is further intended to give government legal power to investigate what force is in the country, competent to act in the shape of pioneers, drivers of waggons, or to perform the various other services which are connected with the operations of an army.[53]

That this inquiry was necessary is alone evidence that the volunteer movement had developed beyond the oversight and control of national administration.

The government foresaw the need, in the event of an invasion, of having to seize land, property, livestock and possessions from ordinary inhabitants, either for use in supplying an army and confronting the enemy, or to prevent them falling into his hands. There was also a concern to ensure that children, the elderly and infirm could be moved rapidly out of danger: '... much cruelty and much inhumanity would be exercised, if, at the time that able-bodied men were employed in the field, some provision was not made for the infants and aged, who would be left unprotected.'[54]

The 1798 Act is clear that it should apply (only) while the current war continued: 'this Act shall have Continuance *during the present War with France*' [emphasis added]. When war was renewed in 1803, similar defensive measures to those initiated five years previously were once again necessary. But since the 1798 Act had effectively expired with the cessation of hostilities in 1802, new legislation was introduced, leading to the passage of the Defence Act 1803 in June of that year.[55]

The text of the 1803 Act is for all practical purposes identical to that of its predecessor.[56] The major constitutional change that it reflects is that of the Act of Union 1800, which united the Kingdom of Great Britain and the Kingdom of Ireland to create the United Kingdom of Great Britain and Ireland. Hence the 1803 Act throughout extends its provisions to Ireland, and adds the responsibilities of Governors and Deputy Governors of Ireland to those of the Lords Lieutenant of Great Britain and their deputies.

---

[53] Cobbett (1818): col 1357 ff.
[54] Ibid.
[55] 43 George III Cap LV: see Appendix 4.
[56] Cf. Appendices 3 and 4.

There is one interesting feature of the new text which is both consistent and deliberate. Where the 1798 Act refers throughout to '… Boats, Barges, Waggons, Carts, Horses …', the 1803 revision has '… Boats, Barges, Waggons, Carts, *Cars*, Horses…' [emphasis added]. This would seem to reflect the ubiquity of the jaunting car in Ireland at the time – a means of transport so popular and common that subsequently the government of the day spotted a revenue opportunity, and proceeded to levy a tax on it.[57]

In setting out the framework for the survey returns published in this volume, it makes sense to consider the provisions of the two Acts together, since they are effectively the same. There are two broad themes: imposing a duty to collect information; and granting powers to act on that information in case of emergency.

The principal duty imposed on Lords Lieutenant (and in 1803 on Governors in Ireland) was to arrange for the collection of detailed returns of information, covering:

- numbers of men between the ages of 15 and 60, identifying those who were incapable of active service; those who were already serving in Volunteer Corps etc.; and those who were willing to be armed and trained for civil defence
- which men were willing to serve as waggon drivers, boatmen and in similar roles, so that invalids, women and children – and provisions – could be moved to safety and out of reach of the invaders
- numbers of those individuals who might have to be evacuated
- details of vehicles, livestock and stockpiles of provisions which could equally be of use to the enemy or employed in civil defence

To achieve these purposes, the Lord Lieutenant was to issue warrants to 'constables, tythingmen, headboroughs, or other officers of every parish or place' to ensure that such returns were made; these returns had to be presented under oath to general and divisional meetings of the county Lieutenancy.

The Lord Lieutenant was given the power to appoint officers to arm and train willing volunteers; and in the event of actual invasion, in effect to declare martial law: to seize any equipment, goods or produce ('cattle, sheep, hay, straw, corn, meal, flour, or provisions of any kind'), to order the evacuation of the local population, and to destroy any property or possessions that might be of use to the enemy. Further powers of compulsory purchase – subject to a

---

[57] 53 George III Cap LIX, Creating Duties on Carriages, etc. (Ireland) Act 1813.

mechanism to ensure fair compensation – and of imposing fines and other punishment completed a draconian package.

Census and surveys

A primary reason why the returns sought under the Defence Acts were necessary is that the authorities were comparatively ignorant of the facts. Over the preceding half-century, Britain – and especially England – had experienced rapid and profound changes as the Industrial Revolution transformed the economic and social landscape. Tens and then hundreds of thousands of people had forsaken life on the land and in the villages of their parents for a future in the newly industrialised towns. Historians remain divided over the balance between 'push' and 'pull' factors, and over how voluntary was the move from the countryside to the cities. But there is no doubt that the transformation was historically unprecedented.

In parallel, and for reasons still not wholly understood, there was a rapid increase in the total population. In 1750, the population of England was an estimated 5.74 million.[58] Fifty years later, it had grown to 8.3 million, an increase of 45 per cent in the space of two generations.[59] Not only were there half as many people again; the mass migration from the country to the town meant that the central government did not even know where they were.

As a result, there was increasing concern, in an era of periodic agricultural slumps and shortages, about the ability of the nation to feed its rapidly increasing numbers – and of the consequences of failure. Among the most influential of commentators on the population issue was Thomas Malthus, whose famous essay on the subject was first published in 1798, the same year as the first Defence Act.[60] Malthus claimed to demonstrate that since population numbers would increase geometrically, while agricultural productivity could increase only arithmetically, Britain would inevitably face a future of famine, starvation and death, the only practical result of continued population growth.

A concrete result of the growing concern was the Census Act 1800, which provided for the first ever national census to be carried out in 1801.[61] Its prime mover was one of the unsung heroes of Georgian Britain, John Rickman. In 1796 he wrote a paper entitled 'Thoughts on the Utility and Facility of a general

---

[58] Wrigley and Schofield (1981).
[59] Jefferies (2005).
[60] Malthus (1798).
[61] 41 George III Cap XV.

Enumeration of the People of the British Empire'. Still in his 20s in 1800, he published a further article 'On Ascertaining the Population'. When this was brought to the attention of Charles Abbot, shortly to be elected as Speaker of the House of Commons, Rickman was appointed as Speaker's Secretary, and became the principal force behind the first four British censuses.

Rickman was a prime mover in the effort to understand and quantify the transformation of British society in the second half of the Industrial Revolution. He very clearly understood the deeper purpose behind gathering his statistics:

> Social science was his study from the time he left Oxford, and he regarded the population returns quite rightly as giving data for the widest political and social deductions.[62]

R. G. Thorne, for the History of Parliament project, commented:

> [Abbot] was responsible for another innovation of public utility, the population bill, which provided for a national census, to be followed by a statistical digest of births, deaths and marriages. While the prevailing food scarcity was its pretext, it was conceived by Abbot as a contribution to defence planning, an aid to government in assessing the country's manpower.[63]

Speaker Abbot bought the estate of Kidbrook near East Grinstead in 1802. He served as a Justice of the Peace; he commanded a troop of cavalry in the North Pevensey Legion under Lord Sheffield; and he supported the Duke of Richmond – no doubt with enthusiasm – as one of his Lieutenancy colleagues.[64]

Feeding the people

Understanding the other side of the Malthusian equation, the capacity of the nation to produce sufficient food to support the population, was proving to be equally problematic. Official concern about the paucity of reliable agricultural data had been mounting since the middle of the century. Charles Smith had published a series of pamphlets and essays in response to harvest failures in the 1750s.[65] Then the late 1780s and the 1790s saw a series of poor harvests in

---

[62] Williams (1912): 15.
[63] Thorne (n.d.).
[64] He is recorded as present at a special meeting of the Lieutenancy on 31 August 1804; cf. ESRO L/C/G/4: 'Army of Reserve, 1804'.
[65] Cf. Smith (1758, 1804).

Southern Britain, as in France. Output was seriously reduced in 1789, 1790, 1792 and 1794.

The rapidly increasing population exacerbated the impact on the ground. In 1795, a particularly cold and wet winter caused severe shortages the following year; the price of wheat doubled in eight months, leading to growing unrest throughout the country.[66] Pitt's government established a Select Committee to 'enquire into the circumstance of the present scarcity and the best means of remedying it'. As a result, pressure mounted to improve the accuracy and coverage of agricultural information.

So at the same time as John Rickman was developing his argument for a survey of the population, in 1788 and 1789 the agricultural commentator Arthur Young called on his correspondents to send him reports on harvest conditions in their areas.[67] Through the 1790s, Young repeated his surveys, publishing the results in the *Annals of Agriculture*, which he edited.[68] These unofficial exercises ran in parallel with a succession of Select Committee enquiries which, however, were hampered by patchy and incomplete returns. Minchinton comments:

> [T]he last decade of the eighteenth century was dimly perceiving, what the nineteenth had to learn through painful experience, that effective remedial measures for social problems can only be taken when enquiry has revealed, preferably in statistical form, the dimensions of the question.[69]

This unenthusiastic attitude was reflected in the apparently half-hearted official approach to the issue. Coppock argued that three conditions had to be satisfied before agricultural returns could be successfully collected: 'the Government had first to be convinced of the usefulness of such information, a satisfactory means of collection had then to be found, and finally opposition on the part of landlords and farmers had to be overcome'.[70] Nevertheless, concern about agricultural shortages and the rising cost of food continued to trouble the government and parliamentarians, and a number of Select Committees reported on the issues in 1800 and 1801.

---

[66] Minchinton (1953): 29.
[67] Remarkably, between these two dates Young made a tour to France, and witnessed the storming of the Bastille in person.
[68] 'Arthur Young was the greatest of all English writers on agriculture' *1911 Encyclopedia Britannia Vol 28.*
[69] Minchinton (1953): 33.
[70] Coppock (1956): 5.

In mid-1801, Addington's Home Secretary, Lord Pelham[71] called on the clergy to make returns of 'the acreage of wheat, barley, oats, potatoes, peas, beans and turnips or rape, and in the northern and western dioceses, of rye also'.[72] The resulting returns are preserved in The National Archives among Home Office papers HO 67; a complete transcript was published by the *List and Index Society*, Vols 189, 190 & 195.[73] The returns for Sussex, included in Vol 195, are outside the scope of this volume, but are an important counterpart to the Defence Act returns for agricultural historians. The information collected by these various initiatives is particularly valuable since, as Coppock went on to note,[74] the collection of agricultural statistics made during the Napoleonic Wars was not immediately followed up: 'little interest seems to have been shown for over twenty years.'

All these efforts at the collection of statistics suffered from perennial doubts over their accuracy. In the case of agricultural returns, farmers and others worried that tithes and taxes would be based on figures submitted, so there was an inevitable tendency to under-reporting. Turner quotes a letter from the Duke of Richmond of 19 February 1797 in which 'he questions the reliability and fullness of the returns arising from the original inquiry of 1796 because of suspicions that the returns might be used for taxation purposes.'[75,76]

However, Turner goes on to argue that since the Defence Acts contained provisions to indemnify farmers should their livestock be requisitioned for military purposes, or if the livestock and other possessions became victims of any scorched-earth policy, the tendency to under-reporting should have been eliminated. (It is even possible that the incentive was reversed, and that over-reporting might be seen as a bet for future compensation.)

In a debate in Parliament on the Military Service Bill in July 1803, Pitt paid tribute to the quality of the information collected under the 1798 Act:

> There is hardly one military district in the kingdom, of which the government have not at this moment in its possession ample memorials, prepared a considerable time before the termination of the late war ... containing a minute statement of the various points of

---

[71] later Earl of Chichester; a colleague of the Duke of Richmond in the Sussex Lieutenancy: cf. Biographical Notes and Proceedings *passim* below.
[72] Henderson (1952b): 338.
[73] Home Office (1982a, 1982b, 1983).
[74] op cit
[75] Turner (1998): 146 fn 12.
[76] TNA HO/42/40 ff 209-10 PRO.

resistance which are to be found on the coasts, and all the intermediate points of military defence between the different coasts and the capital.[77]

Turning to population statistics, it was clearly less straightforward to misreport numbers, and there were fewer incentives to do so. The problem of 'missing' men was observed later, in records of desertions of volunteers. Rickman himself insisted on the value and accuracy of his work on the census. Writing 30 years later, he noted (in splendidly orotund phrases):

> A controversy of some duration had existed as to the increase or diminution of the population; and the result of the Act of 1801 being adverse to the opinions of those who had taken a gloomy view of national resources, insinuations were not wanting against the accuracy of the enumeration.[78]

The imperative to improve statistical understanding of the population and the ability of agriculture to sustain it reinforced the drive to determine the defensive capability of the nation in the face of invasion. It seems reasonable to assume that by the time returns were made under the Defence Acts, the resultant figures were fairly reliable. The indemnity provisions in the legislation should have prevented the systematic under-reporting of agricultural data which it was feared might have coloured previous information gathering; Pitt paid tribute to the quality of the information collected and this assessment must have applied to Sussex at least as much to other counties; Rickman implicitly defended the accuracy of the population figures (which were based largely on volunteerism, not conscription).

The figures were collected rape by rape, parish by parish, on the instructions of deputy lieutenants, superintendents and clerks, and they were all endorsed by the significant landowners and major figures in the county at the Lieutenancy meetings. It seems fair to conclude that participants were confident of their accuracy; and we in turn should be able to treat them as such.

It must not be overlooked, though, that behind these apparently dry statistics was a population living in daily apprehension of violent French invasion.[79] It is

---

[77] Cobbett (1803): col 1657.
[78] Preface to the Abstract of Returns, 1833. For a detailed review of the accuracy of the 1801 census, see Wrigley and Schofield (1989), especially pp. 122-26.
[79] 'Those who have the privilege of aggregating and generalising [demographic data] have a special responsibility to remember that the numbers they are handling are nothing more and nothing less

probably now forgotten that a large French invasion fleet set sail in 1796, bound initially for Ireland, only to be beaten back by bad weather; and that the following year a small force (rapidly captured by volunteers) actually managed to land near Fishguard. Once Napoleon took control of the French army in 1797, the danger to the nation was all too real.

Colley reminds us how widespread were the fears. Quoting in part the recollection of the poet John Clare, she writes:

> Nerves were kept at fever pitch by preparations for evacuation, by long lines of wagons in village streets waiting to transport women, children and the infirm away from the scene of battle, and by instructions distributed by local clergymen and constables, urging people to prepare 'a change of linen, and one blanket for each person, wrapped up in the coverlid of your bed, and bring with you all the food in your possession' in readiness when the order came to flee or fight.[80]

The proceedings published here took place against a profoundly turbulent and fearful background. English society had experienced fifty years of social and economic upheaval; hunger and periodic starvation were far from unknown; large parts of the rural population were on the move into the rapidly-growing towns; army, militias and volunteers were in search of coherent and consistent roles in the national defence. And both government and people feared invasion, especially in front-line counties such as Sussex.

The 3rd Duke of Richmond, Lord Lieutenant

The Lord Lieutenant was the pivotal actor in all the separate but inter-related county defence mechanisms. The Third Duke of Richmond (the 'radical Duke') was a man who had enjoyed a long and distinguished life and career.[81] Richmond was appointed Lord Lieutenant of Sussex in 1763. At the turn of the century, he was nearly 65 years old, and so had served in the office of Lord Lieutenant for nearly 40 years. But there is no suggestion that his energy or commitment were waning. Reese emphasizes that, 'This was a man of great physical energy, active all his life in soldiering, farming on his estate, building, yachting and hunting. When he died at the age of seventy-one he was hoping

---

than the sum of the hopes, loves and fears of every individual human being.' Morland (2019): loc. 652.
[80] Colley (2009): 306.
[81] He was nicknamed the 'Radical Duke' for his strong advocacy of the cause of the American colonists during their war of independence.

that a son would shortly be born to him.'[82] Overseeing the defence of his County was his last major public responsibility.

The master of Goodwood spent the early part of his public career as a firm supporter of the Rockingham Whigs. He served as Master-General of the Ordnance in Rockingham's second ministry from March to July 1782, but resigned after the Fox-North coalition succeeded. When Pitt became Prime Minister in 1784, he brought Richmond back in the same role at the Ordnance. Here he was an agent of reform, revamping payments for officers and instituting a survey of the South Coast which led to the creation of the Ordnance Survey.[83]

He played a significant role in the creation of the Royal Horse Artillery in 1793, which developed from two troops of horse artillery that he raised at Goodwood. He was appointed colonel of the Royal Horse Guards on 18 July 1795, and field marshal in 1796. In 1797 he raised his own troop of yeomanry, the Duke of Richmond's Light Horse Artillery, which trained at Goodwood: this was notable as being one of very few artillery companies which was allowed to be raised outside the regular army: 'Presumably, the exception was made because the Duke was a former Master General of the Ordnance'.[84]

Predictably, his willingness to serve under Pitt led to accusations of opportunism, and criticism that he had tacked towards the Tory camp. But in the end, his half-hearted support of the Pitt administration and his increasing absences from government led to his dismissal in February 1795. He effectively withdrew to Goodwood to see out his declining years. But his commitment to defending the County lasted to the end: 'Only with the militia and his plan of national defence … was he personally active'.[85]

Hudson says:

> He was a particularly hard-working Lord Lieutenant, guiding committees with a firm hand and bombarding officials with pages of

---

[82] Reese (1987): 123.
[83] 'On [21 June] 1791, Ordnance Survey was born. Our arrival was marked by the payment of the princely sum [of] £373.14s to Jesse Ramsden for a three-foot theodolite. That purchase was made at the request of the Master General, the 3rd Duke of Richmond, and is now generally accepted as the founding action of the Ordnance Survey.' *https://www.ordnancesurvey.co.uk/blog/tag/220th-anniversary/*
[84] Hudson (1984): 170.
[85] Reese (1987): 247.

well-informed argument about how the defence of Sussex should best be organized.[86]

However, this is a partial and somewhat flattering summary. By all accounts Richmond was a difficult, irascible and often unpleasant man. Reviewing Olson (1961) in *Sussex Notes and Queries*, L. F. Salzman commented: 'Upright, hardworking and unpopular, his considerable ability failed to achieve success, largely because of a tactlessness which led to his quarrelling with everyone from King George III downwards.'[87] According to Olson, Richmond was also unpopular because of the source of his wealth, a grant made by Charles II to Richmond's grandfather of a tax of a shilling on every chaldron of coal taken out of Newcastle.[88]

Roger Knight concurs:

> Richmond's abrasive personality and unpopularity ensured not only that the separateness of his department was accentuated but also that his personal isolation grew … He was hot-tempered, inconsistent and quarrelsome: he fell out both with the duke of York and with Henry Dundas, and when in 1795 Pitt eventually ejected him from his post no one in government was sorry to see him go.[89]

The historian Holland Rose was simply scathing, alleging basic incompetence (e.g. 'the Duke of Richmond, Master of Ordnance, distinguished himself by his incapacity and his ridiculous orders').[90] Watson summed up: 'In spite of enjoying high office under the younger Pitt, his career was strangely disappointing'.[91]

A further indication of Richmond's character can be gained from his own words, in his altercation with Lt. Col. Powlett, the Government's Inspecting Field Officer, who was seeking his cooperation to make his circuit of Sussex (Appendix 5 has the details). Richmond was blithely obstructive e.g., 'Your Letter seems to think that I, as Lord Lieutenant, should give the necessary Orders; but this I confess I know not how to set about.' His non-cooperation eventually produced Powlett's rather hurt conclusion:

---

[86] Hudson (1984): 166.
[87] Salzman (1961): 252.
[88] Olson (1961): 102.
[89] Knight (2013): 42-3.
[90] Rose (1911): 86.
[91] Watson (1960): 117.

> I cannot help regretting that your Grace did not, in the first Instance, do me the Honour to tell me it never was your Intention to comply in this Case with the Wishes of Government.

Richmond's long identification with the Whig party meant that he did not feel reticent in criticising the military and defence policies of the Pitt and Addington administrations. In particular, this expressed itself in his determination to defeat the policy of 'driving the country'.

Driving the Country

Throughout this period, whenever the threat of invasion increased, the Government flirted with 'driving the country': in the event of a successful invasion, much of coastal Sussex would suffer evacuation and be subject to a scorched-earth policy. (Indeed, later in the Napoleonic Wars, both the Portuguese and Russian authorities were to adopt such a strategy to deny resources to the invaders.)[92]

Glover suggests that the first reference to 'driving the country' dates from 1779, when it was proposed by General William Roy during an earlier invasion threat (although in fact no invasion occurred).[93] In 1796, the policy of 'driving the country' was revived.[94] In a letter of 24 January 1798 to Lord Portland, Home Secretary, the Duke of Richmond protested: he argued that 'the whole issue of driving the country was so complex that Legislative Authority would be necessary to effect it'. He was also concerned about the proposals for obtaining information (which came to be embodied in the 1798 Defence Act) in imitation of what had been done in Dorset.[95]

Three years later, when the danger of invasion once again became acute, 'driving the country' returned to the agenda. In July 1801, a 'secret' circular was sent to District Commanders warning of an imminent French invasion and seeking the information necessary to arrange mass evacuation.[96] This was the immediate trigger for Richmond's convening the Lieutenancy meeting of 13 August 1801. Lord Bolton, Lord Lieutenant of neighbouring Hampshire, was also sceptical of the practicality and wisdom of attempting to drive the country.

---

[92] By contrast with 'driving the country', the earliest attested occurrence of the phrase 'scorched earth', more familiar to a modern audience, is as recent as 1937, in the context of the Sino-Japanese War (*OED*).
[93] Glover (1973): 54.
[94] Cf. also Goodwin (1985): 68 and Chapter 6 generally.
[95] Clammer (2014): 292. He claimed there would be 'imperfections' in the data gathered; but it is difficult to avoid the conclusion that he was simply attemping to frustrate the government.
[96] Kenyon (1950): 60.

Richmond and Bolton formed a united front. On 14 August, Richmond wrote to Lord Hobart, Secretary of State for War and the Colonies, arguing for a change of policy (cf. Appendix 6). And on 29 August he wrote to Lord Bolton with a summary of the deliberations of 13 August, seeking his support (cf. Appendix 7).

As we have seen, the Peace of Amiens brought a temporary respite in 1802. But as soon as war broke out again in 1803, Napoleon began amassing his Armée d'Angleterre at Boulogne and other strategic points on the coast. In June, proposals for recruiting the 'body of the people' to national defence were sent to Lords Lieutenant of coastal counties, and proposals for 'driving the country' were again revived.

Glover notes that Richmond, with his unrivalled experience as Master General of the Ordnance, continued his strong opposition: 'Very cogently, Richmond argued that if it were possible to destroy all supplies in an invaded country, the result would be famine among all those of the inhabitants, notably the elderly and infirm poor, who could not flee; but in fact the job was so vast it was not possible.'[97]

Knight adds:

> [A]t the general meeting of the lieutenancy of Sussex, chaired by Richmond, and attended by General David Dundas as general commanding the Southern District, it was resolved unanimously to ask the king to reconsider laying waste 'one of the richest provinces in England'.[98]

On 20 October 1803 Richmond wrote formally to Charles Philip Yorke, Home Secretary, once again opposing the policy of 'driving the country'. Eventually, it was quietly dropped.

Deliberations

As the Duke of Richmond and his colleagues met to consolidate the results of their surveys into the defensive potential of the county, they were obviously committed to the military organization of a nation under severe threat, but it was one which was struggling to harness its defensive capabilities effectively. They were also, as we have seen, far from content with Government policy on the defence of the crucial southern coast. They dutifully carried into effect – as

---
[97] Glover (1973): 54.
[98] Knight (2013): 252-53.

far as possible – the requirements of the Defence Acts, and collected the statistics and information which are so valuable to us today. But at the same time, they used their understanding of the situation on the ground to press their concerns.

The men who gathered periodically to plan the defence of their county and of the nation were not simply a bunch of local worthies, a Dad's Army assembly of borough councillors or village tradesmen. These were men among the leading powers in the county, major national figures. As the Biographical Notes below show, the Duke of Richmond's colleagues included four earls, a viscount, knights of the shire, the Speaker of the House of Commons and many other individuals of substance. It may be fashionable to decry landed privilege, but the deliberations of these men suggest that they bore the weight of that privilege robustly, and resolved to honour it. This was:

> a social landscape fundamentally different from our own ... a time when the great house in the park was the sole centre of political authority away from the royal court; when its size and magnificence were the one means of expressing political influence and achievement in monumental form. The influence and achievement in question here attached to the resident family and its reigning head.[99]

They met variously at the White Hart and the Star Inn in Lewes, the Half Moon in Petworth, and the Castle Inn in Brighton. These were among the most prominent assembly rooms in the county. The White Hart still exists, advertising itself today as 'the historic meeting place of Lewes'. The Star Inn is now Lewes Town Hall. The Half Moon was situated on the Market Place in Petworth: it was closed and demolished in 1900.

The Castle Inn in Brighton was situated on the North side of Castle Square, but also no longer exists: the site is now occupied by the Royal Bank of Scotland building on Old Steine. It was originally built in the 1740s as a private house, but was later converted to an inn. In 1766, the leading architectural designer John Crunden added the Assembly Rooms to the rear of the building; this was considered to be 'one of the most elegant rooms in the country ... designed in Adam style with a brilliantly decorated ceiling, plaster relief walls, colonnaded recesses, and a musicians' gallery'.[100] Sadly, the only images available of the interior depict its use as a high-class society ballroom rather than as a conference venue. From 1791 to 1809, the inn was run by Thomas Tilt. After the

---

[99] Laslett (1984): 211-13.
[100] Carder (1990).

original inn was demolished in 1823, the Assembly Rooms were converted into a royal chapel. The building was subsequently dismantled and reassembled in a new building in Montpelier Place to form St Stephen's Church.[101]

The deliberations of the Lieutenancy Meetings fall into two main phases: August- October 1801; and July-November 1803; with a postscript from November 1805 to February 1806. However, the proceedings (and schedules) in the volumes presented here are entered continuously.

August-October 1801

On 23 July 1801, as invasion fears mounted, Lord Hobart wrote a circular letter to Lords Lieutenant, asking them to assemble volunteer corps for training. During August, it became apparent that the coastal counties, in particular, were reluctant. On 13 August 1801, Richmond convened a Lieutenancy Meeting. This reviewed the relevant legislation dating back to 1798 (the first Defence Act), along with instructions subsequently received, including those for preparing to drive the country.

The meeting rehearsed in detail the results of the surveys carried out under the 1798 Act (thereby preserving a summary of the returns themselves, apparently now lost). From an analysis of these returns, the meeting concluded that 'there are neither *Carriages*, *Men* or *Draft Cattle* to remove the Grain and Persons incapable of removing themselves, from the District proposed.' They suggested that it would be better to 'avoid the Confusion which an attempt at what cannot be performed is likely to create' and argued that the 'destruction ... of what could not be removed from a large Tract of Fertile Country [would] prove great and unnecessary waste in these times of Scarcity when possibly only a small part of it might fall into the Enemy's Hands.' (cf. p. 6).

On 7 September 1801, Lords Lieutenant were ordered to update the 1798 returns. The Lieutenancy met on 14 September 1801 to appoint Deputy Lieutenants and arrange for collecting the necessary details. Although preliminary proposals for peace were agreed in London on 30 September, the Lieutenancy meeting convened on 8 October 1801 to consider and endorse the detailed schedules. The meeting was adjourned *sine die*, in view of the prospect of peace. (cf. p. 101).

---

[101] Carder (1990).

July-November 1803; 1805-06

The Defence Act 1803 was passed in June 1803, renewing the requirements for information gathering first set out in the 1798 Act. As Napoleon gathered his army on the French coast, the threat of invasion again became acute, and 'driving the country' once more loomed as a realistic prospect. Reese says the Lieutenancy meeting on 7-8 July 1803 was called specifically to reject these resurrected proposals.[102] The meeting resolved that:

> We trust the fate of England can never be reduced to such an Extremity, That it is not by ourselves making a Desert of our own Country that an Enemy will be stopped, but by our own Army backed with that Energy and Spirit with which every Individual will to a Man rise in Arms on Actual Invasion (cf. p. 107).

They reviewed the information they were required to collect, and arranged for the appointment of Inspectors and Superintendants, confirmed at the subsequent meeting on 21 July 1803. In the meantime, however, the Government confused matters by passing the Additional Forces Act (i.e. the Army of Reserve Act). This was 'loathed as alike oppressive and unfair':[103] its real intent was to drive up the number of volunteers out of fear of the impact of the Militia ballot. But men who had paid £10 or £15, often both, to purchase exemption from the Militia, were outraged to find that this did not protect them against the new legislation. Fines paid in lieu of service in the Militia did not count against the Army of Reserve, nor vice versa.

In view of the confusion over the status of exemptions purchased under the previous legislation, the meeting decided to submit the issue to the Law Officers for a determination. They met again on 1 August to review the response, which was, as expected, unsympathetic. The Duke of Richmond wrote to the Secretary of State on 23 August: 'The people ... have become suspicious of the magistrates. They cannot understand how a new Act can violate the engagement of the old. A ballot is a ballot with them, and when they have bought exemption from one, they cannot understand how they are liable to another. I warned Addington of this, and hoped Parliament would make some remedy'.[104]

At the 1 August 1803 meeting, the Lieutenancy received the detailed schedules which form the bulk of this volume. The subsequent meeting on 10 August

---

[102] Reese (1987) 239
[103] Fortescue (1909): 57.
[104] Fortescue (1909): 57.

recorded the offers of service and willingness to raise forces received, which were followed up at the 22 August meeting. A week later, alarmed by the threat of fines for failure to produce the names of balloted men or substitutes, the Lieutenancy recommended holding immediate ballots, and using the sums raised from earlier penalties to help defray the costs of nominating substitutes.

In October and November, the meeting noted the volunteer troops and corps which had been raised; and endorsed a schedule of waggons to be completed (which seems never to have been issued). However, in November and December 1805 a detailed schedule of waggons, drivers etc. was completed, which was received at the meeting on 20 February 1806. By then, however, the invasion threat was effectively over.

By the end of 1805, Lord Hawkesbury, who had succeeded Yorke as Home Secretary under Pitt, was complaining that many counties had yet to raise a single man under the Act. He claimed that this failure was 'chiefly to be attributed to the Supineness and Inactivity of the Parish Officers and the Heritors, and their Agents' and with a scarcely veiled threat noted that 'His Majesty's Government have thought it expedient that an intelligent Officer should be directed to make a Circuit through each County, for the Purpose of meeting the Parish Officers, the Heritors and their Agents, in the Manner least inconvenient to them, and of giving them such Information and Assistance upon the Spot as they may require.' (cf. Appendix 8).

On 21 October 1805, Nelson's fleet destroyed the combined French and Spanish fleet at the battle of Trafalgar, cementing Britain's naval superiority. Napoleon's invasion had already been called off. On 27 August, he marched the assembled troops eastwards as the core of his new Grande Armée, soon to triumph at Ulm, Vienna and Austerlitz.

For Great Britain, the defeat of Napoleon was a defining victory:

> It is possible to argue that cheap and limited government in the early nineteenth century was only made possible by the unusually strong strategic position ... that Britain achieved out of the greatest conflict it had ever fought.[105]

Conclusions

What can we learn from the deliberations of the Lieutenancy meetings between 1801 and 1806, and from the information they collected? For the historian, they

---

[105] Cookson (1997): 15

should reinforce a number of key themes. The most obvious is that grand national narratives inevitably have a local expression and usually local antecedents. The danger of invasion created by Napoleon's army posed an existential threat to the nation as a whole; but national policy had to be based on the response at the level of county and parish. All history is fundamentally local history – in both its origins and its impacts.

Similarly, most figures of national importance wielding substantial power have a hinterland and a grounding in local identity. While national policy is not simply the sum of individual local actions, local perspectives are more powerful than is sometimes admitted. Where an old man in the twilight of his career – by 1806 the 3rd Duke of Richmond was only months from death, and had earned at best a mixed verdict from posterity – takes a stand based on local knowledge and a lifetime of experience he can still have an impact on national policy.

A further theme of contemporary historiography is the importance of recognizing the experience of 'ordinary people', and the way in which this has influenced the development of grand policy. Many of the key figures here emerged from the French historical tradition. Jules Michelet (1798-1874) insisted that history should concentrate on the people, not only its leaders or its institutions:

> 19th-century French historians no longer saw history as the chronicling of royal dynasties, armies, treaties, and great men of state, but as the history of ordinary French people and the landscape of France.[106]

Fernand Braudel stressed the *longue durée*, in the belief that deep structures of society were more powerful in driving history than dates and kings.[107] Emmanuel Le Roy Ladurie used detailed historical records of the peasants of Languedoc in arguing for the primacy of local culture, economics and the experience of the people.[108] The records edited in this volume can be as informative of *le Sussex profond* as the works of Braudel or Ladurie are of *la France profonde*.

A final theme is that geography and demography are crucial underpinnings of historical continuity. The impact of both should be clear from this introduction:

---

[106] Jurkevich (1999): 42.
[107] Cf. Braudel (1949) etc.
[108] e.g. Le Roy Ladurie (1975).

in the position of Sussex in the front-line of invasion defence; and in the attempt to comprehend the growth and distribution of early nineteenth century population in the county.

Much of the content in the returns below is numerical and statistical, but this does not mean it is drily uninteresting. Who were the seven Aliens in Westhampnett in 1801 (p. 19)? It is understandable why there were 34 boats recorded in Bosham in 1801, but why only one in Appledram across the channel (p. 25)? How is it that in 1803 there were more than 70,000 sheep in the Southern Division of Pevensey Rape, but only 2 goats (p. 266)? How were they able to reproduce and breed?

Among the many named individuals, glimpses of character stand out too. From Nuthurst in 1803: 'William and Henry Woolver refuse to act in any capacity whatever, & Hugh Alexander except on Board a Man of War' (p. 182). On 1 August 1803 the Lieutenancy Meeting recorded that John Ovington, Emery Churcher, Robert Follett, Messrs Barber and Hillier, John Pilgrim Boorn, George Woodland and Charles Dendy, all of the Parish of Sidlesham, had refused to return an account of their stock as required, and ordered that their names be entered as Refractory and reported to the Commissary General (p. 129). From New Shoreham 1803: 'The Cavalry Man has no horse' (p. 181). Rusper 1803: 'There's only 1 Mill in the parish & James Caffyn the miller says he can't engage to deliver any flour' (p. 186). Burwash: 'I cannot engage for no certain Quantity but am willing to do the Utmost of my Power if called on Signed Edward Hildar' (p. 298).

There are many detailed points of description. From Lewes Rape: 'There is a bridge in this Parish over the River Ouse for Waggons to pass and repass situated about 3 miles North of Newhaven and by which Artillery may be Transported from the Downs east and West of the River' (p. 197). North Lewes 1805: 'The Roads and Communication in the space of Residence of this Corps at particular seasons almost Impassible' [sic] (p. 341).

These records illuminate the life of the rural Sussex community during a brief period of heightened national danger. They provide greater depth and range of information than the 1801 census; their coverage of livestock and agricultural capacity is unmatched; they offer an unparalleled account of the nation's preparedness (or otherwise) for foreign invasion, complementing the official, national narrative. They reveal a vanished England, a lost England. They record modest and unknown people, working the land, following their trades, poor, often hungry, fearful and facing invasion by foreign armies.

In the particular person of the 3rd Duke of Richmond, we see a major, if fading, national politician struggling to reconcile his duty to sustain civil defence while rejecting a key plank of the strategy of successive governments: in this latter endeavour, he was successful, in that the policy of 'driving the country' was eventually abandoned. Thankfully, the issue was never finally put to the test. The invasion never came. England survived.

BIOGRAPHICAL NOTES

The members of the Lieutenancy meetings included most if not all of the prominent individuals of the county; many of them were of course also major national figures. (ODNB signifies an entry in the *Oxford Dictionary of National Biography*.)

The Lieutenancy Meetings

The Duke of Richmond (1735-1806)

Charles Lennox, Field Marshal His Grace the Duke of Richmond and Lennox KG PC FRS.; of Goodwood.

He served in the army from 1752 until his death, commanding the 33rd and 72nd Regiments of Foot. Nicknamed the 'Radical Duke', he supported the colonists during the American Revolutionary War, argued for lenient policy in Ireland and campaigned for parliamentary reform. He served as Master-General of the Ordnance under Rockingham and then Pitt.

He saw active service during the Seven Years War; and was appointed Lord Lieutenant of Sussex on 18 October 1763.

In 1797, he raised his own troop of Yeomanry, the Duke of Richmond's Light Horse Artillery, which he trained on his estate at Goodwood. (ODNB).

The Earl of Chichester (1756-1826)

Thomas Pelham, 2nd Earl of Chichester PC, PC (Ire), FRS.; of Stanmer House.
He was Surveyor-General of Ordnance under Rockingham; and Chief Secretary for Ireland under Pitt. He served as Home Secretary under Addington from 1801 to 1803.

The family seat was Stanmer House, between Lewes and Brighton. (ODNB).

The Earl of Egremont (1751-1837)

George O'Brien Wyndham, 3rd Earl of Egremont FRS.; of Petworth.

He was a renowned patron of the arts and collector. J M W Turner lived as his guest at his seat at Petworth House for a period. He was also a great canal builder, responsible for the Rother Navigation.

Among his many acquaintances was the agricultural author Revd Arthur Young.

He was Colonel of the Sussex Troops of Gentlemen and Yeoman Cavalry
An eccentric, it is said that he maintained a harem of mistresses at Petworth, and fathered over 40 illegitimate children. 'From his seat at Petworth House, north of the Downs, Egremont exercised a more than benevolent ownership

over his 110,000 acres and into the county beyond.' (Knight 2013: 168). (ODNB).

Viscount Gage (1761-1808)

Henry Gage, 3rd Viscount Gage; of Firle.
He was born in Montreal where his father, General Thomas Gage, was commander of the British forces during the American Revolution.
He rose to Major-General in the British Army; served as a Captain in the Sussex Yeomanry, and as Colonel of the South Pevensey Volunteers.
The seat of the Gage family is Firle Place.

The Earl of Sheffield (1735-1821)

John Baker Holroyd, 1st Earl of Sheffield; of Sheffield Place, Fletching.
As a parliamentarian and author, he wrote and campaigned on agricultural issues, and served as President of the Board of Agriculture.
He was Colonel of his own cavalry regiment, the 22nd Regiment of Light Dragoons.
In 1769, he bought Sheffield Place from Lord De La Warr. (ODNB).

The Earl of Ashburnham (1760-1830)

George Ashburnham, 3rd Earl of Ashburnham, KG, GCH, FSA.
His family held Ashburnham Place for 750 years. He was a godson of the King, George III.

Charles Abbot (1757-1829)

Of Kidbrooke, East Grinstead. MP for Helston 1795-1802, for Heytesbury 1802, for Woodstock 1802-06, for Oxford University 1806-17. Speaker of the House of Commons 1802-17. Baron Colchester from 1817. He purchased Kidbrook in 1802. Commanded a troop of cavalry in the North Pevensey Legion and was Lieut-Col. of the East Grinstead Volunteers in 1803. Abbot's efforts led to the act for taking the first census in 1801. 'The choice of a pugnacious dwarf as Speaker of the House of Commons ... was the subject of much private criticism.' (Thorne n.d.). (ODNB).

Sir Cecil Bisshopp, 12th Baron Zouche (1752–1828)

Of Parham. He was MP for New Shoreham 1790-1806
He raised the Parham Troop of Sussex Yeomanry, which trained on his estate at Parham Park.
He became the 12th Baron in 1815.

Sir John Bridger (c1734-c1816)

He lived at Coombe Place in Hamsey, outside Lewes. High Sheriff of Sussex 1780.

Sir Charles Merrik Burrell, 3rd Baronet (1774–1862)

Of Knepp Castle, West Grinstead.
He succeeded Sir Cecil Bisshopp (qv) as MP for New Shoreham (1806-62); Father of the House of Commons.
He married Frances Wyndham, one of the illegitimate children of George, 3rd Earl of Egremont (qv).

John Thomas Capel (1769-1819)

Hon. John Thomas Capel was the younger son of the 4th Earl of Essex (his son Arthur Algernon Capel succeeded to the title as the 6th Earl).

Thomas Carr, Kt (c1749-1814)

Sir Thomas Carr, Knight of Beddingham. Died 9 Jun 1814 aged 65. High Sheriff of Sussex 1801.

John Marten Cripps (1780-1853)

After Jesus College, Cambridge, he set out on a European tour with his tutor, the Rev. William Otter (afterwards bishop of Chichester) and Thomas Malthus. Fellow of the Society of Antiquaries. In 1797 he inherited the property of his maternal uncle, John Marten, which included possessions in the parish of Chiltington, where he built Novington Lodge. He introduced the kohl-rabi to Britain from Russia. (ODNB).

John Apsley Dalrymple (c1769-1833)

Of Mayfield. His father was General Sir Hew Whiteefoord Dalrymple. Colonel of the 15th Hussars and lord of the manor of Hamerdon in Ticehurst.

Sir David Dundas (1735-1820)

General Sir David Dundas GCB, PC
He saw active service in both the Seven Years War and the French Revolutionary War. He was Colonel of the 7th Light Dragoons and Quartermaster-General; subsequently Colonel of 2nd Dragoons and commander in Kent and Sussex from 1803; later Commander-in-Chief of the Forces. (ODNB).

William Ellis (?-1806)

Horsham solicitor and Clerk of the Peace. Appointed Clerk of the General Meetings by the Duke of Richmond; served in that role until his death in 1806. Succeeded in both offices by William Balcombe Langridge.

William Frankland (1761-1816)

Of Muntham. He was a cousin of Thomas Pelham, Earl of Chichester (qv). Private Secretary to Secretary of State for Home Affairs 1798-1801; Lord of the Admiralty 1806-07. Lt. Col. North Yorks militia 1803-14. MP for Thirsk 1801-06, for Queensborough 1806-07, for Thirsk again 1807-15.

John Fuller of Rose Hill (1757-1834)

Known as 'Mad Jack' Fuller of Rose Hill.
He inherited Rose Hill estate (now Brightling Park).
He was MP for Southampton 1780-84, and for Sussex from 1801 to 1812.
He was Captain of a light infantry company in the Sussex Militia; Captain in the Sussex Gentlemen and Yeomanry Cavalry.
He served as High Sheriff of Sussex (1797).
He was a sponsor of the Royal Institution; mentor and supporter of the young Michael Faraday; patron of J M W Turner. He sponsored the Fuller medal of the RI and founded the Fullerian Chairs of Chemistry and Physiology there. (ODNB).

John Trayton Fuller (1723-1811)

Of Ashdown Park. The Fuller family had its roots in Uckfield and Waldron (East Sussex). He reportedly inherited significant wealth from his father Thomas Fuller, a West India merchant, in 1780. Residence Ashdown House.

Charles Gilbert (1731-1816)

Attorney and solicitor. From 1767 he occupied 23 High Street, Lewes.
He was Commissioner of Newhaven Harbour from 1767; trustee of several turnpikes from 1761; deputy lieutenant of the Cinque Ports in 1804.
He was active in business throughout Sussex: steward of manors and estates, including that of the Duke of Dorset.
In 1792, he purchased a fine mansion adjoining the Gildredge Manor estate in Eastbourne from Stephen Lushington, later extending the family estates in East Dean and Birling.

James Holmes Goble (1759-1814)

James Holmes Goble of Arundel. He was a Major in the Sussex Yeomanry Horse Artillery

Charles Goring (1743-1829)

He inherited Wiston House.
He was MP for New Shoreham 1774-80.
He served as High Sheriff of Sussex (1827).

Sir Charles Foster Goring (1768-1844)

7th Baronet.

Thomas Cecil Grainger (1774-1834)

Of Bridge House Cuckfield.

Thomas Henry Harben (1768-1823)

He was heavily involved in the series of Seaford constituency ('rotten borough') controversies between about 1788 and 1802 (see Sir John Leach). He worked closely with the 3rd Duke of Richmond, and appears to have been responsible for supervising the management of the Treasury interest.
'On 15 July 1800, a grand match of cricket was played near Seaford by seven officers belonging to the Sussex Regiment, commanded by Lt Col Pelham and four gentlemen of the neighbourhood, against eight officers of the Corps of the Cinque Port Volunteers, under the command of Thomas Henry Harben Esq., and three gentlemen, which was won by the latter; Volunteers having beaten the Militia by 18 runs.' *Sussex Weekly Advertiser* 21st July 1800.

Thomas Kemp (c1745-1811)

MP for Lewes 1780-1802; 1806-11
'His politics were those of an honest country gentleman ... but generally inclining to whiggism', wrote the *Gentleman's Magazine* in his obituary notice. His son Thomas Read Kemp developed the Kemp Town estate in Brighton

Thomas Davis Lamb (1775-1818)

He was the eldest son of Thomas Phillipps Lamb.
He was Private Secretary to Lord Hawkesbury, Secretary of State for Foreign Affairs, 1801–02.
He was MP for Rye from 1802–1806; and Mayor of Rye from 1803–04, 1809–10 and 1816–17.

Thomas Phillipps Lamb (?1752-1819)

>Politician. He lived at Mountsfield Lodge, near Rye, and served as Government agent in Rye.
>He was MP for Rye 1812–16 and 1819
>He and his son Thomas Davis Lamb (qv) served as Mayor of Rye some 18 times from 1775–1817.

Sir John Leach (1760-1834)

>He was an English judge; Master of the Rolls (1827). In 1792 he was engaged as counsel in the Seaford election petition; recorder of Seaford 1797. MP for Seaford 1806-16. Deputy Speaker of the House of Lords (1827). (ODNB).

Major-Gen Charles Lennox (1764-1819)

>Charles Lennox, 4th Duke of Richmond, 4th Duke of Lennox, 4th Duke of Aubigny, KG, PC.
>He was the nephew of the 3rd Duke of Richmond: he succeeded to the title since there were no legitimate heirs.
>He was a colonel in the Duke of York's regiment; then lieutenant-colonel in the 35th Regiment of Foot. He fought against the French in the Revolutionary Wars; and served in the Napoleonic Wars. He was later Governor-General of British North America (i.e. Canada).
>He was MP for Sussex until he succeeded his uncle. (ODNB).

Sir James Martin Lloyd (1762-1844)

>(1762–1844) 1st Baronet. He was a Sussex landowner, militia officer and long-serving MP. He served in the Sussex Militia: major 1783, lieutenant-colonel 1803. In 1790 and 1791 he was elected MP for Steyning, but was forced on both occasions to stand down on petition. He regained the seat in 1796, holding it until 1818. Then MP for New Shoreham 1818-26.

William Margesson

>High Sheriff of Sussex (1805).

William Mitford

>Of Pitshill, in the Parish of Tillington, frequently described as one of the most important country houses in West Sussex.

John Napper (c1740-1822)

>Died 22 May 1822 aged 82 (memorial St Peter ad Vincula Wisborough Green).

Francis Newbery (1743-1818)

> He purchased Heathfield Park, the estate of Lord Heathfield, in 1791.
> Publisher and businessman.
> He served as High Sheriff of Sussex (1796). (ODNB).

John Newnham (1735-1809)

> He died 19 June 1809 West Grinstead.

William Newton (1744-1808)

> Colonel William Newton. He was a Major and then Lieutenant Colonel in the 10th Light Dragoons (Hussars).
> He was a personal friend of the Prince of Wales, who often visited him at Southover Grange.
> He commanded the 10th Light Dragoons 1786-93.

Thomas Partington (1760-1841)

> Of Offham in the parish of Hamsey near Lewes. Barrister. Magistrate, Chairman of the Quarter Sessions of the East Division of Sussex.

William Stephen Poyntz (1770-1840)

> He had seats at Midgham House in Berkshire and Cowdray Park.
> A serial parliamentarian, he was MP for St Albans 1800-07, MP for Callington (Cornwall) 1810-18, MP for Chichester 1823-30, MP for Ashburton 1831-35, MP for Midhurst 1835-37.

Sir James Pulteney (1755-1811)

> General Sir James Murray Pulteney, 7th Baronet PC.
> He served in the 19th and 57th Regiments of Foot; twice wounded during the American War of Independence. He then served with the 4th and 94th Regiments of Foot, and later as aide-de-camp to the King, George III.
> He was General Officer Commanding Eastern District in 1805 and later was appointed Secretary at War. (ODNB).

John Quantock (c1770-1820)

> Justice of the Peace. His memorial in Chichester Cathedral states 'for many years a resident magistrate in this city and county; died 10 September 1820 in the 50th year of his age.'

Charles Scrase-Dickins

He was High Sheriff of Sussex (1798).

Henry Thurloe Shadwell (c1756-1807)

Died 1 Oct 1807

Henry Shelley junior (c1767-1811)

Of Patcham. Died 31 Dec 1811. MP for Lewes, 1802-11 (succeeded Thomas Kemp qv), Cornet, 1st Life Guards 1790; Lieutenant 1791; Captain 1794. Aide-de-camp to General Hulse in Holland. He underwent hardships subsequently blamed as 'the foundation of all his sufferings'. He was the last of the male line of the Shelleys of Patcham.

Timothy Shelley (1753-1844)

Sir Timothy Shelley, 2nd Baronet of Castle Goring
He was the son of Sir Bysshe Shelley, 1st Baronet, and father of Percy Bysshe Shelley the poet.
He was MP for New Shoreham 1802-18.

George Shiffner (1762-1842)

Sir George Shiffner, 1st Baronet, of Coombe in Hamsey. Son-in-law of Sir John Bridger (qv).
He was a Cornet in the Regiment of Light Dragoons
Justice of the Peace; Captain of the Lewes Troop of Yeomanry and of the South Lewes Volunteer Battalion.
He was MP for Lewes 1812-26.
He was the cousin-in-law of 'Mad Jack' Fuller (qv)

Inigo Freeman Thomas (1767-1847)

Inigo Freeman Thomas of Ratton in Willingdon was the son of Margaret (née Thomas) and Arthur Freeman of Antigua, and the grandson of Sir George Thomas, 1st Baronet of Yapton and Ratton and Governor of the Leeward Islands.
After inheriting the Thomas family estates he took the surname Thomas.
He was MP for Weobley in Herefordshire 1796-1800
He was Captain of the Eastbourne Yeomanry Cavalry from 1798. In 1807-08, as Major Inigo Thomas, he acted as a senior officer for Pevensey Rape, in charge of Volunteers.

Sir George Thomas, 3rd Baronet (1740–1815)

> The son of Sir William Thomas, 2nd Baronet, he succeeded to the baronetcy in 1777.
> He created Dale Park near Madehurst, built by the architect Joseph Bonomi.
> He served as MP for Arundel 1790-97.

Nathaniel Tredcroft (1747-1825)

> Baptised, lived and died in Horsham. His second son was the Rev Robert Tredcroft, Prebendary of Lincoln and Chichester.

Samuel Twyford (?-1826)

> High Sheriff of Sussex (1795).

Major-General John Whyte

> Major-General Whyte's Regiment of Foot (later The 1st West India Regiment) was created in May 1795, Major-General John Whyte, from the 6th Foot, appointed colonel.

National figures

William Pitt the Younger (1759-1806)

> Younger son of William Pitt, Earl of Chatham.
> He became the youngest ever Prime Minister of Britain, at the age of 24: Prime Minister 1783-1801; and 1804-06.
> Characterised as a Tory at the time, he was initially comfortable working with Whigs such as Charles James Fox, and served under Shelburne as Chancellor of the Exchequer.
> He was Prime Minister throughout the French Revolutionary Wars; his return to power coincided with the early Napoleonic Wars. (ODNB).

Henry Addington, Viscount Sidmouth (1757-1844)

> He was a childhood friend of Pitt, and succeeded him as Prime Minister in 1801, serving until 1804. He oversaw the Treaty of Amiens in 1802, which led to an uneasy peace.
> He was criticized for his lack of energy and defensiveness in prosecuting the subsequent Napoleonic Wars. After Pitt's return, Addington was raised to the peerage as Viscount Sidmouth, and served as Lord President of the Council. Later, he served as Home Secretary from 1812-22. (ODNB).

Henry Dundas, Viscount Melville (1742-1811)

He was a Tory, a dominant figure in the 'Scottish Enlightenment', and a lawyer. A good friend of Pitt, he served under Pitt and Addington as Home Secretary (1791-94), Secretary of State for War (1794-1801) and First Lord of the Admiralty (1804-05).

He was subject to impeachment proceedings in 1806, the last ever attempt to impeach a member of the House of Lords, but was acquitted of misappropriation of public money. (ODNB).

Charles James Fox (1749-1806)

He was a leading Whig statesman who became a bitter political rival of Pitt. Adopting radical opinions, he became a supporter of the American colonists and cheerleader for the French Revolution.

He spent most of his career in opposition, save for a brief spell as Foreign Secretary under Rockingham and North, and later under Grenville.

As the Revolutionary Wars proceeded, he found himself increasingly isolated politically, and finally conceded that his belief in Napoleon's good intentions was unfounded.

He was a nephew of the Duke of Richmond. (ODNB).

Charles Philip Yorke (1764-1834)

A Tory, MP for Cambridgeshire 1790-1810, and for Liskeard 1812-18. Addington appointed him Secretary at War in 1801, and Home Secretary in 1803, in which role he oversaw the Proceedings under the Defence Acts recorded in this volume.

He served as First Lord of the Admiralty in the later years of the Napoleonic Wars. (ODNB).

Edmund Burke (1729-1797)

Irish author, philosopher, statesman.

MP for Wendover 1765-74; for Bristol 1774-80; for Malton 1780-94.

He was a supporter of the Rockingham Whigs; and supported the American colonists during the War of Independence. Today seen as one of the philosophical founders of modern conservatism.

His *Speech to the Electors at Bristol at the Conclusion of the Poll* (1774) is a classic statement of the system of representative government. *Reflections on the Revolution in France* (1790) was an instant best-seller, forecasting accurately the disaster to which the Revolution would lead. (ODNB).

Thomas Malthus (1766-1834)

An Anglican cleric, political economist, statistician and student of demography.

His famous essay *On the Principle of Population* (1798) argued that population numbers increase geometrically, while food production increases only arithmetically. Hence the population would inevitably increase until the agricultural capacity to feed them was exhausted, leading to disease and famine.

The resultant controversy stimulated an intense interest in measuring both population numbers and agricultural productivity; later, his theories were debated by Ricardo, Mill and subsequent generations of political economists. (ODNB).

John Rickman (1771-1840)

Civil servant; statistician; FRS; father of the United Kingdom census.
Charles Abbot (qv), Speaker of the House of Commons, appointed him as his Private Secretary. He drafted the 1800 Census Act, which led to the first ever national census in 1801, and continued to oversee the censuses until his death. In parallel, he served as Speaker's Secretary and as Assistant Clerk to the House of Commons. (ODNB).

BIBLIOGRAPHY

(place of publication is London unless otherwise indicated)

Aspinall, A., and E. A. Smith (eds). 1959. *English Historical Documents 11* (Routledge)

Beckett, I. F. W. 1985. *The Buckinghamshire Posse Comitatus 1798* (Buckinghamshire Record Society No 22)

— — 2011. *Britain's Part-Time Soldiers: The Amateur Military Tradition: 1558–1945*. (Pen & Sword Military, Barnsley)

Braudel, Fernand. 1949. *La Méditerranée et le Monde Méditerranéen a l'époque de Philippe II* (3 vols) (Armand Colin, Paris)

Burke, Edmund. 1790. *Reflections on the Revolution in France etc.* (printed by James Dodsley, Pall Mall)

Carder, Tim. 1990. The Encyclopaedia of Brighton. (Brighton and Hove Libraries) https://www.mybrightonandhove.org.uk/places/placestree/castle-square/castle-square

Clammer, David. 2014. 'Driving the Country. Counter Invasion Planning in Dorset, 1793-1803'. *Journal of the Society for Army Historical Research* Vol 92 No 372

Cobban, Alfred. 1957. *A History of Modern France Vol 1: 1715-1799* (Penguin)

Cobbett, William. 1818. *Parliamentary History Vol XXXIII (1797-98)* (Hansard)

— — 1820. *Parliamentary History Vol XXXVI (1801-03)* (Hansard)

Colley, Linda. 2009. *Britons: Forging the Nation 1707-1837,* revised edition (Yale University Press)

Cookson, J. E. 1985. 'British Society and the French Wars, 1793–1815', *Australian Journal of Politics and History* 31 (2)

— — 1997. *The British Armed Nation, 1793–1815* (Clarendon Press, Oxford)

Coppock, J. T. 1956. 'The Statistical Assessment of British Agriculture', *Agricultural History Review* 4, pp. 4-21

Crook, Malcolm. 2002. *Revolutionary France* (Oxford University Press)

Cruikshank, George. 1803. *A pop-gun fired off by George Cruikshank: in defence of the British volunteers of 1803 etc.* (W. Kent & Co)

Davey, James. 2017. *In Nelson's Wake: The Navy and the Napoleonic Wars* (Yale University Press)

Dickinson, H. T. 1985. *British Radicalism and the French Revolution, 1789-1815* (Blackwell)

— — (ed) 1989. *Britain and the French Revolution, 1789–1815* (Macmillan)

Emsley, Clive. 1979. *British Society and the French Wars 1793–1815* (Macmillan)

—— 1985. 'The Impact of War and Military Participation on Britain and France 1792-1815', in Emsley, C. and J. Wavin (eds), *Artisans, Peasants and Proletarians 1760-1860* (Croom Helm)

Englund, Steven. 2004. *Napoleon: A Political Life* (Harvard University Press)

Evans, Chris. 2006. *Debating the Revolution: Britain in the 1790s* (I. B. Tauris)

Fortescue, J. W. 1909. *The County Lieutenancies and the Army 1803-14* (Macmillan)

Gee, Austin. 1989. *The British Volunteer Movement, 1793–1807,* (PhD thesis, Faculty of Modern History, Oxford University)

—— 2003. *The British Volunteer Movement, 1794–1814* (Clarendon Press, Oxford)

Glover, R. C. 1973. *Britain at Bay: Defence against Bonaparte 1803-14* (Allen & Unwin)

Goodwin, John. 1985. *The Military Defence of West Sussex: 500 Years of Fortification of Coast Between Brighton & Selsey* (Middleton Press, Midhurst)

Hampshire Archives & Local Studies. Retrieved 14 October 2018, 'Discovering Waterloo and the Napoleonic Wars through the Archives', n.d., http://documents.hants.gov.uk/archives/DiscoveringWaterlooNapoleonicwarsthroughthearchives.pdf

Henderson, H. C. K. 1952a. 'The 1801 Crop Returns for Sussex', *Sussex Archaeological Collections* 90, pp. 51-59

—— 1952b. 'Agriculture in England and Wales in 1801', *Geographical Journal* CXVIII, pp. 338-45

Hicks, Peter 2008. 'The Militarization of Society in Georgian Britain and Napoleonic France' *Napoleonica. La Revue*, n°1, mai – août

Holland Rose, John. 1911. *William Pitt and the Great War* (G Bell & Sons)

Home Office: Acreage Returns (HO 67): List and Analysis Part I Bedfordshire to Isle of Wight, 1801, List and Index Society Vol 189, 1982

Home Office: Acreage Returns (HO 67): List and Analysis Part II Jersey to Somerset, 1801, List and Index Society Vol 190, 1982

Home Office: Acreage Returns (HO 67), Transcript and Analysis, Pt. III, Staffs.-Worcs, 1801, List and Index Society Vol 195, 1983

Hudson, Ann. 1984. 'Volunteer Soldiers in Sussex During the Revolutionary and Napoleonic Wars, 1793-1815' *SAC* 122, pp. 165-81

Jefferies, Julie. 2005. 'The UK population: past, present and future', *People and Migration 2005 edition (ed) Roma Chappell* (HMSO)

Jurkevich, Gayana. 2000. *In Pursuit of the Natural Sign*. (Bucknell University Press, Pennsylvania USA)

Kenyon, G. H. 1950. 'The Civil Defence and Livestock Returns for Sussex in 1801: with particular reference to the returns for Kirdford Parish in 1798', *Sussex Archaeological Collections* 89, pp. 57-84

—— 1954. 'Livestock in Icklesham, 1798 and comparative livestock figures for Sussex and Essex, 1798 and 1801', *Sussex Notes and Queries* 14, pp. 48-50

Kitchen, Frank. 1991. 'Aspects of the defence of the south coast of England: 1756-1805', *Fort* 19, pp. 11-22

Knight, Roger. 2013. *Britain Against Napoleon: The Organization of Victory, 1793–1815* (Allen Lane)

Le Roy Ladurie, Emmanuel. 1975. *Montaillou, village occitan de 1294 à 1324* (Folio, Paris)

Laslett, Peter. 1984. *The World We Have Lost, further explored* (Charles Scribner's Sons, New York)

Leslie, Kim C. and Brian Short. 1999. *An Historical Atlas of Sussex* (Phillimore & Co, Bognor Regis)

Lloyd, Peter A. 1991. *The French are Coming: the Invasion Scare 1803-5* (Spellmount Ltd, Tunbridge Wells)

Longstaff-Tyrell, Peter. 2000. *Front-Line Sussex: Napoleon Bonaparte to the Cold War* (Sutton Publishing, Stroud)

Ludlum, David M. 1989. 'Bad Weather and the Bastille', *Weatherwise*, vol 42, Issue 3 pp. 141-42

Malthus, Thomas. 1798. *On the Principle of Population*

Minchinton, W. E. 1953. 'Agricultural Returns and the Government during the Napoleonic Wars', *Agricultural History Review* I, pp. 29-43

Mori, Jennifer. 2000. *Britain in the Age of the French Revolution: 1785-1820* (Routledge)

Morland, Paul. 2019. *The Human Tide: How Population Shaped the Modern World* (John Murray Press)

Neumann, J. 1977. 'Great Historical Events that were Significantly Affected by the Weather: 2, the Year Leading to the Revolution of 1789 in France'. *Bulletin American Meteorological Society,* vol 58 No 2

—— and J. Dettwiller. 1990. 'Great Historical Events that were Significantly Affected by the Weather: Part 9, the Year Leading to the Revolution of 1789 in France (II)'. *Bulletin American Meteorological Society*, vol 71 No 1

Norman, Jesse (ed). 2015. *Edmund Burke. Reflections on the Revolution in France and Other Writings* (Everyman)

Olson, Alison Gilbert. 1961. *The Radical Duke: The Career and Correspondence of Charles Lennox, Third Duke of Richmond* (Oxford University Press)

Knight, Roger. Britain Against Napoleon: The Organization of Victory, 1793-1815 (p. 571). Penguin Books Ltd. Kindle Edition.

Philp, Mark (ed). 2006. *Resisting Napoleon: The British Response to the Threat of Invasion 1797–1815* (Routledge)

Philp, Mark. 2011. 'Britain and the French Revolution'. 17 February 2011. www.bbc.co.uk/history/british/empire_seapower/british_french_rev_01.shtml retrieved 24 November 2018

Rashid, Salim. 1980. 'The Scarcity of 1800: a Contemporary Account', *Agricultural History Review*, 48, 2, pp. 115-119

Reese, M. M. 1987. *Goodwood's Oak. The Life and Times of the Third Duke of Richmond, Lennox and Aubigny* (Threshold Books)

Salzman, L. F. 1961. Review of Olson (1961), *Sussex Notes and Queries* November 1961

Schama, Simon. 1989. *Citizens. A Chronicle of the French Revolution* (Random House, New York)

Sebag-Montefiori, Cecil. 1908. *A History of the Volunteer Forces From The Earliest Times To The Year 1860: Being A Recital Of The Citizen Duty* (Constable)

Smith, Charles. 1758. *Three Tracts On The Corn-trade And Corn-laws: Viz: A Short Essay On The Corn-trade And The Corn-laws etc.*

— — 1804. *Tracts on the Corn-Trade and Corn-Laws. New edition*

Tamplin, Steve. n.d. 'Britain's Volunteer Movement 1794 – 1815', retrieved 21 October 2018, http://www.loyalvolunteers.org/history/britains_volunteer_movement.htm

Thorne, R. G. n.d. Charles Abbot. http://www.historyofparliamentonline.org/volume/1790-1820/member/abbot-charles-1757-1829 retrieved 28 December 2018

Tombs, Robert. 2014. *The English and their History: The First Thirteen Centuries* (Penguin)

Turner, Michael (ed). 1983. *Home Office: Acreage Returns (HO 67), Transcript and Analysis, Pt. 3, Staffs.-Worcs, 1801*, List and Index Society, Vol 195

— — 1998. 'Counting Sheep: Waking up to New Estimates of Livestock Numbers in England c 1800', *Agricultural History Review*, 46, 2, pp. 142-161

Walton, Clifford. 1894. *History of the British Standing Army A.D. 1660 to 1700.* (Harrison and Sons)

Watson, J. Steven. 1960. *The Reign of George III 1760-1815* (Oxford University Press)

Western, J. R. 1965. *The English militia in the eighteenth century: the story of a political issue 1660-1802* (Routledge)

Wheeler, H. F. B., and Alexander Broadley. 1908. *Napoleon and the Invasion of England: The Story of the Great Terror* (London)

Williams, Noel T. St John. 1994. *Redcoats and courtesans: the birth of the British Army (1660–1690)* (Brassey's)

Williams, Orlo. 1912. *Lamb's Friend the Census-Taker. Life and Letters of John Rickman* (Houghton Mifflin, New York)

Williamson, Philip, Alisdair Raffe, Stephen Taylor and Natalie Mears (eds) 2017 *National Prayers: Special Worship Since the Reformation, Volume 2: General Fasts, Thanksgivings and Special Prayers in the British Isles, 1689-1870* (Church of England Record Society 22)

Wrigley, E. A. and R. S. Schofield. 1981. *The Population History of England 1541-1871: a Reconstruction* (Cambridge University Press)

Young, Arthur. 1797. *National Danger and the Means of Safety*

Young, Rev. Arthur. 1793. *General View of the Agriculture of the County of Sussex*, (1813 edition, David & Charles reprints, 1970)

EDITORIAL POLICIES

I have aimed to reproduce the deliberations of the Lieutenancy meetings, and the schedules of data they endorsed, in a way which does justice to the source material in terms of layout, pagination etc.; but which also aids contemporary review and research.

In the great majority of cases of the 1801 returns, the pagination of the main schedules here follows the pagination of the original; I have only occasionally had to take a small number of rows to a following page. In the various schedules, I have occasionally rationalised column headings and layout for consistency and to facilitate internal comparison. However, the great majority of the schedule entries are laid out to represent their original layout (as the illustrative samples show).

The schedules in the 1803 returns are rather more complex, and often scrappily completed; in addition, the clerks tended to create their own variations of layout, column headings etc. Here, I have more often broken a table at a more convenient point, or rationalized headings and layout for greater consistency. Nevertheless, all content has been preserved and faithfully transcribed.

Occasionally, Remarks have been moved to a note below the table to facilitate presentation.

Where a figure of nil was returned, the clerks variously, and inconsistently, recorded this as either a dash (-), a zero (0) or a blank ( ). I have standardized all these as dashes.

Where proper names are abbreviated in the manuscript, I have silently expanded them (William for Wm, James for Jas etc.): names are referenced in full in the Index, and there was little benefit in retaining the abbreviated forms in the text. (The practice of the clerks was inconsistent.) There is one exception to this policy: where individual signatures are written with an abbreviation — most notably in the case of Wm Ellis, Clerk to the General Meetings — I have retained the abbreviated form as representing the writer's original intention. Similarly, I have silently expanded 'Jan' to 'January', 'Feb' to 'February' etc.

Some names have been quietly modernised for consistency (e.g. Arundel for Arundell), especially in the headings to schedules; obvious scribal errors (e.g. Fortington for Tortington, Newhurst for Ewhurst) have occasionally been amended, again for consistency and to facilitate searching and indexing. I have generally retained titles and honorifics as per the original (William Ellis used

'Esq' and 'Esquire' variously), although I have silently expanded some of the more idiosyncratic ones (e.g. 'Honourable' for 'Honble').[109]

I have transcribed variant spellings and/or errors as they exist in the original, mainly without comment, although I have reverted sparingly to the occasional use of [sic] to offer assurance of a faithful reading. Where appropriate, initial capital letters have been silently inserted at the start of quotations.

The Schedules published here were – obviously – compiled without the benefit of modern spreadsheets or electronic calculators, and must have involved substantial manual arithmetic. In preparing this edition, all the Schedules have been checked and re-calculated, not least to confirm the accuracy of the present transcription. It is perhaps surprising, not that there were errors in the original tallies but that there were comparatively few. Where there are errors in the Schedules, the original figures have been retained in the transcription, with notes to the tables recording corrections where necessary.

It is not possible to trace definitively the source of the arithmetical errors, whether they were in the schedules as originally submitted, in their intermediate summaries or in their final consolidation. However, it is suggestive that the Schedules for Arundel are significantly less accurate in this respect than those for other Rapes. This perhaps suggests that the subdivision clerk for Arundel was less competent or diligent than the others; or that William Ellis, Clerk to the Lieutenancy Meetings, copied rather than recalculated the entries and totals submitted to him. But this may be to speculate too far on the process of producing these Schedules.

---

[109] William Ellis preferred the spelling 'honorable' to 'honourable' when he used the full form.

FACING INVASION:
PROCEEDINGS UNDER THE DEFENCE ACTS 1801-1805

PROCEEDINGS UNDER THE DEFENCE ACTS

[13 August 1801]

> Proceedings at a Meeting of Lieutenancy held at the White Hart Inn in Lewes in the County of Sussex the thirteenth Day of August One thousand eight hundred and one pursuant to an Advertizement in the Lewes Paper signed by his Majesty's Lieutenant of the said County for that purpose

Present

> His Grace the Duke of Richmond in the Chair
> Earl of Egremont
> Lord Pelham
> John Fuller, Rosehill
> Francis Newberry
> Captain Shiffner
> Edmund Cranston
> John Trayton Fuller
> Inigo Freeman Thomas
> Henry Thurloe Shadwell
> Colonel Newton
> William Green
> Thomas Kemp
> J M Lloyd
> Mr Poyntz
> Henry Shelley His Majesty's Deputy Lieutenant
>
> Justices of the Peace and Captains of Yeomanry Corps in the said County[110]

Read the Act of Parliament of the 38th of the King Chap 27 entitled 'an Act to enable his Majesty more effectually to provide for the Defence and Security of the Realm during the present War, and for indemnifying Persons who may suffer in their Property by such Measures as may be necessary for that purpose 5th April 1798.'

Read His Majesty's Warrant under sign Manual to the Lieutenant of this County bearing date the 6th of April 1798.

Read two Letters from Mr Dundas when Secretary of State of the 6th and 7th of April 1798 to His Majesty's Lieutenant of this County.

---

[110] Also present were Lieutenant General Hulse, District Commander, and Major General Whyte, Commander in Sussex; cf. Richmond to Hobart, 14 August 1801, Appendix 5.

Read the Paper entitled Proposed Arrangement for removing the Live Stock from the Coast of the County of Sussex dated the 7th April 1798 and given in by General Sir Charles (now Lord) Grey to the General Meeting of Lieutenancy held the 27th of May 1798 which Paper also contains proposed arrangements for the removal of the Dead Stock.

Read a paper entitled 'addition to the arrangement for removing the Live Stock from Sussex in consequence of the Act of Parliament confirming the Indemnity to the Inhabitants'.

Read a Letter of Lord Hobart's one of His Majesty's Principal Secretaries of State to His Majesty's Lieutenant of this County bearing date the 15th of June 1801.

Read a printed Paper transmitted in the said Letter entitled 'a Plan for removing the live Stock from the Coast of Great Britain etc etc etc'.

Read a Letter from Lieutenant General Hulse commanding in the Southern District of the 23rd June 1801 to his Majesty's Lieutenant for this County in Consequence of the offer he states to have made to him to attend him at any time and place he should appoint pursuant to his Majesty's Commands.

Read Lieut Genl Hulse's Orders of the 1st of August 1801 communicated to his Majesty's Lieutenant by Major General Whyte.

Resolved

That it is the most Anxious wish of this Meeting zealously and cordially either in their Public or Private Capacities to cooperate as far as they are able with such arrangements as His Majesty shall in his Wisdom think proper to direct for carrying into execution the Provisions of the Act of Parliament of the 38th of the King Chap 27 or for otherwise providing for the Defence of the Kingdom in which this County having near ninety Miles of Coast immediately opposite to and within twelve Hours Sail of the Enemy feels itself most deeply and particularly interested.

That it appears by the Act of the 38th of the King Chap 27 Sect 7 That it is lawfull for his Majesty to authorize and empower by order under his Majesty's Sign Manual his Lieutenants and Deputy Lieutenants or any of them on any Emergency and on the Requisition of such other Person as his Majesty shall specially empower to make such Requisition to give all such orders as shall be necessary for the removal of all Cattle Corn and the other Articles therein specified, and also in case of necessity to destroy such Cattle, Corn and other Articles which may be of advantage to the Enemy.

And by Section 8 that the giving Orders for the removal of Cattle, Corn, or any other Article which may be of advantage to the Enemy or useful to the Public Service, is left to the Lieutenants, Deputy Lieutenants or any of them when actual Invasion or the actual appearance of the Enemy on the Coast, or the Danger of Invasion is deemed so imminent as to make it adviseable for them to give such orders.

That Mr Dundas's dispatch of the 6th of April 1798 enjoins it as His Majesty's express command that the Provisions of the Act then transmitted of the 38th of the King Chap 27 should be punctually attended to (as far as they are applicable) in the County of Sussex.

That the said Letter states that some Allowance must be made in the application so general and extensive for unforeseen Contingencies and that in this case His Majesty trusting to his Lieutenant and His Deputy Lieutenants not to lose sight of the Principle of the Measures is graciously pleased to leave it to their joint Discretion to act according to Circumstances. But in another part of the said Letter it mentions that the General of the District will attend the Meeting of the Lieutenancy and submit and explain to them the Plans and local Arrangements prepared and determined upon by Him in concert with his Royal Highness the Commander in Cheif and his Majesty's Ministers upon each of the Heads in which the Assistance of the Civil Power acting in Concert with Him will be necessary for carrying them into execution.

That Mr Dundas's Letter of 7th April 1798 states that his foregoing Instructions were framed to give additional energy and extension to the Plans of Defence recommended by the General and liable to such deviation (if any) as might be necessary to accommodate them to those plans: that the Grounds which may have been stated to justify any departure from the General system of Measures specified in his Instructions should be reported to him. And that the degree of Latitude His Majesty's Lieutenant should possess in the arrangement of Defence to be made in the County of Sussex should be both for the purpose of placing it on the same Footing as the remainder of the District and in order to ensure the concurrence of the General intrusted with the Defence of the same in whatever steps may be adopted with that view.

That the Letter of Lord Hobart one of His Majesty's present Secretaries of State dated the 15th of June 1801 transmitting to His Majesty's Lieutenant another plan that has been arranged for facilitating the Measures which should be adopted with a view to the security of the Inhabitants and their Property and the Prevention of Confusion in the event of any attempt being made by the Enemy to effect a Landing upon the Coast of Great Britain particularly recommends it to him to communicate with the General Officer Commanding the District in which the County of Sussex is situated upon the subject of it: And informs him that he will be instructed by His Royal Highness the Commander in Chief to act in Concert with him and His Majesty expects that they will together arrange the Measures which it may be proper to adopt if circumstances should at any time occur to render it necessary that this plan should be carried into quick and effectual Execution.

That Lieutenant General Hulse's Letter to his Majesty's Lieutenant of the 23rd June 1801 and His General Orders dated the 1st August 1801 explain that the plan of Sir Charles (now Lord) Grey is to be pointedly attended to.

That the Plan given in by Sir Charles (now Lord) Grey in 1798 divides this County first into two great Divisions of North and South and afterwards the North into eight and the South into nine Subdivisions, making in all seventeen Subdivisions.

That in two of the cases there pointed out of a landing being effected five of the Southern Divisions are to be cleared immediately, that is to say 5/17 of the County supposing the Divisions to be nearly equal but if the produce in Corn of the Southern Divisions be much greater, as it is believed they are, than in the Northern Divisions it will not be too much to say that the five Southern Divisions to be cleared will be equal to one-third of the County, and if the Northern Divisions immediately behind them are afterwards cleared it will exceed one half of the County.

That it appears from the aggregate of the Returns made in 1798 that there were at that time in the County

   89990 Quarters of Wheat
   52742 do of Oats
    7294 do of Barley
    3127 do of Pease and Beans
   23740 do of Malt

   176893 Quarters of Grain

That if the Grain from one third of the County amounting to 58,964 Quarters is to be removed, supposing ten Quarters to be carried in a Waggon drawn by four Horses, or Oxen it will require 5896 Teams and the foregoing Return of Grain having been made in the Month of May when only one Third of the Produce may be supposed to have been left unconsumed. This Quantity must be Treble immediately after Harvest, which would require 17,688 Waggons, to remove the Grain from only one third of the County.

That it appears by the same Returns that there were then in the County 35040 Loads of Hay, one third of which would require 11680 Teams to remove, and as the Quantity at this Season of the Year may be supposed treble to what it was in May it would now require 35040 Waggons to remove the Hay.

That it appears by the same Returns that the Number of Persons who from Age, Infancy, Infirmity or other causes may probably be incapable of removing themselves, amounted in the whole County to 57837 one third of which is 19279 and supposing 30 persons could be removed in one Waggon it would require 642 Waggons for this purpose.

That the Total Number of Waggons as above stated requisite to remove only the Grain and Persons incapable of removing themselves would be 18330 Waggons.

That the number of Waggons reported in the said Returns to be in the whole County is 6434 and Carts 11,232 and allowing two Carts to carry as much as one Waggon they will be equal to 5616 making in all 12,050 Waggons in the whole County, one third of which supposed to belong to the third of the County to be cleared will amount to 4016 Waggons which is 14314 Waggons short of what would be wanted for removing only the Grain and Persons incapable of removing themselves independently of what would be wanted for removing valuable Effects and Flour, Potatoes, Pork, Bacon and other Salt Meat, Cheese and Liquor of which no Account is here taken. If the Hay were also to be removed there would be the deficiency of 25994 Teams.

That it appears by the said Returns that the number of Persons between the age of 15 and 60 willing to serve as Servants with Teams or as drivers of Carriages amounted to 5126 in the whole County one third of which is 1708 and allowing two Men to each Team they would supply only 854 Teams.

That it appears by the said Returns that the total Number of Men in the whole County between the ages of 15 and 60 is 30,686 from which being deducted the Number of Persons infirm or incapable of active Service amounting to 2738 the remainder is 27,948. That if 18330 Waggons are necessary to remove only the Grain and Persons incapable of removing themselves from one third of the

County, and each Waggon requires two Men to attend it, it would amount to 36,660 Men wanted for this Service which is one third more than there are Men between the age of 15 and 60 fit for Service in the whole County.

That it further appears by the above mentioned Returns that the total Number of Draft Horses in the whole County was but 18,414. The draft Oxen are not distinguished, but supposing them to amount to the same number which is probably much overrating them, the total of the Draft Cattle would be 36828 and taking one third for the District to be cleared would give 12276 Draft Cattle which for 18330 Teams is only about two thirds of one Draft Cattle for each Team.

That altho' these Returns may and probably in many particulars are very erroneous, yet it appears to this Meeting of the Lieutenancy that they are sufficient from the foregoing statements to prove that there are neither *Carriages, Men* or *Draft Cattle* to remove the Grain and Persons incapable of removing themselves, from the District proposed. They therefore wish to submit it to the Consideration of the General commanding in the Southern District, and to his Majesty's Ministers whether the local Circumstances of this County proving the impracticability of removing the Grain soon after Harvest or indeed at a later Period with the Persons incapable of removing themselves from so large an extent of Territory it may not be more advantageous for the Defence of the County to avoid the Confusion which an attempt at what cannot be performed is likely to create, especially as it is presumed that if the Mills are rendered for a time unserviceable unthreshed Corn would be of little use to an Enemy, and whether the previous destruction pointed out of what could not be removed from a large Tract of Fertile Country might not prove great and unnecessary waste in these times of Scarcity when possibly only a small part of it might fall into the Enemy's Hands.

That it is further submitted to the General that if as directed in Mr Dundas's Letter the depriving the Enemy of Supplies is to be combined with the means of furnishing our own Forces with every requisite, the removal of Dead Stock cannot be attempted without depriving Him of Horses for the Artillery and Waggons for the supplies of his Army. That he be requested to state what number of Draft Horses, Oxen, Waggons and Carts He will want for this Service and that of the Commissary and the Terms on which he would retain them; after which, when the new Returns come in the Lieutenancy will use their best endeavours to forward such an arrangement.

That it appears by the aforementioned Returns that the number of Oxen, Cows and young Cattle in the whole County then amounted to 60885 and Sheep, Deer, Goats and Pigs to 549,991.

That if the General thinks any considerable part of these or only the Carriages, Horses and Draft Oxen can be removed without creating much Confusion, it is submitted to him, whether for this Purpose and indeed at all Events it would not be better to subdivide the Districts proposed by Sir Charles (now Lord) Grey into smaller Portions, perhaps reverting to the old Division of Parishes or hundreds would facilitate the Execution as far as regards the civil Power, and the General having a Map of the County with the Parishes and Hundreds marked on it, would then be enabled as occasion might require to make His requisition to a Deputy Lieutenant for the removal the sort of Cattle he would think proper from such places only as he would wish to have the Cattle drove from, without in the least hindering Him from making his Requisition that the Cattle from the whole of the Districts as marked out by Sir Charles now Lord Grey should be driven, if he should judge so extensive a measure to be necessary and practicable.

That as far as removing the Carriages Draft Horses or Oxen from a few Hundreds the Lieutenancy conceive such an operation (which they understand is the most essential of any) could easily be performed with regularity and they will readily apply themselves to arrange the Execution of it.

They will also if the General will suggest such a Plan as shall be approved by Government for engaging a Corps of Pioneers to serve in this County and the retaining Bounties that should be given to them, give it every assistance in their power.

As to the Corps of Gamekeepers the Lieutenancy imagine that the Officers of Yeomanry will easily induce Men of that Description to join them in case of actual Invasion, when they trust that they may in the first Instance and being so immediately on the spot be employed in attacking or annoying the Enemy rather than in retiring from Him and driving away the Cattle.

That is respect to the Commissary General the Lieutenancy trust he will be better able to make his Contracts with Individuals than by their fixing a Price for Grain or Carriage which moreover they are not apprized of their being authorized by Law to do.

That the Lieutenancy do not find themselves authorized by any Law to call upon the Clergy to take the Returns proposed in the plan transmitted in Lord

Hobart's Letter but will direct such as shall be approved by the General to be made out by the Peace Officers Church Wardens and Overseers of the Poor as by Law is directed in this County.

That his Majesty's Lieutenant for this County be requested to communicate the proceedings of this Meeting and the above resolutions to the General Commanding in the Southern District and to one of his Majesty's Principal Secretaries of State repeating the Assurances of their Zeal to promote all such Measures as His Majesty shall think fit to adopt for the Defence of the Realm. But when called upon to carry into Execution Measures that from the nature and local Circumstances of this County it is out of their power to perform they submit with all Duty and respect the Grounds for such Modifications of the plan proposed as shall enable them really to fulfill His Majesty's just Expectations from the known Loyalty of this County.

NB. Since the above calculation has been made it appears by measuring on the Map the several Districts in a rough way that they contain of square miles as follows.

1st	District of the Southern Division of Sussex	78	square miles
2nd	Do	116	Do
3rd	Do	116	Do
4th	Do	129	Do
5th	Do	144	Do
6th	Do	112	Do
7th	Do	141	Do
8th	Do	108	Do
9th	Do	112	Do

	Northern Division		
1st	District	12	square miles
2nd	Do	36	Do
3rd	Do	42	Do
4th	Do	60	Do
5th	Do	36	Do
6th	Do	32	Do
7th	Do	80	Do
8th	Do	72	Do

In the two cases where the 2nd, 3rd, 4th, 5th and 6th, and 5th, 6th, 7th, 8th and 9th Southern Districts are to be cleared it will appear that each of those Lots of five Districts contain 617 square miles.

And the whole County appearing to contain only about 1426 square Miles either of these parcels of five Districts would amount to about 3/7 of the whole County. The foregoing Calculations having been made upon a supposition that they contained only one third of the County is therefore too little by about one tenth as to the quantity of Grain to be removed, and the Means of removing it remaining the same they are of course by one tenth more Deficient than has been stated.

This Meeting is adjourned to the Star Inn in Lewes aforesaid until the 14th Day of September next to be then and there held at Eleven o'clock in the forenoon.

Wm. Ellis [clerk]

[14 September 1801]

Proceedings of a Meeting of Lieutenancy held at the Star Inn in Lewes in the County of Sussex the 14th Day of September 1801 Pursuant to an Advertisement in the Lewes Paper signed by His Majesty's Lieutenant of the said County for that Purpose

Present

His Grace the Duke of Richmond in the Chair
Inigo Freeman Thomas
John Trayton Fuller
Thomas Phillips Lamb
William Green
John Luxford
Charles Goring
Thomas Kemp
Henry Thurloe Shadwell
William John Campion
William Newton
Edward Harvey
Henry Shelley
George Shiffner
Earl of Egremont

His Majesty's Deputy Lieutenants
Justices of the Peace and Captains of Yeomanry Corps in the said County

The following Papers were read, Vizt

At the Court of Weymouth the 7th of September 1801

Present
The King's Most Excellent Majesty in Council

Whereas by an Act passed in the 38th year of His Majesty's reign Intituled 'An Act to enable His Majesty more effectually to provide for the Defence and Security of the Realm during the present War, and for indemnifying Persons who may suffer in their Property, by such Measures as may be Necessary for that Purpose' His Majesty is empowered, by and with the advice of his Privy Council to order and require from time to time, as His Majesty shall see occasion, the Lieutenants of the several Counties, Ridings and Places within that Part of Great Britain called England and of the several Counties, Stewartries, Cities and Places within that Part of Great Britain called Scotland

and their Deputy Lieutenants acting as Lieutenants under the Law now in force, to appoint proper Officers to be ready for arraying, Training, Exercising and Commanding such Men as shall be willing to engage themselves to be armed trained and exercised for the Defence of the Kingdom and also proper Persons to be in like Manner ready in case of need, for superintending and directing the Execution of the several other Duties which may be necessary to be done for the several Purposes mentioned in the said Act. His Majesty in Pursuance of the Powers given by the said Act, is pleased, by and with the advice of his Privy Council, to order and require, and doth hereby order and require the Lieutenant or Deputy Lieutenants acting as Lieutenants of the County of Sussex to appoint proper Officers to be ready for Arraying, Training, Exercising and Commanding such Men as shall be willing to engage themselves to be armed, trained and exercised as aforesaid; and the said Lieutenant or Deputy Lieutenants acting as Lieutenants as aforesaid, are hereby further ordered and required to appoint proper Persons to be in like Manner ready, in case of need, to superintend and direct the Execution of the several other Duties which may be necessary to be done for the several purposes mentioned in the said Act; But as it is His Majesty's Pleasure nevertheless, that such Officers and other Persons shall be appointed in such Numbers and under such Regulations, and Restrictions only as His Majesty shall think fit to order and direct, the said Lieutenant or Deputy Lieutenants acting as Lieutenants as aforesaid are hereby Ordered and Directed to signify to His Majesty the Names and Ranks of all Officers so to be appointed and the Purposes for which they are so To be appointed, on or before the tenth Day of October next in order that such Officers and Persons only may be appointed as His Majesty shall approve.   Steph. Cottrell

George R

Whereas by an Act passed in the thirty-eighth year of our reign intituled 'An Act to enable His Majesty more effectually to provide for the Defence and Security of the Realm, and for indemnifying Persons who may suffer in their Property by such Measures as may be Necessary for that Purpose' divers Provisions are made for procuring the Returns of the Number of Men residing within the several Counties Ridings Stewartries Cities and Places in Great Britain of the Age of Fifteen and under the Age of Sixty Years and of divers other Particulars in the said Act mentioned and specified and of such other Particulars as We shall require for the Purpose of enabling Us and the Persons acting under Our Authority to give such Orders as may be necessary for the Purposes in the said Act mentioned And We are by the said Act empowered by Order under our Sign Manual to authorize and require the several Lieutenants and Deputy Lieutenants of such Counties Ridings Stewartries Cities and Places respectively to hold such General and Subdivision Meetings in their respective Counties Ridings Stewartries Cities and places as We shall think fit and as shall be necessary for the Execution of the said Act and to require for such Purposes the attendance of such Persons as in the said Act mentioned and general Power and Authority is thereby given to the said Lieutenants and Deputy Lieutenants and all Justices of the Peace Constables Tythingmen Headboroughs and other Officers to do within their respective Counties Ridings Stewartries Cities and Places all such Acts Matters and Things as shall be required by Us to be done by them respectively in the execution of the said Act as they have to do the several Matters and Things by Law required to be done by them respectively by any Act now in force concerning the Militia Forces of this Kingdom We do hereby in Pursuance of the said Act authorize and require you your several Deputy Lieutenants and the Justices of the Peace of our County of Sussex and all others whom it may concern to hold a General Meeting of the Lieutenancy of Our said County at such a Place as you shall think fit to appoint for that Purpose on or before the first Day of October next and then and there and also from time to time afterwards as occasion may require to appoint such General and Subdivision Meetings of Lieutenancy within the said County to be held at such Place and at such Times as you shall find necessary and expedient for the Purposes of procuring such Returns as in the said Act is mentioned and of executing these Our Orders and any other Orders which you may receive from Us through one of Our Principal Secretaries of State in Conformity to the Provisions of the said Act and for the due Execution of the same And We do further order and require you and such Deputy Lieutenants and Justices of the Peace as shall be present at such Subdivision Meetings respectively and all Constables and other Officers within such Subdivisions respectively to do all Acts Matters and Things necessary for these purposes which you and they are enabled to do respectively by the Laws now in force concerning the Militia Forces of the Kingdom And for so doing this shall be your Warrant Given at our Court at St James's the twelfth Day of September 1801 in the forty first year of our Reign

To
Our Right Trusty and Right
Entirely Beloved Cousin and
Councillor Charles Duke of   By His Majesty's
Richmond Our Lieutenant of our   Command
County of Sussex or in his
Absence to the Deputy Lieutenants   Hobart
of our said County

My Lord   Downing Street Sept 12th 1801

It being judged expedient under the present Circumstances that every possible preparation should be made in the County of Sussex for enabling your Grace to carry into effect the several Provisions of the Act of the 38th of the King in Case His Majesty should hereafter see especial cause to direct the execution of the Provisions of the said Act in Manner pointed out in the 7th and 8th Clauses thereof, I herewith transmit to your Grace, His Majesty's Warrant authorizing you to hold a General Meeting of the Lieutenancy of the County and such further General Meetings as may be requisite for that Purpose, together with His Majesty's Order in Council of the seventh Instant under which your Grace will proceed to the Appointment of such Persons as you may think proper to recommend for His Majesty's Approbation to superintend and direct the execution of the several Duties which may arise in carrying into effect the measures adopted by your Grace in conformity to the Act above mentioned I have the Honour to be My Lord Duke your Grace's most Obedient humble servant Hobart

P.S. Your Grace is earnestly requested to call the first Meeting of your County as much before the 1st of October as you conveniently can

To
The Lord Lieutenant of the County of Sussex

Ordered

That a copy of the Letter from H. M. Lieutenant of the 29th August 1801 to several Gentlemen requesting to know whether they would lend their Assistance to superintend or direct the Removal of the live Stock in case of Invasion and the Parishes they would undertake for together with the answers received be referred to the several Subdivision Meetings to which they belong

And that the Deputy Lieutenants and Justices of the Peace as such Subdivision Meetings do take such Offers into Consideration and form a Plan for the distribution of Parishes into such Districts as may appear to them most convenient to be placed under a superintendant of Removals. That they would recommend such Gentlemen as are willing and they think most proper to be so appointed Superintendants for each District. And such Persons as are willing and they think most proper to be appointed Directors of Removals in each Parish. And to make their Report accordingly to the next General Meeting to be held at Lewes on the 8th day of October next at the white Hart Inn at Eleven O'Clock in the forenoon.

And the several Letters above mentioned were delivered to the several Subdivision Clerks accordingly.

At this Meeting the several Subdivision Meetings for this County were appointed as follows (Vizt)

Hastings Rape, on Wednesday the 30th Inst. at the George Inn in Battle.
Pevensey, the same Day at the Sheffield Arms in Fletching.
Lewes, the same Day at the White Hart Inn in Lewes.
Bramber, the same Day, at the Chequers Inn in Steyning.
Arundell, the same Day, at the Half Moon in Petworth.
Chichester, the same Day, at the Swan Inn in Chichester.

At this Meeting the several Deputy Lieutenants hereunder mentioned were appointed as hereunder mentioned for the purpose of directing the Stock in case of Invasion to be removed and for fully putting the said Act into Execution (Vizt)

Hastings Rape	Henry Cresset Pelham William Markwick & John Fuller of Parkgate Esqs
Pevensey	Edward Cranston and Charles Gilbert Esquires
Lewes	John Lord Sheffield Henry Shelley and William Green Esquires
Bramber	Charles Goring and Nathaniel Tredcroft Esquires
Arundell	Walter Smyth Esquire and Sir George Thomas Baronet
Chichester	William Brereton and Samuel Twyford Esquires

And this Meeting is adjourned until the 8th Day of October accordingly to be then held at the White Hart Inn in Lewes aforesaid.
                    Wm Ellis [Clerk]

[8 October 1801]

Further Proceedings of a Meeting held at the White Hart Inn in Lewes in the County of Sussex on Thursday the 8th of October 1801 pursuant to the Adjournment of that last Meeting for that Purpose

Present

John Lord Sheffield
Mr Shadwell
Mr Kemp
Mr Fuller ParkGate
Mr Cranston
Mr Lamb
Captain Shiffner
Colonel Newton
Captain I F Thomas
His Majesty's Deputy Lieutenants Justices of the Peace and Captains of Yeomanry Corps in the said County

[At this meeting]

At this Meeting the Clerks to the Justices of the several and respective Subdivision Meetings in the said County returned the following Schedules pursuant to an Order of the last general Meeting for that Purpose (Vizt)

Chichester Rape Schedule No 1

A summary of the Returns made by the Churchwardens and Overseers of the Poor Rape the 30th September and 3rd October 1801 pursuant to the Act of Parliament for Realm etc

Names of Hundreds and Parishes	No of men and boys between the ages of 15 and 60 who are capable of active service	No of men and boys between the ages of 15 and 60 who are incapable of active service	No of men above the age of 60 who are capable of active service	No of men above the age of 60 who are incapable of active service	No of men above the age of 60 who are capable of removing themselves	No of men above the age of 60 who are incapable of removing themselves
Aldwick Hundred						
Southbersted	104	11	5	13	3	1
Pagham	119	12	9	11	-	5
Slindon	100	17	-	15	11	11
Tangmere	36	3	2	3	3	-
E. & W. Lavant	65	5	4	3	3	1
	424	48	20	45	20	18
Manwood Hd						
Sidlesham	114	9	-	1	7	5
Selsea	130	1	-	11	4	5
Earnley	34	2	-	-	3	1
East Wittering	62	4	-	-	-	2
West Wittering	92	3	5	3	4	2
Itchenor	31	2	4	1	3	1
Birdham	85	5	2	6	6	6
	548	26	11	22	27	22
Bosham Hd						
West Thorney	No return					
Chidham	43	8	2	2	3	1
Bosham	161	16	1	21	22	4
Funtingdon	141	21	2	39	30	11
West Stoke	26	9	8	-	-	-
	371	54	13	62	55	16

of the several Parishes of the said Rape at two Subdivision Meetings held for the said enabling His Majesty more effectually to provide for the Defence and Security of the

No of women or girls above 7 years of age who are capable of removing themselves	No of women or girls above 7 years of age who are not capable of removing themselves and of women with children at the breast	No of boys under 7 years of age	No of girls under 7 years of age	No of persons serving in Yeomanry or Volunteer Corps — Yeomanry	Yeomanry Infantry — Infantry	Aliens	Quakers
160	84	69	70	1			
196	33	98	99	–			
102	46	24	36	2			
28	13	16	13	2			
64	14	20	32	5			
550	190	227	250	10			
211	72	79	85	1	6		
64	68	36	53		100		
26	8	11	12				
54	6	27	21	1			
119	7	32	26				
46	12	24	17				
103	31	39	48		4		
623	204	248	262	2	110		
41	7	15	17		1		
270	64	95	98	2			
240	45	84	63	3	2		1
25	5	2	2	1		1	
576	121	196	180	6	3	1	1

[Chichester Rape Schedule No 1 continued]

Names of Hundreds and Parishes	No of men and boys between the ages of 15 and 60 who are capable of active service	No of men and boys between the ages of 15 and 60 who are incapable of active service	No of men above the age of 60 who are capable of active service	No of men above the age of 60 who are incapable of active service	No of men above the age of 60 who are capable of removing themselves	No of men above the age of 60 who are incapable of removing themselves
Box and Stockbridae Hd						
Aldingbourne	76	3	-	-	5	7
Appledram	31	-	-	4	4	-
Boxgrove	148	2	7	4	4	17
Donnington	46	3	1	1	-	-
Eartham	13	4	-	2	2	2
Hunston	29	1	2	5	4	2
Merston	23	-	-	-	-	2
New Fishbourne	No return					
Northmundham	40	2	-	-	-	4
The Close	31	-	5	-	-	-
Oving	115	5	-	9	6	4
Rumboldsweek	52	5	6	1	-	2
St Bartholomew	52	-	-	6	7	1
Upwaltham	19	-	-	-	-	-
Westhampnett	49	1	-	9	9	9
	724	26	21	41	41	50
City of Chichester						
Subdeanry	221	8	-	24	22	7
St Peter the Less	70	-	1	-	4	3
Saint Olave	41	5	1	1	1	-
Saint Martin	52	12	6	5	1	4
Saint Andrew	90	10	-	1	3	1
Saint Pancrass	186	12	15	20	-	-
The Pallant	41	4	-	4	5	10
	701	51	23	55	36	25

No of women or girls above 7 years of age who are capable of removing themselves	No of women or girls above 7 years of age who are not capable of removing themselves and of women with children at the breast	No of boys under 7 years of age	No of girls under 7 years of age	Yeomanry	Infantry	Aliens	Quakers
175	56	84	94	2	-	-	-
12	15	14	15	-	-	-	-
201	100	58	42	14	-	4	-
63	9	4	19	-	-	-	-
29	9	9	7	1	-	-	-
25	21	16	16	-	-	-	-
14	25	8	-	-	-	-	-
112	26	38	22	-	-	-	-
70	5	11	6	1	1	-	-
153	49	43	37	1	-	-	-
76	11	21	25	2	-	-	-
72	4	41	22	-	-	-	-
20	3	7	4	2	-	-	-
102	26	35	36	8	-	7	-
1124	359	389	345	31	1	11	-
490	71	98	96	4	6	2	-
137	17	20	19	-	11	-	-
118	13	6	9	-	7	1	-
85	29	34	29	-	3	-	-
164	106	40	47	3	6	1	11
271	60	78	93	-	3	-	10
85	50	31	28	-	4	-	-
1350	346	307	321	7	40	4	21

Column headers for "No of persons serving in Yeomanry or Volunteer Corps": Yeomanry, Infantry

[Chichester Rape Schedule No 1 continued]

Names of Hundreds and Parishes	No of men and boys between the ages of 15 and 60 who are capable of active service	No of men and boys between the ages of 15 and 60 who are incapable of active service	No of men above the age of 60 who are capable of active service	No of men above the age of 60 who are incapable of active service	No of men above the age of 60 who are capable of removing themselves	No of men above the age of 60 who are incapable of removing themselves
Westbourne & Singleton Hd						
Binderton	19	-	1	2	-	-
Compton	51	3	-	9	-	2
East Dean	No return					
Eastmarden	No return					
Midlavant	No return					
Northmarden	9	-	-	-	-	-
Racton	25	-	-	-	1	-
Singleton	99	4	5	9	3	6
Stoughton	No return					
Upmarden	36	1	2	1	4	2
Westbourne	270	15	10	19	20	26
West Dean	No return					
	509	23	18	40	28	36
Midhurst Borough & St John's	169	29	-	2	11	24
	16	7	-	2	-	-
	185	36	-	4	11	24
Easbourn Hund						
Bepton	23	-	-	12	10	4
Cocking	77	-	9	6	-	2
Easbourn	150	1	2	4	22	9
Graffham	57	2	10	7	2	5
Farnhurst	97	-	3	8	8	9
Hesyshott*	62	1	-	-	8	-
Iping	-	-	-	-	-	-
Linch	23	3	-	-	3	2

No of women or girls above 7 years of age who are capable of removing themselves	No of women or girls above 7 years of age who are not capable of removing themselves and cf women with children at the breast	No of boys under 7 years of age	No of girls under 7 years of age	No of persons serving in Yeomanry or Volunteer Corps Yeomanry Infantry		Aliens	Quakers
				Yeomanry	Infantry		
27	-	2	3	1	-	-	-
65	22	23	20	-	1	-	-
4	3	-	-	-	-	-	-
22	5	12	9	-	-	-	-
139	14	27	36	9	-	-	-
33	18	22	20	2	-	-	-
452	156	302	154	-	17	-	-
742	218	388	242	12	18		
202	175	70	72	7	-	3	-
30	25	9	6	-	-	-	-
232	200	79	78	7	-	3	-
27	7	11	8	-	-	-	-
28	36	30	28	2	-	-	-
175	22	70	66	13	-	-	-
52	9	20	25	-	-	-	-
128	53	93	74	-	-	-	-
73	30	33	29	-	-	-	-
-	-	-	-	-	-	-	-
26	2	11	7	-	-	-	-

[Chichester Rape Schedule No 1 continued]

Names of Hundreds and Parishes	No of men and boys between the ages of 15 and 60 who are capable of active service	No of men and boys between the ages of 15 and 60 who are incapable of active service	No of men above the age of 60 who are capable of active service	No of men above the age of 60 who are incapable of active service	No of men above the age of 60 who are capable of removing themselves	No of men above the age of 60 who are incapable of removing themselves
Linchmere	-	-	-	-	-	-
Lodsworth	82	3	5	4	5	9
Selham	20	1	-	2	-	-
Stedham	47	8	5	5	-	3
Woolbeding	56	7	1	-	1	2
	694	26	35	48	59	45
Dumpford Hundred						
Chithurst	25	-	1	6	1	3
Didling	19					
Elsted	37	3	1	-	5	3
Harting	212	10	6	27	2	4
Rogate	86	12	8			15
Treyford	32	-	-	-	-	-
Trotton	51	13	2	6	3	4
Terwick	25	1	-	-	1	1
	487	49†	18	39	12	30
[Totals]	4643	339	159	356	289	266

*.sic

† error: should read 39

No of women or girls above 7 years of age who are capable of removing themselves	No of women or girls above 7 years of age who are not capable of removing themselves and of women with children at the breast	No of boys under 7 years of age	No of girls under 7 years of age	Yeomanry	Infantry	Aliens	Quakers
-	-	-	-	-	-	-	-
104	50	38	45	4	-	-	-
20	17	6	10	1	-	-	-
49	30	17	10	1	-	-	-
62	17	20	11	1	-	2	-
744	273	349	313	22	-	2	-
32	5	4	10	-	-	-	-
19	5	11	7	-	-	-	-
25	9	15	6	-	-	-	-
263	24	102	87	-	-	-	-
-	-	8	10	2	-	-	-
22	11	7	12	-	1	-	-
56	22	24	21	1	-	-	-
28	9	13	7	-	-	-	-
445	85	184	160	3	1	-	-
6386	1996	2267*	2151	100	173	21	22

* error: should be 2367

Chichester Rape Schedule No 2

Names of Hundreds and Parishes	Fatting oxen	Cows	Steers Heifers and Calves	Colts	Sheep	Lambs	Hogs	Sows	Pigs	Riding Horses	No of other number that can	
											Waggons	carts
Aldwick Hundred												
Southbersted	72	90	22	5	407	-	121	26	212	19	33	50
Pagham	61	89	60	12	931	211	195	70	344	26	44	76
Slindon	-	35	5	6	1282	80	93	17	220	23	14	26
Tangmere	-	11	1	-	154	-	52	8	50	6	6	10
E. & W. Lavant	9	30	18	3	2090	410	82	22	58	10	21	22
	142	255	106	26	4864	701	543	143	884	84	118	184
Manwood Hd												
Sidlesham	52	102	53	16	638	146	115	42	170	26	45	62
Selsea	-	61	31	11	1450	-	120	28	129	12	23	32
Earnley	-	23	13	6	338	22	108	9	50	9	11	19
East Wittering	9	49	24	3	51	6	78	24	33	8	12	23
West Wittering	-	59	22	-	716	-	146	30	151	14	29	43
Itchenor	-	10	4	1	54	-	4	4	11	1	3	4
Birdham	-	45	6	1	175	-	93	26	134	13	26	39
	61	349	153	38	3422	174	664	163	678	83	149	222
Bosham Hd												
West Thorney	No return											
Chidham	-	14	53	6	438	-	48	16	119	7	16	25
Bosham	5	84	45	8	275	9	196	56	207	18	44	66
Funtingdon	-	61	51	7	1549	21	172	41	164	32	37	51
West Stoke	-	15	-	1	750	-	100	-	-	5	5	8
	5	174	149	22	3012	30	516	113	490	62	102	150
Box and Stockbridge Hd												
Aldingbourne	29	65	47	9	1104	130	250	58	272	33	37	63
Appledram	27	23	5	7	170	5	77	9	58	4	10	13
Boxgrove	16	69	22	10	1020	677	207	41	262	26	27	42
Donnington	-	16	5	2	311	30	48	14	41	5	14	22

other Carriages	Draft Horses	Draft Oxen	Wind	Water	Quantity of corn they can grind in 24 hours	Bakers	Private	Amt of bread they can bake in 24 hours	No of Bridges	No of Boats	No of Barges
7	113	-	-	-	-	2	58	146	-	5	-
14	157	10	1	-	96	-	57	195	-	19	-
3	50	-	-	-	-	3	38	57	-	-	-
-	22	-	-	-	-	2	21	208	-	-	-
2	45	6	1	-		1	28	57	-	-	-
26	385*	16	2	-	96	8	202	663	-	24	-
4	155	-	-	1	120	-	32	64	-	-	-
2	69	20	1	-	16	-	20	54	-	2	-
3	39	-	1	-	12	-	6	23	-	-	-
-	49	-	-	-	-	25	-	-	-	-	-
2	108	13	-	-	-	-	17	74	-	-	-
-	23	-	-	-	-	1	2	3	-	-	-
-	92	-	1	1	80	-	39	-	-	-	-
11	535	33	3	2	228	26	116	218	-	2	-
2	42	-	-	1	32	-	25	96	-	-	-
7	131	-	1	3	232	1	49	250	2	34	-
10	94	-	1	2	120	2	103	420	-	-	-
2	19	-	-	-	-	1	7	32	-	-	-
21	286	-	2	6	384	4	184	798	2	34	-
10	122	8	1	1	80	-	102	288	-	-	-
1	45	-	1	-	160	-	17	72	-	1	-
5	85	18	1	-	20	-	106	675	-	-	-
1	43	14	-	-	-	-	7	11	-	-	-

(Column groups: Waggons Carts or Carriages with the of horses or oxen be supplied to draw them — other Carriages, Draft Horses, Draft Oxen; Corn Mills — Wind, Water, Quantity of corn they can grind in 24 hours; Ovens — Bakers, Private, Amt of bread they can bake in 24 hours; No of Bridges; No of Boats; No of Barges)

* error: should read 387

[Chichester Rape Schedule No 2 continued]

Names of Hundreds and Parishes	Fatting oxen	Cows	Steers Heifers and Calves	Colts	Sheep	Lambs	Hogs	Sows	Pigs	Riding Horses	Waggons	carts
Eartham	-	6	-	-	400	100	10	5	33	4	1	2
Hunston	11	32	7	7	144	-	65	10	43	5	7	15
Merston	2	14	8	1	129	-	64	6	16	4	9	11
New Fishbourn	No return											
Northmundham	23	69	-	2	479	23	117	16	119	10	23	36
The Close	-	3	-	-	-	-	3	-	-	5	-	1
Oving	74	106	57	20	698	47	318	52	175	22	36	54
Rumboldsweek	23	15	9	-	121	-	21	6	46	2	8	12
St Bartholomew	6	68	-	-	-	-	9	-	2	4	-	2
Upwaltham	-	3	1	-	680	365	40	8	47	2	6	6
Westhampnett	-	24	11	19	1303	104	150	15	43	53	31	40
	211	513	172	77	6559	1481	1379	240	1157	179	209	319
City of Chichester												
Subdeanry	18	45	54	2	95	20	66	12	78	32	7	17
St Peter the Less	-	3	-	-	13	1	35	-	11	9	6	12
Saint Olave	-	-	-	-	-	-	16	1	10	2	2	8
Saint Martin	-	10	3	1	10	-	24	-	-	5	3	10
Saint Andrew	-	21	11	1	66	-	29	1	16	15	2	8
Saint Pancrass	13	40	3	-	140	-	40	8	54	10	12	20
The Pallant	-	-	-	-	-	-	13	-	-	20	4	8
	31	118	71	4	324	21	223	22	169	93	36	83
Westbourne & Singleton												
Binderton	17	13	2	1	1140	260	54	-	-	7	7	8
Compton	6	20	10	-	1306	-	75	8	14	8	8	12
East Dean	No return											

Waggons Carts or Carriages with the of horses or oxen be supplied to draw them			Corn Mills			Ovens					
other Carriages	Draft Horses	Draft Oxen	Wind	Water	Quantity of corn they can grind in 24 hours	Bakers	Private	Amt of bread they can bake in 24 hours	No of Bridges	No of Boats	No of Barges
-	8	-	-	-	-	-	-	-	-	-	-
-	-	-	-	-	-	-	16	72	-	-	-
2	27	6	-	-	-	-	11	27	-	-	-
6	65	-	1	1	80	-	54	143	-	-	-
2	-	-	-	-	-	-	-	-	-	-	-
4	96	10	3	1	92	1	63	170	-	-	-
-	29	-	-	-	-	2	12	50	-	-	-
-	9	-	-	-	-	2	-	18	-	-	-
-	18	-	-	-	-	-	4	60	-	-	-
6	84	-	-	1	80	-	39	70	-	-	-
37	631	56	7	4	512	5	431	1656	-	-	-
11	39	8	-	-	-	9	2	148	-	-	-
7	41	-	-	-	-	3	-	61	-	-	-
2	8	-	-	-	-	3	1	30	-	-	-
2	8	-	-	-	-	1	-	-	-	-	-
12	18	-	-	-	-	2	2	34	-	-	-
2	32	-	-	-	-	5	6	72	-	-	-
4	13	-	-	-	-	1	1	35	-	-	-
40	159	8	-	-	-	24	12	380	-	-	-
2	20	-	-	-	-	-	4	7	-	-	-
1	28	-	-	-	-	2	34	60	-	-	-

[Chichester Rape Schedule No 2 continued]

Names of Hundreds and Parishes	Fatting oxen	Cows	Steers Heifers and Calves	Colts	Sheep	Lambs	Hogs	Sows	Pigs	Riding Horses	No of other number that can	
											Waggons	carts
Eastmarden	No return											
Midlavant	No return											
Northmarden	-	3	-	-	200	80	7	1	11	1	2	3
Racton	-	49	13	1	400	-	36	10	71	3	8	8
Singleton	2	39	8	2	2050	552	97	22	105	24	23	38
Stoughton	No return											
Upmarden	-	40	23	1	1794	442	59	9	64	16	20	26
Westbourne	6	148	86	6	694	54	271	48	183	27	55	108
West Dean	No return											
	31	312	142	11	7584	1388	599	90	448	86	123	203
Midhurst	5	63	58	10	590	-	75	32	202	24	22	11
& St John's	-	4	-	-	-	-	7	1	10	2	1	4
	5	67	58	10	590	-	82	33	212	26	23	15
Easbourn Hund												
Bepton	2	20	4	1	150	1	30	10	21	2	4	6
Cocking	20	44	46	2	1168	156	93	13	76	10	18	26
Easbourn	33	82	96	9	1021	-	333	9	98	32	34	43
Graffham	-	25	45	2	97	65	19	11	100	2	10	14
Farnhurst	-	91	86	13	244	79	76	24	128	7	23	24
Heyshott	6	35	53	7	270	50	48	7	60	4	11	19
Iping	No return											
Linch	-	43	34	5	309	100	40	4	22	2	5	6

Waggons Carts or Carriages with the of horses or oxen be supplied to draw them				Corn Mills			Ovens					
other Carriages	Draft Horses	Draft Oxen	Wind	Water	Quantity of corn they can grind in 24 hours	Bakers	Private	Amt of bread they can bake in 24 hours	No of Bridges	No of Boats	No of Barges
-	4	-	-	-	-	-	-	4	-	-	-
2	20	-	-	-	-	-	11	20	-	-	-
2	55	-	-	-	-	2	38	245	-	-	-
2	53	-	2	-	-	-	49	153	-	-	-
12	179	-	2	5	368	4	167	820	1	14	6
21	359	-	4	5	368	8	303	1309	1	14	6
-	53	8	-	-	-	6	26	64	3	1	
-	6	-	-	-	-	-	2	14	-	-	-
-	59	8	-	-	-	6	28	78	3	1	-
-	16	8	-	-	-	-	18	36	-	-	-
2	53	4	-	1	40	-	-	79	-	-	-
4	93	18	-	-	-	-	40	174	1½	-	-
2	38	-	-	-	-	4	36	102	-	-	-
2	88	6	-	-	-	-	86	252	-	-	-
1	48	6	-	1	192	-	38	144	-	-	-
-	22	8	-	-	-	-	12	22	-	-	-

[Chichester Rape Schedule No 2 continued]

Names of Hundreds and Parishes	Fatting oxen	Cows	Steers Heifers and Calves	Colts	Sheep	Lambs	Hogs	Sows	Pigs	Riding Horses	Waggons	carts
Eastmarden	No return											
Linchmere	No return											
Lodsworth	2	18	38	7	185	72	80	23	107	10	9	23
Selham	17	15	20	-	25	-	36	6	49	1	7	13
Stedham	17	43	54	6	264	-	103	12	83	13	18	26
Woolbeding	2	45	52	14	260	101	33	13	58	13	12	17
	99	461	528	66	3993	624	891	132	802	96	151	217
Dumpford Hundred												
Chithurst	-	15	15	4	13	30	24	2	54	2	4	11
Didling	6	17	17	10	318	122	25	7	18	2	7	7
Elsted		24	25	2	366	120	33	4	24	5	8	13
Harting	40	166	69	15	1994	535	98	13	155	15	42	65
Rogate	32	103	60	1	1310	-	124	12	54	15	22	19
Treyford	-	24	14	5	228	168	30	2	27	4	7	6
Trotton	-	125	114	22	923	86	72	15	121	15	17	20
Terwick	4	44	19	2	279	-	14	7	43	3	7	8
	82	518	333	61	5431	1061	420	62	496	61	114	149
[Totals]	667	2767	1412	315	35779	5480	5317	998	5336	770	1025	1542

Waggons Carts or Carriages with the of horses or oxen be supplied to draw them				Corn Mills			Ovens					
other Carriages	Draft Horses	Draft Oxen	Wind	Water	Quantity of corn they can grind in 24 hours	Bakers	Private	Amt of bread they can bake in 24 hours	No of Bridges	No of Boats	No of Barges
2	31	6	1	3	30	5	76	379	3	-	-
-	22	2	-	-	-	-	11	54	-	-	-
-	49	-	-	-	-	-	46	180	-	-	-
2	46	-	-	-	-	2	35	78	-	-	-
15	506	38*	1	5	262	11	398	1500	4½	-	-
-	27	-	-	-	-	-	18	26	-	-	-
-	14	-	-	-	-	-	10	63	-	-	-
-	26	-	-	-	-	1	19	46	-	-	-
-	133	-	1	2	-	-	81	288	-	-	-
-	73	-	-	1	60	1	59	260	-	-	-
-	24	-	-	-	-	1	12	30	-	-	-
2	64	6	-	1	10	-	43	145	-	-	-
-	22	-	-	1	64	-	15	48	-	-	-
2	383	6	1	5	134	3	257	906	-	-	-
173	3303	165†	20	27	1984	95	1931	7508	10½	112	6

* error: should read 58

† error: should read 185

Chichester Rape Schedule No 3

Names of Hundreds and Parishes	No of Persons between 15 and 60 willing to serve — Horseback	Foot	How they can arm themselves — Swords	Pistols	Firelocks	Pikes	No of Persons willing to serve as Pioneers
Aldwick Hundred							
Southbersted	28	24	1	1	-	-	36
Pagham	22	31	-	5	4	-	1
Slindon	-	-	-	-	-	-	30
Tangmere	2	8	2	-	7	1	16
E. & W. Lavant	6	15	5	1	-	-	7
	58	78	8	7	11	1	110*
Manwood Hd							
Sidlesham	3	-	-	-	3	-	-
Selsea	2	-	-	-	1	-	2
Earnley	-	-	-	-	-	-	9
East Wittering	-	-	-	-	-	-	-
West Wittering	6	16	-	2	8	-	2
Itchenor	-	-	-	-	-	-	2
Birdham	2	14	-	-	-	-	16
	13	30	-	2	12	-	31
Bosham Hd							
West Thorney	No return						
Chidham	-	-	-	-	-	-	-
Bosham	6	25	3	4	6	2	11
Funtingdon	8	16	1	3	5	-	6
West Stoke	-	-	-	-	-	-	11
	14	31†	4	7	11	2	28
Box and Stockbridge Hd							
Aldingbourne	14	53	13	13	33	20	54
Appledram	1	3	-	-	-	-	-
Boxgrove	22	17	4	5	3	-	20
Donnington	2	15	2	2	13	-	6
Eartham	-	-	-	-	-	-	-
Hunston	1	12	-	-	-	-	5

* error: should read 90

Felling Axes	Pick Axes	Spades	Shovels	Bill Hooks	Saws				No of Persons between 15 and 60 willing to act as drivers of cattle	Do of sheep	Do of Teams	Do Boatmen or Bargemen
3	14	15	9	2	7	-	-	-	17	18	19	9
12	21	23	39	21	29	-	-	-	27	-	-	-
12	9	4	9	2	11	-	-	-	32	5	25	-
2	3	8	1	-	2	-	-	-	5	2	6	-
5	6	5	1	5	2	-	-	-	7	6	14	-
34	53	55	59	30	51	-	-	-	88	31	64	9
-	-	-	-	-	-	-	-	-	25	24	31	5
1	1	-	-	-	-	-	-	-	9	8	14	2
-	3	2	-	3	1	-	-	-	4	3	3	-
-	-	-	-	-	-	-	-	-	-	2	4	-
-	-	-	1	-	1	-	-	-	3	4	9	3
-	1	1	-	-	-	-	-	-	2	-	-	3
3	2	1	1	1	2	-	-	-	7	3	26	1
4	7	4	2	4	4	-	-	-	50	44	87	14
-	-	-	-	-	-	-	-	-	5	4	6	-
-	2	-	-	3	4	-	-	-	18	20	45	31
-	3	1	-	1	1	-	-	-	5	8	5	-
-	1	2	1	2	-	-	-	-	7	9	2	-
-	6	3	1	6	5	-	-	-	35	41	58	31
15	13	7	13	1	5	-	-	-	15	28	16	-
-	-	-	-	-	-	-	-	-	4	4	9	1
12	10	10	11	12	13	-	-	-	23	23	25	-
-	-	-	-	-	-	-	-	-	7	5	12	1
-	-	-	-	-	-	-	-	-	12	6	3	-
2	3	2	3	2	2	-	-	-	4	4	7	-

[Chichester Rape Schedule No 3 continued]

Names of Hundreds and Parishes	No of Persons between 15 and 60 willing to serve — Horseback	Foot	How they can arm themselves — Swords	Pistols	Firelocks	Pikes	No of Persons willing to serve as Pioneers
Merston	1	1	-	-	1	-	7
New Fishbourn	No return						
Northmundham	-	5	-	-	4	1	20
The Close	-	4	1	-	-	1	-
Oving	-	4	2	-	2	-	18
Rumboldsweek	-	-	-	-	-	-	1
St Bartholomew	-	2	-	-	-	-	-
Upwaltham	-	4	-	-	1	-	4
Westhampnett	6	1	6	-	1	-	36
	47	121	28	20	58	22	171
City of Chichester							
Subdeanry	16	20	2	2	17	-	2
St Peter the Less	1	-	-	-	-	-	-
Saint Olave	-	4	-	-	-	-	-
Saint Martin	4	3	-	1	-	-	-
Saint Andrew	13	16	-	-	-	-	-
Saint Pancrass	-	4	-	-	-	-	-
The Pallant	3	8	-	-	23	2	-
	37	55	2	3	30	2	2
Westbourne & Singleton							
Binderton	-	-	-	-	-	-	7
Compton	2	8	-	-	-	-	23
East Dean	No return						
Eastmarden	No return						
Midlavant	No return						
Northmarden	-	-	-	-	-	-	5
Racton	-	-	-	-	-	-	12
Singleton	11	6	9	10	7	-	14
Stoughton	No return						
Upmarden	-	1	-	-	1	-	10
Westbourne	19	97	19	19	80	17	56

Felling Axes	Pick Axes	Spades	Shovels	Bill Hooks	Saws				No of Persons between 15 and 60 willing to act as drivers of cattle	Do of sheep	Do of Teams	Do Boatmen or Bargemen
-	3	6	2	-	-	-	-	-	2	2	5	-
6	5	-	3	-	6	-	-	-	10	6	16	-
-	-	-	-	-	-	-	-	-	-	-	-	-
6	6	4	-	2	-	-	-	-	19	9	31	-
-	1	-	-	-	-	-	-	-	-	-	-	-
-	-	-	-	-	-	-	-	-	11	-	-	-
-	-	1	2	1	-	-	-	-	2	3	6	-
-	13	13	4	-	6	-	-	-	9	5	9	-
41	54	43	38	18	32	-	-	-	118	95	139	2
-	-	-	-	-	2	-	-	-	3	2	14	-
-	-	-	-	-	-	-	-	-	-	-	1	-
-	-	-	-	-	-	-	-	-	2	-	-	-
-	-	-	-	-	-	-	-	-	4	-	1	-
-	-	-	-	-	-	-	-	-	-	4	-	-
-	--	-	-	-	-	-	-	-	3	1	-	-
-	-	-	-	-	-	-	-	-	-	2	-	-
-	-	-	-	-	2	-	-	-	12	9	16	-
3	1	-	1	2	-	-	-	-	5	4	4	-
5	8	1	10	8	1	-	-	-	1	8	8	-
1	1	1	1	1	-	-	-	-	2	1	1	-
2	2	1	3	2	-	-	-	-	4	2	7	-
11	3	1	4	7	4	-	-	-	23	22	19	-
6	2	1	-	1	-	-	-	-	3	4	9	-

Implements they can bring

[Chichester Rape Schedule No 3 continued]

Names of Hundreds and Parishes	No of Persons between 15 and 60 willing to serve		How they can arm themselves					No of Persons willing to serve as Pioneers
	Horseback	Foot	Swords	Pistols	Firelocks	Pikes		
West Dean	No return							
	32	112	28	29	88	17		127
Midhurst	10	34	6	3	22	3		60
& St John's	-	3	1	-	-	2		6
	10	37	7	3	22	5		66
Easbourn Hund								
Bepton	-	-	-	-	-	-		9
Cocking	-	20	-	-	1	-		29
Easbourn	1	36	1	-	35	1		38
Graffham	-	5	-	-	2	-		4
Farnhurst	6	16	2	-	16	-		59
Heyshott	-	20	4	-	5	3		13
Iping	No return							
Linch	-	1	-	-	-	-		1
Linchmere	No return							
Lodsworth	2	2	8	8	1	-		31
Selham	-	-	-	-	-	-		17
Stedham	5	-	-	-	5	-		17
Woolbeding	5	2	2	-	2	-		12
	19	102	17	8	67	4		230
Dumpford Hundred								
Chithurst	-	6	-	-	5	2		3
Didling	-	-	-	-	-	-		2
Elsted	1	1	1	2	1	-		6
Harting	5	27	10	7	8	4		61
Rogate	-	32	-	-	1	-		11
Treyford	3	1	3	4	-	1		7
Trotton	1	-	1	1	-	-		13
Terwick	2	2	2	-	2	-		6
	12	69	17	14	17	7		109
[Totals]	242	635	111	93	316	60		874

Proceedings and Schedules

Felling Axes	Pick Axes	Spades	Shovels	Bill Hooks	Saws				No of Persons between 15 and 60 willing to act as	Do of sheep	Do of Teams	Do Boatmen or
54	41	9	20	21	6	-	-	-	71	72	85	21
15	22	10	8	-	5	-	-	-	20	18	14	-
1	2	1	1	-	1	-	-	-	3	-	3	-
16	24	11	9	-	6	-	-	-	23	18	17	-
-	-	9	-	-	-	-	-	-	3	5	5	-
2	2	5	-	-	1	-	-	-	12	7	16	-
4	17	4	4	-	9	-	-	-	24	22	23	-
-	-	-	-	-	-	-	-	-	-	5	-	-
29	14	4	3	4	4	-	-	-	14	11	17	-
10	8	-	-	-	-	-	-	-	13	3	12	-
1	-	-	-	-	-	-	-	-	6	6	8	-
26	16	28	14	12	18	-	-	-	17	17	13	-
2	1	2	-	-	-	-	-	-	5	2	8	-
8	9	17	7	8	3	-	-	-	10	7	10	-
6	5	5	2	-	1	-	-	-	11	7	13	-
88	72	74	30	24	36	-	-	-	115	82	125	-
2	-	2	-	2	-	-	-	-	6	5	7	-
2	-	-	-	-	-	-	-	-	7	6	4	-
-	-	3	2	2	1	-	-	-	6	5	6	-
13	10	9	6	8	8	-	-	-	13	7	24	-
7	2	10	4	6	2	-	-	-	8	6	10	-
2	4	1	4	1	1	-	-	-	3	1	5	-
3	4	3	2	1	-	-	-	-	13	13	12	-
-	1	2	-	-	3	-	-	-	5	4	7	-
29	21	30	18	20	15	-	-	-	61	47	75	-
266	278	229	177	123	157	-	-	573	439	666	77	

[signed]   R Wilmot Clerk to the Sub[division] Meetings for Chichester Rape

Lewes Rape Schedule No 1

Extract List of Parishes on

Names of Hundreds and Parishes	No of men and boys between the ages of 15 and 60 who are capable of active service	No of men and boys between the ages of 15 and 60 who are incapable of active service	No of men above the age of 60 who are capable of active service	No of men above the age of 60 who are incapable of active service	No of men above the age of 60 who are capable of removing themselves	No of men above the age of 60 who are incapable of removing themselves
Saint Peter & St Mary Westout	97	2	6	5	3	8
St Michael	189	3	6	7	7	8
St John under the Castle	125	20	-	6	1	5
All Saints	258	10	8	13	9	3
St John the Baptist Southover	99	8	-	14	11	2
Patcham	76	9	7	7	-	1
Kingston	31	3	-	3	-	5
Iford	30	4	-	1	-	1
Meeching als Newhaven	18	7	-	1	4	2
Piddinghoe	55	1	1	3	-	-
Southease	26	5	-	2	-	2
Rodmell	55	-	3	-	3	4
Telscombe	26	-	4	-	-	-
Hamsey	73	7	5	1	-	3
Barcomb	196	1	2	12	-	-
Newick	35	4	2	2	13	5
Poynings	28	4	-	-	-	1
Newtimber	45	3	1	2	2	-
Piecomb	41	7	-	-	3	3
Fulking	30	2	2	-	1	4
Brighthelmstone	272	121	32	48	22	17
West Blatchington	12	-	2	1	-	1
Portslade	80	-	1	8	2	6
Hangleton	15	3	-	1	-	-

the Defence Act

Year 1801

No of women or girls above 7 years of age who are capable of removing themselves	No of women or girls above 7 years of age who are not capable of removing themselves and of women with children at the breast, must be carried with such Children	No of boys under 7 years of age	No of girls under 7 years of age	No of persons serving in Yeomanry or Volunteer Corps of Infantry—	Aliens	Quakers
125	66	39	32	3	-	-
255	64	81	68	14	2	-
160	163	78	76	13	-	9
450	70	103	128	19	4	4
57	4	130	76	-	-	-
74	41	41	23	2	-	-
28	13	8	8	2	-	-
34	9	12	9	4	-	-
179	70	68	42	59	-	-
49	16	10	27	9	-	-
26	14	11	14	-	-	-
53	36	26	29	2	-	-
23	6	8	8	-	-	-
70	10	32	35	9	-	-
147	45	78	66	2	-	2
143	46	38	47	-	-	-
10	6	4	6	3	-	-
44	10	18	10	3	-	-
37	13	18	12	3	-	-
44	7	15	22	2	-	-
2489	541	901	803	115	42	61
16	1	4	4	-	-	-
80	27	21	15	1	-	-
14	2	3	3	-	-	-

[Lewes Rape Schedule No 1 continued]

Names of Hundreds and Parishes	No of men and boys between the ages of 15 and 60 who are capable of active service	No of men and boys between the ages of 15 and 60 who are incapable of active service	No of men above the age of 60 who are capable of active service	No of men above the age of 60 who are incapable of active service	No of men above the age of 60 who are capable of removing themselves	No of men above the age of 60 who are incapable of removing themselves
East Aldrington	No Inhabitants Particulars inserted in Portslade List					
Clayton	27	4	4	7	6	6
Keymer	155	11	-	1	7	8
Hurstperpoint	259	20	18	28	14	14
Slaugham	51	11	6	9	4	2
Cuckfield	304	27	9	28	16	20
Bolney	108	9	5	10	6	1
Twineham	57	1	1	3	4	-
Crawley	46	-	1	-	5	-
Balcombe	124	1	15	1	-	6
Worth	155	8	3	11	10	6
Westhoathly	128	8	7	15	13	10
Ardingly	120	8	9	7	4	1
Street	26	2	-	2	4	3
Plumpton	58	-	-	-	5	5
Wivelsfield	80	18	1	3	17	2
Chailey	163	7	7	20	7	19
Ditcheling	151	11	11	10	6	6
Westmeston	48	4	5	2	2	2
Chiltington	37	3	-	6	6	2
Preston	44	5	1	4	5	1
Hove	33	-	2	-	-	-
Rottingdean	116	2	3	2	-	7
Ovingdean	25	-	-	1	2	1
Falmer	76	2	-	11	6	5
Totals	4213*	386	190	318	230	208

* error: should read 4303

[signed]   H Shelley
            Wm Newton

No of women or girls above 7 years of age who are capable of removing themselves	No of women or girls above 7 years of age who are not capable of removing themselves and of women with children at the breast, must be carried with such Children	No of boys under 7 years of age	No of girls under 7 years of age	No of persons serving in Yeomanry or Volunteer Corps of Infantry—	Aliens	Quakers
61	23	35	33	2	-	-
122	42	57	42	3	-	-
310	101	100	100	3	-	-
16	34	19	19	-	-	-
319	224	147	159	10	3	-
178	20	34	45	-	1	-
30	2	31	10	1	-	-
45	9	14	26	-	-	4
135	54	36	50	1	-	-
181	16	61	54	6	-	2
162	43	58	48	7	-	-
131	60	53	65	1	-	-
29	20	15	11	2	-	-
60	11	40	25	1	-	-
92	62	47	55	1	-	-
178	36	52	46	-	-	-
208	15	61	64	1	-	-
46	24	25	16	1	-	-
41	23	10	10	1	-	-
46	13	28	25	-	-	1
35	14	13	15	1	-	-
114	40	44	61	2	-	5
24	1	8	3	1	-	-
56	32	33	22	2	-	-
7226	2199	2768	2567	312	52	88

Lewes Rape Schedule No 2

Extract List of Parishes on

Names of Hundreds and Parishes	Fatting oxen	Cows	Steers Heifers and Calves	Colts	Sheep	Lambs	Hogs	Sows	Pigs	Riding Horses	Waggons	carts
Saint Peter & St Mary Westout	-	34	2	10	640	260	47	4	25	18	5	16
St Michael	-	14	3	-	22	-	42	2	13	38	2	9
St John under the Castle	14	45	14	3	1576	130	72	10	57	16	15	21
All Saints	14	18	1	7	19	-	80	21	22	35	2	10
St John the Baptist Southover	-	39	60	1	41	1	102	5	-	13	5	12
Patcham	-	22	2	1	3450	730	94	10	30	9	13	14
Kingston	18	16	16	4	1750	-	51	5	20	7	8	13
Iford	-	31	56	2	1742	122	39	14	42	7	9	18
Meeching als Newhaven	4	8	15	-	900	220	103	19	71	18	8	20
Piddinghoe	-	10	-	1	1950	690	52	9	39	2	13	16
Southease	-	30	23	2	680	148	17	16	18	2	7	12
Rodmell	8	38	27	1	1192	462	31	7	63	5	14	19
Telscombe	-	3	3	-	875	254	12	4	33	4	8	18
Hamsey	18	53	68	7	1838	810	162	20	49	17	22	35
Barcomb	86	158	181	19	1276	210	215	28	152	16	45	63
Newick	-	64	84	7	241	1	62	5	58	12	16	19
Poynings	-	13	22	4	730	400	25	7	30	6	8	11
Newtimber	-	19	20	1	1312	602	56	6	57	16	9	18
Piecomb	-	9	8	-	1157	705	33	7	43	4	7	13
Fulking	-	19	52	8	1160	560	28	5	38	5	8	8
Brighthelmstone	-	43	3	2	1025	360	265	18	155	58	28	74
West Blatchington	-	3	-	-	700	280	18	4	8	2	3	3
Portslade	-	16	1	-	1015	400	116	17	54	12	12	21

Year 1801

the Defence Act

Waggons Carts or Carriages with the of horses or oxen be supplied to draw them			Corn Mills				Ovens					
other Carriages	Draft Horses	Draft Oxen	Wind	Water	Quantity of corn they can grind in 24 hours (quarters)	Bakers (lbs of bread)	Private	Amt of bread they can bake in 24 hours	No of Bridges	No of Boats	No of Barges
11	24	12	2	-	10	1	7	1382	-	-	-
15	32	-	1	-	-	4	3	12740	-	-	-
9	52	24	-	-	-	2	14	10080	-	-	-
12	13	-	-	-	-	3	7	7490	1	-	-
1	15	-	-	-	-	-	-	-	4	4	-
-	48	28	1	-	15	-	40	8400	-	-	-
-	14	72	1	-	3	-	21	2940	-	-	-
-	22	46	-	-	-	-	23	3220	-	1	-
5	27	18	1	-	7½	2	7	1540	1	14	7
1	26	48	-	-	-	-	33	4830	-	-	-
-	16	18	-	-	-	-	16	1610	1	-	-
-	24	52	1	-	7	-	37	5180	-	-	-
-	24	-	-	-	-	-	12	180	-	-	-
5	51	59	1	-	15	-	33	13440	1	-	-
5	86	91	1	1	30	2	71	32480	7	1	3
-	47	33	-	-	-	2	17	2380	2		-
-	21	22	-	1	5	-	10	1400	-	-	-
1	19	18	-	-	-	-	20	7000	-	-	-
1	18	28	-	-	-	-	14	6090	-	-	-
-	18	28	-	-	-	-	23	3640	-	-	-
49	187	-	1	-	15	17	5	24815	-	-	-
-	6	14	-	-	-	-	6	1680	-	-	-
4	38	8	2	-	10	1	12	4340	-	-	-

[Lewes Rape Schedule No 2.continued]

Names of Hundreds and Parishes	Fatting oxen	Cows	Steers Heifers and Calves	Colts	Sheep	Lambs	Hogs	Sows	Pigs	Riding Horses	Waggons	carts
Hangleton	-	3	-	-	1200	460	18	2	19	2	7	9
East Aldrington	\multicolumn{12}{l}{The stock of this Parish inserted in Portslade Schedule}
Clayton	-	55	112	10	657	64	56	18	94	12	18	27
Keymer	56	80	95	14	850	397	108	11	108	12	32	56
Hurstperpoint	131	129	107	5	1615	366	191	48	311	48	53	71
Slaugham	10	81	111	13	212	35	75	16	93	4	25	44
Cuckfield	49	259	387	20	887	94	315	54	375	42	87	141
Bolney	6	79	130	5	198	89	97	3	133	7	29	30
Twineham	92	36	51	9	243	110	93	5	32	9	23	25
Crawley	-	12	19	4	18	-	14	6	33	1	5	6
Balcombe	12	66	166	5	278	58	109	14	82	7	32	48
Worth	7	149	336	10	890	155	127	23	150	6	73	94
Westhoathly	11	117	232	4	467	10	109	22	117	15	43	65
Ardingly	12	87	184	4	280	130	117	19	144	10	35	46
Street	20	43	14	4	485	27	47	6	26	6	8	12
Plumpton	20	43	55	4	658	39	68	1	4	4	16	20
Wivelsfield	11	88	87	14	263	22	140	12	72	7	30	94
Chailey	14	120	157	11	595	299	139	10	106	15	46	63
Ditcheling	54	44	40	2	916	210	165	3	24	10	23	31
Westmeston	89	35	53	5	668	454	77	5	33	4	11	18
Chiltington	10	70	42	5	766	227	71	12	46	8	16	28
Preston	1	9	-	-	1296	440	47	11	51	5	13	19
Hove	-	16	1	-	340	130	21	8	52	4	6	9
Rottingdean	-	14	-	-	2972	1038	69	13	86	19	21	33
Ovingdean	-	5	-	-	1100	-	35	4	30	4	8	9
Falmer	6	14	-	2	3326	976	101	28	106	6	17	22
[Totals]	773	2359	3040	230	46471	13175	4131	597	3404	489*	944	1483

* error: should read 589

    [signed]   H Shelley Wm Newton

Waggons Carts or Carriages with the of horses or oxen be supplied to draw them			Corn Mills			Ovens						
other Carriages	Draft Horses	Draft Oxen	Wind	Water	Quantity of corn they can grind in 24 hours (quarters)	Bakers (lbs of bread)	Private	Amt of bread they can bake in 24 hours	No of Bridges	No of Boats	No of Barges
1	16	14	-	-	-	-	6	376	-	-	-
4	62	12	1	1	13	-	53	5600	3	-	-
-	79	33	2	1	9	-	20	2800	1	-	-
14	140	32	1	2	126	3	162	25865	1	-	-
-	74	6	-	1	6	-	-	-	-	-	-
-	293	63	2	3	15	8	90	3281	3	-	-
1	86	6	1	-	20	9	75	13650	1	-	-
3	55	14	-	-	-	-	31	4410	2	-	-
-	25	-	-	-	-	-	13	1820	-	-	-
3	74	22	-	1	4	2	77	30100	1	-	-
26	110	30	2	1	17	1	51	26530	1	-	-
4	100	54	7	2	22	-	100	28700	1	-	-
3	88	37	-	1	4	-	70	9800	2	-	-
3	15	20	-	-	-	-	7	1960	2	-	-
1	38	26	-	1	24	-	28	3920	-	-	-
1	94	32	-	-	-	-	72	22824	-	-	-
9	128	62	1	-	4	-	100	14000	5	-	-
3	63	22	-	-	-	-	36	5040	-	-	-
1	18	44	-	-	-	-	5	2240	-	-	-
1	44	30	-	-	-	-	-	-	2	-	-
2	29	24	1	-	15	1	24	12250	-	-	-
2	18	-	1	-	15	1	9	3150	-	-	-
2	61	15	1	-	3	3	21	3500	-	-	-
-	20	14	-	-	-	-	7	2870	-	-	-
1	49	46	1	-	7	-	38	10640	-	-	-
204	2607	1277	33	16	4212*	62	1526	392183	42	20	10

* error: should read 421½

[signed]Langridge & Kell cl[er]ks

Lewes

Lewes Rape Schedule No 3 — Parishes Extracted on the Defence Act

Names of Hundreds and Parishes	Horseback	On foot	Swords	Pistols	Firelocks	Pikes	No of Persons between the ages of 15 and 60 willing to act as Pioneers or Labourers
Saint Peter & St Mary Westout	20	13	-	-	2	-	17
St Michael	21	51	4	3	13	-	22
St John under the Castle	13	13	2	4	2	2	7
All Saints	17	19	17	17	14	2	6
St John the Baptist Southover	6	4	-	-	-	-	16
Patcham	-	1	-	-	-	1	31
Kingston	1	-	1	1	-	-	8
Iford	1	1	1	1	-	-	2
Meeching als Newhaven	1	3	3	5	3	3	13
Piddinghoe	1	-	1	-	-	-	14
Southease	-	2	-	-	2	-	3
Rodmell	8	12	-	-	-	-	-
Telscombe	--	-	-	-	-	-	-
Hamsey	-	-	-	-	-	-	4
Barcomb	1	1	-	-	-	-	6
Newick	-	-	-	-	-	-	21
Poynings	3	15	-	-	-	-	6
Newtimber	5	1	1	1	-	-	10
Piecomb	-	-	-	-	-	-	13
Fulking	4	3	4	2	3	-	7
Brighthelmstone	23	75	-	-	-	-	68
West Blatchington	-	11	-	-	-	-	-
Portslade	-	5	-	-	5	-	29
Hangleton	-	-	-	-	-	-	2
East Aldrington	No inhabitants		-	-	-	-	
Clayton	-	-	-	-	-	-	12
Keymer	4	-	-	-	-	-	4
Hurstperpoint	1	9	1	1	9	-	84

Columns under "How they can arm themselves": Cavalry (Swords, Pistols), Infantry (Firelocks, Pikes). "No of Persons between 15 and 60 willing to serve and in what capacity" covers Horseback and On foot.

Implements they can bring					Any other implements				No of Persons between 15 and 60 willing to act as drivers of cattle	Do of sheep	Do of Teams	Do Boatmen or Bargemen
Felling Axes	Pick Axes	Spades	Shovels	Bill Hooks	Saws						
1	3	3	2	5	1	-	-	-	9	8	8	1
-	-	2	1	-	1	-	-	-	27	28	17	-
5	3	2	3	-	9	-	-	-	25	10	10	1
2	1	3	-	-	2	-	-	-	19	16	8	1
10	1	6	6	2	10	-	-	-	6	4	3	-
5	5	10	10	-	-	-	-	-	16	15	12	-
3	2	2	-	-	1	-	-	-	6	3	6	-
2	-	-	-	-	-	-	-	-	13	7	5	-
7	4	2	6	-	7	-	-	-	5	1	6	-
1	1	8	3	-	1	-	-	-	9	8	16	-
-	-	1	-	-	2	-	-	-	13	6	7	-
-	-	-	-	-	-	-	-	-	9	9	14	-
-	-	-	-	-	-	-	-	-	10	10	8	-
1	2	3	3	-	1	-	-	-	21	7	16	-
140	70	55	60	150	60	-	-	-	38	46	29	6
5	3	4	3	3	2	-	-	-	12	9	9	-
6	6	6	16	4	12	-	-	-	6	2	5	-
2	1	6	2	5	1	-	-	-	6	9	6	-
8	2	3	1	-	-	-	-	-	11	7	9	-
3	2	1	1	-	2	-	-	-	6	3	7	-
-	-	-	-	-	-	-	-	-	38	25	12	-
-	-	-	-	-	-	-	-	-	-	4	3	-
4	9	10	1	2	2	-	-	-	11	9	15	-
-	-	-	-	-	4	-	-	-	5	3	3	-
-	-	-	-	-	-	-	-	-	-	-	-	-
5	1	4	-	-	3	-	-	-	6	5	9	-
2	1	1	-	2	1	-	-	-	23	11	6	-
9	21	32	4	2	16	-	-	-	88	11	59	-

[Lewes Rape Schedule No 3.continued]

Names of Hundreds and Parishes	No of Persons between 15 and 60 willing to serve and in what capacity		How they can arm themselves						No of Persons between the ages of 15 and 60 willing to act as Pioneers or Labourers
^	Horseback	On foot	Swords	Pistols	Firelocks	Pikes	^
^	^	^	Cavalry		Infantry		^
Slaugham	3	6	1	1	3	-	21
Cuckfield	46	31	8	16	27	2	76
Bolney	-	-	-	-	-	-	35
Twineham	1	-	1	1	-	-	2
Crawley	13	18	5	1	7	1	-
Balcombe	3	14	4	4	11	1	39
Worth	1	36	-	-	24	-	22
Westhoathly	11	27	2	10	26	1	34
Ardingly	16	20	-	-	-	-	5
Street	-	-	-	-	-	1	5
Plumpton	4	19	-	-	-	-	16
Wivelsfield	-	-	-	-	-	-	8
Chailey	4	4	-	-	-	-	3
Ditcheling	-	1	-	-	1	-	4
Westmeston	-	-	-	-	-	-	5
Chiltington	-	-	-	-	-	-	-
Preston	3	3	4	5	9	1	10
Hove	-	-	-	-	-	-	15
Rottingdean	7	1	2	1	1	-	30
Ovingdean	-	-	-	-	-	-	-
Falmer	-	2	-	-	1	-	4
[Totals]	242	421	62	74	163	15	739

[signed]   H Shelley
           Wm Newton

Implements they can bring					Any other implements				No of Persons between 15 and 60 willing to act as drivers of cattle	Do of sheep	Do of Teams	Do Boatmen or Bargemen
Felling Axes	Pick Axes	Spades	Shovels	Bill Hooks	Saws							
3	5	7	2	3	1	-	-	-	6	2	8	-
30	17	42	25	7	13	-	-	-	66	30	52	-
10	14	10	8	5	4	-	-	-	26	26	23	-
2	-	-	-	-	-	-	-	-	6	5	14	-
5	-	2	1	-	-	-	-	-	13	3	11	-
6	5	16	5	4	-	-	1 pit saw	1 scythe	27	23	26	-
11	14	25	18	29	6	-	-	-	7	9	14	-
21	2	22	6	2	2	-	-	-	14	15	21	-
4	1	4	2	1	5	-	-	-	5	7	8	-
-	1	2	1	-	-	-	-	-	8	4	6	-
5	10	25	14	30	15	-	-	-	11	2	5	-
2	3	1	1	-	1	-	-	-	16	16	17	-
-	-	-	-	-	-	-	-	-	4	4	7	-
-	-	-	4	-	-	-	-	-	5	1	5	-
1	2	-	-	2	1	-	-	-	24	7	18	-
-	-	-	-	-	-	-	-	-	16	9	11	-
1	5	13	18	1	5	-	-	-	14	6	9	-
2	2	7	-	-	3	-	-	-	3	1	3	-
4	2	4	7	-	3	-	-	-	11	16	32	-
-	-	-	-	-	-	-	-	-	7	4	13	-
1	2	1	-	-	-	-	-	-	22	20	24	-
330*	223	345	234	259	197	-	1	1	749	485	635	9

* error: should read 329

[signed]   Langridge & Kell cl[er]ks
Lewes

Pevensey Rape Schedule No 1

to wit

An Abstract of the several Persons mentioned hereunder mentioned within the said Rape

Names of Hundreds and Parishes	No of men and boys between the ages of 15 and 60 who are capable of active service	No of men and boys between the ages of 15 and 60 who are incapable of active service	No of men above the age of 60 who are capable of active service	No of men above the age of 60 who are incapable of active service	No of men above the age of 60 who are capable of removing themselves	No of men above the age of 60 who are incapable of removing themselves
Ringmer	-	2	2	4	2	27
Southmalling	84	4	3	4	6	2
Stanmer	34	2	-	-	-	5
Glynd	36	9	-	11	9	2
Cliff	218	13	7	5	-	-
Friston	-	-	-	-	-	-
Jevington	54	1	2	5	3	1
East Dean	49	2	-	-	2	-
West Dean	29	1	-	1	1	-
Willingdon	55	7	6	8	8	5
Bishopstone	7	2	-	-	4	3
Denton	14	-	-	-	-	-
Bletchington	-	-	-	5	-	-
Heighton	2	-	-	-	2	2
Berwick	41	-	-	6	3	3
Folkington	26	2	2	3	2	1
Litlington	2	-	-	-	-	5
Arlington	32	-	-	-	20	-
Wilmington	55	2	6	5	4	1
Tarring	24	-	2	-	-	-
Selmeston	23	-	-	-	-	4
Eastbourne	72	21	2	11	10	14
Alciston	37	4	4	1	-	2
Lullington	10	-	1	1	-	1

and described in the Schedule marked No 1 and returned for the respective Parishes

No of women or girls above 7 years of age who are capable of removing themselves	No of women or girls above 7 years of age who are not capable of removing themselves and of women with children at the breast, must be carried with such Children	No of boys under 7 years of age	No of girls under 7 years of age	No of persons serving in Yeomanry or Volunteer Corps of Infantry—	Aliens	Quakers
175	71	64	74	6	-	-
86	31	42	41	5	-	-
30	5	20	6	-	-	-
65	48	19	19	4	-	-
329	54	57	56	8	4	11
-	-	-	-	-	-	-
59	13	22	30	2	-	-
96	16	31	30	5	-	-
27	5	9	4	7	-	-
52	46	34	32	6	-	-
38	12	19	11	13	-	-
15	9	5	5	3	-	-
32	17	18	13	12	-	-
19	5	11	16	5	-	-
44	14	27	26	12	-	-
25	19	6	8	2	-	-
25	19	15	13	6	-	-
133	73	62	33	5	-	-
65	16	16	21	2	-	-
23	-	3	1	2	-	-
18	8	3	3	1	-	-
371	100	153	164	44	-	-
46	25	24	23	2	-	-
10	2	4	5	5	-	-

[Pevensey Rape Schedule No 1 continued]

Names of Hundreds and Parishes	No of men and boys between the ages of 15 and 60 who are capable of active service	No of men and boys between the ages of 15 and 60 who are incapable of active service	No of men above the age of 60 who are capable of active service	No of men above the age of 60 who are incapable of active service	No of men above the age of 60 who are capable of removing themselves	No of men above the age of 60 who are incapable of removing themselves
Alfriston	56	16	-	-	2	3
Beddingham	56	2	3	2	-	-
Westfirle	129	6	6	12	5	7
Hailsham	77	20	5	2	3	4
Hellingly	95	8	3	4	4	-
Chalvington	38	-	-	8	6	-
Ripe	70	2	-	-	5	2
Laughton	110	1	8	9	11	3
Eastgrinsted	527	55	10	27	26	27
Hartfield	74	2	11	28	5	372
Wythyham	117	5	4	1	75	31
Lindfield	207	15	23	9	16	11
Buxted	48	22	1	1	6	25
Framfield	86	13	12	7	9	4
Isfield	83	5	2	1	2	4
Uckfield	134	18	-	13	3	8
Mayfield	95	16	13	8	17	7
Wadhurst	-	-	-	-	-	-
Frant	268	47	-	11	-	-
Rotherfield	300	15	-	14	24	25
Fletching	236	-	7	10	12	10
Horstedkeynes	77	6	36	26	111	32
Littlehorsted	-	13	1	1	3	4
Maresfield	204	21	11	8	12	14
Chiddingly	137	9	11	8	3	1
Easthoathly	67	1	3	2	3	5
Waldron	111	5	10	-	13	12
[Total]	4304*	395	217	282	452	691

* error: should read 4306

Proceedings and Schedules

No of women or girls above 7 years of age who are capable of removing themselves	No of women or girls above 7 years of age who are not capable of removing themselves and of women with children at the breast, must be carried with such Children	No of boys under 7 years of age	No of girls under 7 years of age	No of persons serving in Yeomanry or Volunteer Corps of Infantry—	Aliens	Quakers
165	17	87	80	60	-	-
51	19	13	12	4	-	-
154	37	47	45	11	-	-
156	62	66	45	11	-	-
129	17	96	66	4	-	5
36	14	10	14	-	-	-
41	21	36	25	2	-	-
192	18	83	43	5	-	-
644	880	404	234	24	-	-
33	149	122	-	3	-	-
19	107	106	100	4	-	-
299	62	92	13	-	-	-
214	129	82	102	4	-	-
214	25	76	66	2	-	-
72	47	40	40	2	-	-
219	76	160	60	6	1	1
275	88	84	71	-	-	-
-	-	-	-	-	-	-
292	87	201	139	9	-	-
197	117	127	117	-	-	-
297	20	186	207	-	-	-
112	64	49	69	-	-	-
43	24	18	11	-	-	-
290	63	69	86	1	-	-
-	254	34	-	-	-	-
87	56	54	25	5	-	-
88	208	58	67	60	-	-
6102	3269	3064	2471	374	5	17

Pevensey Rape Schedule No 2

to wit ... An Abstract of the several Persons Matters and things mentioned and hereunder mentioned within the said Rape

Names of Hundreds and Parishes	No of Persons*	Fatting oxen	Cows	Steers Heifers and Calves	Colts	Sheep	Lambs	Hogs	Sows	Pigs	Riding Horses	Waggons	carts
Ringmer	86	45	123	161	9	1613	359	235	27	173	29	48	72
Southmalling	14	12	29	39	1	1810	820	162	-	-	13	21	29
Stanmer	24	-	15	-	-	1200	350	37	2	20	10	4	6
Glynd	26	54	39	67	3	711	202	8	10	61	9	4	10
Cliff	56	-	35	-	-	14	-	73	6	26	30	2	5
Friston	-	-	-	-	-	-	-	-	-	-	-	-	-
Jevington	20	10	24	62	6	1623	568	43	5	49	8	10	21
East Dean	45	24	10	22	3	1705	650	41	14	45	9	10	14
West Dean	7	4	7	23	2	1990	829	56	11	30	4	10	14
Willingdon	51	21	89	162	5	1655	795	45	11	59	10	17	34
Bishopstone	3	71	35	40	2	1478	461	36	6	17	6	9	14
Denton	5	7	7	20	-	721	250	8	5	27	3	6	9
Bletchington	8	-	6	-	-	-	-	5	2	10	-	2	7
Heighton	12	-	5	-	-	350	100	19	3	22	3	5	6
Berwick	13	42	35	82	5	800	255	45	8	26	6	9	18
Folkington	12	40	37	32	-	670	320	47	7	-	7	6	14
Litlington	8	5	7	-	1	503	218	21	5	42	4	5	7
Arlington	35	80	106	197	17	1106	629	170	29	43	15	27	36
Wilmington	31	54	71	61	5	1811	392	70	5	20	13	11	17
Tarring	12	-	6	8	1	836	-	40	-	-	2	5	5
Selmeston	8	51	39	21	1	979	339	33	4	63	4	12	16
Eastbourne	145	186	115	156	8	3865	1707	167	38	175	32	41	82
Alciston	32	110	16	-	-	1200	1	30	2	12	1	10	12

* This is the only Schedule 2 return which includes a column for number of persons. It is not clear how these figures relate to the figures in Pevensey Schedule 1

described in the Schedule marked No 2 and returned for the respective Parishes

Waggons Carts or Carriages with the of horses or oxen be supplied to draw them			Corn Mills			Ovens						
other Carriages	Draft Horses	Draft Oxen	Wind	Water	Quantity of corn ea can grind in 24 hours	Bakers (lbs of bread)	Private	Amt of bread ea can bake in 24 hours Bls	No of Bridges	No of Boats	No of Barges
14	87	118	-	-	-	-	55	12620	-	-	-
2	39	66	1	-	6 Qrs	1	7	18	-	-	-
3	16	-	-	-	-	-	18	72	-	-	-
3	17	35	-	-	-	-	25	50	-	-	-
5	25	-	-	-	-	3	3	138	-	-	-
-	-	-	-	-	-	-	17	-	-	-	-
1	22	40	-	-	-	-	44	1807	-	-	-
2	24	41	-	-	-	-	14	105	-	-	-
-	23	56	-	-	-	-	50	56	-	-	-
-	38	65	2	-	20 Qrs	1	17	147	-	-	-
1	21	40	-	1	60 Bls	-	5	61	-	-	-
-	15	20	-	-	-	-	20	10	-	-	-
-	10	-	-	-	-	1	10	44	-	-	-
-	10	8	-	-	-	-	12	44	-	-	-
-	30	34	-	-	-	-	24	12	-	-	-
1	10	24	-	1	48 Bls	-	24	72	-	-	-
1	12	13	-	-	-	-	38	132	-	-	-
4	64	92	2	-	120 Bls	-	17	76	-	-	-
-	28	51	-	-	-	-	10	17	-	-	-
1	7	24	-	-	-	-	7	10	-	-	-
-	26	34	-	-	-	-	32	20	-	-	-
2	144	127	4	-	400 Bls	8	30	117	-	-	-
-	24	24	-	-	-	-	6	4790	-	-	-

[Pevensey Rape Schedule No 2 continued]

Names of Hundreds and Parishes	No of Persons*	Fatting oxen	Cows	Steers Heifers and Calves	Colts	Sheep	Lambs	Hogs	Sows	Pigs	Riding Horses	Waggons	carts
Lullington	5	-	5	8	-	537	180	11	4	3	1	3	4
Alfriston	40	-	21	-	29	1454	270	91	12	14	9	21	37
Beddingham	4	63	31	70	4	930	740	72	17	79	8	19	24
Westfirle	68	155	68	133	12	1547	570	127	27	98	29	23	35
Hailsham	125	82	187	235	10	1428	276	193	33	121	25	67	61
Hellingly	61	174	141	235	2	838	211	170	13	112	22	33	62
Chalvington	21	12	60	37	4	257	-	27	6	40	4	11	16
Ripe	41	32	96	59	4	215	58	2	1	38	6	14	19
Laughton	74	126	162	150	12	1595	596	112	42	142	16	27	48
Eastgrinsted	419	60	327	247	84	1069	324	375	52	307	58	122	217
Hartfield	117	14	181	247	25	443	12	143	21	239	13	52	83
Wythyham	29	13	77	135	12	484	-	130	4	53	4	19	12
Lindfield	173	15	193	800	14	367	446	180	25	306	31	69	104
Buxted	123	5	47	119	26	886	-	291	32	111	22	55	13
Framfield	130	41	212	242	27	977	601	250	50	148	58	66	89
Isfield	44	10	46	80	4	385	114	39	4	153	6	19	27
Uckfield	109	11	58	43	10	245	52	102	25	93	25	31	34
Mayfield	183	116	313	577	29	1083	507	191	39	217	43	71	10
Wadhurst	No return												
Frant	127	3	129	123	9	632	502	122	30	206	23	37	102
Rotherfield	146	33	95	300	43	1814	213	288	45	187	22	167	186
Fletching	155	15	180	329	10	1343	201	267	14	28	22	54	106
Horstedkeynes	84	4	104	218	12	887	-	121	21	128	8	41	71
Littlehorsted	26	6	45	88	7	316	72	47	13	71	10	13	21
Maresfield	144	44	129	531	-	79	69	35	90	21	40	69	4
Chiddingly	78	52	117	57	7	773	419	169	20	78	13	38	60
Easthoathly	65	7	54	47	8	305	31	90	27	74	2	16	33
Waldron	93	184	214	152	11	971	-	222	8	12	15	42	39
	3337	2093	4148	6415	484	48500	15709	5258	875	4029*	753	1473	1965

* error: should read 3999

Waggons Carts or Carriages with the of horses or oxen be supplied to draw them			Corn Mills				Ovens						
other Carriages	Draft Horses	Draft Oxen	Wind	Water	Quantity of corn ea can grind in 24 hours	Bakers (lbs of bread)	Private	Amt of bread ea can bake in 24 hours	No of Bridges	No of Boats	No of Barges
-	8	13	-	-	-	-	6	780 lbs of bread	-	-	-
-	40	44	1	-	-	3	33	4790	-	-	-
1	39	76	1	-	12	-	21	22 Bls	-	-	-
5	70	84	1	-	40	-	68	68	-	-	-
5	100	78	1	1	11	-	111	288	-	-	-
12	89	103	1	-	-	-	60	60	-	-	-
-	29	18	-	-	-	-	21	56	-	-	-
2	30	26	1	-	-	-	41	41	-	-	-
7	86	118	-	-	-	-	77	46	-	-	-
5	280	122	1	4	25 Qrs	4	280	791	-	-	-
12	113	92	-	1	42	-	70	70	-	-	-
-	54	52	-	1	5	2	44	156	-	-	-
12	171	72	-	3	25	2	172	1662	-	-	-
-	164	64	-	2	30	-	114	253	-	-	-
24	141	120	20	3	120	-	123	99	-	-	-
44	54	-	-	-	-	-	25	16	-	-	-
2	55	34	-	1	109	1	98	133	-	-	-
4	209	192	1	3	55	2	148	692	-	-	-
3	33	81	-	3	25	1	107	3925	-	-	-
1	270	214	1	1	54	-	143	715	-	-	-
1	160	120	2	-	160	-	160	2536	-	-	-
4	107	78	-	1	7	1	77	102	-	-	-
-	36	54	-	-	-	-	-	-	-	-	-
2	136	68	2	2	150	-	138	1791	-	-	-
3	103	90	2	1	100	-	77	221	-	-	-
5	59	32	-	2	12	-	58	9526 lbs	-	-	-
-	66	44	-	-	-	1	33	66 Bls	-	-	-
194	3394	3001	44	31	206 Lds 11 Bls	31	2784*	950 Lds 17 Bls 29 lbs-	-	-	

* error: should read 2790

Pevensey Rape Schedule No 3

to wit ...   An Abstract of the several Persons Matters and things mentioned and hereunder mentioned within the said Rape

| Names of Hundreds and Parishes | No of Persons between 15 and 60 willing to serve and in what capacity ||| How they can arm themselves |||||| No of Persons between the ages of 15 and 60 willing to act as Pioneers or Labourers |
| | Horseback | On foot | | Cavalry ||| Infantry ||| |
				Swords	Pistols		Firelocks	Pikes		
Ringmer	-	31		-	-		29	-		44
Southmalling	2	-		2	4		-	-		37
Stanmer	-	7		-	-		2	-		-
Glynd	4	7		4	5		4	4		10
Cliff	-	-		-	-		-	-		-
Friston	No return									
Jevington	-	3		-	-		-	-		13
East Dean	-	-		-	-		-	-		1
West Dean	-	-		-	-		-	-		-
Willingdon	-	1		-	-		1	-		24
Bishopstone	-	-		-	-		-	-		10
Denton	-	-		-	-		-	-		-
Bletchington	-	-		-	-		-	-		4
Heighton	1	3		1	1		3	-		-
Berwick	2	12		2	2		6	-		7
Folkington	-	1		-	-		-	-		5
Litlington	-	-		-	-		-	-		-
Arlington	-	-		-	-		-	-		30
Wilmington	4	3		1	3		-	3		8
Tarring	3	-		-	-		3	-		8
Selmeston	-	-		-	-		-	-		4
Eastbourne	4	5		3	8		6	2		54
Alciston	-	-		-	-		-	-		3
Lullington	-	-		-	-		-	-		-
Alfriston	-	-		-	-		-	-		-
Beddingham	-	-		-	-		-	-		10
Westfirle	-	16		-	-		16	-		28

described in the Schedule marked No 2 and returned for the respective Parishes

Implements they can bring				Any other implements					No of Persons between 15 and 60 willing to act as drivers of cattle	Do of sheep	Do of Teams	Do Boatmen or Bargemen
Felling Axes	Pick Axes	Spades	Shovels	Bill Hooks	Saws	Sledges						
22	75	19	6	7	19	-	-	-	46	38	29	-
24	-	-	-	-	-	-	-	-	17	16	17	-
-	-	-	-	-	-	-	-	-	13	7	6	-
3	7	5	2	-	3	-	-	-	7	3	13	-
-	-	-	-	-	-	-	-	-	1	-	2	11
5	2	5	-	1	-	-	-	-	16	7	6	-
-	-	-	-	-	-	-	-	-	18	10	15	-
-	-	-	-	-	-	-	-	-	6	9	7	-
10	1	18	6	4	15	-	-	-	14	6	15	-
-	-	-	-	-	-	-	-	-	10	16	8	-
-	-	-	-	-	-	-	-	-	3	5	4	-
2	-	1	-	-	2	-	-	-	6	3	7	-
-	-	-	-	-	-	-	-	-	6	7	3	-
3	2	4	2	3	1	-	-	-	7	6	9	-
-	-	-	-	-	-	-	-	-	6	2	7	-
-	-	-	-	-	-	-	-	-	8	5	7	-
10	4	7	3	4	4	-	-	-	23	17	23	-
7	1	6	-	1	4	-	-	-	7	1	7	-
5	3	10	4	9	9	-	-	-	3	3	9	-
-	1	-	1	2	-	-	-	-	7	3	7	-
31	16	48	53	10	48	-	-	-	68	39	38	-
1	1	-	-	-	-	-	-	-	16	14	10	-
-	-	-	-	-	-	-	-	-	2	2	2	-
-	-	-	-	-	-	-	-	-	7	7	9	-
-	-	-	-	-	-	-	-	-	9	10	11	-
8	4	6	7	1	2	-	-	-	8	6	22	-

[Pevensey Rape Schedule No 3 continued]

Names of Hundreds and Parishes	No of Persons between 15 and 60 willing to serve and in what capacity — Horseback	On foot	Cavalry — Swords	Pistols	Infantry — Firelocks	Pikes	No of Persons between the ages of 15 and 60 willing to act as Pioneers or Labourers
Hailsham	3	10	1	1	8	2	9
Hellingly	5	5	5	-	5	-	25
Chalvington	-	-	-	-	-	-	13
Ripe	-	2	-	-	2	-	23
Laughton	4	5	1	-	2	-	4
Eastgrinsted	64	133	20	28	70	2	60
Hartfield	1	-	-	-	-	-	77
Wythyham	7	16	-	-	3	-	52
Lindfield	6	22	8	9	21	6	68
Buxted	16	22	-	-	-	-	44
Framfield	20	57	10	16	43	14	18
Isfield	-	1	-	-	-	-	21
Uckfield	-	-	-	-	-	-	3
Mayfield	12	10	12	3	6	-	27
Wadhurst	No return						
Frant	2	-	1	1	-	-	4
Rotherfield	21	10	18	8	4	2	11
Fletching	25	20	4	5	9	-	77
Horstedkeynes	-	18	-	-	18	-	36
Littlehorsted	4	3	-	-	-	-	-
Maresfield	18	9	-	4	3	-	14
Chiddingly	4	4	2	4	2	1	4
Easthoathly	7	23	4	4	9	-	13
Waldron	13	48	2	2	34	11	35
[Totals]	252	507	101	108	309	47	938

Implements they can bring					Any other implements				No of Persons between 15 and 60 willing to act as crivers of cattle	Do of sheep	Do of Teams	Do Boatmen or Bargemen
Felling Axes	Pick Axes	Spades	Shovels	Bill Hooks	Saws	Sledges					
6	-	5	3	2	2	2	-	-	28	24	24	-
5	4	6	2	3	3	-	-	-	22	13	16	-
4	5	3	-	-	-	-	-	-	6	9	11	-
18	1	-	2	-	3	-	-	-	8	7	16	-
3	1	-	-	-	-	-	-	-	35	40	10	-
30	17	34	16	16	36	-	-	-	90	49	50	-
48	14	18	12	1	2	-	-	-	49	25	38	-
16	2	14	11	-	9	-	-	-	28	19	40	-
24	8	17	6	4	8	-	-	-	38	21	31	-
8	5	7	11	10	6	-	-	-	27	16	10	
17	11	12	11	6	13	-	-	-	23	18	19	-
9	3	2	1	3	4	-	-	-	15	15	20	-
-	-	-	-	-	-	-	-	-	13	10	7	-
8	14	1	-	-	2	-	-	-	67	45	37	-
1	2	2	3	1	1	-	-	-	6	6	3	-
-	-	1	-	1	-	-	-	-	17	23	20	-
21	14	16	15	3	10	-	-	-	37	25	24	-
14	-	12	2	7	7	-	-	-	43	33	-	2
-	-	-	-	-	-	-	-	-	13	6	16	-
7	6	1	-	-	11	-	-	-	17	19	14	-
3	1	2	-	-	-	-	-	-	6	12	19	-
13	5	3	-	-	3	-	-	-	8	8	11	-
23	29	37	28	9	29	-	-	-	21	19	16	-
409	259	322	207	108	256	2	-	-	951	704	745	13

Hastings Rape Schedule No 1

to wit   An Abstract of the Returns of the Churchwardens and Resolutions of a General Meeting of Lieutenancy held at the Star Inn made and passed in the 38 Year of the Reign of his present Majesty intitled of the Realm during the present War and for indemnifying Persons who may

Names of Hundreds and Parishes	No of men and boys between the ages of 15 and 60 who are capable of active service	No of men and boys between the ages of 15 and 60 who are incapable of active service	No of men above the age of 60 who are capable of active service	No of men above the age of 60 who are incapable of active service	No of men above the age of 60 who are capable of removing themselves	No of men above the age of 60 who are incapable of removing themselves
Goldspur Hundred						
Peasmarsh	82	16	10	2	1	2
Beckley	78	11	6	8	8	7
Iden	60	-	-	6	4	-
Playden	27	3	1	8	2	7
East Guilford	18	-	-	-	-	-
Gostrow Hundred						
Breede	166	2	7	2	6	7
Udimore	85	-	-	17	-	3
Shoyswell Hundred						
Ticehurst	277	26	7	11	20	11
Hawkesborough Hundred						
Burwash	325	26	8	4	11	65
Heathfield	318	13	10	3	4	14
Warbleton	171	7	-	13	12	-
Foxearl Hundred						
Wartling	133	10	3	10	8	9
Hurstmonceux	42	4	7	4	18	3
Ashburnham	35	8	-	12	11	1

Overseers of the Poor of the several Parishes in the said Rape pursuant to the
At Lewes in the said County for carrying into Execution an Act of Parliament
An Act to enable his Majesty more effectually to provide for the Defence and Security
Suffer in their Property by such Measures as may be necessary yfor that Purpose

No of women or girls above 7 years of age who are capable of removing themselves	No of women or girls above 7 years of age who are not capable of removing themselves and of women with children at the breast, must be carried with such Children	No of boys under 7 years of age	No of girls under 7 years of age	No of persons serving in Yeomanry or Volunteer Corps of Infantry—	Aliens	Quakers
92	18	63	48	15	-	-
92	170	20	23	5	-	-
56	15	23	29	11	-	-
60	71	21	25	6	-	-
14	7	7	4	-	-	-
256	40	95	9	83	-	-
87	6	40	47	9	-	-
380	101	120	90	8	-	-
283	91	132	127	6 Cav	-	-
336	65	126	129	3 Cav	-	-
146	103	120	94	3 Do	-	-
172	45	83	65	6 Cav	-	-
25	44	12	40	4 Do	1	-
37	21	37	36	8 Cav 4 each		-

[Hastings Rape Schedule No 1 continued]

Names of Hundreds and Parishes	No of men and boys between the ages of 15 and 60 who are capable of active service	No of men and boys between the ages of 15 and 60 who are incapable of active service	No of men above the age of 60 who are capable of active service	No of men above the age of 60 who are incapable of active service	No of men above the age of 60 who are capable of removing themselves	No of men above the age of 60 who are incapable of removing themselves
Guestling Hundred						
Fairlight	84	2	11	4	3	5
Pett	36	4	4	-	-	4
Guestling	59	-	-	1	1	6
Icklesham	78	6	3	6	1	1
Staple Hundred						
Northiam	203	6	15	21	16	6
Bodiam	53	4	4	2	1	1
Ewhurst	20	5	3	3	2	7
Sedlescombe	114	11	7	9	-	-
Henhurst Hundred						
Etchingham	38	32	-	10	4	8
Salehurst	345	2	17	26	17	32
Netherfield Hundred						
Mountfield	146	-	-	-	9	10
Dallington	36	10	-	-	10	10
Penhurst	10	1	-	1	-	1
Brightling	99	12	6	1	6	10

No of women or girls above 7 years of age who are capable of removing themselves	No of women or girls above 7 years of age who are not capable of removing themselves and of women with children at the breast, must be carried with such Children	No of boys under 7 years of age	No of girls under 7 years of age	No of persons serving in Yeomanry or Volunteer Corps of Infantry—	Aliens	Quakers
106	40	34	34	6 do 3 of each	-	-
63	6	9	12	-	-	-
98	78	45	31	1 Infantry 2 Cavalry	-	-
93	51	38	28	15 Inf	-	-
425	35	87	91	1 Do 2 Cav	-	-
59	39	28	20	-	-	-
39	44	75	70	-	-	-
85	59	44	48	3 Cav	-	-
71	32	25	21	1 Do	-	-
189	472	137	139	6 Do	-	4
166	19	56	66	6 Do	-	-
44	33	18	26	6 Do	-	-
13	6	11	3	2 Do	-	-
130	39	50	40	10 Do	-	-

[Hastings Rape Schedule No 1 continued]

Names of Hundreds and Parishes	No of men and boys between the ages of 15 and 60 who are capable of active service	No of men and boys between the ages of 15 and 60 who are incapable of active service	No of men above the age of 60 who are capable of active service	No of men above the age of 60 who are incapable of active service	No of men above the age of 60 who are capable of removing themselves	No of men above the age of 60 who are incapable of removing themselves
Ninfield Hundred						
Ninfield	108	9	2	6	-	1
Catsfield	104	-	5	7	4	-
Hove	112	-	-	-	18	8
Bexhill Hundred						
Bexhill	243	7	8	7	18	14
Baldsloe Hundred						
Ore	52	-	1	4	1	-
Crowhurst	21	1	-	4	3	3
Hollington	30	2	7	-	3	-
Westfield	132	2	-	4	-	7
Castle	22	13	-	-	-	-
Saint Leonard's	21	-	3	-	-	-
Battle Hundred						
Battle	407	15	15	20	30	12
Whatlington	48	-	3	7	3	4
[Totals]	4438	270	173	243	252	279

No of women or girls above 7 years of age who are capable of removing themselves	No of women or girls above 7 years of age who are not capable of removing themselves and of women with children at the breast, must be carried with such Children	No of boys under 7 years of age	No of girls under 7 years of age	No of persons serving in Yeomanry or Volunteer Corps of Infantry—	Aliens	Quakers
125	11	32	32	2 Do	-	-
142	32	49	38	2 Do	-	-
123	27	39	44	5 Do	-	-
230	133	117	118	4 Do	-	-
69	20	37	15	1 Do	-	-
73	11	34	35	1 Do	-	-
39	-	18	12	-	-	-
61	33	4	236	5 Do	-	-
24	9	11	10	-	-	-
16	5	5	5	1 Do	-	-
572	105	181	187	20 Cav	-	-
63	3	31	19	2 Do	-	-
5154	2139	2114	2235	174 Cavalry 17 Infantry	1	4

Hastings Rape Schedule No 2*

An Abstract of the Returns of the Rape pursuant to the Resolutions of a General Meeting of Lieutenancy held Act of Parliament made and passed in the 38 Year of the Reign of his Provide for the Defence and Security of the Realm during the present Measures as may be necessary for that Purpose'

Names of Hundreds and Parishes	Fatting oxen	Cows	Steers Heifers and Calves	Colts	Sheep	Lambs	Hogs	Sows	Pigs	Riding Horses	Waggons	carts
Goldspur Hundred												
Peasmarsh	54	91	183	6	1639	527	110	4	47	19	27	59
Beckley	56	131	271	6	1285	544	127	14	41	16	45	78
Iden	60	56	77	-	4502	490	81	11	28	4	20	43
Playden	11	25	37	2	1032	513	25	8	27	2	7	18
East Guilford	-	29	47	-	6910	32	20	5	27	-	-	7
Gostrow Hundred												
Breede	20	92	207	9	593	385	253	13	99	19	42	57
Udimore	19	75	124	2	1103	545	80	7	8	8	21	40
Shoyswell Hundred												
Ticehurst	21	265	308	20	2307	1242	261	23	151	33	89	100
Hawkesborough Hundred												
Burwash	30	260	379	11	1633	1092	258	20	135	45	54	103
Heathfield	29	94	256	15	777	80	322	24	122	18	71	108
Warbleton	31	137	325	10	1624	231	233	27	141	13	50	83
Foxearl Hundred												
Wartling	89	105	146	4	1865	486	119	21	111	27	29	42
Hurstmonceux	54	244	154	11	1677	50	201	17	23	21	25	42
Ashburnham	60	80	155	4	1396	330	98	12	191	22	27	51

* This Schedule 2 return omits the final three columns (bridges, boats, barges) which are included in the other Schedule 2 returns

Churchwardens and Overseers of the Poor of the several Parishes in the said
at the Star Inn at Lewes in the said County for carrying into Execution An
present Majesty intitled 'An Act to enable his Majesty more effectually to
War and for indemnifying Persons who may suffer in their Property by such

Waggons Carts or Carriages with the of horses or oxen be supplied to draw them			Corn Mills				Ovens	
other Carriages	Draft Horses	Draft Oxen	Wind	Water	Quantity of corn they can grind in 24 hours (quarters)	Bakers (lbs of bread)	Private	Amt of bread they can bake in 24 hours
1	78	26	1	-	40 Bls	-	26	124 Bls of Flour
5	109	53	1	1	2 Load	-	33	99 Do
-	41	50	-	-	-	-	41	674 Quart Loaves
2	23	12	2	-	8 Quar	-	11	23 Bls
-	8	-	-	-	-	-	12	2400 lb weight of Bread in the wk
1	83	85	1	-	24 Bls	-	102	3 Bls each
-	42	43	1	-	24 Bls	-	22	3 Bls each
16	177	111	1	2	-	-	167	409 Bls each half
18	139	100	2	1	2 Load of Wheat 52 of oats	-	200	72 Sacks of Flour
7	171	136	1	1	4 Quart	2	141	Bakers 8 Bls Private 76 Bls
11	116	142	-	3	24 Bls ea	-	95	3 Bls each
24	72	104	2	2	3 Load	-	82	162 Bls
7	63	108	1	-	-	-	29	156 Gallons
1	62	92	-	-	-	-	50	156 Bushels

[Hastings Rape Schedule No 2 continued]

Names of Hundreds and Parishes	Fatting oxen	Cows	Steers Heifers and Calves	Colts	Sheep	Lambs	Hogs	Sows	Pigs	Riding Horses	Waggons	carts
Guestling												
Fairlight	24	85	131	8	1879	627	92	27	38	1	30	48
Pett	135	34	214	6	2048	282	93	5	54	5	11	19
Guestling	53	107	249	4	1056	233	18	20	78	1	34	59
Icklesham	24	182	220	3	7108	4621	48	20	42	2	29	46
Staple												
Northiam	24	111	195	8	1096	360	20	11	32	2	32	75
Bodiam	15	52	140	8	464	239	47	10	74	7	14	30
Ewhurst	9	89	137	3	794	286	-	-	14	7	33	52
Sedlescomb	42	44	113	3	847	317	12	14	61	1	18	24
Henhurst												
Etchingham	37	102	256	9	760	239	10	3	39	1	28	58
Salehurst	29	177	283	8	1448	817	31	26	20	3	65	82
Netherfield												
Mountfield	18	78	208	12	1130	554	16	16	85	1	25	46
Dallington	18	33	60	5	196	215	51	9	33	3	15	25
Penhurst	8	16	53	2	166	124	25	2	27	4	8	11
Brightling	1	96	133	5	1167	391	12	2	47	1	24	55
Ninfield												
Ninfield	34	71	105	7	699	341	12	6	47	1	19	37
Catsfield	52	78	167	2	1131	509	16	4	23	2	24	36
Hove	15	91	109	1	868	368	91	13	56	2	20	36

No of other number that can

Waggons Carts or Carriages with the of horses or oxen be supplied to draw them			Corn Mills				Ovens		
other Carriages	Draft Horses	Draft Oxen	Wind	Water	Quantity of corn they can grind in 24 hours (quarters)	Bakers (lbs of bread)	Private	Amt of bread they can bake in 24 hours	
4	77	64	1	-	80 Bls	-	39	135 Peck Loaves
1	31	32	-	-	-	-	26	117 Bls of Flour
3	87	63	-	-	-	-	32	101 Do
5	58	92	1	-	60 Bls	-	61	1507 Galls of Flour
5	103	52	4	-	5 Qrs ea	-	112	3 Bls each
2	31	34	-	1	5 Quarts	-	36	216 Bls of Do
-	87	50	2	-	12 Bls	-	26	119 Bls of Do
1	43	51	1	-	24 Bls	-	77	258 Do of Do
1	78	46	-	-	-	-	35	4 Bls ea oven
61	164	51	1	2	390 Do	-	253	1067 Bls
5	62	92	-	-	-	-	-	-
1	24	22	-	-	-	-	27	99 Bls of Flour
2	9	20	-	-	-	-	11	45 Bushels
6	57	74	2	-	140 Bls	-	66	67 Do
-	68	34	-	-	-	-	47	47
-	55	54	1	1	5 Qs ea	-	-61	1135 Galls of Flour
-	43	50	1	-	1 Load ½	-	38	77 Bls

[Hastings Rape Schedule No 2 continued]

Names of Hundreds and Parishes	Fatting oxen	Cows	Steers Heifers and Calves	Colts	Sheep	Lambs	Hogs	Sows	Pigs	Riding Horses	Waggons	Carts
Bexhill												
Bexhill	25	215	424	18	2636	995	253	28	123	31	43	65
Baldsloe												
Ore	10	50	69	1	592	267	95	19	99	3	12	21
Crowhurst	6	69	118	7	1271	480	59	12	37	1	19	36
Hollington	-	38	62	-	112	50	36	-	-	4	10	19
Westfield	11	30	427	9	1697	179	18	3	20	8	45	65
Castle	2	13	27	2	200	-	14	4	18	1	5	9
Saint	2	21	59	-	520	190	11	4	15	3	7	10
Battle												
Battle	30	118	248	12	1073	517	24	41	16	5	56	107
Whatlington	1	32	39	2	120	79	60	1	24	6	13	18
[Totals]]	1159	3716	6915	245	60421*	19327†	5110	506	2645‡	629	1146	1920

* error: should read 59421
† error: should read 19827
‡ error: should read 2745

Waggons Carts or Carriages with the of horses or oxen be supplied to draw them			Corn Mills		Ovens		
other Carriages	Draft Horses	Draft Oxen	Wind	Water	Quantity of corn they can grind in 24 hours (quarters)	Bakers (lbs of bread)	Private	Amt of bread they can bake in 24 hours

other Carriages	Draft Horses	Draft Oxen	Wind	Water	Quantity of corn they can grind in 24 hours (quarters)	Bakers (lbs of bread)	Private	Amt of bread they can bake in 24 hours
2	138	128	2	-	one 10 Qus one 12 Do	1	76	-
3	41	12	-	-	-	-	33	422 Peck Loaves
3	46	22	-	-	-	-	15	114 Bls
-	29	14	-	-	-	-	18	54 Do
3	117	80	1	-	5 Qrs	-	120	360 Do
-	13	12	1	-	-	-	3	12 Gs Ea
-	16	23	-	-	-	-	10	6 Do ea
15	160	138	4	1	5 Qrs ea	-	208	572½ Bls
-	39	18	1	1	5 Qrs Do	-	34	102 Do
216	2880*	2390	36	16	-	3	1175	-

* error: should read 2860

[signed] T Fuller
Thos Phil Lamb

Hastings Rape Schedule No 3*

to wit ... An Abstract of the Returns of the Rape pursuant to the Resolutions of a General Meeting of Lieutenancy held Act of Parliament made and passed in the 38 Year of the Reign of his Provide for the Defence and Security of the Realm during the present Measures as may be necessary for that Purpose'

Names of Hundreds and Parishes	No of Persons between 15 and 60 willing to serve and in what capacity		How they can arm themselves					No of Persons between the ages of 15 and 60 willing to act as Pioneers or Labourers
			Cavalry		Infantry			
	Horseback	On foot	Swords	Pistols	Firelocks	Pikes	
Goldspur Hundred							
Peasmarsh	-	8	2	-	2	4	29
Beckley	1	25	4	-	15	7	18
Iden	-	-	-	-	-	-	14
Playden	1	4	1	1	4	-	6
East Guilford	-	-	-	-	-	-	-
Gostrow Hundred							
Breede	2	1	2	1	1	1	18
Udimore	-	-	-	-	-	-	6
Shoyswell Hundred							
Ticehurst	3	7	2	-	1	-	72
Hawkesborough Hundred							
Burwash	2	-	-	-	-	-	2
Heathfield	13	2	7	10	2	-	26
Warbleton	1	22	1	2	21	-	30
Foxearl Hundred							
Wartling	4	6	2	-	6	2	24
Hurstmonceux	4	-	4	4	-	-	30
Ashburnham	7	-	-	3	3	-	10
Guestling Hundred							
Fairlight	3	-	3	3	-	-	15

* This Schedule 3 return omits the final column (boatmen & bargemen) included in the other Schedule 3 returns

Churchwardens and Overseers of the Poor of the several Parishes in the said at the Star Inn at Lewes in the said County for carrying into Execution An present Majesty intitled 'An Act to enable his Majesty more effectually to War and for indemnifying Persons who may suffer in their Property by such

Implements they can bring							For any other iinstruments the Pioneers may engage to brings			No of Persons between 15 and 60 willing to act as drivers of cattle	Do of sheep	Do of Teams
Felling Axes	Pick Axes	Spades	Shovels	Bill Hooks	Saws						
9	5	4	3	4	3	Axe & Handbill			15	12	12
8	2	4	-	5	4	-	-	-	20	18	20
7	8	14	14	-	8	-	-	-	13	14	19
3	-	3	-	-	1	-	-	-	4	4	11
-	-	-	-	-	-	-	-	-	9	10	-
14	12	18	14	8	12	-	-	-	11	7	18
-	-	-	-	-	-	-	-	-	7	8	13
22	26	28	21	23	14	-	-	-	57	55	56
-	2	-	2	-	-	-	-	-	17	23	36
5	11	7	2	-	1	-	-	-	31	28	29
22	4	16	4	-	4	-	-	-	39	31	33
7	3	6	1	3	3	-	-	-	14	12	15
18	10	11	5	2	1	-	-	-	16	5	30
2	4	3	1	2	2	-	-	-	4	3	16
5	1	2	-	1	-	-	-	-	23	18	19

[Hastings Rape Schedule No 3 continued]

Names of Hundreds and Parishes	No of Persons between 15 and 60 willing to serve and in what capacity - Horseback	No of Persons between 15 and 60 willing to serve and in what capacity - On foot	Cavalry - Swords	Cavalry - Pistols	Infantry - Firelocks	Infantry - Pikes	No of Persons between the ages of 15 and 60 willing to act as Pioneers
Pett	-	-	-	-	-	-	2
Guestling	2	6	2	4	6	6	27
Icklesham	8	-	6	6	-	-	30
Staple Hundred							
Northiam	4	2	-	2	1	-	11
Bodiam	1	1	1	1	1	-	14
Ewhurst	1	-	1	2	-	-	20
Sedlescombe	16	14	4	5	5	2	31
Henhurst Hundred							
Etchingham	2	4	-	2	2	-	11
Salehurst	23	63	23	23	63	63	91
Netherfield							
Mountfield	1	2	1	1	2	2	2
Dallington	-	-	-	-	-	-	1
Penhurst	-	-	-	-	-	-	-
Brightling	7	14	7	7	24	13	37
Ninfield Hundred							
Ninfield	1	1	1	2	1	-	26
Catsfield	9	24	-	-	-	-	5
Hove	22	35	-	-	15	18	24
Bexhill Hundred							
Bexhill	2	4	-	2	-	4	41
Baldsloe Hundred							
Ore	-	1	-	-	-	1	16
Crowhurst	9	2	8	1	-	-	29
Hollington	-	-	-	-	-	-	9
Westfield	-	-	-	-	-	-	21
Castle	-	-	-	-	-	-	-
Saint Leonard's	1	-	1	1	-	-	-
Battle Hundred							
Battle	10	1	-	-	1	-	14
Whatlington	2	-	-	-	1	-	1
[Totals]]	162	249	83	83	177	123	763

Proceedings and Schedules

Felling Axes	Pick Axes	Spades	Shovels	Bill Hooks	Saws	For any other instruments the Pioneers may engage to brings			No of Persons between 15 and 60 willing to act as drivers	Do of sheep	Do of Teams
1	-	2	-	-	1	-	-	-	11	13	10
21	16	4	10	17	-	-	-	-	13	18	16
9	7	8	3	2	1	-	-	-	14	20	24
1	-	1	1	-	-	-	-	-	26	27	18
5	8	8	2	3	1	-	-	-	11	12	17
17	2	16	9	17	10	-	-	-	28	27	31
15	-	9	1	-	-	-	-	-	19	17	23
6	-	4	2	5	1	-	-	-	15	12	15
11	5	16	1	1	-	-	-	-	69	78	44
1	1	1	1	1	1	-	-	-	4	3	3
-	1	1	-	-	-	-	-	-	10	9	8
-	-	-	-	-	-	-	-	-	5	4	6
38	6	21	14	4	15	-	-	-	14	12	12
12	2	6	2	5	6	-	-	-	25	24	25
1	5	7	3	-	5	-	-	-	20	20	12
-	17	-	-	-	6	-	-	-	18	-	14
7	2	4	3	3	7	Thatching rake			37	37	41
13	2	1	1	-	-	-	-	-	16	6	10
9	8	8	1	1	-	-	-	-	15	3	8
3	-	5	-	-	1	-	-	-	21	6	9
12	10	4	4	2	7	-	-	-	40	34	37
-	-	-	-	-	-	-	-	-	14	13	8
-	-	-	-	-	-	-	-	-	6	3	8
11	8	6	8	-	7	-	-	-	46	19	30
1	1	1	1	-	1	Mattock		-	11	7	17
316	189	249	134	109	123	-	-	-	788	672	773

[Arundel Rape]* Schedule No 1

Parishes	No of men and boys between the ages of 15 and 60 who are capable of active service	No of men and boys between the ages of 15 and 60 who are incapable of active service	No of men above the age of 60 who are capable of active service	No of men above the age of 60 who are incapable of active service	No of men above the age of 60 who are capable of removing themselves	No of men above the age of 60 who are incapable of removing themselves
Southstoke	26	-	-	3	2	1
Madehurst	27	14	-	1	1	4
Binsted	24	1	-	2	1	4
Middleton	19	-	-	3	2	1
Tortington	16	1	1	1	1	-
Ford	17	1	2	-	-	-
Yapton	66	1	-	-	2	10
Barnham	32	2	-	-	5	-
Climping	46	2	5	6	-	-
Felpham	129	-	1	7	-	5
Walberton	53	5	-	-	7	3
Eastergate	54	2	1	-	-	-
Northstoke	17	-	-	-	5	2
Leominster	56	17	-	3	2	2
Angmering	156	18	1	13	-	7
Kingston	13	-	1	-	-	-
Rustington	56	2	-	-	7	1
Ferring	54	-	4	6	10	-
Poleing	39	1	-	7	4	5
Burpham	47	7	-	11	-	2
Goring	95	3	-	6	9	-
Warningcamp	28	2	-	4	-	-
Preston	25	4	2	5	1	4
Littlehampton	42	11	4	5	-	-
Borough of Arundell	311	50	3	23	-	6
Petworth	429	17	12	6	14	34
Barlavington	23	-	-	-	-	-
Tillington	148	2	1	12	7	6

* Not specified on Schedule

No of women or girls above 7 years of age who are capable of removing themselves	No of women or girls above 7 years of age who are not capable of removing themselves and of women with children at the breast, must be carried with such Children	No of boys under 7 years of age	No of girls under 7 years of age	Cavalry	Infantry	Aliens	Quakers
38	1	9	11	-	-	-	-
38	9	9	14	2	2	-	-
35	4	10	17	-	-	-	-
13	2	3	-	-	-	-	-
21	3	8	2	-	-	-	-
19	10	5	6	2	1	-	-
128	34	57	46	6	-	-	-
29	10	12	15	1	-	-	-
56	11	23	24	5	-	-	-
83	81	59	60	2	11	-	-
77	56	71	59	2	2	-	-
51	2	20	16	2	-	-	-
12	7	3	2	-	-	-	-
97	22	44	40	5	-	-	-
183	26	61	66	5	2	-	-
5	8	7	4	-	-	-	-
60	14	23	15	3	2	-	-
47	22	15	20	-	-	-	-
47	6	20	6	-	-	-	-
45	32	29	17	2	-	-	-
131	27	37	40	1	-	-	-
41	-	13	12	-	-	-	-
67	2	25	19	1	-	-	-
81	81	76	27	-	7	-	-
760	112	127	147	3	100	4	11
409	181	171	176	30	-	3	-
27	5	4	9	1	-	-	-
208	18	128	66	6	-	-	-

[Arundel Rape Schedule No 1 continued]

Parishes	No of men and boys between the ages of 15 and 60 who are capable of active service	No of men and boys between the ages of 15 and 60 who are incapable of active service	No of men above the age of 60 who are capable of active service	No of men above the age of 60 who are incapable of active service	No of men above the age of 60 who are capable of removing themselves	No of men above the age of 60 who are incapable of removing themselves
Kirdford	291	13	6	26	44	27
Northchapel	172	3	8	3	5	6
Lurgashall	110	3	7	1	1	1
Stopham	29	2	-	4	2	3
Burton	5	-	-	-	-	2
Sutton	53	3	6	15	-	-
Egdean	17	2	-	-	5	-
Duncton	43	-	-	-	4	2
Woollavington	41	9	4	-	5	23
Amberley	67	4	7	3	6	14
Parham	16	-	-	5	2	3
Gritham	15	2	1	3	3	1
Pulborough	275	16	9	23	16	32
Billingshurst	155	12	18	25	35	6
Wiggenholt	9	-	-	1	-	1
Storrington	175	14	8	-	-	-
West Chiltington	110	8	8	6	4	10
Bury	86	1	3	3	5	11
Coldwaltham	46	5	-	14	11	4
Fittleworth	125	1	14	11	9	8
Hardham	27	2	-	8	2	5
Coates	7	-	-	-	-	-
Bignor	25	-	3	1	-	2
Wisborough Green	255	3	15	16	6	11
Houghton	36	9	2	7	5	4
[Totals]	4227*	275	157	303†	250	270‡

* error: should read 4238

† error: should read 299

‡ error: should read 273

No of women or girls above 7 years of age who are capable of removing themselves	No of women or girls above 7 years of age who are not capable of removing themselves and of women with children at the breast, must be carried with such Children	No of boys under 7 years of age	No of girls under 7 years of age	Cavalry	Infantry	Aliens	Quakers
353	114	115	110	6	-	-	-
180	57	50	51	-	-	-	-
50	41	44	46	1	-	-	-
46	19	19	21	1	-	-	-
6	3	4	1	-	-	-	-
89	15	65	43	2	-	-	-
25	3	8	6	2	-	-	-
53	16	27	15	1	-	-	-
50	-	-	-	-	-	-	-
129	29	42	36	1	-	-	-
21	9	4	8	3	-	1	-
14	14	13	8	-	-	-	-
271	189	143	124	2	-	-	-
301	124	114	131	-	-	-	4
13	-	5	2	1	-	-	-
139	33	67	68	-	-	-	5
172	27	51	55	3	-	-	-
102	37	53	36	5	-	-	-
52	33	16	23	3	-	-	-
155	50	49	56	4	-	-	-
24	4	5	5	-	-	-	-
5	3	5	5	-	-	-	-
27	10	11	9	-	-	-	-
339	38	113	165	2	-	-	-
46	12	13	11	2	-	-	-
5470	1676*	2105	1971	118	127	8	21†

* error: should read 1666
† error: should read 20

[Arundel Rape]* Schedule No 2

Names of Hundreds and Parishes	Fatting oxen	Cows	Steers Heifers and Calves	Colts	Sheep	Lambs	Hogs	Sows	Pigs	Riding Horses	Waggons	carts
Southstoke	4	21	74	-	344	221	15	6	46	3	6	9
Madehurst	4	18	17	9	860	430	42	16	89	12	7	13
Binsted	4	16	23	4	297	34	74	4	29	5	8	12
Middleton	6	6	4	1	31	-	40	3	10	5	5	6
Tortington	74	48	-	2	160	-	17	1	-	5	6	9
Ford	53	15	4	4	136	128	41	6	30	1	7	10
Yapton	34	54	25	6	712	27	169	28	168	24	22	44
Barnham	29	19	31	1	209	-	77	12	43	4	8	11
Climping	122	29	24	4	581	8	139	8	56	8	14	19
Felpham	37	102	27	1	306	6	170	36	243	17	20	33
Walberton	-	32	22	7	562	98	124	29	206	27	25	40
Eastergate	-	33	9	3	218	-	143	9	32	8	10	22
Northstoke	8	34	29	3	607	230	15	3	22	2	5	7
Leominster	182	54	26	5	761	-	93	20	64	15	19	34
Angmering	59	86	86	9	2772	344	215	48	234	25	28	45
Kingston	22	11	26	5	467	8	49	6	45	3	6	9
Rustington	4	29	26	1	153	-	137	26	106	8	23	29
Ferring	5	23	11	8	562	1	110	31	109	6	12	18
Poleing	15	25	10	2	3	83	45	17	100	9	13	18
Burpham	2	35	33	1	1433	417	54	16	106	12	8	19
Goring	18	53	19	16	1188	110	206	28	147	16	27	38
Warningcamp	-	18	9	4	243	167	32	12	39	4	7	9
Preston	2	7	17	-	50	-	58	12	77	2	10	10
Littlehampton	-	30	17	4	150	9	143	27	92	21	14	24
Arundell Borough	16	70	26	4	999	77	123	7	110	47	15	35
Petworth	22	91	123	41	1302	422	148	46	214	76	69	85
Barlavington	-	7	9	1	200	100	22	3	39	2	3	3
Tillington	8	81	134	20	367	61	190	42	246	16	39	48

* Not specified on Schedule

Waggons Carts or Carriages with the of horses or oxen be supplied to draw them			Corn Mills				Ovens						
other Carriages	Draft Horses	Draft Oxen	Wind	Water	Quantity of corn ea can grind in 24 hours	Bakers (lbs of bread)	Private	Amt of bread ea can bake in 24 hours in Gallons	No of Bridges	No of Boats	No of Barges
-	16	10	-	-	-	-	16	20	-	1	1
6	33	-	-	-	-	-	18	120	-	-	-
2	21	-	-	-	-	-	13	-	-	-	-
1	15	-	-	-	-	-	6	136	-	1	-
1	17	-	-	-	-	-	5	27	-	-	-
2	21	-	-	-	-	-	10	248	-	2	-
4	73	6	-	-	-	2	47	1448	-	-	-
1	27	12	1	-	5	-	17	504	-	-	-
1	44	9	1	-	10	-	29	145	-	-	-
3	88	-	2	-	20	-	83	3872	1	5	-
8	67	-	2	-	20	-	56	1640	-	-	-
-	38	7	-	-	-	7	13	312	-	-	-
-	11	20	1	-	10	-	11	176	-	3	-
5	59	14	1	-	10	-	34	243	2	-	-
5	89	65	2	-	10	1	79	1896	-	-	-
1	14	8	-	-	-	-	7	288	-	-	-
-	59	8	-	-	-	-	13	312	-	-	-
-	32	10	1	-	-	-	39	880	-	2	-
1	35	-	-	-	-	-	22	512	-	-	-
5	34	19	-	-	-	-	-	-	-	2	-
-	80	8	-	-	-	-	52	2248	-	-	-
-	19	-	-	-	-	-	13	288	-	-	-
1	21	-	-	-	-	-	15	704	-	3	-
6	39	4	1	-	10	2	16	193	-	-	-
15	69	-	1	1	15	16	21	1160	1	13	-
15	188	72	-	1	35	10	60	2800	2	2	-
-	9	-	-	-	-	-	11	320	-	-	-
3	105	42	-	-	-	3	97	-	-	-	-

[Arundel Rape] Schedule No 2 continued

Names of Hundreds and Parishes	Fatting oxen	Cows	Steers Heifers and Calves	Colts	Sheep	Lambs	Hogs	Sows	Pigs	Riding Horses	Waggons	carts
Kirdford	4	189	437	43	884	152	251	88	507	32	94	118
Northchapel	7	62	76	12	142	-	120	11	129	3	30	42
Lurgashall	2	44	77	16	368	-	72	20	120	4	28	35
Stopham	41	27	23	3	744	-	57	6	63	4	10	12
Burton	17	12	31	2	564	260	48	9	46	5	6	14
Sutton	16	21	29	1	500	141	57	15	96	3	7	11
Egdean	-	15	22	2	177	59	10	8	37	3	6	9
Duncton	2	23	28	6	230	124	45	18	93	3	9	13
Woollavington	6	50	82	5	1152	-	91	14	95	5	15	18
Amberley	22	76	148	10	700	280	81	18	137	6	19	27
Parham	-	10	8	3	390	105	15	7	38	5	-	6
Gritham	20	23	90	7	16	51	39	10	79	2	7	8
Pulborough	123	209	265	27	1142	165	424	58	318	39	89	113
Billingshurst	36	134	264	14	358	17	227	31	273	22	63	78
Wiggenholt	24	10	39	6	360	250	4	3	12	1	5	6
Storrington	-	60	68	2	683	127	134	14	169	27	24	39
West	20	79	132	24	408	79	117	40	190	9	31	46
Bury	60	67	90	-	2012	664	149	26	113	10	26	34
Coldwaltham	14	42	30	13	298	-	31	8	43	5	11	14
Fittleworth	16	84	91	19	746	10	184	53	183	22	27	42
Hardham	76	39	51	6	66	223	77	12	73	9	11	12
Coates	-	12	26	8	62	24	12	2	15	1	6	8
Bignor	-	5	-	3	425	168	40	6	43	4	5	8
Wisborough Green	53	175	231	12	1504	-	312	45	385	52	41	104
Houghton	-	17	12	4	980	470	80	10	31	2	8	10
[Totals]†	1189	2591	3211	414	30584	6450	5238	1024	5989	660	1016	1486

* Not specified on Schedule
† multiple errors; correct totals below

| [Totals] | 1289 | 2532 | 3211 | 414 | 30584 | 6350 | 5368 | 1034 | 5990 | 661 | 1014 | 1486 |

other Carriages	Draft Horses	Draft Oxen	Wind	Water	Quantity of corn ea can grind in 24 hours	Bakers (lbs of bread)	Private	Amt of bread ea can bake in 24 hours	No of Bridges	No of Boats	No of Barges
7	254	96	-	5	30	-	202	4568	4	-	-
1	92	12	1	-	20	2	92	2002	-	-	-
-	72	16	-	1	-	2	33	-	1	2	-
3	35	-	-	-	-	1	24	407	1	1	1
-	14	10	-	1	-	-	4	160	-	-	-
-	31	3	-	-	-	-	47	1880	1	-	-
-	20	-	-	-	-	-	12	376	-	-	-
-	30	8	-	1	25	-	30	800	-	-	-
-	39	-	-	1	20	-	25	150	-	-	-
1	66	6	-	1	4	2	58	566	-	-	-
3	13	-	-	-	-	-	9	224	-	-	-
-	17	8	-	-	-	-	10	3648	2	4	-
4	226	14	2	3	40	-	214	1712	6	2	2
4	161	32	1	9	10	4	177	3016	-	-	-
-	6	12	-	-	-	-	7	112	-	-	-
-	97	-	1	1	-	2	29	36	-	-	-
-	85	6	-	-	-	3	83	1856	-	-	-
2	70	16	1	1	30	-	49	2536	-	-	-
-	33	-	1	-	-	-	48	1152	1	6	-
5	83	8	-	3	30	2	101	1688	1	2	1
-	40	-	-	-	-	-	11	264	9	2	-
-	12	8	-	-	-	-	6	72	-	1	-
-	18	-	-	1	7	-	16	768	-	-	-
6	137	128	1	-	10	4	213	3368	6	-	9
-	24	-	-	-	-	-	30	488	1	-	-
122	2988	697	21	30	371	99	2343	54936	39	47	21

Waggons Carts or Carriages with the of horses or oxen be supplied to draw them; Corn Mills; Ovens

* multiple errors; correct totals below

| 122 | 2988 | 697 | 21 | 30 | 371 | 63 | 2333 | 52341 | 39 | 54 | 14 |

[Arundel Rape]* Schedule No 3

Names of Hundreds and Parishes	No of Persons between 15 and 60 willing to serve and in what capacity – Horseback	On foot	Cavalry – Swords	Pistols	Infantry – Firelocks	Pikes	No of Persons between the ages of 15 and 60 willing to act as Pioneers
Southstoke	3	7	-	1	5	4	3
Madehurst	6	8	6	6	7	-	7
Binsted	-	-	-	-	-	-	1
Middleton	-	-	-	-	-	-	7
Tortington	-	-	-	-	-	-	7
Ford	-	2	-	-	2	-	1
Yapton	-	35	-	-	18	17	24
Barnham	-	-	-	-	-	-	10
Climping	2	-	-	-	-	-	-
Felpham	7	47	7	13	25	9	48
Walberton	18	12	1	1	5	-	11
Eastergate	-	9	-	-	9	-	24
Northstoke	-	-	-	-	-	-	3
Leominster	3	-	-	1	-	-	14
Angmering	5	55	5	5	55	-	50
Kingston	-	-	-	-	-	-	2
Rustington	5	7	-	-	-	-	18
Ferring	-	11	-	-	2	9	16
Poleing	-	-	-	-	-	-	16
Burpham	6	4	-	-	55	-	16
Goring	11	12	-	-	12	-	32
Warningcamp	-	14	-	-	-	-	5
Preston	1	1	1	1	-	1	1
Littlehampton	11	32	9	7	22	-	23
Arundel Borough	15	133	1	4	1	7	37
Petworth	27	31	-	-	-	-	29
Barlavington	-	-	-	-	-	-	8
Tillington	2	4	-	-	-	-	68

* Not specified on Schedule

Felling Axes	Pick Axes	Spades	Shovels	Bill Hooks	Saws	Scythes	Knives		No of Persons between 15 and 60 willing to act as drivers of cattle	Do of sheep	Do of Teams	Do Boatmen or Bargemen
-	2	-	-	1	1	-	-	-	4	2	5	2
2	3	1	1	-	-	-	-	-	9	7	5	-
1	-	-	-	-	1	-	-	-	9	8	7	-
4	3	5	2	3	3	-	-	-	4	3	4	-
2	6	6	5	1	1	-	-	-	3	3	5	-
-	1	1	-	-	-	-	-	-	6	7	5	-
2	15	22	13	16	23	-	-	-	3	7	17	-
2	2	2	2	2	-	-	-	-	6	7	9	-
-	-	-	-	-	-	-	-	-	2	7	-	-
10	10	11	10	3	4	-	-	-	9	10	14	-
8	1	2	-	1	9	-	-	-	16	11	6	1
2	7	2	4	6	3	-	-	-	7	8	9	-
-	2	2	4	1	1	-	-	-	5	4	6	1
5	8	5	9	2	9	-	-	-	12	21	17	-
37	8	6	1	-	-	-	-	-	41	16	14	-
-	2	2	-	-	-	-	-	-	5	4	5	-
-	-	-	-	-	-	-	-	-	11	3	10	-
2	7	3	4	-	-	-	-	-	9	9	9	-
12	2	6	2	8	11	-	-	-	8	7	5	1
10	3	15	1	3	3	-	-	-	6	4	9	2
5	7	7	7	-	7	-	-	-	11	10	11	-
3	2	3	2	2	1	-	-	-	4	3	4	-
-	-	1	1	1	-	-	-	-	4	2	13	3
9	8	9	7	6	6	-	-	-	9	10	8	14
2	8	4	9	-	1	-	-	-	31	22	26	5
-	-	-	-	-	-	-	-	-	23	24	27	-
1	3	1	1	2	-	-	-	-	2	1	5	-
12	33	11	11	2	-	-	-	-	2	1	5	-

Column groups: Implements they can bring (Felling Axes, Pick Axes, Spades, Shovels, Bill Hooks, Saws); Any other instruments Pioneers may engage to bring (Scythes, Knives).

[Arundel Rape Schedule No 3 continued]

Names of Hundreds and Parishes	Horseback	On foot	Swords	Pistols	Firelocks	Pikes	No of Persons between the ages of 15 and 60 willing to act as Pioneers
Kirdford	10	16	-	-	4	-	45
Northchapel	-	36	-	-	36	-	52
Lurgashall	2	28	2	-	28	-	38
Stopham	-	1	-	-	-	-	6
Burton	-	-	-	-	-	-	-
Sutton	2	27	2	2	7	-	-
Egdean	-	-	-	-	-	-	5
Duncton	-	-	-	-	-	-	28
Woollavington	-	-	-	-	-	-	6
Amberley	-	17	-	-	-	-	19
Parham	6	3	-	-	2	-	-
Gritham	-	1	-	-	1	-	1
Pulborough	17	47	3	5	37	6	62
Billingshurst	1	-	-	-	-	1	133
Wiggenholt	-	-	-	-	-	-	1
Storrington	-	5	-	-	5	-	1
West Chiltington	12	9	10	2	4	4	27
Bury	6	3	4	4	-	-	20
Coldwaltham	-	8	-	-	7	1	6
Fittleworth	6	37	6	1	37	-	28
Hardham	-	10	-	-	10	-	2
Coates	-	-	-	-	-	-	3
Bignor	5	-	2	4	-	-	7
Wisborough Green	158	31	39	11	26	19	73
Houghton	-	1	-	-	1	-	15
[Totals]	347	704	98	68	423	78	959*

Column groupings: "No of Persons between 15 and 60 willing to serve and in what capacity" (Horseback, On foot); "How they can arm themselves" — Cavalry (Swords, Pistols), Infantry (Firelocks, Pikes).

* error: should read 1059

Proceedings and Schedules

Felling Axes	Pick Axes	Spades	Shovels	Bill Hooks	Saws	Scythes	Knives		No of Persons between 15 and 60 willing to act as drivers of cattle	Do of sheep	Do of Teams	Do Boatmen or Bargemen
35	14	31	8	1	14	-	-	-	43	41	57	-
42	3	2	2	2	1	-	-	-	18	10	25	-
12	12	7	1	3	3	-	-	-	17	15	17	-
2	1	6	5	5	1	-	-	-	7	5	7	-
-	-	-	-	-	-	-	-	-	3	1	2	-
4	6	4	3	2	1	-	-	-	10	7	15	-
3	5	5	2	-	3	-	-	-	4	3	5	-
3	25	6	-	-	-	-	-	-	11	8	10	-
2	1	3	-	-	-	-	-	-	5	2	4	-
-	-	-	-	-	-	-	-	-	12	3	13	-
-	-	-	-	-	-	-	-	-	1	1	4	-
-	-	-	-	-	-	-	-	-	6	5	4	-
7	24	23	18	9	5	-	-	-	48	43	62	18
59	32	15	2	14	3	-	-	-	51	31	44	-
-	1	-	-	-	-	-	-	-	2	3	2	-
1	-	-	-	-	-	-	-	-	4	2	4	-
11	5	5	2	-	1	-	-	-	16	17	4	-
16	15	17	14	5	16	-	-	-	21	21	20	-
3	-	-	-	1	2	1	-	-	10	10	12	-
5	14	3	1	1	3	-	1	-	26	15	19	-
-	-	-	-	-	-	-	-	-	6	6	4	-
1	1	1	-	-	-	-	-	-	1	1	2	-
1	2	2	1	1	-	-	-	-	6	5	5	-
31	28	16	9	5	12	-	-	-	54	29	44	-
6	4	5	-	-	-	-	-	-	7	6	7	-
396*	336	277†	164	109	150	1	1	-	681	512	704‡	50**

* error: should read 375
† error: should read 278
‡ error: should read 677
** error: should read 47

Bramber Rape Schedule No 1

Names of Hundreds Boroughs and Parishes	No of men and boys between the ages of 15 and 60 who are capable of active service	No of men and boys between the ages of 15 and 60 incapable of active service	No of men above the age of 60 who are capable of active service	No of men above the age of 60 who are incapable of active service	No of men above the age of 60 who are capable of removing themselves	No of men above the age of 60 who are incapable of removing themselves
Brightford						
Lancing	116	5	2	7	-	5
Sompting	88	2	4	4	2	1
Broadwater	285	4	13	5	7	2
Clapham	56	-	-	-	-	7
Findon	23	6	1	11	5	2
Durrington	36	6	-	2	2	-
Heene	23	1	2	-	-	2
East Easwrith						
Warminghurst	8	1	-	-	2	-
Itchingfield	58	2	2	9	9	1
Thakeham	6	-	-	2	2	5
Sullington	69	3	2	9	3	6
Fishersgate						
Old Shoreham	50	3	3	2	-	-
Kingston by Sea	24	-	-	-	-	-
Southwick	49	8	-	13	2	7
Burbeach						
Beedingupper H	57	10	2	2	1	5
Beedinglower H	57	-	-	-	2	1
Ifield	38	3	10	1	16	3
Edburton	14	2	-	1	1	-
Singlecross						
Warnham	178	7	-	-	14	8
Rusper	104	5	-	-	13	5
Nuthurst	80	4	1	-	8	5
Steyning						
Washington	85	6	-	11	6	-
Wiston	63	2	-	-	6	4
Buttolphs	12	-	-	-	-	-
Combe	17	1	1	3	1	4

No of women or girls above 7 years of age capable of removing themselves	No of women or girls above 7 years of age who are not capable of removing themselves and of women who having children at the breast must be carried with such children	No of boys under 7 years of age	No of girls under 7 years of age	No of persons serving in Yeomanry or Volunteer Corps of Infantry distinguishing which	Aliens	Quakers	No of boys between the ages of 7 and 15
128	34	74	56	-	-	2	40
136	13	30	50	4 cavalry	-	-	-
339	28	125	122	6 Do	-	-	-
54	5	26	23	-	-	-	-
121	35	24	27	1 Do	-	-	-
32	16	30	15	-	-	-	-
24	11	12	10	-	-	-	-
26	12	12	11	-	-	-	-
65	31	21	22	-	-	-	25
39	25	29	29	1 Do	-	-	-
75	16	19	18	1 Do	-	-	-
68	4	16	20	Gds 2 & 1 Fenc			18
25	1	9	6	-	-	-	-
63	33	30	24	-	-	2	-
66	48	37	38	-	-	-	-
70	6	10	13	-	-	-	18
85	16	59	35	2 Gds	-	9	-
29	6	11	12	-	-	-	-
228	39	54	65	1 Guide			76
112	28	32	37				29
98	54	53	55	-	-	-	-
97	17	39	25	1 Cavalry	-	-	-
84	11	19	30	2 Do	-	-	-
10	4	4	3	-	-	-	-
8	5	6	-	-	-	-	-

[Bramber Rape Schedule No 1 continued]

Names of Hundreds Boroughs and Parishes	No of men and boys between the ages of 15 and 60 capable of active service	No of men and boys between the ages of 15 and 60 incapable of active service	No of men above the age of 60 who are capable of active service	No of men above the age of 60 who are incapable of active service	No of men above the age of 60 who are capable of removing themselves	No of men above the age of 60 who are incapable of removing themselves
Tipnoak						
Henfield	191.	16	11	15	11	11
Woodmancote	47	8	3	1	7	4
Albourne	40	3	3	3	10	8
Westgrinsted						
Ashington	24	-	-	5	-	-
Ashurst	80	2	6	3	3	1
Shipley	-	4	-	-	30	20
Westgrinsted	150	64	-	-	11	12
Windham&Ewhurst						
Cowfold	113	5	2	8	7	10
Shermanbury	70	3	-	3	-	3
Steyning Bor						
Steyning	28	7	5	6	10	20
Horsham Bor						
Horsham	606	37	22	26	26	59
Patching						
Patching	53	17	-	2	2	2
Bramber Bor						
Bramber	17	2	-	8	9	-
Tarring						
Tarring	30	7	2	11	6	2
New Shoreham Bor						
New Shoreham	155	3	13	19	17	14
Westeaswith						
Slinfold	135	10	2	-	8	3
Rudgwick	209	56	14	8	11	6
[Totals]	3544	325	126	200	270	248

No of women or girls above 7 years of age capable of removing themselves	No of women or girls above 7 years of age who are not capable of removing themselves and of women who having children at the breast must be carried with such children	No of boys under 7 years of age	No of girls under 7 years of age	No of persons serving in Yeomanry or Volunteer Corps of Infantry distinguishing which	Aliens	Quakers	No of boys between the ages of 7 and 15
272	95	127	98	3 Yeo	-	-	127
75	14	25	21	3 Cavalry	-	-	-
64	36	26	25	-	-	-	-
43	24	34	22	-	-	-	-
81	120	19	14	2 Cav	-	-	23
198	103	98	75	-	-	1	-
187	129	106	108	-	-	1	-
187	33	53	59	-	-	3	49
82	15	22	30	-	-	-	-
296	82	119	123	2 Cav	-	-	-
853	363	298	343	3 Gds	3	48	219
58	17	26	19	3 Yeo			
23	17	13	11	-	-	-	9
173	33	55	45	I Yeoman	-	-	-
255	64	98	73	1 Do	-	-	67
99	45	54	53	-	-	-	74
217	75	61	80	1 Do	-	-	-
5245	1763	2015	1945	9 Yeo; 8 Gd; 23 Cav; 1 Fenc	3	66	774

[Bramber Rape Schedule No 2

Names of Hundreds and Parishes	Fatting oxen	Cows	Steers Heifers and Calves	Colts	Sheep	Lambs	Hogs	Sows	Pigs	Riding Horses	Waggons	carts
Brightford												
Lancing	24	57	13	3	1637	289	141	33	85	21	26	43
Sompting	3	34	29	4	1570	160	88	20	82	11	17	28
Broadwater	9	70	27	14	1410	657	230	36	147	27	33	65
Clapham	-	28	19	3	2052	1017	86	14	75	4	15	20
Findon	-	31	17	4	3192	605	89	16	80	18	20	27
Durrington	-	14	10	-	555	314	30	9	30	5	8	10
Heene	3	9	5		207	86	44	7	35	3	5	8
East Easwrith												
Warminghurst	25	22	56	4	77	-	36	8	36	9	10	12
Itchingfield	17	61	133	10	226	85	52	14	106	6	25	29
Thakeham	19	66	126	6	164	-	129	12	106	10	22	34
Sullington	8	40	58	2	720	159	99	10	58	11	16	22
Fishersgate												
Old Shoreham	-	20	-	-	1405	637	85	8	28	11	10	15
Kingston by Sea	2	3	-	-	630	265	6	2	37	2	4	6
Southwick	-	9	2	-	1126	240	73	12	75	9	10	26
Burbeach												
Beedingupper H	125	80	117	12	2068	544	73	13	102	13	23	32
Beedinglower H	-	30	42	1	1357	-	99	1	-	7	19	24
Ifield	25	86	124	5	140	60	84	18	83	10	42	44
Edburton	2	10	20	4	508	280	45	2	11	4	6	7
Singlecross												
Warnham	50	98	171	10	325	47	104	23	200	12	21	8
Rusper	12	67	112	6	164	-	63	15	101	4	29	35
Nuthurst	4	101	119	10	220	31	171	21	105	2	37	45
Steyning												
Washington	4	76	80	4	1597	510	118	93	113	18	27	41
Wiston	27	58	131	4	1130	475	134	5	22	7	26	29

Proceedings and Schedules

other Carriages	Draft Horses	Draft Oxen	Wind	Water	Quantity of corn they can grind in 24 hours	Bakers	Private	Amt of bread they can bake in 24 hours	No of Bridges	No of Boats	No of Barges	No of Deer
								Bushells				
1	103	8	1	-	60 Bls	-	52	134	1	1	-	-
3	48	36	-	-	-	1	47	193	-	-	-	-
13	115	20	1	-	2 Lds	6	57	271	-	30	-	-
-	44	30	-	-	-	-	6	17	-	-	-	-
5	54	26	-	-	-	2	40	152	-	-	-	-
10	16	-	-	-	-	-	20	440	-	-	-	-
1	13	10	-	-	-	-	10	20	-	-	-	-
1	31	-	-	-	-	-	14	96	-	-	-	-
2	59	-	-	-	-	-	44	180	-	-	-	-
2	76	6	-	-	-	-	49	176¼				
-	39	37	1	2	3 Lds	-	38	78½	--	-	-	-
4	28	26	1	-	15 qrs	2	19	324	1	-	-	-
1	7	14	-	-	-	-	8	22	-	-	-	-
2	28	22	1	-	96 Bls	-	24	96	-	2	-	-
1	57	20	1	-	10 qrs	-	26	65	2	-	9	-
2	60	-	-	1	100 Bls	-	32	87	1	1	-	-
9	102	10	-	-	-	1	10	-	-	-	-	-
1	18	16	-	-	-	-	20	46	-	-	-	-
1	88	20	-	-	-	-	113	303	5	1	-	-
-	75	4	1	-	24	-	64	196	-	-	-	-
3	96	-	-	1	24 sacks	-	65	340	1	-	-	-
6	63	59	-	-	-	3	73	256	-	-	-	-
3	57	45	-	-	-	-	20	-	-	-	-	400

Column group headers: Waggons Carts or Carriages with the of horses or oxen be supplied to draw them | Corn Mills | Ovens

[Bramber Rape Schedule No 2 continued]

Names of Hundreds and Parishes	Fatting oxen	Cows	Steers Heifers and Calves	Colts	Sheep	Lambs	Hogs	Sows	Pigs	Riding Horses	Waggons	carts (No of other number that can)
Buttolphs	4	10	26	-	921	262	13	5	30	2	3	5
Combe	-	13	20	1	864	303	22	4	24	1	4	7
Tipnoak												
Henfield	208	138	156	16	1741	658	236	52	165	22	53	72
Woodmancote	34	42	64	8	292	33	55	9	90	11	19	24
Albourne	54	21	31	1	83	10	54	8	35	7	20	21
Westgrinsted												
Ashington	6	36	69	3	234	4	51	7	61	4	12	13
Ashurst	81	81	187	4	346	193	156	22	79	16	28	41
Shipley	44	161	362	8	713	-	282	33	242	15	47	43
Westgrinsted	112	156	349	9	814	160	322	25	291	18	66	85
Windham&Ewhurst												
Cowfold	47	102	161	19	298	218	176	24	160	8	43	54
Shermanbury	79	49	74	2	159	84	104	18	138	5	23	28
Steyning Bor												
Steyning	124	79	116	5	2428	579	145	16	138	36	29	49
Horsham Bor												
Horsham	46	325	486	34	1237	266	363	138	695	137	134	180
Patching												
Patching	-	14	2	1	460	-	55	4	24	1	6	8
Bramber Bor												
Bramber	4	11	9	-	762	304	30	3	19	3	3	4
Tarring												
Tarring	-	14	-	1	710	263	102	28	114	13	12	10
New Shoreham Bor												
New Shoreham	-	23	3	-	18	9	21	4	19	17	2	17
Westeaswith												
Slinfold	75	100	234	8	536	53	219	20	129	16	48	59
Rudgwick	83	121	208	17	379	-	237	31	205	22	69	79
[Totals]	1360	2566	3968	243	35475	9860	4722	843	4375	578	1072	1409

Waggons Carts or Carriages with the of horses or oxen be supplied to draw them			Corn Mills				Ovens				No of Bridges	No of Boats	No of Barges	No of Deer
other Carriages	Draft Horses	Draft Oxen	Wind	Water	Quantity of corn they can grind in 24 hours	Bakers	Private	Amt of bread they can bake in 24 hours	No of Bridges	No of Boats	No of Barges	No of Deer
-	8	18	-	-	-	-	5	-	-	-	-	-
1	12	21	-	-	-	-	7	19	1	-	-	-
2	118	30	1	3	3	-	103	400½	2	1	6	-
6	40	36	-	-	-	-	28	73	-	-	-	-
8	47	44	-	-	-	-	39	87	-	-	-	-
-	47	8	1	1	2078 Bls	-	30	150	-	-	-	-
-	62	2	1	-	1 Load	-	50	129	-	-	-	-
-	170	18	1	2	20 Sacks	-	112	171½	-	-	-	-
4	160	8	1	-	1½ Loads	2	123	353	-	-	-	-
6	107	4	-	1	2 Lds	1	89	368	2	-	-	-
2	52	-	-	1	3 Qrs	-	38	78	1	-	-	-
6	113	63	1	2	2 lds 20 Bls	2	61	274	-	-	-	-
59	340	9	7	2	213 Bls	8	297	988	4	-	-	-
-	26	8	-	-	-	-	12	29	-	-	-	-
-	10	12	-	-	-	-	22	79½	1	-	6	-
-	39	-	-	-	-	2	50	169	-	-	-	-
3	19	-	-	-	-	-	5	155	-	26	10	-
4	109	32	1	1	176	-	77	143	2	-	-	-
1	154	46	1	2	6 Lds	3	127	432	4	-	-	-
173	2910	768	22	19	73 Lds 10 Bls	33	2126	189 Lds 31½ Bls	28	62	31	400

Bramber Rape Schedule No 3

Names of Hundreds and Parishes	No of Persons between 15 and 60 willing to serve and in what capacity — Horseback	On foot	Cavalry — Swords	Pistols	Infantry — Firelocks	Pikes	No of Persons between the ages of 15 and 60 willing to act as Pioneers or Labourers
Brightford							
Lancing	15	14	-	-	-	-	27
Sompting	-	10	-	-	10	-	34
Broadwater	9	45	9	8	44	1	38
Clapham	-	-	-	-	-	-	18
Findon	8	17	-	-	-	-	18
Durrington	1	7	1	-	1	-	6
Heene	-	-	-	-	-	-	5
East Easwrith							
Warminghurst	-	8	-	-	8	-	1
Itchingfield	4	7	1	3	7	-	13
Thakeham	3	2	-	-	-	-	16
Sullington	-	4	-	-	2	-	13
Fishersgate							
Old Shoreham	5	4	-	6	4	-	9
Kingston by Sea	-	-	-	-	-	-	10
Southwick	1	1	-	-	3	-	16
Burbeach							
Beedingupper H	6	3	6	6	2	1	17
Beedinglower H	17	11	1	2	28	-	8
Ifield	-	-	-	-	-	-	31
Edburton	3	-	3	-	-	-	11
Singlecross							
Warnham	9	16	-	18	15	1	66
Rusper	-	1	-	-	1	-	1
Nuthurst	8	-	1	4	2	-	34
Steyning							
Washington	11	1	-	-	-	-	68
Wiston	9	8	5	5	5	2	19
Buttolphs	1	-	-	-	-	-	3
Combe	-	-	-	-	-	-	-

Implements they can bring						Any other instruments Pioneers may engage to bring			No of Persons between 15 and 60 willing to act as drivers of cattle	Do of sheep	Do of Teams	Do Boatmen or Bargemen
Felling Axes	Pick Axes	Spades	Shovels	Bill Hooks	Saws	Mattocks	Prongs					
7	10	3	15	1	8	-	-	-	8	23	29	-
1	7	11	8	2	5	-	-	-	22	7	10	-
15	4	7	4	-	8	-	-	-	45	40	54	32
3	6	5	2	-	2	-	-	-	11	8	10	1
5	6	11	3	1	9	-	-	-	7	7	5	1
-	1	2	1	1	1	-	-	-	9	3	4	-
-	-	5	-	-	-	-	-	-	5	2	3	4
-	1	-	-	-	-	-	-	-	9	5	4	-
6	1	3	1	-	2	-	-	-	10	9	16	-
5	7	2	5	-	5	-	-	-	17	16	18	-
1	-	8	1	-	2	-	-	-	10	12	16	-
-	-	4	2	1	-	-	-	-	6	5	5	-
-	-	2	-	-	-	-	-	-	5	3	6	1
8	-	5	1	-	4	-	-	-	8	9	13	4
10	4	3	4	1	11	-	-	-	11	8	9	12
4	1	2	2	1	6	-	-	-	4	3	11	-
14	7	1	4	-	4	-	-	-	19	15	24	-
1	3	2	3	1	2	-	-	-	3	2	6	-
17	13	19	8	1	8	-	-	-	23	24	42	-
1	-	-	-	-	-	-	-	-	1	-	-	-
9	5	7	4	-	10	-	-	-	28	27	23	-
64	40	73	52	98	80	-	-	-	29	29	28	-
8	3	7	7	2	3	-	-	-	12	7	13	-
-	1	2	-	-	-	-	-	-	3	2	3	-
-	-	-	-	-	-	-	-	-	6	2	4	-

[Bramber Rape Schedule No 3 continued]

Names of Hundreds and Parishes	Horseback	On foot	Swords	Pistols	Firelocks	Pikes	No of Persons between the ages of 15 and 60 willing to act as Pioneers or Labourers
Tipnoak							
Henfield	12	9	-	-	-	-	24
Woodmancote	3	4	3	4	4	-	16
Albourne	-	-	-	-	-	-	16
Westgrinsted							
Ashington	1	8	1	-	8	-	11
Ashurst	1	1	1	-	1	-	15
Shipley	2	8	5	6	2	1	91
Westgrinsted	33	128	-	-	13	-	15
Windham&Ewhurst							
Cowfold	11	-	1	3	5	2	75
Shermanbury	-	1	-	-	1	-	18
Steyning Bor							
Steyning	39	33	39	33	32	24	37
Horsham Bor							
Horsham	25	54	4	2	30	-	68
Patching							
Patching	-	9	-	2	1	-	34
Bramber Bor							
Bramber	-	-	-	-	-	-	4
Tarring							
Tarring	9	25	-	-	-	-	11
New Shoreham							
New Shoreham	8	14	3	4	2	-	7
Westeaswith							
Slinfold	24	22	5	15	37	2	43
Rudgwick	-	13	-	-	8	5	75
[Totals]	278	488	89	121	276	39	1042

Column groupings: "No of Persons between 15 and 60 willing to serve and in what capacity" covers Horseback and On foot. "How they can arm themselves" — Cavalry: Swords, Pistols; Infantry: Firelocks, Pikes.

Implements they can bring							Any other instruments Pioneers may engage to bring		No of Persons between 15 and 60 willing to act as drivers of cattle	Do of sheep	Do of Teams	Do Boatmen or Bargemen
Felling Axes	Pick Axes	Spades	Shovels	Bill Hooks	Saws	Mattocks	Prongs				
17	15	20	14	10	17	-	-	-	23	23	14	4
7	2	8	2	1	4	-	-	-	6	8	10	-
2	-	9	3	-	2	-	-	-	12	7	2	-
-	-	-	-	-	-	-	-	-	8	4	7	-
15	14	12	11	11	10	-	-	-	5	3	20	-
21	18	18	20	4	6	-	3	-	35	32	43	-
24	8	-	-	2	-	-	-	-	56	10	30	-
55	32	50	31	25	13	-	-	-	19	21	23	-
4	2	5	2	4	1	-	-	-	12	11	13	-
4	13	5	12	3	11	6	-	-	38	30	39	2
22	1	12	3	7	9	-	-	-	70	71	70	-
3	11	8	9	1	2	-	-	-	14	6	7	-
3	-	2	-	-	3	-	-	-	3	3	5	4
8	-	5	-	-	9	-	-	-	17	13	21	-
6	1	2	2	-	2	-	-	-	17	-	-	13
13	19	3	2	-	6	-	-	-	19	12	18	-
18	4	10	3	7	8	-	-	-	20	12	33	-
401	260	353	241	185	273	6	3	-	685	534	711	78

This Meeting is adjourned sine Die Preliminaries of Peace having been signed

[signed]   Wm Ellis
              Clerk to the General Meetings

Sussex (ss) Proceedings at a Meeting of Lieutenancy held at the White Hart Inn in Lewes in and for the said County on Saturday the 16th Day of January 1802 pursuant to an Advertisement in the Lewes Paper for that purpose

Present

William Newton
George Shiffner } Esqrs
Henry Theo: Shadwell
John Fuller

At this Meeting Mr. William Ellis Clerk of the said General Meetings produced his Bill for his pains and trouble in executing the said Act amounting to the Sum of fifty nine pounds twelve Shillings and Eight pence.

Ordered that the same be now allowed.

Also at this Meeting Mr. William Johnson Clerk of the Subdivision Meetings for the Rape of Arundell in the said County produced his Bill for the like in the said Rape amounting to the Sum of Sixteen pounds and Eight Shillings. —

Also at this Meeting Mr. John Tilden Simpson Clerk of the Subdivision Meetings for the Rape of Hastings in the said County produced his Bill for the like in the said Rape amounting to the Sum of Twenty three pounds and four Shillings.

Also at this Meeting Messrs. Wm. Balcombe Langridge and Christopher Kell Clerks of the Subdivision Meetings for the Rape of Lewes in the said County produced their Bill for the like in the said Rape amounting to the Sum of Twenty three pounds and thirteen Shillings. —

Also at this Meeting Mr. Samuel Gwynne Clerk of the Subdivision Meetings for the Rape of Pevensey in the said County produced his Bill for the like in the said Rape amounting to the Sum of Twenty eight pounds Six Shillings and Eleven pence.

[16 January 1802]

Sussex

Proceedings at a Meeting of Lieutenancy held at the White Hart Inn in Lewes in and for the said County on Saturday the 16th Day of January 1802 Pursuant to an Advertisement in the Lewes Paper for that Purpose

Present

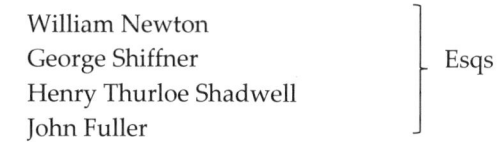

William Newton
George Shiffner } Esqs
Henry Thurloe Shadwell
John Fuller

At this Meeting, Mr William Ellis, Clerk of the said General Meetings produced his Bill for his pains and Trouble in executing the said Act amounting to the Sum of Fifty nine Pounds twelve Shillings and Eight pence.

Ordered

that the same be now allowed.[111]

Also at this Meeting Mr William Johnson Clerk of the Subdivision Meetings for the Rape of Arundell in the said County produced his Bill for the like in the said Rape amounting to the Sum of Sixteen pounds and Eight Shillings.

Also at this Meeting Mr John Tildon Sampson Clerk of the Subdivision Meetings for the Rape of Hastings in the said County produced his Bill for the like in the said Rape amounting to the Sum of Twenty three Pounds and four Shillings.

Also at this Meeting Messrs William Balcombe Langridge and Christopher Kell Clerks of the Subdivision Meetings for the Rape of Lewes in the said County produced their Bill for the like in the said Rape amounting to the Sum of Twenty three Pounds and thirteen Shillings.

Also at this Meeting Mr Samuel Gwynne Clerk of the Subdivision Meetings for the Rape of Pevensey in the said County produced his Bill for the like in the

---

[111] Here, and in subsequent cases, it is not clear how and at whose expense these bills were settled. Since the Lord Lieutenant was a Crown servant, it is likely that the sums were reimbursed from central government by one route or another.

said Rape amounting to the Sum of Twenty eight Pounds Six Shillings and Eleven Pence.

Also at this Meeting Mr William Ellis Clerk of the Subdivision Meetings for the Rape of Bramber in the said County produced his Bill for the like in the said Rape amounting to the Sum of Seventeen Pounds four Shillings and ten pence.

Ordered

that the same be now allowed.

[signed] Wm Ellis Cl[er]k

[7-8 July 1803]

At a Meeting of the Lieutenancy of the County of Sussex held at the Castle Inn at Brighthelmstone on Thursday and Friday the Seventh and Eighth Days of July One Thousand eight Hundred and three in Pursuance of His Majesty's Warrant of the twenty fourth of June directed to His Grace the Duke of Richmond His Majesty's Lieutenant for this County for that purpose.

Present

His Grace the Duke of Richmond His Majesty's Lieutenant
Right Honorable Thomas Lord Pelham
George Obrien Earl of Egremont
Henry Lord Viscount Gage
John Lord Sheffield
Lord St Asaph
Honorable John Thomas Capel
General Sir David Dundas
Lieut General Sir James Pultney
Major General Charles Lennox
Major General Whyte

Sir George Thomas
Sir Cecil Bysshopp   } Baronets
Sir Charles Burrell

Sir John Bridger   } Kts
Sir Thomas Carr

John Fuller of Rose Hill
Francis Newbery
William Sowell
William Mitford
Thomas Phillipps Lamb
John Quantock
Thomas Cecil Grainger
John Trayton Fuller
Edward Cranston   } Esquires
Thomas Kemp
Samuel Twyford
Inigo Freeman Thomas
Henry Thurloe Shadwell
Charles Scrase Dickins
William Newton
Charles Goring

Nathaniel Tredcroft
Walter Smyth
Charles Foster Goring
William Stephen Poyntz
John Napper
James Holmes Goble
George Shiffner   Esquires
Thomas Davis Lamb
John Newnham
James Martin Lloyd
Timothy Shelley
Charles Gilbert

Read His Majesty's said Warrant,

Read A Circular Letter of the same Date from the Right Honorable Lord Hobart one of His Majesty's Principal Secretaries of State to His Majesty's Lieutenant for the County of Sussex,

Read The Act of Parliament therewith transmitted 'To enable His Majesty more effectually to provide for the Defence and Security of the Realm during the Present War; and for indemnifying Persons who may suffer in their Property by such Measures as may be necessary for that Purpose',

Read The Printed Paper entitled 'Proposals for rendering the Body of the People Instrumental to the General [sic] Defined in Case of Invasion' together with the 'Plan for establishing a System of Communication throughout each County' and the nine Schedules therein referred to transmitted in the before mentioned letter of Lord Hobart and requested by him to be submitted to the Consideration of the Lieutenancy at their first Meeting,

Read A Circular letter communicated by General Sir David Dundas K.B. from His Royal Highness the Duke of York Commander in Chief, dated from the Horse Guards 1st July 1803 addressed to General Officers Commanding Districts

Read The Resolution of the Meeting of Lieutenancy of this County held at Lewes on the 13th of August 1801, and the Letter of the Lord Lieutenant of the County of Sussex to Lord Hobart one of His Majesty's Principal Secretaries of State on that occasion

And all the said Papers having been fully considered with all the Attention that their high Importance and the Duty of the Lieutenancy requires

Resolved unanimously

1st That this Meting feels and believes that every Individual in this County feels with them the Most Dutiful Attachment to His Majesty's Royal Person and Government, the Warmest Zeal for the Preservation for the happy and free Constitution of these Realms and the Strongest desire to Contribute by every Means in their Power to repel an Invasion to which this County may in the first Instance be exposed and which from the Experience of other Countries that have been invaded by the French Arms must here involve those who fall within it's [sic] reach in every Misery to which human Nature can be Subject.

2ndly And Unanimously That we have the fullest reliance on the Loyalty, Bravery and good Conduct of the Army Militia Yeomanry and other Forces that may be employed by His Majesty to defend the Country and however prudent the Legislature may have thought it to enable His Majesty to impede the Progress of an Enemy by laying Waste the Country before him, Yet we trust that no Circumstance can arise which can induce His Majesty to carry into Execution so desolating a Measure as to burn and destroy some of the Richest Provinces of England which the Enemy himself might spare, and thereby Anticipate one of the greatest Evils, he could inflict

We trust the fate of England can never be reduced to such an Extremity, That it is not by ourselves making a Desert of our own Country that an Enemy will be stopped, but by our own Army backed with that Energy and Spirit with which every Individual will to a Man rise in Arms on Actual Invasion

3rd And Unanimously That we will exert ourselves to carry into immediate execution those parts of the General Plan which appear to be adapted to the Particular Circumstances of the County of Sussex

4thly And Unanimously That we trust it has been an Oversight in the Act of Parliament of the 43^d of the King Chapter 55, Section 11, where it is enacted That if the Owner or Owners or Person or Persons interested in the removal or Destruction of any Waggons Carts Cars or other Carriages Horses Cattle Sheep Hay Straw Corn Meal Flour or other Provisions or any other Articles whatsoever or in the destruction or injury of any House Mill Bridge or other Building or any Matter or Thing of Value under the directions of the said Act shall not be willing to accept of such Compensation as the Commissioners of His Majesty's Treasury in Great Britain shall upon the report of Persons appointed by them to enquire into and ascertain the Value of such Articles and the Compensation which ought to be made for the same by Way of Purchase or Hire or recompence for Damage or otherwise according to the Nature of the

Case be pleased to offer, His Majesty may order two Justices of the Peace of the County to Settle and Ascertain the Compensation which ought to be made to such Owner or Owners or Persons Interested which Justices shall settle and ascertain the same accordingly and this done without giving any appeal to a Jury although such is allowed in the preceding Clause of the same Act for the Possession or Use of any Piece of Ground marked out by any General Officer or other Person Commissioned for such purpose that may be wanted for the Public Service, certainly an object of less Importance than those contained in the 11th Section which may include the whole Property of many Individuals

We hope therefore for the Interests of the Inhabitants and Proprietors of this County who may be deeply interested in such an Event that His Majesty's Government will recommend it to Parliament to Amend the said Act so as to allow the Subject the same Appeal to a Jury in the Cases contained in the 11th Section as is done in respect to those contained in the 10th Section

5thly And Unanimously That however exceptionable the mode of ascertaining the Value of such Damages may be under this Act Yet as it holds out in Compensation for all Damages & generally and without any Exception, we cannot feel ourselves authorized to narrow the Provisions of an Act of Parliament and intimate to the Inhabitants as is expressed in the plan proposed 'that no Indemnification whatsoever will be allowed for the property of any Person who is of an Age and in a State of Health to aid the Public Service and whose Name does not appear in the Rolls of his Parish for some of the Duties mentioned in the said Plan' no such restrictions or Conditions being imposed by the said Act of Parliament

6thly That with respect to the Plan itself, following its several Divisions First *that of the driving the Country and removals* The Resolutions of the Meeting of the Lieutenancy of this County held at Lewes on the 13th of August 1801 having shewn that from the Returns of Carriages and Draft Cattle of the whole County they were insufficient to remove the Dead Stock from any considerable part of this County in any reasonable time, and that any attempt at so impracticable a Measure to any great extent of Country would only be productive of Confusion and perhaps even of detriment to the Service of the Army, and the Right Honorable Lord Hobart one of His Majesty's Principal Secretaries of State having signified His Majesty's approbation of the said resolutions, we conceive that the now calling for Returns of the Dead Stock is unnecessary, and the more so as from the continual and great Fluctuations in the Various Articles such Returns which even for the Moment could not be depended upon would only tend to Mislead, instead of affording any Real Information on which any Just Estimate could be formed as to the Quantities actually in hand either in the aggregate or separately at any Period subsequent to the Day of taking each Return

Resolved

therefore unanimously That the account of Grain Malt Fodder and Straw be struck out of the Returns in the Schedules required to be made from each Parish.

We also conceive that it will be very difficult to drive Cattle Sheep and Hogs from any great Extent of Country but of these we will endeavour to ascertain the Number (although they must also be continually varying) and follow as far as we find it practicable the mode pointed out in the plan for carrying the removal of Cattle into Execution.

We fully accede to the Propriety of removing Horses of all Kind and Draft Oxen which we conceive to be perfectly practicable and shall give particular Attention to this Article.

In regard to the second Head Vizt The People being called upon to bear Arms and engaging to assemble when an Enemy has landed. We conceive such a Measure to be of great advantage and we will recommend Enrolments for that purpose, but we conceive this Plan may be rendered much more Useful if such Corps when formed were to be United under Gentlemen of influance [sic] in the neighbourhood who as well as all the Officers should be appointed conformably to the King's Prerogative by his Lieutenant of the County under His Majesty's approbation.

We shall therefore adopt the Schedules proposed in the Plan for this Purpose, excepting as to the allowing Companies of Armed Men to chuse their own Leaders from amongst themselves to bear Commissions under His Majesty or his Lieutenant of the County; conceiving such Elections of Military Officers to be a dangerous Invasion of the King's Prerogative of nominating either directly or through Officers of His Appointment all Military Officers whatsoever, and we do not understand what is meant by such appointments being made under the Civil Authority.

As to the third Head relating to Pioneers we adopt the plan of Schedules as amended

The fourth head of Guides is provided for a Troop upon the same Footing as the last War having offered their Services to Government, which has been accepted of.

The fifth head is Waggons which with some small Alterations in the Schedules and Plans we have adopted although to a great part of the Meeting it appeared unnecessary to have any Association for furnishing a partial supply of Waggons at a time when the whole is by Law placed under the disposal of the General Officer commanding in the District

The 6th 7th and 8th Heads relate to Millers Bakers and Barges. We do not apprehend any difficulty in Millers and Bakers stating what they can do, and engaging to do what they can, provided they have sufficient assistance in Hands and proper supplies of Corn and Flour or in the Proprietors of Barges offering the use of them; And we have accordingly adopted the Schedules proposed in respect to them.

Resolved

Unanimously That His Majesty's Lieutenant be requested to Communicate these Resolutions to Lord Hobart

Resolved

Unanimously on the Motion of John Fuller Esquire That the thanks of this Meeting be given to His Grace the Duke of Richmond for his great attention and Zeal for the General Interest of the Kingdom at large, and for this County in particular at this most Important Crisis of Public Affairs

Also at this Meeting the following Deputy Lieutenants were proposed as Lieutenants of Divisions of Rapes and Assistant Lieutenants of the said County for His Majesty's approbation Vizt

For the Northern Division of the Rape of Chichester	William Stephen Poyntz Esq	Lieutenant
	Lord Robert Spencer	Assistant Lieutenants
	Samuel Twyford Esq	
For the Southern Division of the said Rape	John Peachey Esq	Lieutenant
	George White Thomas Esq	Assistant Lieutenants
	John Quantock Esq	
For the Northern Division of the Rape of Arundell	Lord Egremont	Lieutenant
	William Mitford Esq	Assistant Lieutenants
	William Smyth Esq	
For the Southern Division of the said Rape	Sir George Thomas Bart	Lieutenant
	Charles Scrase Dickins Esq	Assistant Lieutenants
	James Holmes Goble Esq	
For the Northern Division of the Rape of Bramber	Nathaniel Tredcroft Esq	Lieutenant
	Honorable John Thomas Capel	Assistant Lieutenants
	Timothy Shelley Esq	
For the Southern Division of the said Rape	Charles Goring Esq	Lieutenant
	Charles Foster Goring Esq	Assistant Lieutenants
	Harry Bridger Esq	
For the Northern Division of the Rape of Lewes	William Sewell Esq	Lieutenant
	and	
	Thomas Cecil Grainger Esq	Assistant Lieutenant
For the Southern Division of the said Rape	George Shiffner Esq	Lieutenant
	William Newton Esq	Assistant Lieutenants
	Thomas Kemp Esq	
For the Northern Division of the Rape of Pevensey	Lord Sheffield	Lieutenant
	John Tray Fuller Esq	Assistant Lieutenants
	Edward Cranston Esq	
For the Southern Division of the said Rape	Lord Gage	Lieutenant
	Inigo F Thomas Esq	Assistant Lieutenants
	Charles Gilbert Esq	
For the Division of Hastings Rape	John Fuller Esq Rosehill	Lieutenant
	Thomas P Lambe Esq	Assistant Lieutenants
	Lord St Asaph	

[8 July 1803 following]

His Majesty having been pleased under his Warrant bearing date the 22 June 1803 to direct his Lieutenant for the County of Sussex, to hold a General Meeting of the Lieutenancy of the said County for making such Preparations as may be necessary for carrying into effect the several Provisions of the Act 'for enabling his Majesty more effectually to provide for the Defence and Security of the Realm during the present War and for indemnifying Persons who may suffer in their property by such measures as may be necessary for that purpose' in case His Majesty should hereafter see especial cause to direct the execution of the same

And the said Meeting of Lieutenancy having been accordingly held at the Castle Inn in Brighton on Thursday 7th July 1803, Subdivisions Meetings are hereby ordered to be held in each Rape as soon as possible, at which Subdivision Meetings the Deputy Lieutenants and Justices of the Peace are requested to divide each Division of their Rape into such a Number of Districts as they may judge most convenient containing from 3 to 6 adjoining Parishes and to find out of each of such District Gentlemen (Magistrates if possible) who will undertake to be Inspectors of such District, as also in each Parish (or uniting 2 adjoining Parishes when one is small for this Purpose) one Gentleman, Clergyman or principal Farmer who will undertake the office of Superintendant of such Parish or Parishes as they shall find willing to accept of such offices and they shall approve of to the 2nd General Meeting appointed to be held at Brighton on Thursday the 21st of this Ins^t July in order that such persons may have (if his Majesty shall approve of them) Commissions from His Majesty's Lieutenant of the County for such Offices

And that the several Persons willing to offer their Services for any of the situations before mention'd may understand what it is that will be expected of them, They are to be acquainted that the Superintendants of Parishes after having received Copies of the Lists of the Number of Horses, Draft Oxen, other Oxen, Cows, Calves, Sheep and Hogs, Waggons, Carts Drivers returned for the Parish or Parishes which they engage to superintend, are as well as they can to verify the said Lists and to Note down and communicate to the Inspectors any Material alteration they may observe to have taken place in them

They are also to make themselves acquainted with the names and persons of the owners and drivers Shepherds or other Person who may attend the Horses, Waggons, Carts, Cattle or Sheep in case of Removal and learn the different Roads by which each Species can best travel to such places of Rendezvous as may be fixed on so as to avoid interfering with each other, or any Column of

Troops on their March. All which information or such other as they thinks [sic] may be useful

They are also to Report on the first Monday in each Month in person or by writing to the Inspector of the District under whom they are placed.

The Superintendants of Parishes may select Agents to act under them with the approbation of the Inspector and of the Deputy Lieutenants and Justices of the Peace at their Subdivision Meetings and are themselves to go with the whole of the Cattle under their charge upon General Removals or send one of their Agents upon particular Removals. They are also to endeavour to induce each Proprietor to mark his Cattle with the District marks and to establish such other Regulations as they may conceive will best tend to establish Regularity and avoid Confusion when any removals are to take place

They are to receive their directions from their directions from the Inspector of the District.[112]

The Inspector of Districts are to receive their orders [sic] from the Lieutenant of the Rape & transmit them to the Superintendants of Parishes who are in general to see that they are properly preparing themselves for the due execution of such Orders as they may Receive

If the whole or the quarter[113] part of the District of the District[114] should remove, the Superintendant are [sic] to attend them

And whereas it is thought expedient that Volunteer Troops or Companies should be formed of such Individuals who are willing to come forth with arms as proposed in the Schedules or as Pioneers and to have their Names enroll'd for that purpose, It will be the Business of the Superintendants of Parishes to attend the Meetings that the Parish Officers shall appoint for receiving of Voluntary Tenders for such Services and to assist the Parish Officers in taking down the Names of Persons so offering, and classing them properly and otherwise in regularly completing their Lists

This Meeting is adjourned to the Castle Inn in Brighton aforesaid to Thursday the 21st Day of July Instant to be there held at 11 o Clock in the forenoon
[signed]   Wm Ellis Cl[er]k

---

[112] Repetition in original
[113] sic: greater?
[114] Repetition in original

[21 July 1803]

Sussex

At a Meeting of the Lieutenancy of the said County held at the Castle Inn in Brighthelmstone in the said County on Thursday the 21st Day of July 1803 for carrying the General Defence Act into further execution

Present

    His Grace the Duke of Richmond His Majesty's Lieutenant in the Chair
    George Obrien Earl of Egremont
    Lord St Asaph
    Major Genl Charles Lennox
    Sir Cecil Bysshopp   )
    Sir Charles Merrick Burrell   ) Baronets
    John William Commerell Esq, Sheriff of the County
    Inigo Freeman Thomas Esq
    William Stephen Poyntz Esq
    William Sewell Esq
    John Fuller Esq of Rosehill
    George Shiffner Esq
    Charles Foster Goring Esq
    Charles Goring Esq
    Sir Thomas Carr Knight
    William Newton Esq
    George Courthope Esq
    Charles Gilbert Esq
    Thomas Kemp Esq
    Francis Newbery Esq
    Henry Thurloe Shadwell Esq
    Henry Shelley Jun Esq
    Timothy Shelley Esq
    Edward Carleton Esq
    Thomas Cecil Grainger Esq
    James Holmes Goble Esq
    Thomas Henry Harben Esq
    Richard Chase Esq
    Harry Bridger Esq

Read A Letter from Brook Watson Esquire Commissary General to Colonel Carnegie Central Commissary for the County of Sussex for fixing the rates to be paid by Government for Services which might be performed or Supplies furnished in Case of Invasion

Also the Resolution of the Lieutenancy at a Meeting held at Lewes the 13th of August 1801 'That in respect to the Commissary General the Lieutenancy trust he will be better able to make his Contracts with Individuals than by their fixing a Price for Grain or Carriage which moreover they are not apprised of their being authorized by Law to do'. And this Meeting being of the same Opinion That he will be better able to make his Contracts with Individuals than by their fixing a Price for Grain or Carriage which moreover they are not apprised of their being authorized by Law to do.

Resolved

That the Clerk of the General Meetings do transmit their opinion to the Commissary General accordingly.

It appearing to this Meeting that the whole County consists of 301 Parishes it was therefore divided into 78 Districts, to each of which there was appointed a Gentleman of some weight and influence in the Neighbourhood as Inspector and under each of these there were appointed a Superintendant for each Parish or united Parishes for the Purpose of the Act which being read were approved of is as follows Vizt

[Appointment of Inspectors and Superintendants]

Inspectors	[Rape, Division, Parish]	Superintendants
	Chichester Rape **Southern Division**	
District: 1st		
Revd Mr Green	Selsea Sidlesham Earnley	Mr John Stubbington Mr Thomas Hobgen Senr Mr Henry Halstead
District 2nd		
Mr William Dearling	Eastwittering Westwittering West Itchenor Birdham Donnington Appledram Hunston	Mr James Butler Mr Thomas Gibbs Mr William Challen Mr Richard Cosens Jun
District 3rd		
Mr John Hasler	Southbersted Pagham Northmundham Merston	Mr Thomas Halsted Mr George Adams Mr Richard Merricks Mr Henry Sparkes
District 4th		
Edward Woods Esq	Aldingbourne Tangmere Oving Rumbaldswick	Miles Row Esq Mr George Osborne Mr Upton of Tolworth Mr Charles Ewen
District 5th		
John Newland Esq	Newfishbourne Bosham Chidham West Thorney	Mr Joseph Boorn Mr John Martin Jun Mr Henry Postlethwaite
District 6th		
Thomas Huskisson Esq	Westhampnett Boxgrove Slindon Eartham	Revd Mr Charles Webber Mr George Lane Mr Joseph Bailey
District 7th		
Henry Hounsom Esq	East Lavant Mid Lavant West Stoke Funtington	Mr John Towler Mr Henry Halsted Mr John Martin

District 8th		
John Woods Esq of Aldsworth	Westbourne	Mr James Woods
	Racton	Mr William Hipkins
	Stoughton	Mr John Hawkins
	Compton	Revd Mr Thwaites
	Northmarden	
	Upmarden	Mr John Hobbs
	Eastmarden	Mr Edward Pinnix
District 9th		
Revd Mr Bayton	West Dean	Mr George Bayton
	Binderton	
	Singleton	Mr William Dearling Jun
	East Dean	
	Upwaltham	Mr John Colebrook
District 10th		
John Drew Esq Lieutenant and John Murray Esq Inspector	City of Chichester	Mr Henry Hobbs and Mr Richard Philpott
	The Close	
	St Bartholomew	
	St Pancras	
	St James's	

	Chichester Rape **Northern Division**	
District 11th		
Mr Joseph Postlethwaite	Linch	Mr John Turner
	Didling	
	Treyford	Mr Thomas Sparkes
	Elsted	
	Harting	Mr William Russell
District 12th		
Revd Mr Skinner	Graffham	Mr Henry Gadd
	Heyshott	
	Cocking	Mr Nicholas Andrews
	Bepton	
District 13th		
Mr Surtees Swinburn	Midhurst	Mr William Whitter
	St John's	
	Easebourne	Mr William Shotter
	Selham	
	Woolbeding	Revd Charles Williams
District 14th		
Lewis Buckle Esq	Stedham	Revd Walter Islip
	Iping	
	Chithurst	Mr James Piggott
	Trotton	Mr Richard Ayling
	Terwick	Mr John Mellersh
	Rogate	

District 15th		
Richard Yaldwin Esq	Lynchmere	Revd I H S Carey
	Fernhurst	Mr George Mullins
	Lodsworth	
	Signed Wm Step Poyntz	

	Arundell Rape **Upper Division**	
Revd William Kinleside	North Stoke	John Sayers
	Poling	Richard Wyatt Esq
	Burpham	Charles Hersee
	Warningcamp	John Holloway
	Angmering	William Amoore
	Ferring	George Henty
Revd John Cheal Green	Leominster	Stephen Blunden
	Kingston	George Olliver
	Rustington	John Peters
	Goring	George Bushby
	Preston	William Holden
	Littlehampton	Richard Marshall
Edward Carleton Esq	Ford	John Brown Staker
	Binsted	William Laker Jun
	Southstoke	Thomas Parlett
	Madehurst	William Parlett
	Climping	John Boniface
	Tortington	William Newland
Revd Robert Hardy	Eastergate	John Burrell
	Felpham	Robert Sparkes
	Barnham	Joseph Murrell
	Yapton	Bernard Staker
	Walberton	Thomas Collens
	Middleton	Thomas Palmer Jun
	Revd William Groome Arundell Boro Stephen Wise	

	Arundell Rape **Lower Division**	
Revd Edward Tredcroft	Amberley	Joseph Forster
	Parham	William Newman
	Wiggenholt	
	Gritham	Thomas Chatfield
	Pulborough	John Jupp Jun
	Hardham	Richard Challen
Revd Thomas Reddish	Storrington	Francis Bennett
	West Chiltington	Maurice Sayers
	Billingshurst	John Towse

Revd John F Stewart	Houghton	William Burchell
	Bury	Robert Fuller
	Bignor	John Neal
	Fittleworth	John Turner
	Stopham	James Blunden
	Coldwaltham	James Ide
Revd William Pierrepoint	Sutton	Richard Skinner
	Barlavington	Richard Boxall
	Duncton	William Broadbridge
	Wollavington	James Miles
	Burton	Henry Budd
Revd Richard Lomax Martin	Tillington	John Colebrook
	Lurgashall	John Lickfold
	Northchapel	Thomas Taylor
Mr Thomas Seward	Kirdford	William Cooper
	Wisboroughgreen	John Sayers
Mr Robert Rice Palmer	Petworth	John Brown
	Coates	Clement Roberts
	Egdean	Francis Hampton
	Signed Egremont William Mitford	

	Bramber Rape **North Part**	
William Ellis of Horsham, Gent	Horsham	Philip Chasemore
	Beeding North Part	William Charman
	Rusper	Henry Chapman
	Ifield	William Cutler
Jonathan Asbridge of Warnham, Clerk	Warnham	John Agate
	Slinfold	John William Comerell Esq
	Rudgwick	John Ireland
	Sullington North Part	
Richard Constable of Cowfold, Clerk	Shermanbury	John Hughes
	Cowfold	Charles White
	Nuthurst	Edward Henderson
Thomas Elles of West Grinsted	West Grinsted	Henry Heasman
	Shipley	Thomas Killick
	Itchingfield	Richard Holland
	Signed B Shelley Nathaniel Tredcroft T Shelley	

	Bramber Rape **South Part**	
Richard B Comber Esq of Steyning	Steyning	Hugh Penfold of Wickham
	Bramber	Thomas Lidbetter
	Ashurst	William Stanford
	Combe	Francis Gell
	Buttolphs	Richard Cook
Thomas Fuller of Sullington Farmer	Washington	Thomas Holmes
	Thakeham	John Chatfield

	Sullington South Part	Michael Agate
John Wood Esq of Henfield	Henfield	John Beckett
	Woodmancoat	Revd John Rideout
	Albourne	William Scrase
	Edburton	Revd John Marshall
George Wyatt of Michelgrove	Durrington	Richard Street
	Patching	Daniel Simmonds
	Clapham	John Amoore
	Findon	William Tate
Revd Henry Warren of Ashington	Wiston	John Baker
	Ashington	John Golds
	Warminghurst	Thomas Golds
Revd Peter Wood of Broadwater	Lancing	Thomas Lidbetter
	Sompting	Edward Barker Esq
	Broadwater	Thomas Richardson Gent
	Heene	William Mitchell
	Tarring	John Cutler
Thomas Ellman of Old Shoreham	Beeding South Part	John Chatfield
	Southwick	Nathaniel Hall
	Kingston by Sea	William Gorringe
	Old Shoreham	John Ellman
	New Shoreham	Revd T Poole Hooper
	Signed C Goring Depy Lieut Charles F Goring Harry Bridger	

	Lewes Rape **Southern Division**	
District 1st		
Revd Edward R Raynes of Lewes	St Peter & St Mary Westout Lewes	John Harrison Esq
	St Michael	Revd Henry West
	St John Do	Revd P G Croft
	All Saints	W F Hick Esq
District 2nd		
Revd William Gabbitas of Rodmell	Southover	William Verrall
	Kingston	Thomas Rogers
	Iford	Richard Hurley
	Rodmell	John Glazebrook
District 3rd		
George Elphick Esq Newhaven	Newhaven	James Tomsett
	Piddinghoe	William Noakes
	Southease	Henry Webb
	Telscombe	Revd James Hutchins
District 4th		
Thomas Partington Esq Offham	Hamsey	James Andrews
	Barcombe	Revd Charles Bathurst
	Chiltington	Thomas Blackman
	Plumpton	William Faulconer

District 5th		
Revd Henry Poole George E Graham Esq	Chailey	William Wicker
	Newick	Revd Henry Clutton
	Wivelsfield	William Tanner
District 6th		
William Hodson	Street	John Stapeley
	Westmeston	Revd R Bingham
	Ditcheling	Richard Hamshar
	Keymer	Thomas Dominick Whitem[an]
District 7th		
Revd Francis Whitcomb	Newtimber	Revd W Whistler
	Poynings	Robert Gallup
	Fulking	William Goddard
District 8th		
Revd John Dodson	Hurstperpoint	William Borrer Esq
	Clayton	John Bull
	Piecomb	Revd Nicholas Heath
District 9th		
John Paine Esq	Preston	William Stanford
	Patcham	John Hamshar
	Hove	John Vallance
District 10th		
Mr John Hardwick of Hangeleton	Portslade	Robert Smith
	West Blatchington	William Hodson
	Hangleton	John Hardwick
District 11th		
Revd Thomas Hudson of Brighton	Brighton	Cornelius Paine
District 12th		
Nathaniel Kemp Esq of Ovingdean	Rottingdean	Revd T R Hooker
	Ovingdean	John Trill
	Falmer	Richard Chrismass
	Stanmer	Revd John Baker
Signed George Shiffner William Newton Thomas Kemp		

	Lewes Rape **Northern Division**	
Division 1st		
Revd Henry Chatfield	Ardingly	Christopher Heasman
	Westhoathly	Arthur Dewdney
	Balcombe	Isaac Clutton
	Worth	Revd Johnson Towers
	Crawley	John Caffin
Division 2nd		
Revd Francis Fearon	Cuckfield	Edward Packham
	Slaugham	John Batchelor
	Bolney	William Blaker
	Twineham	James Wood
Signed W Sewell Lieut Thomas C Grainger Asst		

	Pevensey Rape Upper Division	
Edward Auger	Eastbourne	Moses Fielder
	Willingdon	John Denman
	East Dean	Nicholas Willard Jun
	Friston	Thomas Rason
	Jevington	James Pagden
	West Dean	William Peckham
Edmund Cooper	Denton	Thomas Pratt
	Bishopstone	Edmund Catt
	Bletchington	William Washer
	Hayton	William Chambers
	Tarring	John Body
William Ridge	Alciston	William Boyd
	Alfriston	Walter Rason
	Berwick	William Goldsmith
	Selmeston	John Pankhurst
Revd James Capper	Wilmington	John King
	Lullington	William Woodhams
	Folkington	Thomas Swaine Kine
	Litlington	Ben Ridge
John Ellman	Southmalling	Thomas Berry
	Ringmer	Thomas Lucas Shadwell
	St Thomas in the Cliffe	Thomas Fuller
	Glynd	William Wisdom
Revd Rab Carr Rider	Hailsham	William Long
	Hellingly	Thomas Akehurst
	Arlington	William Child
Revd Mr Baker	Stanmer	Hugh Poole
Richard Attree	Laughton	Richard Sharp
	Chalvington	Edward Cane
	Ripe	Thomas Cruttenden
Sir Thomas Carr Knight	Beddingham	Joseph Martin
	Westfirle	John Stevens
	Signed H T Shadwell Charles Gilbert	

	Pevensey Rape Lower Division	
John Newnham Esq	Maresfield	Revd W P Woodward
	Buxted	Revd Matthias D'Oyley
Richard Chase Esq	Easthoathly	Revd Edward Langdale
	Framfield	John Woodward Esq
	Littlehorsted	Revd Mr Nott
Richard Streatfield Esq	Isfield	John Jenner Jun
	Uckfield	Revd Mr Rose
	Fletching	Revd George Woodward

John Apsley Dalrymple Esq	Chiddingly	Mr Peter Pagden
	Waldron	Revd Thomas Lewis
	Mayfield	Richard Owen Stone Gent
	Wadhurst	Henry Playsted Jun
D J Cameron Esq	Rotherfield	Revd Mr Crawley
	Frant	Sir John McPherson Bart
John Trayton Fuller Esq	Hartfield	Revd Mr Turner
	Withyham	Revd Mr Bale
Edward Cranston Esq	East Grinstead	Revd Mr Bostock
Gibbs Crawford Esq	Lindfield	Mr George Haynes
	Horsted Keynes	Revd Mr Austen
	Signed Sheffield Lieut L Pev	

	Hastings Rape	
George Courthope Esq William Constable Esq	Salehurst	John Langford
	Ticehurst	Revd Thomas Causton
	Burwash	James Philcox
	Etchingham	Revd Hugh Totty
Francis Newbery Esq	Heathfield	Revd Thomas Fuller
	Warbleton	Robert Hawes Esq
	Dallington	John Barber
Jeremy Curteis Esq Revd J Smith Collett Esq	Peasmarsh	Dive Clark
	Iden	John Stonham
	Playden	John Reeves
	East Guldeford	William Morris
Sir William Ashburnham Bart and John Luxford Esq	Brede	Thomas Ades Snr
	Udimore	William Woodhams
	Guestling	Christopher Hoad
	Icklesham	Thomas Cooper
	Pett	Thomas Russell
Francis Hare Naylor Esq	Wartling	Francis Holland
	Herstmonceux	Eardley W Michell Esq
	Ashburnham	Revd William Delves
	Ninfield	John King
	Hove	Ben Blackman
Edward Milward Jun and Wastel Brisco Esq	Fairlight	John Thorpe
	Ore	Christopher Thorpe
	Crowhurst	John Coppard
	Westfield	John Mosely
	Castle	
	St Leonards	Henry Farncombe
	Hollington	
Edward Jeremy Curteis Esq	Beckley	Samuel Reeves
	Northiam	Thomas Pix
	Bodiam	Robert Tourney
	Ewhurst	Nicholas Larkin

Revd Richard Rideoutt	Mountfield	Thomas Hilder
	Sedlescomb	Walter Mason
	Penhurst	James Ellis
	Brightling	James Buss
John Fuller Esq William Markwick Esq	Battle	John Tildon Sampson
	Whatlington	
	Catsfield	Thomas Smith
	Bexhill	Stephen Brook
	Signed St Asaph John Fuller	

Resolved

> That the Names of the before mentioned Superintendants be sent to the above Inspectors and the Names of Men in every Capacity Stock and in the different Schedules to the said Superintendants
>
> This meeting are of opinion and order that the churchwardens and overseers shall be exempt from being balloted under General Defence, Army of Reserve, and Militia Acts and that what the Deputy Lieutenants did at Lewes on Friday 15th July Instant respecting the Army of Reserve Act be confirmed

Resolved

> That it be represented to His Majesty's Ministers that the Deputy Lieutenants and Magistrates of this County having very lately assured the Men who paid Ten Pounds and Fifteen Pounds penalties for not providing Substitutes for the Militia and Supplementary Militia that it was only at the Expiration of Five Years that they should again be liable to serve or provide a Substitute feel themselves in a very disagreeable Predicament if they should now have to inform them that a new Law has passed again subjecting them to a fresh ballot for a still more extensive and disagreable Service to them and under a still higher Penalty
>
> They are however in Doubt upon the Construction of the Acts of Parliament in this respect and therefore would be glad that the following Questions should be submitted to the Law Officers of the Crown—42 Geo 3 c:90 s 45 & 66, & 43 Geo 3 c 82 Sect 6
>
> Are not the Persons who have paid the above penalties to be considered as *serving by Substitute* during the period of Five Years for which this Exemption is granted, so as to entitle them to an Exemption from the Ballot for the Army of Reserve
>
> If this Question is determined in the Negative they are very apprehensive they shall never be able to make such Persons as those concerned understand that this is not a Breach of Faith on the Part of those from whom they were assured they were clear from any ballot for five Years which may greatly tend to indispose the Lower Orders of the People against the Magistrates and perhaps prove Prejudicial to that Spirit of Unanimity and Zeal for the Public Service that this Meeting is endeavouring by all means in their power to inculcate and therefore hope that as there is a power in the Army of Reserve Act for Parliament to amend it during the present Sessions, His Majesty's Government will recommend it to Parliament to exempt from ballot under the Army of

Reserve Act all Persons who have paid Penalties under the Militia Acts during such Periods as they are exempt from ballot under the Militia Act

This Meeting is adjourned to the Castle Inn in Brighton aforesaid to be there held on Monday the 1st Day of August next at 11 o'Clock in the forenoon

[signed]   Wm Ellis Cl[er]k

[1 August 1803]

Sussex (To wit)

At a Meeting of the Lieutenancy of the said County held at the Castle Inn in Brighton in the said County on Monday the first Day of August 1803 for carrying the General Defence Act into further execution

Present

John Fuller Esq of Rosehill in the Chair
Lord St Asaph
Major General Charles Lennox
Honorable John Thomas Capel
Henry Shelley Jun Esq
William Stephen Poyntz Esq
Thomas Kemp Esq
George Shiffner Esq
William Newton Esq
Inigo Freeman Thomas Esq
Nathaniel Tredcroft Esq
William Sewell Esq
Thomas Cecil Grainger Esq
Charles Gilbert Esq
James Martin Lloyd Esq
Charles Goring Esq

Read The Answer of the Attorney and Solicitor General to the Case sent for their Opinion by the last meeting which is as follows (Vizt)

'By comparing the 43rd and 45th Section of the Militia Act 42nd George 3rd Chapter 90 it appears there is a distinction intended between Persons serving in the Militia either as principals or substitutes and the Persons who have paid the Penalty, the one being descriptive of Persons being exempted till it shall again come to their turn, and the other only for five years. That distinction existing in the original Militia Act, it appears to us that the Army of the Reserve Act extending it's [sic] exemptions only to Persons serving personally or by Substitutes in the Militia will not reach the case of him who has only paid the penalty; We therefore think that they are not exempt from the ballot for the Army of Reserve.

'As to the propriety of altering the Law in this respect, it is not within our Province to advise on that point.

'We are aware that some Doubts might be supposed to exist upon this Point by reason of the 66th Section of the 42nd Geo: 3rd Chap: 90 Because the Section directs the fines to be applied to the purpose of procuring Substitutes for the Persons who have paid them, and supposing them to have been applied, then the Persons having paid them might be considered in some sense as persons serving by Substitute, as the Substitute is procured by their fines so applied. But upon the whole we think that the true Construction of the Act is that which we have given in the former part of our Opinion. And the Person intended to be exempted from the Army of Reserve by reason of Service by Substitute is the Person who has himself actually procured such Substitute and not one who indirectly by means of his fine may have so procured one, or may have compelled the parish to a fresh ballot in cases where no Substitute may have been found at all

Sp: Percival,[115] Thos M Sutton
26th July 1803'

At this Meeting the following offers of Service were made Vizt

Lord St Asaph Francis Hare Naylor Thomas Davis Lamb and John Fuller Esqs offered to Command the four Companies which had offered their Services for the Rape of Hastings but they apprehended that new Regulations would be necessary as the Number of Volunteers in that rape was so very considerably advanced.

Lord Gage offered to take the Command of the Infantry in the Neighbouring Parishes to his own.

Sir John Miller Bart offered to raise a Corps of Yeomanry Cavalry and proposed himself as Captain, Samuel Gwynne Lieutenant and John Ellman Cornet.

Lieutenant Colonel Newton offered to take Charge of the Villages of that Part of the County which lay from Lewes South to the Sea (Vizt) Southover Kingston Iford Rodmell Southease Piddinghoe Telscombe and Newhaven and was ready to take the Command of the Volunteers that should come forward to serve in the above mentioned Parishes.

William Sewell and Thomas Cecil Grainger Esquires offered to take the Command of the Volunteers in their District if compatible with their Situations

---

[115] i.e. Spencer Percival, later Prime Minister

in the Yeomanry Cavalry, and stated that the Volunteers wished to be cloathed in some kind of Uniform, a Red Jacket and Pantaloons or any other that might be considered more proper, and the labouring part of them hoped to have some compensation for their loss of time, and were willing to be called out and trained once a Week or oftner if necessary. That the Number of Volunteers in their Division did not much exceed five Hundred but probably might increase their Numbers to seven or eight Hundred as several of the Pioneers and other Classes since the Schedules had been filled up seem inclined to change their Situations and be trained and exercised and that they the said William Sewell and Thomas Cecil Grainger were the more induced to make the above offer of taking the Command of the Volunteers by knowing that they would more cheerfully go with them than with Officers to whom they were perfect Strangers

George Shiffner Esq recommended the following Persons as Commanders of Volunteers in the Southern Division of the Rape of Lewes (Vizt) Lieutenant Colonel Newton G: E: Graham, Thomas Partington, John Martin Cripps, John Newnham of Newtimber and Elijah Impey Esqrs.

It being represented to this Meeting that John Ovington, Emery Churcher, Robert Follett, Messrs Barber & Hillier, John Pilgrim Boorn, George Woodland and Charles Dendy, all of the Parish of Sidlesham, had refused to return an account of their Stock &c to Thomas Hobger Jun and Napper Challen the Churchwardens of the said Parish as required of them by a Schedule delivered to them

It was ordered

that their Names be entered as Refractory and they are not to be indemnified in consequence of such Refusal, and that the Clerk do write to John Peachey Esq the Lieutenant of the Division and to Col Carnegie the Central Commissary to expostulate with them on the impropriety of their Conduct, and that a Copy be sent to Brooke Watson Esq the Commissary General

At this Meeting the Clerks to the Justices of the several and respective Subdivision Meetings in the said County returned the following Schedules pursuant to an Order for that purpose. (Vizt)

William Ellis Clerk

Chichester Rape Schedule No 1

An Abstract of the Returns made the 30th day of July 1803 by the Churchwardens and Overseers of the Poor of the several Parishes within the said Rape Pursuant to the Act for enabling his Majesty to provide for the Defence of the Realm and for indemnifying Persons who may suffer in their Property

Districts	Draught oxen	Fatting oxen	Cows	Young cattle and Colts	Sheeps [sic]	Goats	Hogs and pigs	Draft	Ridings	Waggons	Carts
South Division											
1st District											
Selsey	-	18	93	57	1175	-	210	94	11	26	39
Sidlesham	-	-	8	2	120	-	-	15	2	5	5
Earnley	-	-	43	17	339	-	165	41	6	11	15
	-	18	144	76	1634	-	375	150	19	42	59
2nd District											
East Wittering	-	-	48	29	405	-	77	43	3	9	14
West Wittering	21	-	42	17	526	-	243	42	8	12	19
West Itchenor	-	-	7	6	153	-	43	8	1	2	5
Birdham	-	-	35	11	366	-	351	98	9	27	38
Donnington	6	6	37	33	606	-	300	53	7	18	25
Appledram	-	-	32	27	500	-	156	40	5	11	14
Hunston	6	10	75	22	274	-	117	41	4	9	12
	33	16	276	145	2830	-	1287	325	37	88	127
3rd Division											
South Bersted	10	59	99	16	599	-	364	118	43	34	64
Pagham	6	51	89	30	1389	-	388	143	19	42	72
North Mundham	8	11	70	39	377	-	358	63	7	20	32
Merston	6	-	12	2	295	-	109	23	2	10	13
	30	121	270	87	2660	-	1219	347	71	106	181
4th Division											
Aldingbourne	6	10	81	26	863	-	522	111	20	33	44
Tangmere	-	16	9	11	226	-	107	17	3	4	6
Oving	-	16	107	78	958	-	575	92	27	34	62
Rumboldsweek	-	-	32	11	-	-	72	12	5	5	5
	6	42	229	126	2047	-	1276	232	55	76	117

[Chichester Rape Schedule No 1 continued]

Districts	Draught oxen	Fatting oxen	Cows	Young cattle and Colts	Sheeps [sic]	Goats	Hogs and pigs	Draft	Ridings	Waggons	Carts
5th Division											
New Fishbourne	-	-	39	11	214	-	90	20	8	6	11
Bosham	-	-	88	83	672	1	657	11	17	47	71
Chidham	-	-	24	6	400	-	200	40	7	16	27
West Thorney		No return									
	-	-	151	100	1286	1	947	17	32	69	109
6th Division											
Westhampnett	6	20	24	25	382	-	185	60	35	23	23
Boxgrove	6	12	61	11	3615	3	303	86	17	27	40
Slindon	-	-	20	88	2562	-	402	58	28	15	25
Eartham	-	-	11	5	1074	-	94	31	7	6	12
	12	32	116	49*	7633	3	984	23	87	71	100
7th Division											
East Lavant	-	-	38	17	2577	-	175	44	12	18	23
Mid Lavant	-	3	6	3	1400	-	52	18	2	6	8
West Stoke	-	-	2	-	545	-	37	9	1	3	5
Funtington	-	2	83	22	847	-	534	99	35	43	59
	-	5	129	42	5369	-	798	170	50	70	95
8th Division											
Westbourne	-	6	160	77	1076	-	998	15	31	57	115
Racton	-	18	27	5	510	-	81	22	3	7	9
Stoughton	-	-	37	13	3783	-	421	99	23	31	26
Compton	-	-	16	5	1364	-	90	20	6	8	11
North Marden	-	-	5	3	754	-	18	10	2	3	4
Up Marden	-	-	17	5	2007	-	100	62	16	10	12
East Marden	-	-	4	1	470	-	59	9	2	3	4
	-	24	266	109	9964	-	1767	377	83	119	181
9th Division											
West Dean	-	1	36	8	3410	-	120	62	11	21	31
Binderton	-	-	24	-	910	-	65	17	7	6	11
Singleton	-	-	28	7	3165	-	199	53	16	15	17
East Dean	-	-	22	12	2810	-	170	46	6	9	10
Upwaltham	-	-	3	3	850	-	55	20	-	6	7
	-	1	113	30	11145	-	609	198	40	57	76

* error: should read 129

[Chichester Rape Schedule No 1 continued]

Districts	Draught oxen	Fatting oxen	Cows	Young cattle and Colts	Sheeps [sic]	Goats	Hogs and pigs	Draft	Ridings	Waggons	Carts
City of Chichester	7	-	70	13	631	7	774	177	93	33	81
The Close	-	-	3	1	-	-	6	1	6	-	2
Saint Bartholomew	-	9	46	12	-	-	115	7	3	2	2
Saint Pancras & St James's	-	-	23	2	10	-	230	18	10	5	13
	7	9	142	28	641	7	1125	203	112	40	98
[North Division]											
Lynch	8	4	45	65	626	-	76	29	2	7	8
Didling	-	-	34	23	591	-	71	14	3	5	7
Treyford	-	10	59	13	631	-	52	27	2	7	11
Elsted	-	-	45	16	598	-	112	25	5	10	13
Harting	-	102	184	33	2378	-	289	100	19	33	41
	8	116	367	150	4824	-	600	195	31	62	80
Graffham	-	-	27	28	375	-	138	23	3	7	6
Heyshott	8	-	44	75	470	-	163	45	7	12	19
Cocking	-	5	47	43	1031	-	140	60	6	21	28
Bepton	-	-	29	6	368	-	60	18	1	4	6
	8	5	147	162†	2244	-	501	146	17	44	59
Midhurst & St Johns	-	-	98	86	275	-	382	75	41	23	53
Easebourne	23	7	83	80	1045	-	504	80	21	32	46
Selham	-	3	11	33	132	-	42	18	2	2	3
	23	10	192	199	1452	-	928	173	64	57	102
Woolbeding	-	12	29	28	425	-	137	34	11	10	13
Stedham	-	16	68	97	179	-	166	61	16	23	29
Iping	-	-	117	50	563	-	163	55	11	17	25
Trotten	6	45	175	162	1163	-	268	67	15	16	18
Chithurst	-	-	25	18	70	-	104	18	2	3	7
Ferwick*	4	-	49	56	143	-	64	21	3	7	8
Rogate	-	35	196	109	1491	-	209	96	21	29	43
	10	108	659	520	4034	-	1111	352	79	105	143

* sic: = Terwick
† error: should read 152

[Chichester Rape Schedule No 1 continued]

Districts	Draught oxen	Fatting oxen	Cows	Young cattle and Colts	Sheeps [sic]	Goats	Hogs and pigs	Draft	Ridings	Waggons	Carts
Lynchmere	-	-	56	34	2095	-	1004	41	6	16	10
Fernhurst	6	-	88	107	351	-	234	75	9	24	35
Lodsworth	16	6	27	55	314	-	333	29	8	12	28
	22	6	171	196	2760	-	1571	145	23	52	73
West Stoke	-	-	29	7	330	-	60	14	1	2	3
	22	6	200	203	3090	-	1631	159	24	54	76
[Totals]	159	512*	3401	2026	60853	11	15158	3440	801	1060	1603

* error: should read 513

Chichester Rape Schedule No 2

Districts	No of Persons appointed for the removal of horses and waggons conveying such Persons as are unable to remove themselves	No of Overseers appointed to Superintend this Service	No of Persons appointed for the Removal of Cattle	No of Overseers for the same	No of Persons appointed for the Removal of Sheep and other Live Stock	No of Overseers for the same
South Division						
1st District						
Selsey	13	1	6	1	3	1
Sidlesham						
Earnley						
2nd District						
East Wittering						
West Wittering	21				15	
West Itchenor						
Birdham						
Donnington	12	2	3	2	3	2
Appledram	4		3		9	
Hunston	2	1	5	1	6	1
	39	3	11	3	33	3
3rd Division						
South Bersted	2	-	1	-	-	-
Pagham	3	1	2	2	3	1
North Mundham	16	2	11	-	11	3
Merston	-	-	1	1	1	1
	21	3	15	3	15	5
4th Division						
Aldingbourne	12	1	3	1	3	1
Tangmere	6	1	-	-	5	1
Oving	23	3	4	1	5	1
Rumboldsweek	7	-	3	-	3	-
*						

* Totals not entered

[Chichester Rape Schedule No 2 continued]

Districts	No of Persons appointed for the removal of horses and waggons conveying such Persons as are unable to remove themselves	No of Overseers appointed to Superintend this Service	No of Persons appointed for the Removal of Cattle	No of Overseers for the same	No of Persons appointed for the Removal of Sheep and other Live Stock	No of Overseers for the same
5th Division						
New Fishbourne	3	1	4	1	4	1
Bosham	5	2	4	2	4	2
Chidham	1	1	1	1	1	1
West Thorney	-	-	-	-	-	-
	9	4	9	4	9	4
6th Division						
Westhampnett	9	1	4	2	4	1
Boxgrove	-	-	-	-	-	-
Slindon	10	3	-	-	12	3
Eartham	4	1	2	1	2	1
	23	5	6	3	18	5
7th Division						
East Lavant	9	1	8	1	5	1
Mid Lavant	-	-	-	-	3	1
West Stoke	6	1	9	1	-	-
Funtington	5	3	5	3	5	3
	20	5	22	5	13	5
8th Division						
Westbourne	22	2	10	2	10	2
Racton	5	2	5	2	4	2
Stoughton	7	-	5	-	7	-
Compton	3	1	3	1	4	1
North Marden	2	1	-	-	-	-
Up Marden	5	1	2	1	2	1
East Marden	1	1	1	1	1	1
	45	8	26	7	28	7

[Chichester Rape Schedule No 2 continued]

Districts	No of Persons appointed for the removal of horses and waggons conveying such Persons as are unable to remove themselves	No of Overseers appointed to Superintend this Service	No of Persons appointed for the Removal of Cattle	No of Overseers for the same	No of Persons appointed for the Removal of Sheep and other Live Stock	No of Overseers for the same
9th Division						
West Dean	12	-	-	-	12	-
Binderton	4	1	3	1	8	1
Singleton	-	-	-	-	-	-
East Dean	16	1	2	-	5	1
Upwaltham	6	1	2	2	3	-
	38	3	7	3	28	2
City of Chichester						
The Close						
Saint Bartholomew			2	1	1	
Saint Pancras &						
St James's						
[North Division]						
Lynch	10	1	7	1	6	1
Didling	6	-	4	-	5	-
Treyford	12	1	3	1	3	1
Elsted	9	1	4	1	7	1
Harting	36	3	28	2	23	2
	73	6	46	5	44	5
Graffham	12	1	6	1	4	1
Heyshott	10	1	6	1	6	1
Cocking	15	4	14	1	13	3
Bepton	1	1	1	-	2	-
	38	7	27	3	25	5
Midhurst & St Johns	10	3	37	2	39	-
Easebourne	6	1	14	1	14	2
Selham	3	1	4	1	4	1
	19	5	55	4	57	3

[Chichester Rape Schedule No 2 continued]

Districts	No of Persons appointed for the removal of horses and waggons conveying such Persons as are unable to remove themselves	No of Overseers appointed to Superintend this Service	No of Persons appointed for the Removal of Cattle	No of Overseers for the same	No of Persons appointed for the Removal of Sheep and other Live Stock	No of Overseers for the same
Woolbeding	8	-	4	1	5	1
Stedham	4	1	4	1	6	1
Iping	12	1	4	1	8	1
Trotten	4	2	10	2	8	2
Chithurst	6	1	2	1	4	1
Terwick	8	1	4	1	3	1
Rogate	-	1	5	1	5	1
	42	7	33	8	39	8
Lynchmere	10	-	1	-	1	-
Fernhurst	7	1	8	1	8	1
Lodsworth	4	1	4	1	3	1
	21	2	13	2	12	2
[Totals]	449	64	288	64*	341	58

* error: should read 54

Chichester Rape Schedule No 3

Districts	No	On Horseback	Foot	Cavalry Swords	Cavalry Pistols	Infantry Firelocks	Infantry Pitchforks	Persons to be provided with arms at the place of General Assembly
South Division								
Selsey								
Sidlesham	18	-	18	-	-	15	3	-
Earnley								
	18	-	18	-	-	15	3	-
East Wittering	29	6	23	-	-	23	-	-
West Wittering								
West Itchenor								
Birdham								
Donnington	21	-	21	-	-	-	-	21
Appledram	17	1	16	1	1	-	-	16
Hunston	10	-	10	-	-	6	-	4
	77	7	70	1	1	29	-	41
South Bersted	8	6	2	3	5	-	-	-
Pagham	65	3	62	3	3	-	-	62
North Mundham	11	4	7	-	-	4	-	4
Merston	3	-	3	-	-	-	-	3
	87	13	74	6	8	4	-	69
Aldingbourne								
Tangmere	16	-	16	-	-	3	13	-
Oving	54	4	50	-	-	-	-	54
Rumboldsweek	17	-	17	-	-	-	-	17
	87	4	83	-	-	3	13	71
New Fishbourne								
Bosham								
Chidham	10	3	7	3	3	7	-	-
West Thorney								
	10	3	7	3	3	7	-	-

[Chichester Rape Schedule No 3 continued]

Districts	No	On Horseback	Foot	Cavalry Swords	Cavalry Pistols	Infantry Firelocks	Infantry Pitchforks	Persons to be provided with arms at the place of General Assembly
Westhampnett	2	-	2	-	-	2	-	-
Boxgrove	101	-	101	-	-	5	-	96
Slindon	11	-	-	-	-	-	-	-
Eartham								
	114	-	103	-	-	7		96
East Lavant	40	-	40	-	-	-	-	40
Mid Lavant								
West Stoke	3	-	3	-	-	-	-	3
Funtington	100	-	-	-	-	25	-	75
	143	-	43	-	-	25	-	118
Westbourne	232	15	217	-	-	-	39	178
Racton	2	-	-	-	-	-	2	-
Stoughton	70	-	-	-	-	-	-	70
Compton	14	2	12	-	-	1	-	13
North Marden								
Up Marden	10	2	8	2	2	8	-	-
East Marden	12	-	12	-	-	-	-	12
	340	19	249	2	2	9	41	273
West Dean	50	-	50	-	-	4	8	38
Binderton								
Singleton	40	-	40	-	-	-	-	40
East Dean	39	-	39	-	-	-	-	39
Upwaltham	8	-	8	-	-	-	-	8
	137	-	137	-	-	4	8	125
City of Chichester	105	-	105	-	-	-	-	105
The Close	10	-	10	-	-	1	-	9
Saint Bartholomew	28	-	28	-	-	-	-	28
Saint Pancras & St James's	31	-	31	-	-	-	-	31
	174	-	174	-	-	1	-	173

[Chichester Rape Schedule No 3 continued]

Districts	No	On Horseback	Foot	Cavalry Swords	Cavalry Pistols	Infantry Firelocks	Infantry Pitchforks	Persons to be provided with arms at the place of General Assembly
[North Division]								
Lynch								
Didling	2	2	-	-	-	-	-	2
Treyford	3	-	3	-	-	-	-	3
Elsted	6	-	6	-	-	6	-	-
Harting	18	-	18	-	-	-	-	18
	29	2	27	-	-	6	-	23
Graffham	40	-	40	-	-	10	-	30
Heyshott	34	-	34	-	-	-	-	34
Cocking	5	-	5	-	-	-	-	5
Bepton	3	-	3	-	-	-	-	3
	82	-	82	-	-	10	-	72
Midhurst & St Johns	78	-	78	-	-	-	-	78
Easebourne	30	-	30	-	-	-	-	30
Selham								
	108	-	108	-	-	-	-	108
Woolbeding								
Stedham								
Iping	26	-	26	-	-	-	-	26
Trotten								
Chithurst	4	-	4	-	-	-	-	4
Terwick	6	-	6	-	-	-	-	6
Rogate	73	-	73	-	-	-	-	73
	109	-	109	-	-	-	-	109
Lynchmere	2	-	2	-	-	-	-	2
Fernhurst	37	-	37	-	-	-	-	37
Lodsworth	14	-	14	-	-	6	8	-
[Totals]	53	-	53	-	-	6	8	39
	1568	48	1520*	12	14	119†	73	1317

* error: should read 1337
† error: should read 126

Chichester Rape Schedule No 4

Districts	No	Felling Axes	Pick Axes	Spades	Shovels	Bill Hooks	Saws	Any other Inst they can bring
South Division								
Selsey	8	5	1	-	-	1	1	
Sidlesham								
Earnley								
East Wittering								
West Wittering	6	6	-	-	-	-	-	
West Itchenor	8	-	4	-	4	-	-	
Birdham								
Donnington	4	2	1	-	-	1	-	
Appledram	2	1	1	-	1	-	-	
Hunston	2	2	-	-	-	-	-	
	22	11	6	-	5	1	-	
South Bersted	-	-	-	-	-	-	-	
Pagham	44	6	35	34	3	-	7	
North Mundham	27	7	6	2	3	2	5	
Merston	11	1	4	1	2	1	2	
	82	14	45	37	8	3	14	
Aldingbourne	7	2	2	2	-	-	1	
Tangmere	5	2	2	-	-	1	-	
Oving	13	-	5	3	-	5	-	
Rumboldsweek	1	1	-	-	-	-	-	
	26	5	9	5	-	6	1	
New Fishbourne								
Bosham								
Chidham	1	-	-	-	1	1	-	
West Thorney								

[Chichester Rape Schedule No 4 continued]

Districts	No	Felling Axes	Pick Axes	Spades	Shovels	Bill Hooks	Saws	Any other Inst they can bring
Westhampnett	23	5	2	3	3	5	3	2 Pikes
Boxgrove	28	17	17	19	18	20	17	2 Iron Crows
Slindon	50	6	19	13	12	10	8	
Eartham	-	-	-	-	-	-	-	
	101	28	38	35	33	35	28	
East Lavant	12	-	11	4	2	-	3	
Mid Lavant	30	8	11	5	-	3	1	
West Stoke	20	1	1	1	1	1	2	
Funtington	8	2	3	5	4	4	1	
	70	11	26	15	7	8	7	
Westbourne	69	11	36	4	1	9	8	
Racton	5	5	-	-	-	-	-	
Stoughton	24	8	1	1	3	8	3	
Compton	31	10	11	8	10	9	10	
North Marden								
Up Marden	16	3	5	2	2	1	2	
East Marden								
	145	37	53	15	16	27	23	
West Dean	30	-	-	-	-	6	-	
Binderton	-	-	-	-	-	-	-	
Singleton	36	7	10	8	5	4	2	
East Dean	15	7	6	3	5	3	4	
Upwaltham								
	81	14	16	11	10	13	6	
City of Chichester	25	4	4	4	-	-	2	
The Close								
Saint Bartholomew								
Saint Pancras & St James's	1	-	-	-	-	-	1	
	26	4	4	4	-	-	3	

[Chichester Rape Schedule No 4 continued]

Districts	No	Felling Axes	Pick Axes	Spades	Shovels	Bill Hooks	Saws	Any other Inst they can bring
[North Division]								
Lynch								
Didling	5	4	-	-	-	-	1	
Treyford								
Elsted	7	7	7	7	7	7	7	
Harting	64	35	8	10	1	-	2	
	76	46	15	17	8	7	10	
Graffham	10	1	6	2	1	-	-	
Heyshott	12	6	1	4	1	-	-	
Cocking	3	-	2	-	-	-	1	
Bepton	11	2	3	5	-	-	-	
	36	9	12	11	2	-	1	
Midhurst & St Johns	29	5	7	6	2	-	3	
Easebourne	37	12	9	12	1	-	2	
Selham								
	66	17	16	18	3	-	5	
Woolbeding	33	3	7	11	5	6	3	
Stedham	24	1	9	20	1	12	-	
Iping	11	3	-	3	-	-	2	
Trotten	38	11	5	8	4	5	5	
Chithurst	4	2	1	3	1	-	-	
Ferwick*	6	-	-	-	-	-	-	
Rogate	15	8	7	7	-	-	8	
	131	28	29	52	11	23	18	
Lynchmere	21	6	3	5	2	3	2	
Fernhurst	24	9	10	4	-	-	2	
Lodsworth	49	11	7	12	3	9	6	
[Totals]	94	26	20	21	5	12	10	
	820†	255	320‡	242**	109	136	127	

* sic: = Terwick

† error: should read 965

‡ error: should read 290

** error: should read 241

Chichester Rape Schedule No 6

Districts	Subscribers	No of Waggons with Tilts and Four Horses or more	No of Waggons with Tilts and Three Horses	No of Carts with tilts and Three Horses or more	No of Carts with tilts and Two Horses	No of Persons appd to act as Servants with Teams	No conductors for the same in proportion of one to every Ten Waggons	No of General Agents for the Parish of Hundred to whom Requisition is to be made to call forth the Cart
South Division								
Selsey	6	5nt	3nt	-	18nt	-	1	-
Sidlesham	8	4do	5do	-	1do	8	-	-
Earnley								
	14	9	8		19	8	1	-
East Wittering								
West Wittering								
West Itchenor								
Birdham								
Donnington								
Appledram								
Hunston	4	4do	-	-	-	4	1	-
South Bersted	26	28do	6do	-	64do	-	-	-
Pagham	12	8do	15do	5nt	9do	26	4	1
North Mundham								
Merston								
	38	36	21	-	73	-	-	-
Aldingbourne	9	4do	5do	-	-	-	-	-
Tangmere	3	2do	2do	-	6do	6	-	-
Oving	15	16do	5do	-	2do	23	3	1
Rumboldsweek	3	1do	1do	-	4do	2	-	-
	30	23	13	-	12	31	3	-
New Fishbourne								
Bosham								
Chidham	6	2do	4do	-	1do	7	1	1
West Thorney								

[Chichester Rape Schedule No 6 continued]

Districts	Subscribers	No of Waggons with Tilts and Four Horses or more	No of Waggons with Tilts and Three Horses	No of Carts with tilts and Three Horses or more	No of Carts with tilts and Two Horses	No of Persons appd to act as Servants with Teams	No conductors for the same in proportion of one to every Ten Waggons	No of General Agents for the Parish of Hundred to whom Requisition is to be made to call forth the Cart
Westhampnett								
Boxgrove	13	-	19Do	-	14Do	-	-	-
Slindon	16		15Do	-	27Do	19	3	1
Eartham								
	29	-	34	-	41	19	3	1
East Lavant								
Mid Lavant	4	-	2Do	-	2Do	6		
West Stoke								
Funtington								
Westbourne								
Racton								
Stoughton								
Compton	2	2Do	-	-	-	-	-	-
North Marden								
Up Marden	4	-	5Do					
East Marden	1	-	-	-	3Do	4		
	7	2	5	-	3	4		
West Dean								
Binderton								
Singleton	7	11Do	-	-	-	-		
East Dean	4	-	4Do					
Upwaltham	1	-	1Do	-	-	2		
	12	-	5	-	-	2		
City of Chichester								
The Close								
Saint Bartholomew								
Saint Pancras &								
St James's								

[Chichester Rape Schedule No 6 continued]

Districts	Subscribers	No of Waggons with Tilts and Four Horses or more	No of Waggons with Tilts and Three Horses	No of Carts with tilts and Three Horses or more	No of Carts with tilts and Two Horses	No of Persons appd to act as Servants with Teams	No conductors for the same in proportion of one to every Ten Waggons	No of General Agents for the Parish of Hundred to whom Requisition is to be made to call forth the Cart
[North Division]								
Lynch	3	4Do						
Didling	4		2Do	-				
Treyford	5	4Do	-	1Do				
Elsted	6	5Do				12	1	
Harting	14	17Do	2Do	-	1Do	37	2	1
	32	30	4	-	-	49	3	1
Graffham								
Heyshott								
Cocking								
Bepton								
Midhurst & St Johns	8	8	-	-	2Do	12	-	1
Easebourne	8	7	1Do	-	-	16	1	--
Selham	1	-	1Do	-	-	2	-	-
	17	15	2	-	2	30	1	1
Woolbeding	5	4Do	1Do	-	-	9	1	-
Stedham	9	6Do	-	-	-	16	1	-
Iping	11	7Do	3Do	1Do	-	22	1	-
Trotten	10	10Do	-	-	-	20	1	-
Chithurst								
Ferwick*	3	1Do	1Do	-	1Do	5	1	-
Rogate	17	14Do	3Do	-	-	36	2	1
	55	42	8	-	-	108	7	1
Lynchmere	7	4Do	1Do	-	1Do	9	1	-
Fernhurst	5	3Do	2Do	-	-	10	1	1
Lodsworth	5	3Do	1Do	-	1Do	6	1	-
[Totals]	17	10	4	-	2	25	3	1
	265	184	136	7	157	319	27	

* sic: = Terwick

Chichester Rape Schedule No 7

Districts	Subscribers No	No & Situations of Water Mills	Names and Situations of Wind Mills	No of Sacks of Flour of 280 lbs net each to be furnished by each Mill very 24 Hours	Will the Subscribers provide the Wheat or not Answer Yes or No
South Division					
Selsey					
Sidlesham					
Earnley					
East Wittering					
West Wittering					
West Itchenor					
Birdham					
Donnington					
Appledram					
Hunston					
South Bersted					
Pagham			1 Pagham Point		
North Mundham		1 Northmundham	1 Northmundham		
Merston					
Aldingbourne					
Tangmere					
Oving					
Rumboldsweek					
New Fishbourne					
Bosham					
Chidham					
West Thorney					

[Chichester Rape Schedule No 7 continued]

Districts	Subscribers No	No & Situations of Water Mills	Names and Situations of Wind Mills	No of Sacks of Flour of 280 lbs net each to be furnished by each Mill very 24 Hours	Will the Subscribers provide the Wheat or not Answer Yes or No
Westhampnett Boxgrove Slindon Eartham East Lavant Mid Lavant West Stoke Funtington Westbourne Racton Stoughton Compton North Marden Up Marden East Marden West Dean Binderton Singleton East Dean Upwaltham City of Chichester The Close Saint Bartholomew Saint Pancras & St James's	6	1 Westhampnett 5 Westbourne	1 Westbourne	27	Yes

[Chichester Rape Schedule No 7 continued]

Districts	Subscribers No	No & Situations of Water Mills	Names and Situations of Wind Mills	No of Sacks of Flour of 280 lbs net each to be furnished by each Mill very 24 Hours	Will the Subscribers provide the Wheat or not Answer Yes or No
[North Division]					
Lynch					
Didling					
Treyford					
Elsted					
Harting					
Graffham					
Heyshott					
Cocking					
Bepton					
Midhurst & St Johns					
Easebourne					
Selham					
Woolbeding					
Stedham					
Iping					
Trotten	1	1 Trotten		3	
Chithurst					
Terwick					
Rogate	1	1 Rogate	-	4	No
	2	2		7	
Lynchmere	1	1 Lynchmere	-	2	No
Fernhurst					
Lodsworth	1	1 Lodsworth	1 Lodsworth	9	No
[Totals]	2	2	1	11	
	10	11	4	45	

Chichester Rape Schedule No 8

Districts	No of Subscribers in each Parish	No of Loaves of 3 lbs to be furnished by each subscriber every 24 Hours - By their usual number of Hands - For a constancy	On Emergency	By the help of aditional Journeymen for a constancy	No of addl Journeymen required	For what kind of fuel the Ovens are Calculated	What Quanty is required every 24 Hours to keep each Oven consty at work supposing 6 Batches to be baked	Wher. Fuel is abundant or not Answer Yes or No
South Division								
Selsey	1	36	216	-	2	Wood	13 fags	No
Sidlesham								
Earnley								
East Wittering								
West Wittering								
West Itchenor								
Birdham								
Donnington								
Appledram								
Hunston								
South Bersted	1	500	1000	3	2	Wood	20 fag	Yes
Pagham								
North Mundham								
Merston								
Aldingbourne								
Tangmere								
Oving								
Rumboldsweek	1	250	-	1	-	Wood	-	No
New Fishbourne								
Bosham								
Chidham								
West Thorney								

[Chichester Rape Schedule No 8 continued]

Districts	No of Subscribers in each Parish	No of Loaves of 3 lbs to be furnished by each subscriber every 24 Hours — By their usual number of Hands — For a constancy	On Emergency	By the help of addl Journeymen for a constancy	No of addl Journeymen required	For what kind of fuel the Ovens are Calculated	What Quanty is required every 24 Hours to keep each Oven consty at work supposing 6 Batches to be baked	Wher. Fuel is abundant or not Answer Yes or No
Westhampnett Boxgrove Slindon Eartham								
East Lavant Mid Lavant West Stoke Funtington	1	150	200	1	-	Wood	2 Bavins and Yeast	
Westbourne Racton Stoughton	5	5654	-	-	-	-	-	-
Compton North Marden Up Marden East Marden	1	100	150	500	2	Wood	25 Fags	Yes
	6	5754	150	500	2	-	25	-
West Dean Binderton Singleton East Dean Upwaltham								
City of Chichester The Close Saint Bartholomew Saint Pancras & St James	14	4890				Wood		No

[Chichester Rape Schedule No 8 continued]

Districts	No of Subscribers in each Parish	No of Loaves of 3 lbs to be furnished by each subscriber every 24 Hours — For a constancy	By their usual number of Hands — On Emergency	By the help of aditional Journeymen for a constancy	No of addl Journeymen required	For what kind of fuel the Ovens are Calculated	What Quanty is required every 24 Hours to keep each Oven consty at work supposing 6 Batches to be baked	Wher. Fuel is abundant or not Answer Yes or No
[North Division]								
Lynch								
Didling	1	75	-	-	-	Wood	12 fag	Yes
Treyford	1	10	80	-	-	Do	20 Do	No
Elsted	1	60	80	-	-	Do	6 Do	No
Harting								
	3	145	160	-	-	-	38	
Graffham								
Heyshott								
Cocking	1	-	48	64				
Bepton								
Midhurst & St Johns	7	1368	48	54	-	Wood		No
Easebourne								
Selham								
Woolbeding	3	288	-	-	-	Wood		Yes
Stedham	2	130				Wood		Yes
Iping								
Trotten								
Chithurst								
Terwick								
Rogate								
	5	418						
Lynchmere								
Fernhurst								
Lodsworth								
	40	13511						

Schedule N°. 8. cont.ᵈ

Westbourne	5	5654	-	-	-	-	-
Racton							
Stoughton							
Compton	1	100	150	500	2	Wood 25 Jaʸ	yes
Northmarden							
Upmarden							
East Marden							
	6	5754	150	500	2	-	25
West Dean							
Binderton							
Singleton							
East Dean							
Upwaltham							
City of Chichester	14	1890	-	-		Wood	-	No
The Close							
Saint Bartholomew							
Saint Pancras							
& St James							
North Division							
Lynch							
Didling	1	75				Wood 12 Jaʸ	yes
Treyford	1	10	80			Dᵒ 20 Dᵒ	No
Elsted	1	60	80	-	-	Dᵒ 6 Dᵒ	No
Harting							
	3	145	160	-		38	
Graffham							
Heyshott							
Cocking	1	-	148	64			
Bepton							
Midhurst & St Johns	7	1368	48	54	-	wood	-	No
Easebourne							
Selham							
Woolbeding	3	288	-			wood	-	yes
Stedham	2	130	-			wood		No
Iping							
Trotton							
Chithurst							
Terwick							
Rogate							
	5	410					
Lynchmere							
Fernhurst							
Lodsworth							

Chichester Rape Schedule No 9

Districts	No of Proprietors	Proprietors Residence	No of Masters	Masters Residence	Parish District or Hundred to which the Craft belongs
South Division Selsey Sidlesham Earnley	1	Sidlesham	1	Fishbourne	Sidlesham
East Wittering West Wittering West Itchenor Birdham Donnington Appledram Hunston	1	Itchenor	2	Itchenor	Itchenor
South Bersted Pagham North Mundham Merston	12	Bognor & Pagham	9	Bognor & Pagham	Pagham
Aldingbourne Tangmere Oving Rumboldsweek					
New Fishbourne Bosham Chidham West Thorney	1	New Fishbourne	1	New Fishbourne	New Fishbourne

Proceedings and Schedules

In What County	Number of Name of the Craft	Tonnage	Whether Deck'd or not	River or Canal on which employ'd	Place to which the Craft usually Tradees
Sussex	Ann & Elizabeth	30	Not		Chichester
Sussex	2	70	Not	Chichester River	
Sussex		77	8 Not		
Sussex	Industry	16	Deck'd	Chichester	Portsmouth

[Chichester Rape Schedule No 9 continued]

Districts	No of Proprietors	Proprietors Residence	No of Masters	Masters Residence	Parish District or Hundred to which the Craft belongs
Westhampnett Boxgrove Slindon Eartham East Lavant Mid Lavant West Stoke Funtington Westbourne Racton Stoughton Compton North Marden Up Marden East Marden West Dean Binderton Singleton East Dean Upwaltham City of Chichester The Close Saint Bartholomew Saint Pancras & St James	6	Westbourne	7	Westbourne	Westbourne

In What County	Number of Name of the Craft	Tonnage	Whether Deck'd or not	River or Canal on which employ'd	Place to which the Craft usually Tradees
Sussex		363	Deck'd	Emsworth Harbor	Portsmouth

[Chichester Rape Schedule No 9 continued]

Districts	No of Proprietors	Proprietors Residence	No of Masters	Masters Residence	Parish District or Hundred to which the Craft belongs
[North Division]					
Lynch					
Didling					
Treyford					
Elsted					
Harting					
Graffham					
Heyshott					
Cocking					
Bepton					
Midhurst & St Johns					
Easebourne					
Selham					
Woolbeding					
Stedham					
Iping					
Trotten					
Chithurst					
Terwick					
Rogate					
Lynchmere					
Fernhurst					
Lodsworth					
	21		20		

In What County	Number of Name of the Craft	Tonnage	Whether Deck'd or not	River or Canal on which employ'd	Place to which the Craft usually Tradees
		556			

Arundel Rape Schedule No 1

Parishes	Draught oxen	Fatting oxen	Cows	Young cattle and Colts	Sheep	Goats	Hogs and Pease [sic]	Draft Horses	Riding Horses	Waggons	Carts
Southstoke	8	12	42	31	656	-	79	18	4	7	8
Madehurst	-	-	19	-	1700	-	71	26	8	7	10
Binsted	-	2	12	21	870	-	80	23	6	7	10
Middleton	-	-	9	3	-	-	46	16	5	5	1
Tortington	-	78	34	2	321	-	35	19	6	6	9
Ford	-	62	5	4	350	-	40	12	2	4	6
Yapton	8	10	74	13	650	-	314	78	24	22	11
Barnham	8	18	17	21	64	-	89	18	5	6	9
Climping	6	91	59	34	1038	-	228	44	11	18	21
Felpham	9	9	68	31	516	-	295	77	10	26	3
Walberton	6	-	40	32	529	-	433	68	26	17	11
Eastergate	4	-	26	19	310	-	256	26	10	11	15
Northstoke	20	15	40	37	1194	-	48	13	2	5	6
Leominster	22	280	59	39	1736	-	372	61	24	26	42
Angmering	67	34	81	114	3968	-	367	74	24	28	48
Kingston	8	17	6	16	294	-	75	13	3	6	9
Rustington	13	7	25	38	147	-	270	50	9	23	27
Ferring	6	6	26	18	741	-	277	36	7	14	20
Poling	10	24	27	26	294	-	128	32	9	13	17
Burpham	16	-	38	50	2950	-	163	38	4	12	17
Goring	6	6	52	19	974	-	462	84	15	33	45
Warningcamp	-	-	17	8	321	-	177	19	6	8	10
Preston	-	-	11	9	120	7	81	20	1	10	10
Little Hampton	6	-	23	38	258	-	155	33	7	12	22
Arundell Boro	-	2	69	13	1053	-	278	47	34	10	39
Petworth	44	15	116	204	2319	-	407	152	88	56	70
Barlavington	-	8	12	5	350	-	45	9	1	4	-
Tillington	46	3	82	170	439	-	368	99	12	36	12

[Arundel Rape Schedule No 1 continued]

Parishes	Draught oxen	Fatting oxen	Cows	Young cattle and Colts	Sheep	Goats	Hogs and Pease [sic]	Draft Horses	Riding Horses	Waggons	Carts
Kirdford	101	3	210	491	1518	-	1010	245	30	92	115
Northchapel	8	16	64	145	540	-	378	89	10	24	1
Lurgashall	8	2	39	67	173	-	252	77	9	21	26
Stopham	-	26	28	49	929	-	134	34	8	10	14
Burton	13	8	17	50	989	-	72	23	4	9	12
Sutton	11	-	32	48	811	-	118	28	5	9	1
Egdean	-	5	9	21	263	-	71	20	2	7	9
Duncton	6	6	7	20	100	-	22	6	1	3	6
Woollavington	20	-	51	45	1422	-	144	50	9	13	26
Amberley	10	10	90	264	1566	-	404	60	7	19	30
Parham	-	1	11	7	753	4	54	15	6	6	10
Gritham	16	10	24	69	310	-	149	14	1	6	6
Pulborough	22	114	197	241	1218	-	710	207	56	83	101
Billingshurst	41	33	147	301	594	-	521	178	26	70	88
Wiggenholt	14	14	14	50	620	-	47	6	1	4	6
Storrington	-	2	65	87	2090	-	354	84	37	26	41
West Chiltington	8	9	86	172	360	-	390	98	12	33	43
Bury	20	16	116	112	3004	-	278	80	14	32	43
Coldwaltham	-	10	42	51	528	-	159	42	3	8	13
Fittleworth	6	2	85	140	957	-	416	79	17	29	41
Hardham	-	74	44	45	440	-	140	28	6	12	1
Coates	-	-	8	8	103	-	19	7	1	3	3
Bignor	-	4	19	8	828	-	99	19	5	6	1
Wisborough Green	108	78	214	283	2755	-	635	189	39	86	104
Houghton	-	-	15	24	1940	-	104	23	3	8	10
	725	1142	2723	3813	48973	11	12219*	2906	675	1051	1259

* error: should read 12319

Arundel Rape Schedule No 2

Parishes	No of Persons appointed for the removal of horses and waggons conveying such Persons as are unable to remove themselves	No of Overseers appointed to Superintend this Service	No of Persons appointed for the Removal of Cattle	No of Overseers for the same	No of Persons appointed for the Removal of Sheep and other Live Stock	No of Overseers for the same
Southstoke	7	1	4	1	3	1
Madehurst	7	1	5	1	6	1
Binsted	7	1	7	1	5	1
Middleton	5	1	1	-	1	1
Tortington	6	1	4	1	4	1
Ford	3	1	2	1	4	1
Yapton	-	3	-	2	-	-
Barnham	2	1	2	1	2	1
Climping	10	1	3	-	4	-
Felpham	8	2	2	1	2	2
Walberton	10	2	2	1	8	2
Eastergate	1	1	7	1	6	1
Northstoke	10	1	5	1	2	1
Leominster	10	4	3	3	5	2
Angmering	8	1	16	1	19	1
Kingston	5	1	1	1	1	1
Rustington	-	1	4	2	4	2
Ferring	3	2	3	2	2	2
Poling	8	1	8	1	9	1
Burpham	8	2	5	2	4	2
Goring	-	-	17	1	-	-
Warningcamp	6	1	7	1	8	1
Preston	4	1	-	-	-	-
Littlehampton	2	1	1	1	2	1
Arundell Borough	3	1	2	1	2	-
Petworth	16	4	11	3	6	4
Barlavington	-	-	2	1	1	1
Tillington	24	1	15	1	10	1

[Arundel Rape Schedule No 2 continued]

Parishes	No of Persons appointed for the removal of horses and waggons conveying such Persons as are unable to remove themselves	No of Overseers appointed to Superintend this Service	No of Persons appointed for the Removal of Cattle	No of Overseers for the same	No of Persons appointed for the Removal of Sheep and other Live Stock	No of Overseers for the same
Kirdford	4	1	4	1	4	1
Northchapel	21	1	21	1	20	1
Lurgashall	5	1	5	1	7	1
Stopham	5	1	4	1	4	1
Burton	-	-	1	-	1	-
Sutton	2	1	9	1	6	1
Egdean	6	1	3	1	3	1
Duncton	3	1	5	1	6	1
Woollavington	7	-	4	-	4	-
Amberley	3	1	13	2	5	2
Parham	1	-	1	-	1	-
Gritham	1	3	3	1	3	1
Pulborough	8	1	10	1	5	1
Billingshurst	3	1	4	1	6	1
Wiggenholt	1	1	2	-	2	1
Storrington	3	1	2	5	5	2
West Chiltington	4	1	7	2	7	2
Bury	6	1	6	2	7	4
Coldwaltham	2	1	3	1	3	1
Fittleworth	2	1	12	2	13	1
Hardham	2	1	4	1	4	1
Coates	2	1	1	-	1	-
Bignor	5	1	5	1	-	1
Wisborough Green	25	4	31	6	35	7
Houghton	5	1	9	1	5	1
[Totals]	298*	65	311†	67‡	256**	65

* error: should read 299
† error: should read 308
‡ error: should read 66
** error: should read 277

Arundel Rape Schedule No 3

Parishes	No of Men willing to serve on Horseback	No of Men willing to serve on Foot	Cavalry Swords	Cavalry Pistols	Infantry Firelocks	Infantry Pitchforks	Persons to be provided with arms at the place of General Assembly
Southstoke							
Madehurst	-	4	-	-	4	-	4
Binsted							
Middleton							
Tortington							
Ford							
Yapton	8	43	-	-	-	-	51
Barnham	-	13	-	-	12	1	-
Climping	-	3	-	-	3	-	3
Felpham							
Walberton	9	37	4	3	15	-	-
Eastergate	-	11	-	-	-	-	11
Northstoke							
Leominster							
Angmering		59	-	-	8	-	51
Kingston	3	1	-	-	-	-	4
Rustington	3	-	-	-	-	-	3
Ferring	1	3	1	1	3	-	3
Poling	-	2	-	-	-	-	2
Burpham	-	5	-	-	5	-	5
Goring	4	-	-	-	-	-	4
Warningcamp							
Preston	-	5	-	-	2	2	3
Littlehampton	9	26	9	21	7	6	-
Arundell Borough	9	55	1	1	5	4	53
Petworth	3	173	-	-	-	-	176
Barlavington	-	3	-	-	-	-	3
Tillington	7	-	-	-	5	2	-

[Arundel Rape Schedule No 3 continued]

Parishes	No of Men willing to serve on Horseback	No of Men willing to serve on Foot	Cavalry Swords	Cavalry Pistols	Infantry Firelocks	Infantry Pitchforks	Persons to be provided with arms at the place of General Assembly
Kirdford	10	37	-	-	5	-	43
Northchapel	1	7	1	-	7	-	2
Lurgashall	-	13	-	-	-	-	13
Stopham	2	10	-	-	-	-	12
Burton							
Sutton	-	1	-	-	1	-	-
Egdean							
Duncton	-	12	-	-	-	-	12
Woollavington	2	25	1	1	7	18	-
Amberley	-	14	-	-	10	3	1
Parham	1	9	-	-	4	-	6
Gritham							
Pulborough	10	78	12	-	48	3	88
Billingshurst							
Wiggenholt							
Storrington	11	15	3	5	18	3	-
West Chiltington	3	24	4	-	20	3	-
Bury	-	10	-	-	-	-	-
Coldwaltham	-	6	-	-	-	-	-
Fittleworth	1	36	1	1	35	-	34
Hardham	-	1	-	-	-	-	1
Coates							
Bignor	-	8	-	-	8	-	-
Wisborough Green	-	34	-	-	34	-	34
Houghton	2	8	2	2	8	-	10
[Totals]	99	791	39	35	274	45	656*

* error: should read 632

Arundel Rape Schedule No 4

Parishes	No of Men willing to serve as Pioneers or Labourers	Felling Axes	Pick Axes	Spades	Shovels	Bill Hooks	Saws	Hd Bills	Axes
Southstoke	9	3	4	4	1	2	2	-	-
Madehurst	10	-	7	2	-	-	1	-	-
Binsted									
Middleton	5	1	4	4	1	-	-	-	-
Tortington	3	1	1	2	1	-	-	-	-
Ford	3	-	3	2	-	-	-	-	-
Yapton	22	15	11	21	9	18	29	-	-
Barnham	2	-	-	-	-	1	1	-	-
Climping	23	3	8	9	5	-	3	-	-
Felpham	32	6	17	12	8	-	5	-	-
Walberton	36	4	26	8	22	2	5	-	-
Eastergate	8	6	1	1	-	-	-	-	-
Northstoke									
Leominster	45	3	14	14	9	2	5	-	-
Angmering	39	15	8	7	7	1	3	-	-
Kingston	4	-	2	1	1	-	-	-	-
Rustington	6	-	2	4	-	-	1	-	-
Ferring	42	1	5	24	9	-	3	-	-
Poling	3	3	-	-	-	-	3	-	-
Burpham	25	5	6	7	2	1	4	-	-
Goring	35	6	6	5	5	7	4	-	-
Warningcamp	1	1	-	-	-	-	1	-	-
Preston	14	1	1	5	3	1	1	-	-
Littlehampton	7	2	2	3	2	-	1	-	-
Arundel Borough	73	3	25	7	4	35	35	-	-
Petworth	233	70	78	107	60	35	83	28	-
Barlavington	6	-	2	2	1	-	1	-	-
Tillington	61	7	19	18	5	5	1	-	-

Implements they can bring

[Arundel Rape Schedule No 4 continued]

Parishes	No of Men willing to serve as Pioneers or Labourers	Felling Axes	Pick Axes	Spades	Shovels	Bill Hooks	Saws	Hd Bills	Axes
Kirdford	234	76	46	49	17	13	24	-	-
Northchapel	86	75	6	1	-	-	2	-	-
Lurgashall	25	9	7	2	3	-	2	-	-
Stopham	2	2	-	-	-	-	-	-	-
Burton									
Sutton	15	2	-	4	-	8	1	-	-
Egdean									
Duncton	14	2	4	3	4	1	-	-	-
Woollavington	7	2	2	1	-	-	1	-	2
Amberley	18	3	5	5	2	1	2	-	-
Parham									
Gritham									
Pulborough	64	11	19	17	8	1	7	-	-
Billingshurst									
Wiggenholt									
Storrington	66	21	10	19	10	-	9	-	-
West Chiltington	39	9	5	10	2	4	9	-	-
Bury	20	11	11	17	12	3	7	-	-
Coldwaltham	7	-	1	7	-	-	-	-	-
Fittleworth	37	7	10	7	5	4	4	-	-
Hardham	2	-	1	1	-	-	-	-	-
Coates	2	1	1	-	-	-	-	-	-
Bignor	5	2	1	4	-	1	3	-	-
Wisborough Green	73	24	12	19	5	2	7	-	-
Houghton	8	1	3	-	2	1	1	-	-
[Totals]	1471	413*	396	435	225	149	271	28	2

* error: should read 414

Arundel Rape Schedule No 6

Parishes	No of persons who are willing to provide waggons etc accord to the 1st Art. of the Plan for Waggons	Number of Waggons Four Horses or more Tilt	Number of Waggons Four Horses or more NT	Number of Waggons Three Horses T	Number of Waggons Three Horses NT	Number of Carts Three Horses or more T	Number of Carts Three Horses or more NT	Number of Carts 2 Horses T	Number of Carts 2 Horses NT	No of Persons appd to act as Servants with Teams	No of conductors for the same in proportion of one to every Ten Waggons	No of General Agents to whom Requisition is to be made to call for Waggons or Carriages
Southstoke												
Madehurst												
Binsted												
Middleton												
Tortington	1	-	-	5								
Ford	1	-	2	-	-	-	-	-	-	5		
Yapton										14		
Barnham	4	-	6	-	-	-	-	-	-	7	-	1
Climping												
Felpham												
Walberton	4	-	7	-	9	-	1	-	8	11	2	1
Eastergate										6		
Northstoke	1	-	5	-	-	-	-	1	-	10	-	-
Leominster												
Angmering	10	-	10	-	1	-	-	-	-	17	1	1
Kingston												
Rustington	11	-	21	-	2	-	27	-	-	10	2	-
Ferring												
Poling	5	-	5	-	2	-	-	-	-	8	1	1
Burpham												
Goring	-	-	-	-	-	-	-	-	-	7	-	-
Warningcamp												
Preston	6	-	-	-	4	-	-	-	2	6	-	-
Littlehampton	4	-	5	-	-	-	-	-	-	7	-	-
Arundel Boro	6	-	8	-	-	-	-	-	-	8	1	1
Petworth	-	-	22	-	1	-	-	-	1	-	-	-
Barlavington	2	-	2	-	-	-	-	-	1	4	-	-
Tillington	6	1	6	-	-	-	-	-	-	-	-	1

[Arundel Rape Schedule No 6 continued]

Parishes	No of persons who are willing to provide waggons etc accord to the 1st Art. of the Plan for Waggons	Number of Waggons Four Horses or more Tilt	Number of Waggons Four Horses or more NT	Number of Waggons Three Horses T	Number of Waggons Three Horses NT	Number of Carts Three Horses or more T	Number of Carts Three Horses or more NT	Number of Carts 2 Horses T	Number of Carts 2 Horses NT	No of Persons appd to act as Servants with Teams	No of conductors for the same in proportion of one to every Ten Waggons	No of General Agents to whom Requisition is to be made to call for Waggons or Carriages
Kirdford	25	-	21	-	7	-	1	-	-	46	-	-
Northchapel	18	-	18	-	-	-	1	-	1	25	2	1
Lurgashall	7	-	5	-	-	-	-	-	2	12	-	-
Stopham												
Burton	1	1	-	-	-	-	-	-	-	1	-	-
Sutton	4	-	3	1	-	1	-	1	-	12	-	-
Egdean	4	-	3	-	2	-	-	1	-	6	1	-
Duncton	4	-	5	-	1	-	-	1	-	8	1	1
Woollavington	1	-	1	-	1	-	-	-	-	-	-	-
Amberley	13	-	11	-	3	-	-	-	-	15	2	1
Parham	2	-	3	-	-	-	-	-	-	2	-	1
Gritham												
Pulborough												
Billingshurst	3	-	3	-	-	-	-	-	1	4	-	-
Wiggenholt	1	-	1	-	-	-	-	-	1	4	-	-
Storrington	23	-	13	-	-	-	-	-	17	24	3	-
West Chiltington	20	-	14	-	7-	-	1	-	3	24	2	1
Bury												
Coldwaltham	3	-	3	-	-	-	-	-	-	3	1	1
Fittleworth	12	-	13	-	-	-	-	-	1	18	2	1
Hardham												
Coates	1	-	1	-	1	-	-	-	-	-	-	-
Bignor												
Wisborough Green	10	-	8	-	-	-	-	-	2	18	1	1
Houghton												
[Totals]	213	2	225	6	41	1	31	4	40	342	22	15*

* error: should read 14

Arundel Rape Schedule No 7

Parishes	No of Subscribers or Undertakers to deliver certain Quantities of Flour etc	No of Water Mills	No of Wind Mills	No of Sacks of Flour of 280 lbs nett each to be furnished every 24 Hours	No of Subscribers who will or will not provide Wheat Yes	No of Subscribers who will or will not provide Wheat No
Southstoke						
Madehurst						
Binsted						
Middleton						
Tortington						
Ford						
Yapton						
Barnham						
Climping						
Felpham	2	-	2	7	-	-
Walberton	2	-	2	-	-	-
Eastergate						
Northstoke	1	-	1	-	-	-
Leominster	1	-	-	-	-	-
Angmering	2 no Cloths		2	-	-	2
Kingston						
Rustington	1 no Cloth	-	1	4	-	1
Ferring	1 no Cloth	-	1	-	-	1
Poling						
Burpham						
Goring						
Warningcamp						
Preston						
Littlehampton	1	-	1	2	-	1
Arundel Boro	2 (1 no Cloth)	1	1	35	-	2
Petworth	1	1	-	20	-	1
Barlavington						
Tillington						

[Arundel Rape Schedule No 7 continued]

Parishes	No of Subscribers or Undertakers to deliver certain Quantities of Flour etc	No of Water Mills	No of Wind Mills	No of Sacks of Flour of 280 lbs nett each to be furnished every 24 Hours	No of Subscribers who will or will not provide Wheat Yes	No
Kirdford	1	1	-	8	-	1
Northchapel	1	-	1	-	-	-
Lurgashall	1	1	-	6	-	1
Stopham						
Burton	1	1	-	14	-	1
Sutton						
Egdean						
Duncton	1 no Cloth	1	-	5	-	1
Woollavington	2 no Cloth	2	-	13	2	-
Amberley	1 no Cloth	1	-	1	1	-
Parham						
Gritham						
Pulborough						
Billingshurst						
Wiggenholt						
Storrington	2	2	-	14	2	-
West Chiltington						
Bury	1 no Cloth	1	-	8	-	1
Coldwaltham						
Fittleworth	2	2	-	42	2	-
Hardham						
Coates						
Bignor	1 no Cloth	1	-	-	-	-
Wisborough green	1	1	-	-	-	-
Houghton						
[Totals]	18 with Cloth 11 no Cloth	16	12	179	7	13

Arundel Rape Schedule No 8

Parishes	No of Subscribers who engage to deliver certain Quantities of Bread	No of Loaves of 3 lbs to be furnished by each subscriber every 24 Hours - By their usual number of Hands - For a constancy	On an Emergency	By the help of aditional Journeymen for a constancy	How many addl Journeymen	For what kind of fuel the Ovens are Calculated - Wood	Furze	What Quanty is required every 24 Hours	What. Fuel is abundant	What. Fuel is not abundant
Southstoke										
Madehurst										
Binsted										
Middleton										
Tortington										
Ford										
Yapton	2	174	348	-	-	2	-	236 fagg	-	No
Barnham										
Climping										
Felpham										
Walberton										
Eastergate	3	100	-	-	-	3		36 fagg	Yes	-
Northstoke										
Leominster										
Angmering										
Kingston										
Rustington										
Ferring	1	24					1	-	-	No
Poling										
Burpham										
Goring										
Warningcamp										
Preston										
Littlehampton	3	96	168	264	4	3	-	60 fagg	-	No
Arundel Boro	7	1020	1310	1660	6	7	-	134 Do	Yes	
Petworth	1	-	400	-	-	1	-	12 Do	-	No
Barlavington										
Tillington	3	301								

[Arundel Rape Schedule No 8 continued]

Parishes	No of Subscribers who engage to deliver certain Quantities of Bread	No of Loaves of 3 lbs to be furnished by each subscriber every 24 Hours			How many addl Journeymen	For what kind of fuel the Ovens are Calculated		What Quanty is required every 24 Hours	What. Fuel is abundant	What. Fuel is not abundant
		By their usual number of Hands									
		For a constancy	On an Emergency	By the help of aditional Journeymen for a constancy		Wood	Furze			
Kirdford	2	240	-	-	-	1	-	25 Do	-	No
Northchapel	2	288	-	-	-	-	-	-	Yes	-
Lurgashall	4	297	-	-	-	1	-	43 Do	Yes	-
Stopham										
Burton										
Sutton										
Egdean										
Duncton										
Woollavington										
Amberley	2	71	-	-	-	1	-	-	Yes	-
Parham										
Gritham										
Pulborough	2	72	-	-	-	1	-	-	-	No
Billingshurst	1	50	-	100	1	1	-	-	Yes	-
Wiggenholt										
Storrington	13	984	-	-	-	1	-	-	-	No
West Chiltington										
Bury	1	24	39	-	-	1	-	-	-	No
Coldwaltham										
Fittleworth	2	120								
Hardham										
Coates										
Bignor										
Wisborough Green	3	270	-	-	-	1	-	40 Do	Yes	-
Houghton										
[Totals]	52	4131	2265	2024	11	24	1	3861 Faggots	7	8

Arundel Rape Schedule No 9

Parishes	No of Boats	Tonnage	Decked	Not Decked	Remarks
Southstoke					
Madehurst					
Binsted					
Middleton					
Tortington					
Ford					
Yapton					
Barnham					
Climping					
Felpham					
Walberton					
Eastergate					
Northstoke					
Leominster					
Angmering					
Kingston					
Rustington					
Ferring					
Poling					
Burpham					
Goring					
Warningcamp					
Preston	2	6	-	2	
Littlehampton	11				
Arundel Boro	15	266	3	12	
Petworth	8	16	-	8	4 Boats belonging to Hardham, 1 to Stopham & 3 to Pulborough
Barlavington					
Tillington					

[Arundel Rape Schedule No 9 continued]

Parishes	No of Boats	Tonnage	Decked	Not Decked	Remarks
Kirdford					
Northchapel					
Lurgashall					
Stopham	2	54	2		
Burton					
Sutton					
Egdean					
Duncton					
Woollavington					
Amberley					
Parham					
Gritham					
Pulborough	5	171	-	5	
Billingshurst					
Wiggenholt					
Storrington					
West Chiltington					
Bury					
Coldwaltham					
Fittleworth					
Hardham	3	77	-	3	
Coates					
Bignor					
Wisborough Green	13	304	-	13	2 belong to Arundel, 1 to Leominster and 10 to Wisborough Green
Houghton	4				
[Totals]	63	894	5	43	

Bramber Rape Schedule No 1

	Live Stock							Horses					
	Draught oxen	Fatting oxen	Cows	Young cattle and Colts	Sheep	Goats	Hogs and Pease [sic]	Draft	Ridings	Waggons	Carts	Vans	Deer
Lancing	8	49	56	27	3542	-	309	78	19	30	44		
Sompting	43	-	44	21	3032	-	185	56	15	20	29		
Broadwater	22	4	55	50	3000	-	250	87	20	25	56		
Clapham	35	2	29	35	3895	-	181	43	9	12	19		
Findon	35	-	34	14	5302	-	200	52	21	19	24		
Durrington	-	-	20	16	1123	-	139	25	4	8	11		
Heene	14	1	12	10	480	-	91	14	3	6	10		
Warminghurst	-	19	22	61	113	-	83	31	9	9	12		
Thakeham	6	6	68	150	305	-	315	73	8	20	8		
Itchingfield	2	8	57	143	210	-	158	54	1	21	25		
Sullington	35	17	39	55	1560	-	154	43	8	12	18		
Old Shoreham	23	-	16	-	2551	-	92	26	9	8	15		
Kingston by Sea	12	-	2	-	1200	-	40	7	2	3	6		
Southwick	18	-	11	-	1887	-	102	36	10	12	20		
Beeding upper	31	112	68	37	4685	-	218	58	11	24	34		
Beeding lower	6	-	52	85	1185	-	143	77	5	26	33	-	58
Ifield	20	40	104	211	516	-	321	111	16	50	55	3	-
Edburton	10	-	12	15	671	-	30	11	5	4	5		
Warnham	41	37	123	186	592	-	293	106	10	54	57		
Rusper	-	5	79	140	60	-	144	63	4	23	17		
Nuthurst	-	8	102	169	811	-	289	91	1	38	54		
Washington	45	5	67	78	2762	-	189	84	12	26	38		
Wiston	29	24	63	120	1728	-	118	48	12	21	31	-	450
Buttolphs	18	9	7	23	1535	-	33	7	2	3	5		

[Bramber Rape Schedule No 1 continued]

	\multicolumn{6}{c}{Live Stock}	\multicolumn{2}{c}{Horses}				
	Draught oxen	Fatting oxen	Cows	Young cattle and Colts	Sheep	Goats	Hogs and Pease [sic]	Draft	Ridings	Waggons	Carts	Vans	Deer
Combe	20	-	10	14	1744	-	82	12	1	4	5		
Ashington	9	5	33	95	261	-	98	40	6	11	17		
Ashurst	-	65	84	189	629	-	253	67	13	25	36		
Shipley	8	86	183	464	909	8	589	184	23	80	89		
Westgrinstead	-	106	56	378	1115	-	363	144	23	70	73		
Henfield	33	115	190	179	2405	-	487	148	20	54	81		
Woodmancote	47	58	40	99	922	-	106	48	10	20	28		
Albourne	30	28	46	72	795	-	37	37	7	15	17		
Cowfold	10	62	107	250	519	-	298	114	12	51	57		
Shermanbury	-	53	49	85	343	-	106	43	6	25	25		
Steyning	44	154	74	109	3076	-	166	94	19	24	41		
Horsham	54	26	355	415	2057	4	871	326	67	117	144		
Patching	-	-	18	3	1050	-	115	20	3	4	6		
Bramber	17	-	11	12	1188	-	55	9	2	3	4		
Tarring	8	-	18	2	934	-	190	61	11	19	29		
New Shoreham	-	-	10	-	20	-	109	20	16	3	20		
Slinfold	30	43	102	256	561	-	293	109	50	18	62		
Rudgwick	36	48	141	223	486	-	432	149	20	63	71		
[Totals]	799	1195	2769	4491	61759	12	8727	2906	493*	1112†	1431	3	508

* error: should read 525
† error: should read 1080

Bramber Rape Schedule No 2

	No of Persons appointed for the removal of horses and waggons conveying such Persons as are unable to remove themselves	No of Overseers appointed to Superintend this Service	No of Persons appointed for the Removal of Cattle	No of Overseers for the same	No of Persons appointed for the Removal of Sheep and other Live Stock	No of Overseers for the same
Lancing	1	1	3	2	6	1
Sompting	7	4	6	3	7	3
Broadwater	20	8	20	2	14	2
Clapham	8	1	4	1	4	1
Findon	10	3	19	3	19	3
Durrington	7	1	9	1	4	1
Heene	4	1	4	1	2	1
Warminghurst	2	1	4	1	3	1
Thakeham	8	1	7	1	7	1
Itchingfield	6	6	6	6	6	6
Sullington	8	2	19	2	6	2
Old Shoreham	2	1	7	2	7	2
Kingston by Sea	2	1	5	1	2	1
Southwick	4	1	5	2	7	2
Beeding upper	1	1	12	2	10	1
Beeding lower	19	-	3	-	3	-
Ifield	10	4	10	4	10	4
Edburton	4	2	3	1	2	1
Warnham	2	1	3	2	2	1
Rusper	15	2	3	1	3	1
Nuthurst	8	2	8	4	9	1
Washington	22	2	11	1	10	1
Wiston	4	1	10	1	1	1
Buttolphs	2	1	3	1	3	1

[Bramber Rape Schedule No 2 continued]

	No of Persons appointed for the removal of horses and waggons conveying such Persons as are unable to remove themselves	No of Overseers appointed to Superintend this Service	No of Persons appointed for the Removal of Cattle	No of Overseers for the same	No of Persons appointed for the Removal of Sheep and other Live Stock	No of Overseers for the same
Combe	3	1	2	1	5	1
Ashington	2	1	2	2	2	1
Ashurst	31	3	7	3	6	3
Shipley	3	2	33	6	33	6
Westgrinstead	8	4	21	7	20	6
Henfield	5	1	1	1	3	1
Woodmancote	2	1	9	2	5	2
Albourne	14	1	2	2	2	1
Cowfold	12	3	9	2	5	2
Shermanbury	2	2	3	2	3	1
Steyning	22	2	26	2	24	2
Horsham	6	4	26	6	11	5
Patching	4	1	3	1	3	1
Bramber	4	2	4	3	2	2
Tarring	12	4	7	3	14	2
New Shoreham	8	2	3	1	5	2
Slinfold	17	3	10	2	9	2
Rudgwick	13	2	12	2	5	2
[Totals]	334*	87	364	93	304	81

* error: should read 344

Bramber Rape Schedule No 3

Parishes	No of persons	On Horseback	On Foot	Swords (Cavalry)	Pistols (Cavalry)	Firelocks (Infantry)	Pitchforks (Infantry)	Persons to be provided with arms at the place of General Assembly	Remarks
Lancing	11	4	7	1	4	7	-	-	
Sompting	-	-	-	-	-	-	-	-	No return
Broadwater	46	6	40	6	-	40	-	-	
Clapham	-	-	-	-	-	-	-	-	No return
Findon	7	4	3	4	4	2	1	-	
Durrington	9	-	9	-	-	9	-	-	
Heene	-	-	-	-	-	-	-	-	No return
Warminghurst	7	-	7	-	-	7	-	-	
Thakeham	14	1	13	1	-	13	-	-	
Itchingfield	-	-	-	-	-	-	-	-	No return
Sullington	5	5	-	5	5	-	-	-	Three have horses but no arms
Old Shoreham	4	4	-	4	4	-	-	-	No horses or arms
Kingston by Sea	-	-	-	-	-	-	-	-	No return
Southwick	-	-	-	-	-	-	-	-	Do have entered as Pioneers and Drivers in Schedule 4
Beeding upper	13	-	6	2	2	5	6	-	
Beeding lower	4	4	-	4	4	-	-	-	
Ifield	4	1	3	-	-	3	-	-	No arms
Edburton	-	-	-	-	-	-	-	-	No return
Warnham	37	2	-	5	6	7	25	-	
Rusper	4	-	4	-	-	4	-	-	
Nuthurst	-	-	-	-	-	-	-	-	No return
Washington	15	-	15	-	-	15	-	-	*
Wiston	15	1	12	1	1	11	1	-	
Buttolphs	-	-	-	-	-	-	-	-	No return

*[Remark] Jus[t] having Firelocks and those not being provided with moulds for Balls it will be necessary for them to be provided with Arms at the place of General Assembly

[Bramber Rape Schedule No 3 continued]

Parishes	No of persons	On Horseback	On Foot	Swords (Cavalry)	Pistols (Cavalry)	Firelocks (Infantry)	Pitchforks (Infantry)	Persons to be provided with arms at the place of General Assembly	Remarks
Combe	-	-	-	-	-	-	-	-	No return
Ashington	5	-	5	-	-	5	-	-	
Ashurst	1	1	-	1	1				*
Shipley	37	-	10	-	-	15	23	-	
Westgrinstead	14	3	2	1	-	8	3	-	
Henfield	4	-	-	-	-	3	1	-	
Woodmancote	6	-	6	-	-	6	-	-	
Albourne	-	-	-	-	-	-	-	-	No return
Cowfold	32	6	21	-	-	2	1	-	The Cavalry can find their own horses
Shermanbury	-	-	-	-	-	-	-	-	No return
Steyning	107	31	76	31	31	76	-	-	
Horsham	40	11	29	-	-	29	-	-	
Patching	-	-	-	-	-	-	-	-	No return
Bramber	-	-	-	-	-	-	-	-	No return
Tarring	28	7	19	7	7	19	2	-	
New Shoreham	26	1	25	2	-	26	-	-	The Cavalry man has no horse
Slinfold	55	25	15	25	25	23	7	-	
Rudgwick	46	1	45	1	1	30	14	-	
[Totals]	596	118	372	101	95	365	84	-	†

* [Remark] No other person wishes to know the Use of Arms but in Case of Invasion would all willingly assist

† [Remark] NB Horses Arms and Accoutrements will be wanting for the whole except 9 persons who can find their own Horses

Bramber Rape Schedule No 4

Parishes	No of Persons	Felling Axes	Pick Axes	Spades	Shovels	Bill Hooks	Saws	Hand Bills	Scythes	Hatchets	Pikes	Spades	Mattocks	Remarks
Lancing	43	7	18	17	19	1	8	-		-	-	-	-	
Sompting	63	10	16	20	13	3	3	-		-	-	-	-	
Broadwater	32	6	6	6	3	1	10	-		-	-	-	-	
Clapham	34	4	3	6	3	2	-	-		-	-	-	-	
Findon	25	11	8	14	9	-	11	-		-	-	-	-	
Durrington	9	-	2	2	1	-	1	-		-	-	-	-	
Heene	11	-	3	4	3	1	-	-		-	-	-	-	
Warminghurst	2	-	2	-	-	-	-	-		-	-	-	-	
Thakeham	23	4	8	4	3	-	4	-		-	-	-	-	
Itchingfield	9	-	3	1	1	1	5	-		-	-	-	-	
Sullington	5	2	-	1	1	-	2	-		-	-	-	-	
Old Shoreham	5	-	-	3	2	-	-	-		-	-	-	-	
Kingston by Sea	6	-	-	3	1	1	2	-		-	-	-	-	
Southwick	12	7	-	1	3	-	7	-		-	-	-	-	
Beeding upper	14	5	9	3	1	-	3	-		-	-	-	-	
Beeding lower	-	-	-	-	-	-	-	-		-	-	-	-	No return
Ifield	11	5	2	4	4	2	3	-		-	-	-	-	
Edburton	6	1	1	1	1	1	1	-		-	-	-	-	
Warnham	90	33	6	19	6	18	8	-		-	-	-	-	
Rusper	5	-	3	2	-	-	1	-		-	-	-	-	
Nuthurst	50	7	10	8	3	4	16	1	1	-	-	-	-	*
Washington	52	13	23	5	8	2	2	-		1	-	-	-	
Wiston	6	8	7	5	5	2	6	-		-	-	-	-	
Buttolphs	2	2	2	-	-	-	-	-		-	-	-	-	

* [Remark] William and Henry Woolver refuse to act in any capacity whatever, & Hugh Alexander except on Board a Man of War

[Bramber Rape Schedule No 4 continued]

Parishes	No of Persons	Felling Axes	Pick Axes	Spades	Shovels	Bill Hooks	Saws	Hand Bills	Scythes	Hatchets	Pikes	Spades	Mattocks	Remarks
Combe	-	-	-	-	-	-	-	-	-	-	-	-	-	No return
Ashington	7	1	1	2	1	-	2	-	-	-	-	-	-	
Ashurst	30	28	27	28	27	27	20	-	-	-	-	-	-	
Shipley	61	20	16	8	6	7	5	-	-	-	-	-	-	*
Westgrinstead	74	27	11	19	4	9	5	-	-	-	-	-	-	
Henfield	-	-	-	-	-	-	-	-	-	-	-	-	-	No return
Woodmancote	15	4	1	4	1	3	2	-	-	-	-	-	-	
Albourne	25	6	12	15	5	5	5	-	-	-	-	-	-	
Cowfold	25	9	2	4	-	-	7	-	-	-	-	-	-	
Shermanbury	2	-	1	-	-	-	1	-	-	-	-	-	-	
Steyning	54	1	11	-	-	-	1	-	-	-	41	-	-	
Horsham	62	7	4	4	-	1	-	-	-	-	-	-	-	
Patching	16	4	3	3	-	3	3	-	-	-	-	-	-	
Bramber	-	-	-	-	-	-	-	-	-	-	-	-	-	No return
Tarring	13	3	6	7	6	-	4	-	-	-	-	-	-	
New Shoreham	11	11	5	-	4	-	10	-	-	-	-	-	-	
Slinfold	32	15	7	2	3	2	3	-	-	-	-	-	-	
Rudgwick	60	22	8	6	5	4	16	1	2	4	-	1	1	
[Totals]	1002	283	247	231	152	100	177	2	3	5	41	1	1	

For any other instrument the Pioneers may engage to bring

* [Remark] Henry Charman and John Penfold refuse to Act in any capacity whatsoever

Bramber Rape Schedule No 6

Subscribers names		Number of Waggons with tilts and		Number of Carts with tilts and		No of Persons appointed to act as Servants with Teams	Conductors for the same in proportion of 1 to every 10 Waggons	Names of General Agents	Remarks
		Four Horses or more	Three Horses	Three Horses or more	2 Horses				
Lancing	12	NT 20	-	-	-	22	2	1	
Sompting	11	Do 12	-	NT 2	NT 2	13	2	1	
Broadwater	25	Do 9	NT 8	-	Do 6	5	7	2	
Clapham	5	Do 11	Do 4	-	Do 1	8	1	2	
Findon	5	Do 7	-	Do 1	Do 2	15	-	-	
Durrington	4	Do 2	Do 4	-	Do 2	4	1	1	
Heene	2	Do 1	Do 2	-	-	2	-	1	
Warminghurst	4	Do 4	-	-	Do 3	5	-	-	
Thakeham	12	13	3	-	-	17	2	1	
Itchingfield	-	-	-	-	-	-	-	-	No return
Sullington	7	Do 7	Do 1	-	1	10	2	-	
Old Shoreham	4	Do 4	-	1	2	11	1	-	
Kingston by Sea	1	-	Do 3	-	Do 1	3	-	1	
Southwick	2	-	Do 6	-	Do 8	11	2	1	
Beeding upper	8	Do 8	-	Do 1	Do 2	14	2	1	
Beeding lower	13	Do 12	Do 5	-	Do 7	23	-	-	
Ifield	20	Do 7	Do 2	1	Do 5	25	2	1	
Edburton	1	-	Do 1	-	-	1	-	-	
Warnham	24	Do 9	Do 19	-	Do 5	56	-	-	
Rusper	16	Do 12	Do 3	-	Do 3	18	2	1	
Nuthurst	13	Do 9	Do 1	Do 1	Do 3	16	2	-	
Washington	18	Do 12	Do 4	-	Do 7	23	2	2	
Wiston	9	Do 9	-	-	-	9	1	1	
Buttolphs	1	Do 1	-	-	Do 1	1	-	1	

[Bramber Rape Schedule No 6 continued]

Subscribers names		Number of Waggons with tilts and		Number of Carts with tilts and		No of Persons appointed to act as Servants with Teams	Conductors for the same in proportion of 1 to every 10 Waggons	Names of General Agents	Remarks
		Four Horses or more	Three Horses	Three Horses or more	2 Horses				
Combe	1	Do 3	-	-	-	-	-	-	
Ashington	9	Do 6	Do 2	-	Do 1	9	1	1	
Ashurst	19	Do 2	Do 17	-	Do 2	29	2	1	*
Shipley	36	Do 29	-	Do 5	Do 12	38	3	-	
Westgrinstead	29	Do 17	Do 8	-	Do 4	50	3	-	
Henfield	3	-	3	-	4	4	3	1	
Woodmancote	6	8	3	-	-	11	1	1	
Albourne	8	Do 5	Do 4	-	Do 1	13	1	2	Will assist
Cowfold	9	Do 11	-	-	-	22	1	1	
Shermanbury	10	Do 8	-	-	Do 2	8	1	1	
Steyning	13	13	2	-	3	10	-	-	
Horsham	6	Do 1	Do 3 with T 4	-	-	6	2	1	
Patching	4	Do 5	-	-	-	3	-	-	
Bramber	1	Do 1	NT 1	-	-	-	-	-	
Tarring	-	-	-	-	-	-	-	-	Nobody would subscribe
New Shoreham	6	Do 2	-	-	3	2	-	-	
Slinfold	21	-	NT 22	-	13	17	3	1	
Rudgwick	9	Do 4	Do 4	-	3	10	-	-	
[Totals]	1277?	294	139	12	115†	540‡	51**	27‡‡	

* [Remark] All agree to find any Quantity of Wheat Oats Hay and Straw they may have to spare
? column total is 407
† error: should read 109
‡ error: should read 544
** error: should read 52
‡‡ error: should read 28

Bramber Rape Schedule No 7

Subscribers	Names	Names and situations of Water Mills	Names and situations of Wind Mills	No of Sacks of Flour of 280 lbs nett each to be furnished by each Miller every 24 Hours	Will the Subscribers provide the Wheat or not Answer yes or no
Lancing	1 no Cloth		1 Lancing	8	No
Sompting	None	-	1 Offington Hill	5 at Mill	No
Broadwater	1 no Cloth				
Clapham	None				
Findon	Do				
Durrington	1		1 Durrington		No
Heene	None				
Warminghurst	Do				
Thakeham	Do				
Itchingfield	Do				
Sullington		There are 4 Mills in this Parish but owing to the smallness of the Streams they with difficulty can supply their regular customers			
Old Shoreham	1 no Cloth		Old Shoreham	1 at the Mill	No
Kingston by Sea	None				
Southwick	1		1 near Southwick	7 at the Mill	No
Beeding upper	1		1 Beeding Mill	12 Do	Yes
Beeding lower		1 Bewbush Grist Mill		None	
Ifield	1 no Cloth	1 Ifield Mill		16	No
Edburton	None				
Warnham	None				
Rusper	Do	There's only 1 Mill in the parish & James Caffyn the miller says he can't engage to deliver any flour			
Nuthurst		Birchen Bridge in Nuthurst	Says it is a Toll Mill and nothing further		
Washington	1 no Cloth		1 Ashington	2	Yes
Wiston	None				
Buttolphs	Do				

1 Storming of the Bastille 14 July 1789

2 Charles Philip Yorke

3 Francis Newbery

4 Thomas Malthus

5 Edmund Burke

6 John Rickman

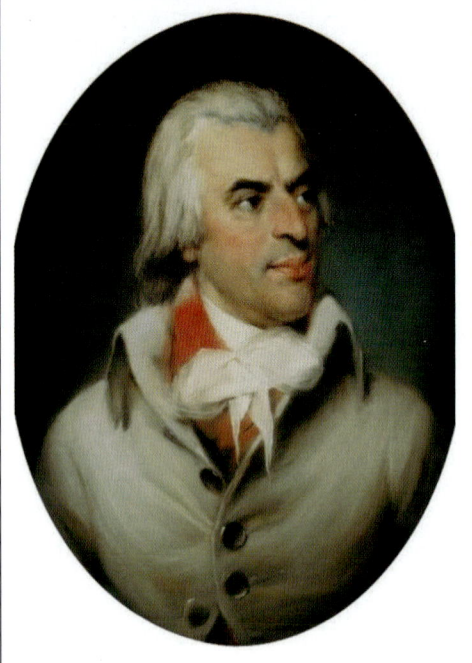

7 Arthur Young

8 Charles Goring

9 Charles Lennox 4th Duke

10 Sir Charles Merrik Burrell

11 George Wyndham Earl of Egremont

Bramber Schedule.

Names of Hundreds and Parishes	No. of Men and Boys between the ages of 15 and 60 who are capable of active service	No. of Men and Boys between the ages of 15 and 60 who are incapable of active service	No. of Men above the age of 60 who are capable of active service	No. of Men above the age of 60 who are incapable of active service	No. of Men above the age of 60 capable of carrying Musquets	No. of Men above the age of 60 incapable of carrying the Musquet
H.d Brightford						
Lancing	116	5	2	7	.	5
Sompting	80	2	4	4	4	1
Broadwater	205	4	13	5	7	9
Clapham	56	.	.	.	.	7
Findon	27	6	1	11	5	2
Durrington	36	6	.	2	2	.
Heene	27	1	3	.	.	2
H.d Easeswrith						
Warminghurst	8	1	..	.	2	.
Itchingfield	50	2	2	9	9	1
Shakeham	6	.	.	2	2	5
Sullington	69	3	2	9	3	6
H.d Fishersgate						
Old Shoreham	50	3	3	3	.	.
Kingstonby Sea	24					
Southwick	40	0	.	12	9	7
H.d Burbeach						
Beedingupper st.	57	10	2	2	1	5
Beedinglower st.	57	.	.	.	2	1
Shield	30	3	10	1	16	3
Edburton	14	2	.	1	1	.
H.d Singlecross						
Warnham	178	7	.	.	14	8
Rusper	104	5	.	.	13	5
Slinfurst	80	4	1	.	8	5

Bramber Rape Schedule No 1 1801 cf. pp. 90-91

Rape —
No. 1.

No. of Women or Girls above 7 years of age who are capable of conveying themselves	No. of Women or Girls above 7 years of age who are not capable of carrying themselves and of women who having Christians at the breast must be carried with such Children	No. of Boys under 7 years of Age	No. of Girls under 7 years of Age	No. of Persons serving in Yeomanry or Volunteer Corps of Infantry &c. distinguishing which	Horses	Oxen	No. of Boys between the ages of 7 and 16
128	34	74	56	....	.	2	40
136	13	30	50	1 Cavalry	.	.	.
239	20	125	122	6 Do	.	.	.
54	6	26	23	....	.	.	.
121	35	24	27	1 Do	.	.	.
32	16	30	15	----	.	.	.
24	11	12	10	----	.	.	.
26	12	12	11	.	.	.	.
65	31	21	22	.	.	.	25
39	25	29	29	1 Do	.	.	.
75	16	19	18	1 Do	.	.	.
60	4	16	20	Cav. 2 & 1 Fenc.	.	.	10
25	1	9	6	----	.	.	.
63	33	30	24	..	.	2	.
66	40	37	30	.	.	.	.
70	6	10	12	.	.	.	10
65	16	59	25	2 Cav	.	9	.
29	6	11	12	.	.	.	.
220	39	64	65	1 Guide	..	..	76
112	70	32	27	----	..	..	29
90	54	53	55	..	.	.	..

Bramber

Hundreds (and) Parishes	Fatting Oxen	Cows	Steers, Heifers and Calves	Colts	Sheep	Lambs	Hogs	Sows	Pigs	Riding Horses	Waggons	Carts
Brightford H.d												
Lancing	24	67	13	3	1637	209	141	33	06	21	26	43
Sompting	3	34	29	4	1570	160	00	20	02	11	17	20
Broadwater	9	70	27	14	1410	657	230	26	147	27	33	65
Clapham	.	20	19	3	2052	1017	06	14	15	4	15	20
Findon	.	31	17	4	2192	605	09	16	00	10	20	27
Durrington	.	14	10	.	555	314	30	9	30	5	0	10
Kerne	3	9	5	.	207	06	44	7	35	3	5	0
Easwrith H.d												
Warminghurst	25	22	56	4	77	.	36	0	36	9	10	12
Ichingfield	17	61	133	10	226	05	52	14	106	6	25	29
Thakeham	19	66	126	6	164	.	129	12	106	10	22	34
Sullington	8	40	50	2	720	159	99	10	50	11	16	22
Fishersgate H.d												
Old Shoreham	.	20	.	.	1405	637	05	0	20	11	10	15
Kingston by Sea	2	3	.	.	630	265	6	2	37	2	4	6
Southwick	.	9	2	.	1126	240	73	13	75	9	10	26
Burbeach H.d												
Woodmancote	125	00	117	12	2060	544	73	12	102	13	23	32
Edingworth	.	30	42	1	1357	..	99	1	.	7	19	24
Ifield	25	06	124	5	140	60	84	10	02	10	42	44
Edburton	2	10	20	4	500	200	45	2	11	4	6	7

Bramber Rape Schedule No 2 1801 cf. pp. 94-95

Rape 2.

Waggons Carts or Carriages with the No of Horses or Oxen required to draw them			Corn Mills			Ovens					
other Carriages	Draft Horses	Draft Oxen	Wind	Water	Quantity of Corn they can grind in 24 Hours	Bakers	Private	Quant. of Bread they can bake in 24 Hours	No. of Forages	No. of Boats	No. of Barges	No. of Deer
1	103	0	1	.	60	.	52	124	1	1	.
3	40	36	.	.	.	1	47	193	.	.	.
13	115	20	1	.	28d	6	57	271	.	30	.
.	44	30	.	.	.	.	6	17	.	.	.
5	64	26	.	.	.	2	40	152	.	.	.
10	16	.	.	.	.	.	20	440	.	.	.
1	13	10	.	.	.	.	10	20	.	.	.
1	31	.	.	.	.	.	14	96	.	.	.
2	59	.	.	.	.	.	44	100	.	.	.
9	76	6	.	.	.	.	49	176½	.	.	.
.	39	37	1	2	32d	.	30	78½	.	.	.
4	20	26	1	.	15qu	2	19	324	1	.	.
1	7	14	.	.	.	.	0	22	.	.	.
2	20	22	1	.	96	.	24	96	.	2	.
1	57	20	1	.	102qu	.	26	65	2	.	9
2	60	.	.	1	100	.	32	67	1	1	.
9	102	10	.	.	.	1	10	.	.	.	.
1	10	16	.	.	.	.	20	46	.	.	.

12 Inigo Freeman Thomas

13 Gen Sir James Murray Pulteney

14 John Baker Holroyd Earl of Sheffield

15 John ('Mad Jack') Fuller

16 Sir George Shiffner

17 Sir Timothy Shelley

18 Thomas Davis Lamb

19 Thomas Pelham Earl of Chichester

20 William Stephen Poyntz

21 Gen Sir David Dundas

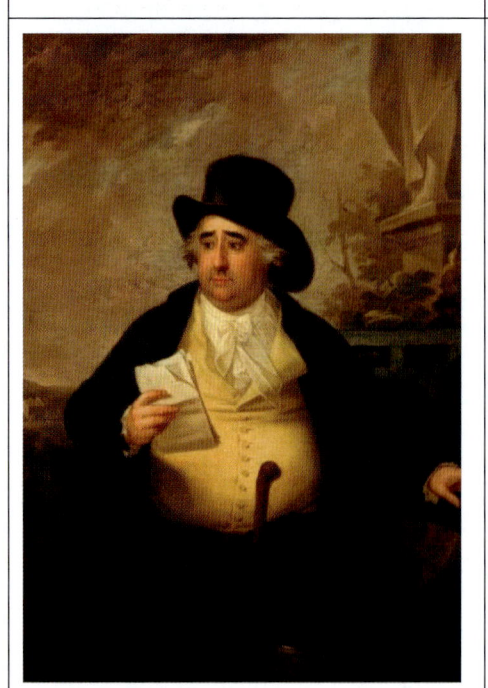

22 Charles James Fox

23 William Pitt the Younger

24 Charles Abbot Baron Colchester

25 Sir John Leach

26 Thomas Partington

27 William Frankland

28 Sir Henry Dundas

29 Henry Addington

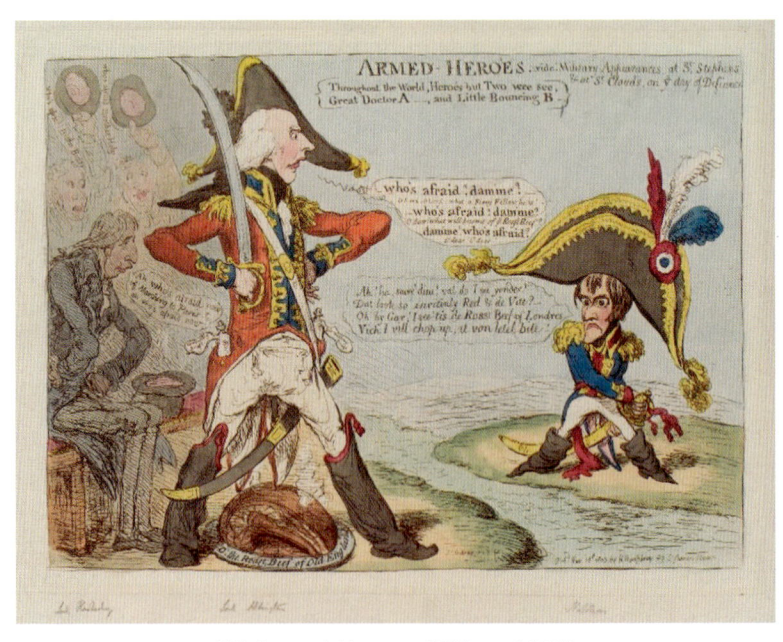

30 Armed Heroes (Gillray 1803)
Hawkesbury (L) and Addington (C) confronting Napoléon

[Bramber Rape Schedule No 7 continued]

Subscribers	Names	Names and situations of Water Mills	Names and situations of Wind Mills	No of Sacks of Flour of 280 lbs nett each to be furnished by each Miller every 24 Hours	Will the Subscribers provide the Wheat or not Answer yes or no
Combe	Do				
Ashington	None				
Ashurst	1		1 Ashurst near Wappingthorn	Willing to supply what flour he may have in hand to spare	
Shipley	2 no Cloth	1 Knep in Shipley	1 Bayley in Shipley	2 sack the Water Mill	No
Westgrinstead	None				
Henfield	Do				
Woodmancote	Do				
Albourne	Do				
Cowfold	1 no Cloth	1 Gose Dean in Cowfold		10 Sacks	No
Shermanbury	1	1 Shermanbury		Can't tell	No
Steyning	2	2 Steyning	1 Steyning	8 sack	Yes
Horsham	3	2 Warnham & Horsham Town Mill	1 Smock Mill on Horsham Common	1 each water mill 3 windmill	Yes
Patching	None				
Bramber	None				
Tarring	Do				
New Shoreham	Do				
Slinfold	1		1 Rough Hook in Slinfold	12 sacks fair wind	Yes
Rudgwick	2 at the Mill	1 Wandford and 1 Gibbins	1 near Rudgwick Street	23 Sacks & 10 gallons each a week	No
[Totals]	21	16	13		

Bramber Rape Schedule No 8

No of Subscribers Names*		No of Loaves of 3 lbs to be furnished by each subscriber every 24 Hours			No of addl Journeymen	For what kind of fuel the Ovens are Calculated	What Quanty is required every 24 Hours to keep each overn constantly at work supposing 6 batches to be baked	Whether. Fuel is abundant or not abundant	Remarks
		By their usual number of Hands		By the help of aditional Journeymen for a constancy					
		For a constancy	On an Emergency						
Lancing	none	-	-	-	-	-	-	-	
Sompting	Do	-	-	-	-	-	-	-	No baker in the Parish
Broadwater	4	560	840	1750	7	Coal Furzes and wood	6 Bu of coal	No	
Clapham	none	-	-	-	-	-	-	-	Do
Findon	Do	-	-	-	-	-	-	-	Do
Durrington	Do	-	-	-	-	-	-	-	Do
Heene	Do	-	-	-	-	-	-	-	Do
Warminghurst	Do	-	-	-	-	-	-	-	Do
Thakeham	Do	-	-	-	-	-	-	-	Do
Itchingfield	1	83	-	-	-	Faggots	6 Faggots	No	Do
Sullington	none	-	-	-	-	-	-	-	
Old Shoreham	2	-	78	-	-	Wood	12 Do	No	
Kingston by Sea	none	-	-	-	-	-	-	-	Do about 12 vacant ovens
Southwick	1	144	not more	-	-	Faggots Furze	6 Bu coals	Yes	25 small vacant ovens
Beeding upper	1	208	-	-	2	Wood	30 Faggots	Do	
Beeding lower	none								
Ifield	2	120	170	760	3	Wood & Faggots	10½ Do	No	70 ovens in use by private families
Edburton	none	-	-	-	-	-	-	-	
Warnham	none	-	-	-	-	-	-	-	No Baker for sale
Rusper	Do	-	-	-	-	-	-	-	
Nuthurst	Do	-	-	-	-	-	-	-	
Washington	1	150	200	350	2	Wood	12 Faggots	No	
Wiston	none	-	-	-	-	-	-	-	
Buttolphs	Do	-	-	-	-	-	-	-	

* Distinguishing the vacant ovens at the Foot of the List

[Bramber Rape Schedule No 8 continued]

	No of Subscribers Names*	No of Loaves of 3 lbs to be furnished by each subscriber every 24 Hours By their usual number of Hands For a constancy	On an Emergency	By the help of aditional Journeymen for a constancy	No of addl Journeymen	For what kind of fuel the Ovens are Calculated	What Quantity is required every 24 hours to keep each oven constantly at work supposing 6 batches to be baked	Whether Fuel is abundant or not	Remarks
Combe	Do	-	-	-	-	-	-	-	
Ashington	Do	-	-	-	-	-	-	-	
Ashurst	1	170	-	-	-	Lash Faggots	8 Do	Yes	
Shipley	Do	-	-	-	-	-	-	-	
Westgrinstead	Do	-	-	-	-	-	-	-	
Henfield	Do	-	-	-	-	-	-	-	
Woodmancote	Do	-	-	-	-	-	-	-	
Albourne	Do	-	-	-	-	-	-	-	
Cowfold	Do	-	-	-	-	-	-	-	
Shermanbury	Do	-	-	-	-	-	-	-	
Steyning	4	1344	-	-	-	-	-	No	Are willing to provide as much flour as they can probably about 70 bushells
Horsham	4	1400	-	-	4	3 wood & 1 coal	12 faggots 1½ bushells coal	Yes	
Patching	none	-	-	-	-	-	-	-	
Bramber	Do	-	-	-	-	-	-	-	
Tarring	2	360	-	-	3	Wood	15 bushells	Yes	
New Shoreham	3	850	1700	4	9	Coals & Wood	2 bushells coal 6 faggots	1 Yes 2 No	
Slinfold	2	170	190	-	4	Wood	7½ faggots	No	
Rudgwick	none	-	-	-	-	-	-	-	
[Totals]	28	5559	3178	2864	34	-	-	-	

Bramber Rape Schedule No 9

Parish	No of Proprietors	Proprietors Residence	Names of the Masters	Masters Residence	Parish District or Hundred to which the craft belongs	In what county	No or name of the craft	Tonnage	Whether decked or not	River or canal on which employed	Place to which the craft usually trades
Lancing	none										
Sompting	Do										
Broadwater	5	Worthing & Broadwater		-	Broadwater in Brightford Hundred	Sussex	Fishing boat	2 each	Yes	At sea	On the sea coast
Clapham	none										
Findon	Do										
Durrington	Do										
Heene	Do										
Warminghurst	Do										
Thakeham	Do										
Itchingfield	Do										
Sullington	Do										
Old Shoreham	Do										
Kingston by Sea	Do										
Southwick	2	Southwick		2	Southwick ½ Hundred Fishersgate	Sussex	none	none	no	River Adur	*
Beeding upper	4	Beeding		-	- Beeding	Sussex	4 1 3 2	36 14 26 22	no	Beeding river	
Beeding lower	none										
Ifield	Do										
Edburton	Do										
Warnham	Do										
Rusper	Do										
Nuthurst	Do										
Washington	Do										
Wiston	Do										
Buttolphs	Do										

* They have each a small boat able to convey 12 men in the river

[Bramber Rape Schedule No 9 continued]

	No of Proprietors	Proprietors Residence	Names of the Masters	Masters Residence	Parish District or Hundred to which the craft belongs	In what county	No or name of the craft	Tonnage	Whether decked or not	River or canal on which employed	Place to which the craft usually trades
Combe		Do									
Ashington		Do									
Ashurst		Do									
Shipley		Do									
Westgrinstead		Do									
Henfield	3	Henfield	3	Henfield	Henfied	Do	2 1 2	25 11 24	No	River Adur	To Shoreham
Woodmancote		none									
Albourne		Do									
Cowfold		Do									
Shermanbury		Do									
Steyning	2	Steyning	2	Steyning	Steyning	Do	-	10 ea	Do	Beeding river	To Do & Moat bridge
Horsham		none									
Patching		none									
Bramber	1	Bramber	1	Bramber	Bramber	Do	3 Barges	10 ea			
Shoreham	1	Shoreham	2	Do	Do	Do	-	15 18 14	Do	River Adur	To Shoreham
Mouscombe	1	Mouscombe	1	Do	Do	Do	-	-	-		
Tarring		none									
New Shoreham	2	New Shoreham	3	Bramber & Shoreham	Shoreham	Do	7 craft total one	90 7	Do	Do	
Slinfold		none									
Rudgwick		Do									
[Totals]	21	-	14					362			

Lewes Rape Schedule No 1 [Southern Division]

Parishes	Draught oxen	Fatting oxen	Cows	Young cattle and Colts	Sheep	Goats	Hogs and Pigs	Draft [Horses]	Riding [Horses]	Waggons	Carts
Saint Peter & St Mary Westout	8	-	23	8	1312	-	76	31	12	6	19
St Michaels	-	-	9	-	-	-	61	29	33	3	4
St John under the Castle	45	6	52	11	3442	-	197	42	15	15	21
All Saints	-	-	14	19	30	-	117	25	24	4	11
Southover	6	2	37	32	20	-	151	15	13	3	11
Kingston	38	-	14	-	2200	-	119	16	2	7	16
Iford	40	12	30	170	3973	-	113	20	7	11	16
Rodmell*	56	27	43	28	3070	-	161	26	10	14	23
Newhaven	22	3	13	3	2032	-	183	31	16	8	20
Piddinghoe	40	-	9	9	4189	-	121	20	4	14	18
Southease	28	-	30	17	1400	-	55	18	1	7	14
Telscombe	-	-	2	2	1791	-	44	22	2	8	12
Hamsey	39	27	59	76	3367	1	162	51	22	25	30
Barcombe	104	17	110	247	881	-	332	86	11	44	58
Chiltington	37	28	68	46	2640	1	125	40	12	17	32
Plumpton	26	15	54	56	1477	-	83	43	4	10	15
Chailey	62	17	150	198	722	-	353	112	19	42	57
Newick	50	-	68	129	469	-	245	52	14	26	39
Wivelsfield	36	8	85	121	555	-	248	78	10	28	43
Street	36	12	53	40	1213	-	101	17	6	8	13
Westmeston	36	29	48	34	1463	-	104	26	8	11	17
Ditchelling	20	63	81	82	4456	-	214	88	15	32	44
Keymer	37	42	118	113	1499	-	267	89	12	31	54
Newtimber	22	-	19	27	2760	-	97	16	10	11	19
Poynings	24	-	12	33	1510	-	125	28	4	7	13
Fulking	28	4	24	55	1920	-	56	18	3	8	8
Hurstpierpoint	46	68	130	132	1657	2	306	137	30	57	66

* [Remark] of the 14 Waggons returned for Rodmell 5 are constructed to be drawn by Oxen and 9 by Horses

[Lewes Rape Schedule No 1 continued [Southern Division]]

Southern Division Parishes	Live Stock							Draft [Horses]	Riding [Horses]	Waggons	Carts
	Draught oxen	Fatting oxen	Cows	Young cattle and Colts	Sheep	Goats	Hogs and Pigs				
Clayton	20	3	59	104	717	-	162	60	8	18	31
Piecomb	33	-	8	-	2910	-	60	16	4	7	9
Preston	24	-	27	1	2830	-	111	27	6	7	18
Patcham	42	-	12	1	6593	-	86	49	6	11	10
Hove	-	-	16	2	750	-	87	18	8	6	11
Portslade	12	-	27	6	2737	-	234	40	11	12	25
Westblatchington	10	-	1	3	1607	-	31	9	2	4	7
Hangleton	4	-	2	1	2450	-	34	22	2	8	13
Brighthelmston	-	-	52	3	2840	6	526	217	79	29	105
Rottingdean	12	6	12	3	5738	-	226	58	21	21	32
Ovingdean	4	-	5	-	2300	-	60	16	5	7	9
Falmer	24	-	13	4	6182	-	237	47	10	16	25
Hanmer	-	-	-	-	-	-	-	-	-	-	-
[Totals]	1071	389	1589	1816	87702	10	6070	1755	481	603	988

Lewes Rape Schedule No 2 [Southern Division]

Southern Division	No of Persons appointed for the removal of horses and waggons conveying such Persons as are unable to remove themselves	No of Overseers appointed to Superintend this Service	No of Persons appointed for the Removal of Cattle	No of Overseers for the same	No of Persons appointed for the Removal of Sheep and other Live Stock	No of Overseers for the same
Saint Peter & St Mary Westout*	11	2	2	1	9	1
St Michaels	5	1	-	-	2	1
St John under the Castle	26	2	2	1	8	1
All Saints	6	8	3	1	3	2
Southover	8	1	12	1	7	1
Kingston	4	1	3	1	5	1
Iford	9	2	11	2	10	2
Rodmell	14	2	11	2	11	2
Newhaven	6	1	6	1	8	2
Piddinghoe	11	1	5	1	10	2
Southease	6	1	2	1	8	1
Telscombe	5	2	1	-	4	1
Hamsey	24	1	5	1	4	1
Barcombe†	5	1	18	1	7	1
Chiltington	4	1	7	1	1	-
Plumpton	14	1	7	1	11	1
Chailey	2	1	2	1	3	1
Newick	16	2	8	2	6	2
Wivelsfield	20	1	13	1	14	1
Street	20	2	5	1	10	1
Westmeston	22	2	6	2	12	2
Ditchelling	16	1	12	1	10	2

* [Remark] Upon a computation it appears that this Parish has about 180 Persons unable to remove themselves and therefore will require draft Oxen or Horses for 4 Waggons

† [Remark] There are many persons in this Parish who have offered their Services in those Capacities but are not at present wanted

[Lewes Rape Schedule No 2 continued [Southern Division]]

Southern Division	No of Persons appointed for the removal of horses and waggons conveying such Persons as are unable to remove themselves	No of Overseers appointed to Superintend this Service	No of Persons appointed for the Removal of Cattle	No of Overseers for the same	No of Persons appointed for the Removal of Sheep and other Live Stock	No of Overseers for the same
Keymer	19	2	16	2	9	2
Newtimber	7	1	5	1	5	1
Poynings	6	1	5	1	6	1
Fulking	3	1	3	1	3	1
Hurstpierpoint	35	3	27	2	5	2
Clayton	2	1	15	1	15	1
Piecomb	7	1	3	1	4	1
Preston	5	1	2	1	3	1
Patcham	11	1	2	1	14	1
Hove	3	1	1	1	2	1
Portslade	11	1	3	1	7	1
Westblatchington	3	1	5	1	5	1
Hangleton	-	-	5	1	6	1
Brighthelmston	18	4	5	2	4	1
Rottingdean	15	4	13	2	15	2
Ovingdean	11	1	1	-	5	1
Falmer	27	2	5	2	13	3
Hanmer	-	-	-	-	-	-
[Totals]	437	63	257	45	284	51

Lewes Rape Schedule No 3 [Southern Division]

Southern Division Parishes	No of persons in each Parish between the ages of 15 and 60 willing to serve with arms and who will agree to assemble for troops or companies under such persons from the neighbourhood	On Horseback	On Foot	Cavalry — Swords	Cavalry — Pistols	Infantry — Firelocks	Infantry — Pitchforks	Persons to be provided with arms at the place of General Assembly
Saint Peter & St Mary Westout	29	1	28	-	2	4	6	18
St Michael	41	4	37	9	2	6	4	36
St John	104	4	100	-	-	-	-	104
All Saints	138	7	131	11	71	111	11	108
Southover	10	2	8	-	-	-	-	10
Kingston	2	-	2	-	-	2	-	-
Iford	4	-	4	-	-	-	-	4
Rodmell	20	-	20	-	-	-	-	20
Newhaven	11	5	6	7	16	8	2	-
Piddinghoe	-	-	-	-	-	-	-	-
Southease	-	-	-	-	-	-	-	-
Telscomb	9	-	9	-	-	-	-	9
Hamsey	19	3	16	2	2	12	9	7
Barcomb	38	3	35	3	3	34	1	-
Chiltington	27	5	22	5	5	2	-	20
Plumpton	-	-	-	-	-	-	-	-
Chailey	10	4	6	4	4	5	1	-
Newick	No special return made							
Wivelsfield	3	-	3	-	-	-	-	3
Street	No offers made from this Parish of Men willing							
Westmeston	No offers made from this Parish of Men willing to							
Ditchelling	2	2	-	-	-	-	-	1

Remarks
There are in this Parish 19 persons who offered their Services as Driving of Cattle Sheep Waggons &c but who at Present are not wanted in those Capacities, appointments having been made as per Schedule 2
Thomas Blair MD offered to serve as a Physician to the Army in this Division
The Swords Pistols and Firelocks returned in this Parish arise chiefly from Mr Weston a Gunsmith who has offered his services
This is a very small Parish
Do
There are a number of persons returned from this Parish, but the whole except the aforesaid are stated to have Engaged in the Corps of Coast of Artillery and Sea Fencible
There is a bridge in this Parish over the River Ouse for Waggons to pass and repass situated about 3 miles North of Newhaven and by which Artillery may be Transported from the Downs east and West of the River
The Return of this Parish is that there are no persons willing to serve with Arms
The General Remark on this Schedule as returned is that the Subscribers in General are willing to come forth in any capacity
to serve with Arms there being not more than will be sufficient to attend to Waggons and Cattle
serve with Arms the Parish being very small & the whole men and boys appointed to Waggons and Cattle

[Lewes Rape Schedule No 3 continued [Southern Division]]

Southern Division Parishes	No of persons in each Parish between the ages of 15 and 60 willing to serve with arms and who will agree to assemble for troops or companies under such persons from the neighbourhood	On Horseback	On Foot	Cavalry Swords	Cavalry Pistols	Infantry Firelocks	Infantry Pitchforks	Persons to be provided with arms at the place of General Assembly
Keymer	\multicolumn{8}{l}{No offers made from this Parish of Men willing to}								
Newtimber	12	-	12	-	-	-	12	-
Poynings	10	-	10	-	-	6	30	-
Fulking	2	-	2	-	-	-	-	2
Hurstpierpoint	25	-	25	-	-	18	-	8
Clayton	11	1	10	1	-	10	-	-
Piecomb	No persons in this Parish to serve								
Preston	13	-	13	-	-	4	3	6
Patcham	3	0	3	-	-	1	2	-
Hove	6	1	5	1	-	-	-	5
Portslade	22	-	22	-	-	-	-	22
Westblatchington	There is only one Farm in the Parish consequently								
Hangleton	2	-	2	-	-	2	-	-
Brighthelmston	276	11	265	9	10	8	1	264
Rottingdean	18	9	9	7	7	1	3	6
Ovingdean	-	-	-	-	-	-	-	-
Falmer	-	-	-	-	-	-	-	-
Hanmer	-	-	-	-	-	-	-	-
[Totals]	867	62	805	59	122	235*	85	653

NB The service required of such as turn out Volunteers being but ill understood by the People in the different Parishes during the Time that the Schedules were preparing, the Number stated in the Southern Division of Lewes Rape appears very small but since the Schedules have been delivered the offers have encreased very considerably and are still encreasing so that the Deputy Lieutenants are convinced the Number of Volunteers will be very large in a short period.

* error: should read 234

Remarks
Serve with Arms but a Remark is made that as there is an Act passing for the Enforcing to Assemble to Exercise they have not returned the Few who offered, who wait further Instructions and their Particulars
no more pesons than required for the Duty specified in Schedule 2
no more persons in this Parish than will be required to drive Cattle Sheep &c
no more persons in this Parish than will be required to drive Cattle Sheep &c

Lewes Rape Schedule No 4 [Southern Division]

No of Districts in which the said Parishes are classed	No of Parishes in each such District and within the said Division	No of Persons willing to act as Pioneers & Labourers	Felling Axes	Pick Axes	Spades	Shovels	Bill Hooks	Saws	Other implements they can bring	Remarks
No 1	Saint Peter & St Mary Westout	12	4	2	6	5	2	7		
	St Michael	44	4	-	1	1	1	9		
	St John	10	7	1	6	7	7	14	2 Prongs	
	All Saints	43	11	6	11	4	2	14		*
2	Southover	15	13	2	-	2	-	11		
	Kingston	6	3	-	3	1	-	2		
	Iford	2	1	-	1	-	-	1		
	Rodmell	2	-	2	-	2	-	-		
3	Newhaven	31	7	3	12	13	-	7		
	Piddinghoe	15	4	2	9	2	0	6		
	Southease	2	2	-	-	-	-	-		
	Telscomb	5	1	2	2	1	3	2		
4	Hamsey	18	6	6	3	1	-	2		
	Barcomb	12	11	1	-	-	10	1		
	Chiltington	16	5	1	4	-	2	2	2 Hatchets	
	Plumpton	17	5	9	12	4	-	1		
5	Chailey	11	2	3	2	2	-	2		†
	Newick	10	7	2	5	2	2	7		‡
	Wivelsfield	8	5	3	-	3	-	-		

* [Remark] Besides the foregoing implements returned for the Parish of All Saints Mr A Wilds a Builder who has returned himself a pioneer & artificer can furnish numerous other implements and will be a most useful Member to Head a Body of Pioneers a service he will most readily undertake if necessary

† [Remark] The Inhabitants in General seem willing to act in any Capacity when called upon

‡ [Remark] All willing to come forward in any Capacity if required when they are likely to be of most service

[Lewes Rape Schedule No 4 continued [Southern Division]]

No of Districts in which the said Parishes are classed	No of Parishes in each such District and within the said Division	No of Persons willing to act as Pioneers & Labourers	Felling Axes	Pick Axes	Spades	Shovels	Bill Hooks	Saws	Other implements they can bring	Remarks
6	Street	No offer made from this Parish of men to act as Pioneers or Labourers there being an insufficient number to attend Waggons and Cattle							
	Westmeston	1	1	-	1	-	-	1		
	Ditchelling	8	-	3	2	3	-	-		
	Keymer	No offer made from this Parish of men to act as Pioneers or Labourers, there is however a Remark returned that the Inhabitants wish to know under whom they are to Mass before they are set down							
7	Newtimber	5	5	5	5	5	5	5		
	Poynings	9	4	3	9	7	-	12		
	Fulking	14	3	2	3	2	2	2		
8	Hurstpierpoint	11	4	2	4	-	-	1		
	Clayton	19	6	2	8	1	-	3	3 Wheelbarrows	
	Piecomb	3	2	2	1	-	-	1		
9	Preston	9	-	1	4	2	1	1		
	Patcham	20	2	7	3	2	2	4		
	Hove	17	2	1	5	7	1	7	4 Pitchforks	
10	Portslade	12	1	-	4	-	1	5	1 Mattock	
	Westchiltington*	9	-	3	3	3	-	-		
	Hangleton	-	-	-	-	-	-	-		
11	Brighthelmstone	59	13	8	3	6	-	18	3 Pitchforks	
12	Rottingdean	36	3	4	7	7	2	4		†
	Ovingdean	-	-	-	-	-	-	-		‡
	Falmer	-	-	-	-	-	-	-		
	Hanmer	-	-	-	-	-	-	-		
	[Totals]									

* error: Westchiltington should read West Blatchington

† [Remark] No more in this Parish than will be required to Drive Sheep Cattle &c

‡ [Remark] No more in this Parish than will be required to Drive Sheep Cattle &c

Lewes Rape Schedule No 6 [Southern Division]

No of District in which the several Parishes are Classed	Names of Parishes in each District and within the said Division	Names of persons in each such Parish who agree to furnish Waggons Carts Horses and also Flour Wheat &c as above	Number of Waggons with tilts and		Number of Carts with tilts and	
			Four Horses or more	Three Horses	Three Horses or more	2 Horses
No 1	Saint Peter & St Mary Westout	-	-	-	-	-
	St Michael	John Shelley Thomas Tourle Esq John Verrell Richard Combes Esq Robert Cooper Christopher Chitty James William Camp William Pettitt John Duplock Richard Ashley John Dennett Edward Weller	3 Tilts 1 Tilted	2 no Tilt 1 no Tilt 1 no Tilt 1 no Tilt	1 cart 2 Horses no Tilt 1 cart 1 Horse Tilted 1 cart 1 Horse no Tilt 1 cart 1 Horse no Tilt 1 cart 1 Horse no Tilt 1 cart 1 Horse no Tilt	
	All Saints	-	-	-	-	-
2	Southover	William Verrell Joseph Fuller Colonel Newton	1 no Tilt		1 Cart 1 Horse no Tilt 1 Cart 1 Horse no Tilt	
	Kingston	-	-		-	
	Iford	-	-		-	
	Rodmell	-				
	Newhaven	Joseph Thomset James Carter Edward Dean Messrs Vine & Brook Lucy Balcombe George Elphick		2 no Tilt 1 no Tilt 2 no Tilt		1 no Tilt 1 no Tilt 1 no Tilt w 1 Horse

Number of persons appointed to act as Servants with Teams	Names of conductors for the same in proportion of 1 to every 10 Waggons	Names of General Agents for the said Parishes to whom requisition is to be made to call forth the Carts or Waggons	Remarks
-	-	No subscription in this Parish their [sic] not being more Waggons than sufficient to conduct the ordinary business	
	John Shelley	John Shelley	These three Waggons are public carriage Waggons capable of carrying a very considerable Weight & Bulk if laden full they will require 8 Horses each
	Christopher Chitty		Christopher Chitty
		Edward Wellers 4 Horse Waggon offered has a Tilt and is a public carriage Waggon capable of carrying a considerable Weight & Bulk if laden full they will require 8 Horses	
		No Waggon or Carts in the Parish capable of Service	
William Simmonds A William Acton James Edwards William Duplock		William Verrell	
There are only 4 Teams of Horses within this Parish for all purposes not more than Suffice for the Ordinary business consequently none do offer			
There are only 5 Teams of Horses within this Parish for all purposes not more than Suffice for the Ordinary business consequently none do offer			
There is in this Parish only 26 Draft Horses although there are 14 Waggons returned as per Schedule 1 of which No 5 are constructed to be drawn by Oxen and 9 by Horses no Offer made on account of the small number of Draft Horses			
		George Elphick	

[Lewes Rape Schedule No 6 continued [Southern Division]]

No of District in which the several Parishes are Classed	Names of Parishes in each District and within the said Division	Names of persons in each such Parish who agree to furnish Waggons Carts Horses and also Flour Wheat &c as above	Number of Waggons with tilts and Four Horses or more	Number of Waggons with tilts and Three Horses	Number of Carts with tilts and Three Horses or more	Number of Carts with tilts and 2 Horses
3	Piddinghoe	Francis Winton Sarah Elmes T Faulconer	2 no Tilt 2 no Tilt 8 no Tilt	-	-	-
	Southease	William Knight Tourle Henry Webb William Knight Tourle James Wenham James Kent	1 no Tilt 3 no Tilt 1 no Tilt 2 no Tilt 1 no Tilt			
	Telscombe	Thomas Roswell John Martin Richard Hobden William Bussby	1 no Tilt 1 no Tilt 1 no Tilt 1 no Tilt			
4	Hamsey	George Shiffner Esq Richard Knight James Andrews Thomas Ellis Mrs Berry	1 no Tilt 1 no Tilt 1 no Tilt 1 no Tilt 1 no Tilt			
	Barcombe	George Verrall Thomas Rickman William Kenward Joseph Smith Mary Skinner Richard Attlee J Verrall Thomas Lucas Shadwell James Coppard William Roser Thomas P Brook Thomas Reed Thomas A Ball Benjamin Beal John Cheesman John Howell Thomas Wickens John Morley John Verrall	1 no Tilt 1 no Tilt 1 no Tilt 1 no Tilt 1 no Tilt 1 no Tilt 1 no Tilt 1 no Tilt 2 no Tilt 1 no Tilt		1 no Tilt 1 no Tilt 1 no Tilt 1 no Tilt 1 no Tilt 1 no Tilt 1 no Tilt 1 no Tilt	

Number of persons appointed to act as Servants with Teams	Names of conductors for the same in proportion of 1 to every 10 Waggons	Names of General Agents for the said Parishes to whom requisition is to be made to call forth the Carts or Waggons	Remarks
	Edmund Davey Jonton Waterman	Francis Winton	
		Henry Webb	
		Thomas Roswell	
	Henry Nye William Scrase John Smith Edward Holder Samuel Barber	Richard Knight	
1 no Tilt	Charles Foord William Chandler John Hollands Daniel Friend Thomas Gorringe James Hoadley Richard Hemsley Henry Phillips James Coppard Edward Roves Humphrey Hillman William Reed Thomas Harman snr Thomas Harman jnr Benjamin Beal John Bryant John Howell Thomas Wickens John Morley Richard Cox		

[Lewes Rape Schedule No 6 continued [Southern Division]]

No of District in which the several Parishes are Classed	Names of Parishes in each District and within the said Division	Names of persons in each such Parish who agree to furnish Waggons Carts Horses and also Flour Wheat &c as above	Number of Waggons with tilts and		Number of Carts with tilts and	
			Four Horses or more	Three Horses	Three Horses or more	2 Horses
4 [cont]	Chiltington	John Martin Cripps Esq		2 no Tilt		
	Plumpton	No Subscribers in this Parish. No reason assignd why				
5	Chailey	John Markwick Esq	1 no Tilt			1 no Tilt
		William Wicker	1 no Tilt			
		Benjamin Kemp Walls	1 no Tilt			
		John Shelley	1 no Tilt			
		Edward May				1 no Tilt
		Susan Morris		1 no Tilt		
		John Ingram	2 no Tilt			
		Benjamin Ridge	1 no Tilt			
		Richard Verrall	1 no Tilt			
		Thomas R Beard			1 no Tilt	
		T Jenner of Wapsbourne	1 no Tilt			
		T Jenner of Wars	1 no Tilt			
		Joseph Wakelin	1 no Tilt			
		Richard Hamshar	1 no Tilt			
		Revd H Poole	1 no Tilt			
	Newick	William Shirt	1 no Tilt			
		John Snashall	1 no Tilt			
		Thomas Johnson	1 no Tilt		1 no Tilt	
		Henry Harmer			1 with Tilt	
		James Hobbs				
6	Wivelsfield	No Subscribers in this Parish. The reason assigned that they have				
	Street	No Subsccribers in this Parish. The reason assigned is that they have				
	Westmeston	No Subscribers in this Parish. The reason assigned is that as there are only				

Number of persons appointed to act as Servants with Teams	Names of conductors for the same in proportion of 1 to every 10 Waggons	Names of General Agents for the said Parishes to whom requisition is to be made to call forth the Carts or Waggons	Remarks
Charles Holman John King	James Harland William Nye Philip Berry	Thomas Blackman	
2 app not named 1 Do Do 1 Do Do 1 Do Do 1 Do Do 1 Do Do 2 Do Do 1 Do Do 1 Do Do 1 Do Do 1 Do Do 1 Do Do 1 Do Do 1 Do Do None appointed	Thomas Jenner of Wars & T R Beard		
Do Do Do Do Do			
not more than sufficient for the Ordinary Business			
no Waggon or Cart but such as will be required to remove Inhabitants			
9 Waggons the whole will be required for the removal of the Inhabitants and their Provisions			

[Lewes Rape Schedule No 6 continued [Southern Division]]

No of District in which the several Parishes are Classed	Names of Parishes in each District and within the said Division	Names of persons in each such Parish who agree to furnish Waggons Carts Horses and also Flour Wheat &c as above	Number of Waggons with tilts and Four Horses or more	Three Horses	Number of Carts with tilts and Three Horses or more	2 Horses
6	Ditcheling	John Bull	1 no Tilt			
		Stephen Martin		1 no Tilt		
		Messrs Caffyn & Foster	1 no Tilt		1 no Tilt	
		Thomas Privilly	1 no Tilt			
		Albert Smith				1 no Tilt
		Richard Hamshar	1 no Tilt			1 no Tilt
		Peter Rowland			1 no Tilt	
		Samuel Denman			1 no Tilt	
		John Borer jnr	1 no Tilt			
		Robert Chatfield	1 no Tilt		1 no Tilt	
		John Wood	1 no Tilt			
		John Wood	2 no Tilt			
		John Borer snr	1 no Tilt			
		Thomas Linfield		1 no Tilt		
		Anthony Tanner				1 no Tilt
		Thomas Herriott		1 no Tilt		
	Keymer	No Subscribers names returned from this Parish but the Schedules offers Neither any arrangement made as to appointment of Senior Conductors				
7	Newtimber	Revd William Tilt	3 no Tilt			
		Stephen Bine	2 no Tilt			
	Poynings Fulking	Thomas Whitcomb		1 no Tilt		
		John Osborne	2 no Tilt			
		Robert Gallup	4 no Tilt			
8	Hurstpierpoint	Revd Doctor Dodson				1 no Tilt
		H S Campion Esq	1 no Tilt	1 no Tilt		
		William Borer Esq	3 no Tilt			
		John Marchant	1 no Tilt			
		William Lindfield	2 no Tilt			
		William Jenner	1 no Tilt			
		Stephen Croskey	2 no Tilt			
		John Mitchell	1 no Tilt			
		John Batten		1 no Tilt		
		Anthony Ede			1 no Tilt	
		John Webber		2 no Tilt		
		George Bishop		1 no Tilt		1 no Tilt
		Henry Wickham	1 no Tilt			

Number of persons appointed to act as Servants with Teams	Names of conductors for the same in proportion of 1 to every 10 Waggons	Names of General Agents for the said Parishes to whom requisition is to be made to call forth the Carts or Waggons	Remarks
16 Persons appointed but not named	Henry Hubbard And Anthony Tanner	John Wood	

generally 21 without specifying particularly either as to Number of Horses or with or without Tilts or Agents			
3 appointed but not names appointed 4 Do		Stephen Bine	
2 Do 2 Do 8 Do	No conductor appointed	John Osborn	
1 Do 2 Do 4 Do 1 Do 2 Do 1 Do 2 Do 1 Do 1 Do 1 Do 2 Do 2 Do 1 Do	William Jenner John Mitchell	 John Marchant	

[Lewes Rape Schedule No 6 continued [Southern Division]]

No of District in which the several Parishes are Classed	Names of Parishes in each District and within the said Division	Names of persons in each such Parish who agree to furnish Waggons Carts Horses and also Flour Wheat &c as above	Number of Waggons with tilts and Four Horses or more	Three Horses	Number of Carts with tilts and Three Horses or more	2 Horses
8	Hurstpierpoint [cont]	William English				1 no Tilt
		William Sawyers	1 no Tilt			
		Edward Harland	1 no Tilt			
		John Geere		1 no Tilt		1 no Tilt
		J P Roberts		1 no Tilt		
		Thomas Wickham	1 no Tilt			
		William Marshall jnr	1 no Tilt			
		John Pratt	1 no Tilt			
		Thomas Pratt		1 no Tilt		
		Thomas King		1 no Tilt		
		Henry Hider	1 no Tilt			
		John Ashfold	1 no Tilt			
		James Harmer	1 no Tilt			
		William Goddard	1 no Tilt			
		John Coulstock	1 no Tilt			
		John Standen				1 no Tilt
		William Broomfield				1 no Tilt
		Henry Davey		2 no Tilt		
		Thomas Wadey		1 no Tilt		
		Thomas Pollard	1 no Tilt			
	Clayton	James Burtenshaw	1 no Tilt			
		John Bartley	1 no Tilt			
		William Ockenden	1 no Tilt			
		Thomas Kitchener	1 no Tilt			
		Nathaniel Helford	1 no Tilt			
		Mrs Tulley	1 no Tilt			
		John Broomfield	1 no Tilt			
		Herbert Brooker			1 no Tilt	
		John Busson	1 no Tilt			
		John Dennett	1 no Tilt			
		William Ede			1 no Tilt	
		Thomas Taley		1 no Tilt		
		John Godley	1 no Tilt			
	Piecomb	John Bull	1 no Tilt			
		Do	10 teams with Oxen			

Number of persons appointed to act as Servants with Teams	Names of conductors for the same in proportion of 1 to every 10 Waggons	Names of General Agents for the said Parishes to whom requisition is to be made to call forth the Carts or Waggons	Remarks
1 Do			
1 Do			
1 Do			
2 Do			
1 Do	James Harmer		
1 Do			
1 Do			
1 Do			
1 Do			
1 Do			
1 Do			
1 Do			
1 Do			
1 Do			
1 Do			
1 Do			
2 Do			
1 Do			
1 Do			
2 appointed but not named			
2 Do			
2 Do			
2 Do			
2 Do			
2 Do			
2 Do		George Webber	John Broomfield
1 Do			
2 Do			
2 Do			
1 Do			
1 Do			
2 Do			
Henry Burtenshaw William Harland	Thomas Hollands	John Bull jnr	

[Lewes Rape Schedule No 6 continued [Southern Division]]

No of District in which the several Parishes are Classed	Names of Parishes in each District and within the said Division	Names of persons in each such Parish who agree to furnish Waggons Carts Horses and also Flour Wheat &c as above	Number of Waggons with tilts and Four Horses or more	Number of Waggons with tilts and Three Horses	Number of Carts with tilts and Three Horses or more	Number of Carts with tilts and 2 Horses
9	Preston	The Offer made by this Parish is 5 Waggons 7 Carts but no Tilts on Horses					
	Patcham	B Tillston Esq	1 no Tilt			
		John Gree	1 no Tilt			
		Edward Sayers	1 no Tilt			
		John Hamshar	1 no Tilt			
	Hove	John Vallance		2 no Tilt		
		Messrs Vallance	2 no Tilt			
	Portslade	Robert Smith	1 no Tilt			
		R S Dyer		no Tilt		
10	West Chiltington*	There are no Waggons within this Parish that can be spared from the					
	Hangleton	No offers The Waggons and Carts being all required in the					
11	Brighthelmstone	William Wigney				2 no Tilt
		Messrs Vallances		2 one without Tilt		
		Messrs Hargrave Brown and Lashmar				1 no Tilt
		John Grenville	1 no Tilt		1 no Tilt	
		Thomas Pocock			1 no Tilt	
		John Pollard				1 no Tilt
		Richard Russell				1 no Tilt
		James Gregory	1 no Tilt			3 carts no Tilts or Horses
		Henry Hobdin		1 no Tilt		
		James Davidson	1 no Tilt			
		Francis Spratley			1 no Tilt	1 no Tilt

* error: West Chiltington should read West Blatchington

Number of persons appointed to act as Servants with Teams	Names of conductors for the same in proportion of 1 to every 10 Waggons	Names of General Agents for the said Parishes to whom requisition is to be made to call forth the Carts or Waggons	Remarks
and the Subscribers Names not inserted			
William Gregory Wiliam Hobbs Thomas Marchant Charles Cutress Thomas Barber John Ashdown & [?] Johnson	None appointed	Edward Sayers	
3 not named	John Sturt	John Vallance	
2 Do			
Ordinary business			
Ordinary business			
2 Do 2 Do 1 Do 2 Do 1 Do 1 Do 1 Do 3 Do 2 Do 1 Do 1 Do	None appointed	William Wigney	

[Lewes Rape Schedule No 6 continued [Southern Division]]

No of District in which the several Parishes are Classed	Names of Parishes in each District and within the said Division	Names of persons in each such Parish who agree to furnish Waggons Carts Horses and also Flour Wheat &c as above	Number of Waggons with tilts and Four Horses or more	Number of Waggons with tilts and Three Horses	Number of Carts with tilts and Three Horses or more	2 Horses
12	Rottingdean	William Alexander		1 no Tilt		
		James Ingram		2 no Tilt		
		Thomas Beard		2 no Tilt		
		Richard Hamshar		1 no Tilt		
		Thomas Geere		1 no Tilt		
		Richard Dumbrell		1 no Tilt		
		Nathaniel Beard		1 no Tilt		
		Henry Godfrey			1 Cart 1 Horse only no Tilt	
		Henry Tinley			1 Do	
		John Botting			1 Do	
		Richard Moorey			1 Do	
		Thomas Lower			1 Do	
	Ovingdean	No Waggons or Carts in the Parish to be spared from the				
	Falmer	Richard Hart	6 no Tilts	NB 3 or Horse Teams		3 Ox Teams
		Richard Verrell	1 no Tilt			1 no Tilt
		Hugh Poole	1 no Tilt	1 no Tilt		
		James Randall		1 no Tilt		
	Stanmer	Robert Henley	1 no Tilt			1 no Tilt
		James Hardcan				
		Rt Hon Thomas Pelham	2 no Tilt			
[Totals]			11	11	-	7
			32	10	-	12
			27	11	3	3
			40	13	5	7
			26	10	4	11
			11	11	-	7
			136	55	12	40

Number of persons appointed to act as Servants with Teams	Names of conductors for the same in proportion of 1 to every 10 Waggons	Names of General Agents for the said Parishes to whom requisition is to be made to call forth the Carts or Waggons	Remarks
23 not named	2 not named	James Ingram	
Ordinary Business			
12 servants not named 3 Do 4 Do 2 Do	William Brown Thomas Brown	Edward Dowlan	
2 Do 1 Do 4 Do			
1st side Schedule 6 2 Do 3 Do 4 Do 5 Do			
Totals	(23) [sic]		

Lewes Rape Schedule No 7 [Southern Division]

No of Distict in which the several Parishes are Classed	Names of Parishes in each Distict and within the said Division	Number and Names of persons in each Parish who engage to deliver as above with answer whether they have a 12 [?] Cloth or not	Names and situations of Water Mills
1	Saint Peter & St Mary Westout	John Hennard at the mill no cloth	
	St Michael	William Lee Joseph Goldsmith and John Whiteman commit for managing the public Town Mill at the mill no cloth	
	St John	No Mill in the Parish	
	All Saints	No Mill in this Parish but Mr Rickman who resides therein has a very Is by persuasion a Quaker	
2	Southover	Thomas Judge at the Mill no cloth George Pescot Do	
	Kingston	There is a Mill in this Parish but the proprietor resides in Southover.	
	Iford	No mill in the Parish	
	Rodmell	John Glazebrook at the Mill no Cloth	
3	Newhaven	James Botten at the Mill Do	
	Piddinghoe	No Mill in this Parish	
	Southease	Do	
	Telscomb	Do	
4	Hamsey	John Sicklemore at the Mill no Cloth	
	Barcomb	Thomas Rickman at the Mill a Cloth Barcomb Mill on the River Ouse 3 miles from Lewes northwards Richard Staples at the Mill no Cloth	
	Chiltington	William Olive at the Mill no Cloth	
	Plumpton	Francis Homewood at the Mill no Cloth	Pllumpton Mill near the village
5	Chailey	Thomas Rook Beard at the Mill no Cloth	
	Newick	John Marshall at the Mill Combe no Cloth	

Names and situations of Wind Mills	No of Sacks of Flour of 280 lbs net each to be furnished by each Miller every 24 Hours	Whether such Subscribers will find Wheat or not Answer yes or no	Remarks
Spittal Hill near Lewes	4	No	
Town Mill in Lewes	5	No	
large Water Mill at Barcomb near Lewes from whence he is ready to furnish flour			
It is returned with that Parish and is described as above Kingston Mill			
Rodmer Mill	Can't ascertain the quantity	No	
His Mill wthin a quarter mile of the village	None	No	
Hamsey Mill near the Racecourse	3	Yes	
Barcomb Mill near the village of Barcomb	20 with proper servants or assistants will provide Wheat for 21 days supply of flour 2	Will provide Wheat for 14 days supply of flour	
Chiltington Mill near Chailey South Common	No quantity mentioned	No	Thomas Olive returns no quantity he is willing to spare all he can
		No	*
Chailey North Common Mill	No quantity returned	No	
Combe Mill near the Village	5	Yes	

* [Remark] The return made by Homewood is that he can't ascertain any particulars in answer to this Schedule on account of the failure of water but if he is furnished with Wheat and a Cloth he will do all in his Power

[Lewes Rape Schedule No 7 continued [Southern Division]]

No of District in which the several Parishes are Classed	Names of Parishes in each Distict and within the said Division	Number and Names of persons in each Parish who engage to deliver as above with answer whether they have a 12 [?] Cloth or not	Names and situations of Water Mills
5	Wivelsfield	No Mill in this Parish	
6	Street	Do	
	Westmeston	Do	
	Ditcheling	Do	
	Keymer	Thomas Turner at the Mill no Cloth Thomas Foord at the Mill Do John Eager at the Mill no Cloth	
7	Newtimber	No Mill in this Parish	
	Poynings	Robert Loase at the Mill no Cloth	
	Fulking	No Mill in the Parish	
8	Hurstpierpoint	Jonathan Ede at the Mill no Cloth George Bishop Do William Peskett Do	Cobbs Mill Ruckford Mill
	Clayton	John Godley at the Mill no Cloth John Geer at the Mill Do	Hammonds Mill
	Piecomb	No Mill in the Parish	
9	Preston	John Streeter at the Mill no Cloth Mary Float at the Mill no Do	
	Patcham	John Streeter at the Mill no Cloth	
	Hove	No Mill in this Parish	
10	Portslade	Two windmills but no offer made	
	Westblatchington	No Mill in this Parish	
	Hangleton	No Do	
11	Brighthelmston	Henry Hobden at the Mill no Cloth	
12	Rottingdean	Thomas Beard at the Mill no Cloth John Botting Do	
	Ovingdean	No Mill in this Parish	
	Falmer	Richard Christmas at the Mill no Cloth	
	Hanmer		
	[Totals]	0 7 0	7 15 7
	Total Water Mills	7	22

Proceedings and Schedules

Names and situations of Wind Mills	No of Sacks of Flour of 280 lbs net each to be furnished by each Miller every 24 Hours	Whether such Subscribers will find Wheat or not Answer yes or no	Remarks
Old Land Mill near Ditchelling Village	4	No	
Vale Bridge Common	4	No	
St John's Mill or St John's Common	4	No	
	No quantity returned	No	
Poynings Mill at Poynings Village			
West Town Mill	4	No	
	5	No	
	Refuses to give answer		
	10	No	
Clayton Mill on Clayton Hill	5	No	
Preston Mill on Preston Hill	5 Bushells in 24 hours	Yes	
Do	Do		
Patcham Mill near Patcham	6 Bushells	Yes	
Ex Cliffe Mill	10	No	
Smock Mill on the Beacon Hill	8	Yes for ready money or at a months credit	
Post Mill near the former	No quantity	Yes Do	
Falmer Mill on Falmer Hill	No quantity	No	
The quantity not	enumerated as some are	returned in Bushells	
1st side schedule 7			
2nd Do			
Windmills total			

Lewes Rape Schedule No 8 [Southern Division]

No of District in which the several Parishes are Classed	Names of Parishes in each District and within the said Division	Names of Subscribers	For a constancy	On an Emergency	By the help of an additional Journeymen for a constancy	No of addl Journeymen required
			\multicolumn{3}{c	}{No of Loaves of 3 lbs to be furnished by each subscriber every 24 Hours}	
			\multicolumn{2}{c	}{By their usual number of Hands}		
1	Saint Peter & St Mary Westout	No public ovens in this Parish				
	St Michael	William Smart	600	800		2
		Thomas Kenward	180	1000		2
		William Kennard	600	800		2
	St John	William J Camp	400	600		2
		Lucy Trigg	400	500	1000	2
		Thomas HIll	600	600	1000	1
	All Saints	Thomas Hill	1200		1800	3
		Stephen Steer	340	510	1020	2
		James Nutley Steele	340	510	1000	2
2	Southover	Sarah Smith		96		
		William Penfold		96		
	Kingston	No publick Oven or Bakers in this Parish				
	Iford	Do				
	Rodmell	Do				
3	Newhaven	Thomas Cruttenden	30	90	180	1
	Piddinghoe	No publick oven or Bakers in this Parish				
	Southease	No publick Do				
	Telscomb	No publick Do				
4	Hamsey	\multicolumn{4}{l	}{No publick Oven in this Parish but about 50 Private Ovens 20 of which}	
	Barcomb	Thomas Weller	100	150		2
		John Adams	100	15		2
	Chiltington	No public Oven in this Parish				
	Plumpton	Do				
	Chailey	Do	\multicolumn{4}{l	}{Most of the Cottages have Ovens though}
5	Newick	Do	\multicolumn{4}{l	}{Several private ones but in General}
	Wivelsfield	Do				
6	Street	Do	\multicolumn{4}{l	}{There are however about 24 small private}
	Westmeston	Do	\multicolumn{4}{l	}{There are however a few small ones}

For what kind of fuel the Ovens are Calculated	What Quantity is required every 24 Hours to keep each overn continuously at work supposing 6 batches to be baked	Whether. Fuel is abundant or not Answer Yes or no	Remarks
		Yes	
Wood or Cole [sic]	12 faggots or 3 Bushells of coals	Yes	
Wood	32	Yes	
Wood	12	Yes	
Wood or Coale	20 Faggots or 6 Bushells coal		
Coal	6 Bushells	Yes	
Wood	No quantity mentioned	Yes	
Coal	Do	Yes	
Wood	15 Faggots	Yes	
Wood	Do	Yes	
Wood	No quantity mentioned	No	These ovens not constantly in use
Wood	Do	No	
Coal	6 Bushells	Yes	
are in the Village the remainder in detached Houses and Cottages			
Wood	9 Faggots	No	*
Wood	9 Do	No	
small in General			
very small			
Ovens			
In private Houses			

* [Remark] There are in this Parish about 90 private Ovens which upon an averadge [sic] will bake 36 Gallons each in 24 Hours with proper assistance

[Lewes Rape Schedule No 8 continued [Southern Division]]

No of District in which the several Parishes are Classed	Names of Parishes in each District and within the said Division	Names of Subscribers	No of Loaves of 3 lbs to be furnished by each subscriber every 24 Hours			By the help of an additional Journeymen	No of addl Journeymen required
				By their usual number of Hands ||		
			For a constancy	On an Emergency			
6	Ditcheling	Thomas Giles	40	80	120	2
		Daniel Parsons	20	40	60	1
	Keymer	No public Oven in this Parish there are many private Ones					
7	Newtimber	No Do					
	Poynings	No Do					
	Fulking	No Do					
8	Hurstpierpoint	No publick Oven in this Parish there are however about 60 private one					
	Clayton	No public Oven in this Parish there are however about 25 private ones					
	Piecomb	Do	15 of which are				
9	Preston	There is one publick oven in this Parish only and that used solely for the 13 Gallons of Flour in 24 Hours					
	Patcham	No public Oven in this Parish there are however several private ones					
	Hove	Do					
	Portslade	Do					
10	West Chiltington*	Do There are however 5 private ones capable of Baking at 1 batch in the For Fewell plenty the Ovens will require in the whole 36 Faggots					
	Hangleton	Do there are four private ones but they are very small					
11	Brighthelmston	Thomas Kent	300	400	400	3
		John Hilton	300	400	400	3
		Richard Streeter	200	200	300	2
		William Sharpe	130	300	200	2
		Thomas Warner	400	600	600	2
		John Lashmar	400	500	500	2
		Edward Streeter	200	300	300	2
		George Newding	300	600	600	3
		William Arnold	300	400	400	3
		William Sicklemore	400	500	500	3
		John Wymark	200	300	300	2
		James Carter	200	300	300	2
		Samuel Akehurst	200	300	300	2
		Thomas Buckwell	130	200	200	2
		James Sicklemore	400	300	600	3
		James Carter	200	300	300	2
		Henry Kennett	200	200	300	2
		Edward Cornford	100	300	200	2
		Thomas Shackleford	200	200	300	2

* The clerk once again confuses (West) Chiltington with West Blatchington

For what kind of fuel the Ovens are Calculated	What Quantity is required every 24 Hours to keep each oven continuously at work supposing 6 batches to be baked	Whether. Fuel is abundant or not Answer Yes or no	Remarks
Wood	16 Faggots	No	
Wood	10 Do	No	
capable of Baking upon an average each 20 Gallons of Flour in 24 Hours Fuel very scarce			
very small & unconnected			
use of Preston Barracks there are also 15 small private ones which on average will be able to bake			
whole 44 Gallons of Flour	Furzes		
Coal	6 Bushells	Yes	
Coals	Do	Yes	
Coal	5 Bushells	Yes	
Coal	4 Bushells	Yes	
Coal	7 Bushells	Yes	
Wood	12 Faggotts	No	
Coal	5 Bushells	Yes	
Wood	15 Faggotts	No	
Wood	12 Do	No	
Coal	6½ Bushells	Yes	
Coal & Wood	4 Bushells & 3 Faggotts	No answer	
Wood	5 Bushells	Yes	
Coal & Wood	4 Bushells & 3 Faggotts	No answer	
Coal	4 Bushells	Yes	
Wood	24 Faggotts	No	
Do	No quantity	No	
Do	Do	Yes	
Coal	4 Bushells	Yes	
Wood	No quantity	No	

[Lewes Rape Schedule No 8 continued [Southern Division]]

No of District in which the several Parishes are Classed	Names of Parishes in each District and within the said Division	Names of Subscribers	No of Loaves of 3 lbs to be furnished by each subscriber every 24 Hours			By the help of an additional Journeymen for a constancy	No of addl Journeymen required
			By their usual number of Hands				
			For a constancy	On an Emergency			
12	Rottingdean	Mary Rowland	120	200	200	-	-
		Henry Lower	120	200	240	1	1
		Elizabeth Taylor	120	200	200	1	1
	Ovingdean		No public Oven in this Parish only 3 Houses in the same					
	Falmer		Do					
	Stanmer	-	-	-	-	-	-
		[Totals]	5120	7600	7640		
			4950	6022	7180		
			5120	7600	7640		
			10070	13622*	14820†		

* error: should read 13087

† error: should read 13820

For what kind of fuel the Ovens are Calculated	What Quantity is required every 24 Hours to keep each overn continuously at work supposing 6 batches to be baked	Whether. Fuel is abundant or not Answer Yes or no	Remarks
Furzes	12 Faggotts	Yes	
Coal or Wood	2 Bushells or 24 Faggotts	Yes	
Furzes	18 Faggots	Yes	
1st side Schedule 8 2nd side			

Lewes Rape Schedule No 9 [Southern Division]

No of District in which the several Parishes are Classed	Names of Parishes within said District and within the said Division	Names of Proprietors	Proprietors Residence	Names of Masters	Masters Residence
1	Saint Peter & St Mary Westout	No Barges Boats or other Craft in the Parish			
1	St Michael	No Barges Boats or other Craft in the Parish			
1	St John	No Barges Boats or other Craft in the Parish			
1	All Saints	No Barges Boats or other Craft in the Parish			
2	Southease*	Do			
2	Kingston	Do			
2	Iford	Do			
2	Rodmell	Do			
3	Newhaven	John Greatherd	Newhaven	John Greatherd	Newhaven
3	Newhaven	John Greatherd	Do		
3	Newhaven	William Brown	Do	James Kitchener	Newhaven
3	Newhaven	William Brown	Do	None appointed	
3	Newhaven	William Brown	Do	Do	
3	Newhaven	William Brown	Do		
3	Newhaven	William Brown	Do		
3	Newhaven	William Brown	Do		
3	Newhaven	Charles Geere	Do	None appointed	
3	Newhaven	Charles Geere	Do		
3	Newhaven	Charles Geere	Do		
3	Newhaven	William Smith	Do	William Smith	Newhaven
3	Newhaven	William Smith	Do	John Smith	Newhaven
3	Newhaven	William Smith	Do		
3	Newhaven	William Smith	Do		
3	Newhaven	William Smith	Do		
3	Newhaven	William Waters jun	Do	William Waters	Newhaven
3	Newhaven	William Waters jun	Do	William Waters Snr	Do
3	Newhaven	William Waters jun	Do		
3	Newhaven	James Ashcroft	Do		
3	Newhaven	James Ashcroft	Do		
3	Newhaven	James Ashcroft	Do		
3	Newhaven	Messrs Vine & Brook	Do		
3	Newhaven	Messrs Vine & Brook	Do		
3	Newhaven	Collector of the Customs	Do		
3	Newhaven	Joseph Stephens	Do		

* error: should read Southover

Parish to which craft belong	No or name of craft	Tonnage of Barges	Whether decked or not	Rivers or canal on which employed	Place to which the craft usually trades
save a few Small Punts and Pleasure Boats					
Newhaven	Bean	15	Decked	Ouse	Newhaven to Lewes
Do	Swift	Boat	No Deck	-	Employed in the Harbour Pilotting
Newhaven	Simpson	20	Decked	Ouse	Newhaven to Lewes
Do	Tilly by Night	18	Decked	Do	Do
Do	Duck	12	Not Decked	Do	Do
Do	Squib	A boat	Not Decked	Do	And in the Harbour
Do	Duck	Do	Not Decked	Do	And in the Harbour
Do	No name	Do	Not Decked	Do	And in the Harbour
Do	Two Charles	24	Decked	Do	Newhaven to Lewes
Do	No name	A small boat	Not Decked	Do	And in the Harbour
Do	No name	Do	Do	Do	And in the Harbour
Do	Prince	20	Decked	Do	Newhaven to Lewes
Do	Mercury	10	Not Decked	Do	Do
Do	Volunteer	A boat	Do		Employed in the Harbour Pilotting
Do	Lilly	Do	Do		Do
Do	Fox	Do	Do		Do
Do	Three Brothers	20	Decked	Ouse	Newhaven to Lewes
Do	3 Sisters	17	Do	Do	Newhaven to Glynd
Do	Drowsey	A Boat	Not Decked		Employed with the Barge
Do	Endeavour	A boat	Do		Fishing & Pilotting
Do	Fox	A small boat	Do		Do
Do	Francis	8	Do		Do
Do	Viper	A Boat	Do		In the Harbour
Do	Snake	Do	Do		Do
Do	No name	A large boat	Do		At sea and in the Harbour protecting the Revenue
Do	Do	A Boat	Do		Employed in the Harbour Pilotting

[Lewes Rape Schedule No 9 continued [Southern Division]]

No of District in which the several Parishes are Classed	Names of Parishes within said District and within the said Division	Names of Proprietors	Proprietors Residence	Names of Masters	Masters Residence
3	Piddinghoe	No Barges Boats or other Craft in this Parish			
	Southease	Do			
	Telscomb	Do			
4	Hamsey	George Shiffner Esq	Combe Place Hamsey		
	Barcomb	Thomas Adams	Barcomb	Thomas Adams	Barcomb
		James & Thomas Day	Do	James and Thomas Day	Barcomb
	Chiltington	No Barges Boats or other Craft in this Parish			
	Plumpton	Do			
	Chailey	No Barges Boats or other Craft in this Parish			
	Newick	Do			
	Wivelsfield	Do			
	Street	Do			
	Westmeston	Do			
	Ditcheling	Do			
	Keymer	Do			
	Newtimber	Do			
	Poynings	Do			
	Fulking	Do			
	Hurstpierpoint	Do			
	Clayton	Do			
	Piecomb	Do			
	Preston	Do			
	Patcham	Do			
	Hove	Do			
	Portslade	Do			
	West Blatchington	Do			
	Hangleton	Do			
	Brighthelmstone	Do			
	Rottingdean	Do			
	Ovingdean	Do			
	Falmer	Do			
	Stanmer	Do			

Parish to which craft belong	No or name of craft	Tonnage of Barges	Whether decked or not	Rivers or canal on which employed	Place to which the craft usually trades
Hamsey	No name	18	Decked	Ouse	Newhaven to Sheffield
Barcomb	Victory	16	Not Decked	Do	Lewes to Uckfield
Barcomb	Lark	16	Not decked	Do	Do
Total no of Barges	13	214	Total amount of tonnage		

Lewes Rape Schedule No 1 [Northern Division]

Parishes	Draught oxen	Fatting oxen	Cows	Young cattle and Colts	Sheep	Goats	Hogs and Pigs	Draft	Riding	Waggons	Carts
			Live Stock					Horses			
Ardingly	50	5	102	186	582	-	286	89	10	34	50
Westhoathly	96	-	144	274	647	-	375	124	10	55	72
Balcombe	31	13	80	178	382	-	192	81	4	34	52
Worth	27	1	197	337	1387	-	374	170	15	77	96
Crawley	-	3	15	49	115	-	73	36	4	9	13
Cuckfield	126	39	339	549	1715	-	765	332	50	121	180
Slaugham	-	-	85	122	270	-	280	91	2	28	48
Bolney	16	28	80	142	369	-	254	67	-	29	40
Twineham	12	93	35	39	301	-	126	52	7	20	19
Totals	358	182	1067*	1876	5768	-	2725	1043†	102	407	580‡

* error: should read 1077
† error: should read 1042
‡ error: should read 570

Sussex North
Division of
Lewes Rape

Schedule N.º 1

Parishes	Draught Oxen	Fatting Oxen	Cows	Young Cattle & Colts	Sheep	Goats	Hogs & Pigs	Draft	Ridings	Waggons	Carts
Ardingly	50	5	102	186	582	–	206	89	10	34	50
Westhoathly	96	..	144	274	647	–	375	124	10	55	72
Balcombe	31	13	80	179	382	–	192	81	4	34	52
Worth	27	1	197	337	1387	–	374	170	15	77	96
Crawley	..	3	15	49	115	.	73	36	4	9	13
Cuckfield	126	39	339	549	1715	–	765	332	50	121	186
Slaugham	..	..	85	122	270	–	280	91	2	28	40
Bolney	16	20	80	142	369	.	254	67	..	29	40
Twineham	12	93	35	39	301	.	126	52	7	20	19
Total	358	182	1067	1876	5768	=	2725	1043	102	407	580

Lewes Rape Schedule No 2 [Northern Division]

Parishes	Names of Persons appointed for the removal of horses and waggons conveying such Persons as are unable to remove themselves	Names of the Overseers appointed to Superintend this Service	Names of Persons appointed for the Removal of Cattle
Ardingly	John Read John Holman	Edward Tester	Edward Dench John Russell Allen Anscombe John Box
Westhoathly	George Watson Richard Mial John Dalton Thomas Budgen William Woodman William Arkwell Edward Isted John Riste Samuel Balcombe Richard Kimber John Knight William Jarden Thomas Coak Michael Waters William Parker John Comber James Michell John Norman Isaac Gates Joseph Browne Joseph Parker	Arthur Duedney	Edward Pelland Thomas Clifford jun William Francis James Towse Benjamin Nicholas Obadiah Budgen James Woodman Thomas Browne Isaac Waters William Shirley James Rose Joseph Tingley William Bingham Thomas Parker John Wing Philip Childs William Leopard William Lock Thomas Comber John Morley Thomas Waller James Budgen
Balcombe	Thomas Jeffery Henry Bishop Richard Tester John Potter John Skinner John Browne William Tester James Wood Thomas Walder John Tulley William Holman John Streatfield Benjamin Jeffery James Tester William Jeffery	James Potter Richard Booker	John Comber jun William Feldwick William Streatfield William Goring William Rice Martin Hoath James Tester John Stepney Thomas Steadman Edward Knowles

Names of Overseers for the same	Names of Persons appointed for the Removal of Sheep and other Live Stock	Name of Overseers for the same	Remarks
Thomas Martin William Newnham	Richard Creasey William Elsey Thomas Pain Samuel Webber William Turner Charles Atterton	Benjamin Wheeler Isaac Brown	
Thomas Clifford	Richard Langridge Simeon Buckman Thomas Turner John Backshall Henry Nicholas Francis Acton John Sherlock George Norman	John Bannister	
John Comber and William Wood	Thomas Gibbs John Bourne jun George Tester sen John Streatfield jun? [sic] Richard Streatfield Allen Smith Michael Humphrey Richard Stedman Joseph Browne Edmund Muddle	Thomas Turner	

[Lewes Rape Schedule No 2 [Northern Division] continued]

Parishes	Names of Persons appointed for the removal of horses and waggons conveying such Persons as are unable to remove themselves	Names of the Overseers appointed to Superintend this Service	Names of Persons appointed for the Removal of Cattle
Worth	Thomas Maynard Henry Alfry William Russell	William Brooker	Thomas Brooker Edward Braizer James Dench John Elliott Richard Apted
Crawley	James Snelling jun William Chart Edward Sayers Henry Cheal	John Michell	James Humphrey James Braizer Charles Elphick
Cuckfield	William Smith John Legg Edward Michell James Attree jun Thomas Norris Edward Picknell James Stone James Upton James Jenner John Jennings Nathaniel Haylor James Stanford William Packham John Dancy John Virgoe Henry Burtenshaw John Packham John Michell Charles Packham James Packham William Packham Henry Packham James Stenning William Osborn Edward Jenner John Lee John Penfold John Stoner John Hobden John Juniper jun John Thornton jun Thomas Agate jun Thomas Agate	James Attree John Coppard William Jennings James Burtenshaw Thomas Packham Richard Uwins Joseph Freeman Thomas Fiest John Thornton John McGeorge	Thomas Parker Philip Hollands Samuel Molinieux John Kennard John Homewood Henry Packham Harry Packham John Packham George Packham James Stenning jun William Booker James Steere John Juniper William Agate Allen Anscombe William Parsons Benjamin Flint Edward Michell John Gatford James Field Charles Upton John Ede William Upton Michael Godsmark

Names of Overseers for the same	Names of Persons appointed for the Removal of Sheep and other Live Stock	Name of Overseers for the same	Remarks
Samuel Braizer	Thomas Ridley William Beal Thomas Cuckney George Knight James HIlls	John Franks	
James Woodyer	William Snelling jun John Stammer William Holden Charles Bartley	Charles Tullett	
Isaac Leney George Homewood James Johnson William Packham Nathaniel Bechely Richard Beal Thomas Cooke Joseph Dancy	William Marchant John Short John Godsmark John Whitehurst Stephen Peters William Humphrey William Vaughans John Barnett William Bennett Thomas Stoner John Streater Samuel Mitchell Charles Ayers James Ockenden John Betts Richard Ede James Walder Richard Betts Richard Blower	John Pace Samuel Picknell John Mitchell James Goddard William Bechely John Knight	There are upwards of 550 Persons in the Parish of Cuckfield incapable of removing themselves

[Lewes Rape Schedule No 2 [Northern Division] continued]

Parishes	Names of Persons appointed for the removal of horses and waggons conveying such Persons as are unable to remove themselves	Names of the Overseers appointed to Superintend this Service	Names of Persons appointed for the Removal of Cattle
Cuckfield [continued]	Thomas Uwins James Pink John Packham Richard Chatfield John Michell John Broad		
[Slaugham]*	William Kensell William Stoveld Stephen Comber William Whiting Thomas King Thomas Betts George Gardener Joseph Izard Thomas Warren John West John Longhurst William Hemsley James Etheridge Matthew Mitchell Robert Stoner Daniel Ethridge	Michael Dancy John Knight George Cremer Henry Leppard Richard Dancy	John Knight Richard Bartley William Sumner William Taylor John Gatford Greenfield Botting Samuel Warnham Thomas Isted sen John Hollands John Ashford John Ellsey William Ede John Tulley Joseph Thomsett sen John Lindfield Thomas Jupp
Bolney	Thomas King John Anscombe William Bray William Shirley Henry Heasman John Beeching	Michael Tulley	Thomas Jupp William Godsmark John Shaw William Standen Edward Dowlen Henry Loxley Philip Tulley John Bandfield John Bashford John Bennett John Crosskey John Henty James Field
Twineham	Richard Hamshar John Hills Peter Wood Henry Clear	James Broad	John Saunders William Randall Henry Botting Richard Gearon Thomas Sanders
Total number	110	23	112

* not specified on Schedule

Names of Overseers for the same	Names of Persons appointed for the Removal of Sheep and other Live Stock	Name of Overseers for the same	Remarks
William Comber William Longhurst John Welsh	George Orton James Linfield Charles Lintott Thomas Mitchell John Ellyott Francis Ellyott William Batchelor Thomas Tullett Henry Mitchell James Hollands John Comber Noah Wells William Heasman	Samuel Whapham William Heaver William Wells	
John Booker John Weeden	John Batchelor John Fiest Walter Hubarne John Barber James Chambers James Mansbridge James King James Booker Richard Greenfield John Taylor Stephen Stanford Richard Bray William Steadman Richard Mitchell William Wood Thomas Edwards	Henry Beeching John Steadman	
William Wood	William Rowland Richard Paine Henry Wood Edmund Davey	James Wood	[signed] Wm Sewell Lieut Thos C Grainger Depy Lieut
21	86	18	

Lewes Rape Schedule No 3 [Northern Division]

Parishes	No of men willing to serve on Horseback	No of men willing to serve on foot	Swords (Cavalry)	Pistols (Cavalry)	Firelocks (Infantry)	Pitchforks (Infantry)	Numbers of Persons to be provided with arms		Remarks
									We recommend the following Gentlemen as Officers
Ardingly	-	56	-	-	-	-	56	135 men	Fasham Nairne Esq Captain William Ward John Clifford Reynolds Lieutenants Martin Ensign
Westhoathly	5	79	3	2	-	-	79		
Balcombe	1	44	-	-	-	1	43	151	William Seaton Esq Captain Mr Isaac Clutton Revd Charles Bethune Lieutenants Thomas Caffyn Ensign
Worth	7	102	6	6	-	1	101		
Crawley	2	6	1	2	-	-	7		
Cuckfield	11	125	9	5	75	137	125	210	Thomas Cecil Grainger Esq Captain Revd Joseph Francis Fearon Thomas Wileman Lieutenants William Morfew Ensign
Slaugham	-	58	-	-	-	-	58		
Bolney	-	22	-	-	3	-	22		
Twineham	-	5	-	-	-	-	5		
Total	26	497	19	15	78	139	496		

Lewes Rape Schedule No 4 [Northern Division]

Parishes	No of Persons willing to serve as Pioneers &	Felling Axes	Pick Axes	Spades	Shovels	Bill Hooks	Saws	[Other implements they can bring]	Remarks
Ardingly	10	9	2	9	3	10	7	4 Pitchforks 1 sledge	65 Pioneers John Harding Captain Richard Harding Francis Childs Leaders
Westhoathly	17	17	1	8	2	-	8		
Balcombe	38	11	3	4	8	7	4		
Worth	56	13	22	13	7	2	3		64 William Allfrey Captain John Jeal Leader George Wales Do
Crawley	8	2	1	2	2	1	1		
Cuckfield	55	26	25	30	27	5	17		William Foakes Captain James Anscombe John Burt Leaders
Slaugham	38	5	-	7	1	1	2	22 Pitchforks	64 John Ellis Captain John Mason Abraham Berry Leaders
Bolney	9	6	-	2	-	1	-		
Twineham	17	5	5	1	5	2	3		
Totals	248	94	59	76	55	29	45		

Lewes Rape Schedule No 6 [Northern Division]

Parishes	Names of persons willing to furnish Waggons and Carts	Number of Waggons with tilts and			Number of Carts with tilts and	
		Four Horses or more	Three Horses	Three Horses or more	2 Horses
Ardingly	Admiral Poynton	1 N T			
	Revd T Browne	1 N T			
	J & W Francis	1 N T			
	Thomas Martin	1 N T			
	Richard Hards	1 N T			
	John Pannett	1 N T			
	John Walder	1 N T			
	John Hollands				1 N T
	Charles Heasman	1 N T			
	Richard Cook	1 N T			
	William Bannister	1 N T			
	Richard Comber	1 N T			
	Edward Tester	1 N T			
	John Burtenshaw	1 N T			
Westhoathly	Mrs Har[?] Clifford	1 N T			
	William Sewell Esq		1 N T		
	Walter Hurst				1
	Thomas Cook	1 N T			
	Fasham Nairne Esq	1 N T			
Balcombe	Revd H[enry] Chatfield	1 N T			
	James Potter	1			
	John Comber	1 N T			
	Thomas Steadman	1 N T			
	John Booker			1 N T	
	Richard Tester	1 N T			
Worth	Thomas Dench		1 N T		
	John Knight		1 N T		
	William Russell		1 N T		
	Mrs Bethune		1 N T		
	William Tydy				1 N T
	John Francis	1 N T			
	James Brookes		1 N T		
	Revd J Towers		1 N T		
	Thomas Privatt		1 N T		

Number of persons appointed to act as Servants with Teams	Conductors for the same in proportion of 1 to every 10 Waggons	Name of the General Agent for the Parish to whom requisition is to be made to call forth the Carts or Waggons	Remarks
1 1 1 1 1 1 1 1 1 1 1 1 1	William Bannister Edward Tester	Richard Comber	
1 1 1 1 1	Walter Hurst	James Axford	
1 1 1 1 1 1	James Potter	Thomas Comber	
1 1 1 1 1 1 1 1	James Brooker Thomas Maynard	Samuel Braizer	

[Lewes Rape Schedule No 6 [Northern Division] continued]

Parishes	Names of persons willing to furnish Waggons and Carts	Number of Waggons with tilts and		Number of Carts with tilts and	
		Four Horses or more	Three Horses	Three Horses or more	2 Horses
Worth [cont]	Thomas Maynard				1 N T
	William Rice				1 N T
	Samuel Brazier		1		
	Thomas Brooker		1		
Crawley	John Caffyn	1 N T			
Cuckfield	Thomas C Grainger Esq	1 N T			
	Henry Michell	1 N T			
	Henry Sayers	1 N T			
	Thomas Tester		1 N T		
	William Becheley		1 N T		
	William Tester		1 N T		
	John Dancy	1 N T			
	Isaac Sayers	1			
	Mary Knight	1 N T			
	Thomas Cooke	1 N T			
	William Burt	1 N T			
	John Croucher		1 N T		
	Stephen Ashfield		1 N T		
	James Knowles	1			
	John Wileman	1			
	William Clutton	1 N T			
Slaugham	William Heaver		1 N T		
	Joseph Thomsett		1 N T		
	Miles McCabe				1 N T
	William Hemsley	1 N T			
	Nahaniel Welsh	1 N T			
	Thomas Young	1 N T			
Bolney	William Blaker	1 N T			
	Jane Renville	1 N T			
	Walter Hubarne	1 N T			1
	John Barber				
	William Bray	1 N T			
	John Walder			1 N T	
	John Burtenshaw	1 N T			

Number of persons appointed to act as Servants with Teams	Conductors for the same in proportion of 1 to every 10 Waggons	Name of the General Agent for the Parish to whom requisition is to be made to call forth the Carts or Waggons	Remarks
2		John Caffyn	
1	James Knowles	James Cooke	
1	Henry Michell		
1			
1			
1			
1			
1			
1			
1			
1			
1			
1			
1			
1			
1			
1			
1	William Kinsett	John Batchelor	
1			
1			
1			
1			
1			
1	William Leopard	William Blaker	
1	Thomas Ings		
1			
1			
1			
1			
1			

[Lewes Rape Schedule No 6 [Northern Division] continued]

Parishes	Names of persons willing to furnish Waggons and Carts	Number of Waggons with tilts and		Number of Carts with tilts and	
		Four Horses or more	Three Horses	Three Horses or more	2 Horses
Bolney [cont]	William Leopard	1 N T			
	Thomas Ings	1 N T			
	Michal Tully			1 N T	
	William Marshall	1 N T			
	Michal Harmer				1 N T
	Henry Beeching	1 N T			
	Stephen Stoffell	1 N T			
Twineham	James Wood Esq	1 N T			
	Richard Hamshar		1 N T		
	Mary Wood	1 N T			
	Edmund Davey	1 N T			
	William Broad	1 N T			
	James Wood of Wapses	1 N T			
	John Botting	1 N T			
	John Wood of Park	1 N T			
	Richard Flint	1 N T			
[Totals]		55	19	2	8

Number of persons appointed to act as Servants with Teams	Conductors for the same in proportion of 1 to every 10 Waggons	Name of the General Agent for the Parish to whom requisition is to be made to call forth the Carts or Waggons	Remarks
1			
1			
1			
1			
1			
1			
1			
1	Richard Hamshar	John Botting	
1			
1			
1			
1			
1			
1			
1			
83	12	10	

[signed] W Sewell Lieut
Thomas C Grainger Asst Lieut

Lewes Rape Schedule No 7 [Northern Division]

Parishes	Subscribers Names	Names and situations of Water Mills	Names and situations of Wind Mills	No of Sacks of Flour of 280 lbs net each to be furnished by each Miller every 24 Hours	Whether such Subscribers will provide Wheat or not
Ardingly	John Hollands	Ardingly near the road leading from Lindfield to Turners Hill		Two of Water	No
Westhoathly	Walter Hurst at the Mill	Sheriff near Burstow Bridge		One	No
	John Harland at the Mill		Selsfield Selsfield Common	One	No
Balcombe	John Booker at the Mill no Cloth	Balcombe in Mill Lane near the Street		Four	Np
Worth	William Seaton at the Mill	Tilgate near Crawley		Three	No
	William Tidy at the Mill	Haselwick in the Road from Crawley to Turners Hill		One	No
	Thomas Stone at the Mill	Furnall near Copthorne		Nine of Water	No
	John Lock		Copthorne	Three	No
Crawley	No mill within the Parish				
Cuckfield	John Pace no Cloth at the Mill	Bridgers near Haywards Heath	Haywards Heath	Three	No
	Jacob Caffyn no Cloth	Cuckfield near Cuckfield Town		Two	Yes
	Henry Jeffery no Cloth at the Mill		Whitemans Green near Cuckfield	Two	No
Slaugham	William Heaver at the Mill	Slaugham		Six	No
Bolney	John Barber no Cloth		Bolney on Bolney Common	One	No
Twineham	No Mill within the Parish				

Total 13 Subscribers
Total 38 Sacks of Flour

[signed] W Sewell Lieut
Thomas C Grainger Asst Lieut

Schedule N.º 7

Parishes	Subscribers Names	Names and Situations of Water Mills	Names and Situations of Wind Mills	N.º of Sacks of Flour of 280. not to be furnished by each Miller every 24 hours	Whether the Subscribers will provide Wheat or not
Ardingly	John Hollands	Ardingly near the road leading from Lindfield to Turners Hill	—	Two of Water	No
Westhoathly	Walter Hurst at the Mill	Sheriff near Burstow Bridge	—	One	No
	John Harland at the Mill	—	Selsfield Selsfield Common	One	No
Balcombe	John Booker, no cloth at the Mill	Balcombe in Mill Lane near the Street	—	Four	No
Worth	W.m Seaton at the Mill	Tilgate near Crawley	—	Three	No
	W.m Tidy at the Mill	Haselwick in the road from Crawley to Turners Hill	—	One	No
	Tho.s Stone at the Mill	Furnall near Copthorne	—	Nine of Water	No
	John Lock	—	Copthorne	Three	No
Crawley	No Mill within the Parish				
Cuckfield	John Pace no Cloth at the Mill	Bridges near Haywards Heath	Hayward Heath	Three	No
	Jacob Taffyn no Cloth	Cuckfield near Cuckfield Town	—	Two	Yes
	Henry Jeffery no Cloth at the Mill	—	Whitemans Green near Cuckfield	Two	No
Slaugham	W.m Weaver at the Mill	Slaugham	—	Six	No
Bolney	John Barber no Cloth	—	Bolney on Bolney Common	One	No
Twineham	No Mill within the Parish				

Total 13 Subscribers
Total 38 Sacks of Flour

W.
Tho.s C

Lewes Rape Schedule No 8 [Northern Division]

Parishes	Subscribers names	By their usual number of Hands — For a constancy	By their usual number of Hands — On an Emergency	By the help of an additional Journeymen for a constancy	No of addl Journeymen required
Ardingly	No public Baker in the Parish				
Westhoathly	The same				
Balcombe	The same				
Worth	The same				
Crawley	The same				
Cuckfield	James Anscombe	100	150	200	2
	Edward Jenner	100	150	200	2
	Mary Ede	80	120	160	2
Slaugham	John Gatford	50	80	120	1
Bolney	No public Baker in the Parish				
Twineham	The same				
	Total	330	520*	680	7

Column header: No of Loaves of 3 lbs to be furnished by each subscriber every 24 Hours

* error: should read 500

Lewes Rape Schedule No 9 [Northern Division]

From the Schedules returned to us upon Oath there appears to be no Boats or Barges within the North Division of the Rape of Lewes

[signed] W Sewell Lieut
Thos C Grainger Asst Lieut

For what kind of fuel the Ovens are Calculated	What Quantity is required every 24 Hours to keep each oven continuously at work supposing 6 batches to be baked	Whether. Fuel is abundant or not Answer Yes or no	Remarks
		\multicolumn{2}{l	}{In these Parishes each House has an oven capable of baking two Bushells of flour that is those belonging to the larger Houses & those belonging to the Cottages one Bushell are heated with Wood and require the former two faggots and the latter one to heat them Fuel everywhere abundant}
Wood	10 Faggots	No	
Wood	8 Faggots	No	
Wood	6 Faggots	No	
Wood	10 Faggots	Yes	
		\multicolumn{2}{l	}{The same remark applies to these Parishes}

[signed] W Sewell Lieut
Thos C Grainger Asst Lieut

Pevensey Rape Schedule No 1 [Northern Division]

Parishes	Draught oxen	Fatting oxen	Cows	Young cattle and Colts	Sheep	Goats	Hogs and Pigs	Draft	Riding	Waggons	Carts
1st District											
Maresfield	70	7	151	210	779	-	388	121	23	42	75
Buxted	97	-	168	182	1861	-	282	144	19	44	26
2nd District											
Easthoathly	32	6	53	79	463	2	188	57	6	19	32
Framfield	143	9	239	274	1520	-	431	160	29	63	119
Little Horsted	60	4	58	93	539	-	107	32	9	19	30
3rd District											
Isfield	46	6	40	92	595	-	167	38	7	13	20
Uckfield	34	3	59	59	320	-	290	56	22	18	36
Fletching	-	-	-	-	-	-	-	-	-	-	-
4th District											
Chiddingly	87	81	107	106	1662	-	337	94	17	41	69
Waldron	72	37	147	200	858	-	161	99	14	33	61
Mayfield	294	87	368	840	2953	1	742	271	48	123	179
Wadhurst	126	32	243	414	2161	-	372	177	19	96	105
5th District											
Rotherfield	286	16	343	484	1755	-	975	276	32	111	184
Frant	122	-	169	220	1208	4	370	136	36	48	133
6th District											
Hartfield	129	6	178	424	1095	2	407	120	16	56	89
Wythyham	164	28	217	431	1682	-	608	162	24	69	113
7th District											
East Grinsted	251	50	292	598	1494	-	902	302	64	129	209
8th District											
Linfield	85	7	199	329	975	-	541	171	34	71	109
Horsted Keynes	74	-	107	216	375	-	283	110	9	39	68
[Totals]	2302	394	3247	5573	24010	9	7694	2482	450	1104	1784

[note: the clerk seems to have had a major arithmetical failure here; correct totals are below]

	2172	379	3138	5251	22295	9	7551	2526	428	1034	1657

Pevensey Rape Schedule No 2 [Northern Division]

Parishes	No of Persons appointed for the removal of horses and waggons and conveying such Persons as are unable to remove themselves	No of the Overseers appointed to Superintend this Service	No of Persons appointed for the Removal of Cattle	No of Overseers for the same	No of Persons appointed for the Removal of Sheep and other Live Stock	No of Overseers for the same
1st District						
Maresfield	23	2	19	2	33	2
Buxted	7	2	4	1	4	2
2nd District						
Easthoathly	9	2	3	2	3	1
Framfield	24	7	34	9	34	4
Little Horsted	15	2	4	3	4	3
3rd District						
Isfield	13	1	3	1	3	1
Uckfield	6	4	5	2	1	1
Fletching	12	3	14	3	15	3
4th District						
Chiddingly	12	2	5	2	5	2
Waldron	7	2	16	2	16	2
Mayfield	13	5	13	4	10	3
Wadhurst	18	2	14	2	10	2
5th District						
Rotherfield	6	2	18	2	16	2
Frant	9	2	14	1	9	1
6th District						
Hartfield	4	2	8	2	8	2
Withyham	8	2	5	1	5	1
7th District						
East Grinsted	6	4	12	2	10	2
8th District						
Lindfield	6	2	12	2	8	1
Horsted Keynes	2	1	2	1	2	1
[Totals]	200	49	205	44	196	36

Pevensey Rape Schedule No 3 [Northern Division]

Parishes	No of persons	On Horseback	On Foot	Cavalry - Swords	Cavalry - Pistols	Infantry - Firelocks	Infantry - Pitchforks	Persons to be provided with arms at the place of General Assembly	Remarks
1st District									
Maresfield									
Buxted									
2nd District									
Easthoathly	27	-	27	-	-	27	-	27	
Framfield	40	17	23	-	-	23	23	-	
Little Horsted	26	26	-	-	-	26	-	-	
3rd District									
Isfield	68	4	64						No arms
Uckfield									
Fletching	66	18	48	19	36	27			No arms
4th District									
Chiddingly									
Waldron									
Mayfield	237	21	216	-	-	87	40		Several want arms
Wadhurst	131	12	119						
5th District									
Rotherfield									
Frant									
6th District									
Hartfield									
Withyham									
7th District									
East Grinsted	87								No arms
8th District									
Lindfield	194	15	179						
Horsted Keynes									
[Totals]		113	676	19	36	190	63	27	

Pevensey Rape Schedule No 4 [Northern Division]

Parishes	No of Persons	Felling Axes	Pick Axes	Spades	Shovels	Bill Hooks	Saws
1st District							
Maresfield							
Buxted							
2nd District							
Easthoathly	16	8	4	8	1	10	3
Framfield	36	22	10	24	12	5	9
Little Horsted	3	1	1	1	-	-	-
3rd District							
Isfield							
Uckfield							
Fletching	22	8	8	4	3	1	6
4th District							
Chiddingly							
Waldron	22	18	19	22	18	7	16
Mayfield	29	22	4	1	-	-	-
Wadhurst	22	8	10	8	4	2	4
5th District							
Rotherfield							
Frant							
6th District							
Hartfield							
Withyham	29	6	5	10	5	1	6
7th District							
East Grinsted	23	5	2	2	1	1	4
8th District							
Lindfield	26	20	4	3	4	2	10
Horsted Keynes							
[Totals]	228	118	76*	83	48	29	58

* error: should read 67

Pevensey Rape Schedule No 6 [Northern Division]

Parishes	Names of persons willing to furnish Waggons and Carts	Number of Waggons with tilts and Four Horses or more	Number of Waggons with tilts and Three Horses	Number of Carts with tilts and Three Horses or more	2 Horses
1st District					
Maresfield	NB There are no more Waggons in the Parish than will be necessary for their own				
Buxted					
2nd District					
Easthoathly					
Framfield					
Little Horsted					
3rd District					
Isfield					
Uckfield	R T Streatfield William Kenward John Simmonds	1 3 No Tilt 1 1			1 3 2
Fletching					
4th District					
Chiddingly					
Waldron					
Mayfield					
Wadhurst					
5th District					
Rotherfield	Robert Fry Samuel Wickens John Moon jun John Pollington Thomas Stapley William Miles Nicholas Martin William Alcorn Ed O Dadsell John Boara Thomas Page	1 1 1 1 1 No Tilt 1 1 1 1 1 1			
Frant					

Number of persons appointed to act as Servants with Teams	Conductors for the same in proportion of 1 to every 10 Waggons	Name of the General Agent for the Parish to whom requisition is to be made to call forth the Carts or Waggons	Remarks
Purposes			
2 5 3	1 Lidbetter	No Tilt No Tilt	
22	1	Revd Mr Crawley	

[Pevensey Rape Schedule No 6 [Northern Division] continued]

Parishes	Names of persons willing to furnish Waggons and Carts	Number of Waggons with tilts and Four Horses or more	Three Horses	Number of Carts with tilts and Three Horses or more	2 Horses
6th District					
Hartfield	Henry Atheroll	1			
	Thomas Tourle	1			
Withyham	John Turner	2			
	Robert Neve	1			
	Richard Nash	No Tilt 1			
	William Garrett	1			
	John Friend	1			
	William Reynard	1			
	Leonard Hooper	1			
7th District					
East Grinsted					
8th District					
Linfield	John Shirley	1			
	John Stevens	1			
	Robert Wood	1			
Horsted Keynes					
[Totals]		27			6

Number of persons appointed to act as Servants with Teams	Conductors for the same in proportion of 1 to every 10 Waggons	Name of the General Agent for the Parish to whom requisition is to be made to call forth the Carts or Waggons	Remarks
2			
9			
3			
46	2		

Pevensey Rape Schedule No 7 [Northern Division]

Parishes	Subscribers Names	Names and situations of Water Mills	Names and situations of Wind Mills
1st District			
Maresfield			
Buxted			
2nd District			
Easthoathly			
Framfield	William Newnham John Smith Isaac Gurr	Framfield Mill Do Do	
Little Horsted			
3rd District			
Isfield	Benjamin Heaver	Isfield Mill	
Uckfield	Caleb Pierce	Uckfield Mill	
Fletching	John Peckham Henry Weston James Brook	Shortbridge Mill Fletching Mill Sheffield Mill	
4th District			
Chiddingly	John Lashmar Edward Elphick William Guy & Co	Chiddingly Mill	Dicker Mill Dicker New Mill
Waldron	John Saunders James Colman	Huggetts Mill	Cross in Hand Mill
Mayfield	Samuel Thomson John Standen Nicholas Dadswell	Moal Mill Mousehall Mill Huggett Furnace Mill	
Wadhurst	Edward Terry John Standen	River Hall Mill	Besbridge Hill Mill
5th District			
Rotherfield	Ann Wickens John Ashby James Ashby	Rudgate Mill Stone Mill	Crowboro Mill

No of Sacks of Flour of 280 lbs net each to be furnished by each Miller every 24 Hours	Whether such Subscribers will provide Wheat or not	Remarks
2	No	
3	No	
4	No	
8	No	At the Mill no Cloth
12		Undertakes to deliver Flour for the space of I Month within 10 Miles of his Mill
5	No	No Cloth
5	No	No Cloth
5	No	No Cloth
2	Yes	No Cloth
2	Yes	No Cloth
1	Yes	No Cloth
	No	No Cloth at this Mill
	No	No Cloth at this MIll
3	No	At the Mill No Cloth
4	No	At the Mill No Cloth
2	Yes	At the Mill No Cloth
16	No	At the Mill No Cloth
14	No	At the Mill No Cloth
	No	At the Mill No Cloth

Pevensey Rape Schedule No 7 [Northern Division] continued

Parishes	Subscribers Names	Names and situations of Water Mills	Names and situations of Wind Mills
5th District [cont]			
Frant	Richard Jones Thomas Ashby Henry Latter	Bushell Mill Bartley Mill Eridge Mill	
6th District			
Hartfield			
Withyham			
7th District			
East Grinsted	Peter Everest Thomas Brown Richard Heather Edward Heaver William Durrant	Framepost Mill Fanplace Mill Tablehurst Mill Bramblety Mill	East Grinsted Com[mon] Mill
8th District			
Lindfield	Anthony Harland John Stevens Thomas Pain	Cockease Mill East Maskells Mill Dean Mill	
Horsted Keynes			

No of Sacks of Flour of 280 lbs net each to be furnished by each Miller every 24 Hours	Whether such Subscribers will provide Wheat or not	Remarks
2 2 2	Yes	
1 1 1 10 10	Yes	At the Mill no Cloth
4 2 4	No No No	No Cloth No Cloth

Pevensey Rape Schedule No 8 [Northern Division]

Parishes	Subscribers names	No of Loaves of 3 lbs to be furnished by each subscriber every 24 Hours — By their usual number of Hands — For a constancy	On an Emergency	By the help of an additional Journeymen for a constancy	No of addl Journeymen required
District 1st					
Maresfield	No public Ovens in the Parish				
Buxted					
District 2nd					
Easthoathly					
Framfield					
Little Horsted					
District 3rd					
Isfield					
Uckfield	William Weller	120	150		
Fletching					
District 4th					
Chiddingly					
Waldron	Nicholas Crowhurst	360	450		
	William Bryan	200	300		
Mayfield	Henry Kemp	180	200		
Wadhurst					
District 5th					
Rotherfield					
Frant					
District 6th					
Hartfield					
Withyham					
District 7th					
East Grinsted	Francis Meads	100	200	630	3
	Henry Hart Grove	10	80	200	1
	Sarah Charlwood	60	120	300	2
	Rebecca Garland	50	100	250	2
District 8th					
[no parish named]	John Stedman	200	400	1	
	George Haynes	64	128	1	

For what kind of fuel the Ovens are Calculated	What Quantity is required every 24 Hours to keep each overn continuously at work supposing 6 batches to be baked	Whether. Fuel is abundant or not Answer Yes or no	Remarks
Wood	18 Faggotts	Yes	
Wood	Faggotts 15	Yes	
Wood	Do 9	No	
Wood	Do 6	No	
Wood	Do 25		
Wood	Do 18	No	
Wood	Do 21		
Wood	Do 20		
Wood	Do 16	Yes–	
Wood	Do 12		

Pevensey Rape Schedule No 9 [Northern Division]

	Name of the Proprietor	Proprietors Residence	Name of the Master	Masters Residence	Parish District or Hundred to which the craft belongs
1st District					
Maresfield	No Barges or Boats within the Parish				
Buxted					
2nd District					
Easthoathly					
Framfield					
Little Horsted					
3rd District					
Isfield	Abraham Shaw Abraham Shaw	Isfield Isfield	James Grover Richard King	Isfield Isfield	Isfield Isfield
Uckfield	R T Streatfield	Uckfield			Uckfield
Fletching	Thomas Grover Thomas Smith J Kennard Jethro Turner William Hobbs Richard Newnham	Fletching Do Do Do Do Do	John Goley Thomas Smith Thomas Grover William Langridge William Hobbs Richard Newnham	Fletching Do Do Do Do Do	Fletching Do Do Do Do Do
4th District					
Chiddingly					
Waldron					
Mayfield					
Wadhurst					
5th District					
Rotherfield					
Frant					
6th District					
Hartfield					
Withyham					
7th District					
East Grinsted					
8th District					
Lindfield					
Horsted Keynes	Edward Tester Thomas Hill & Co	Ardingly Horsted Keynes	Edward Tester Nathaniel Coppard	Ardingly Horsted Keynes	Horsted Keynes Do

In what county	Number or name of the craft	Tonnage	Whether decked or not	River or canal on which employed	Place to which the craft usually trades
Sussex	Lily	15	Decked	River Ouse	both from Newhaven to Freshfield
Sussex	Old Mill	18	Not Decked	River Ouse	
Sussex	Shortbridge	16	Not Decked	River Ouse	from Shortsbride to Lewes
Sussex		14	Not Decked	River Ouse	All from Newhaven to Freshfield Wharf
Do		14	Do	Do	
Do		14	Do	Do	
Do		14	Do	Do	
Do		14	Do	Do	
Do		16	Not Decked	Do	Do
Do	Ninety	16	Do	Do	Do

Pevensey Rape Schedule No 1 [Southern Division]

Parishes	Draught oxen	Fatting oxen	Cows	Young cattle and Colts	Sheep	Goats	Hogs and Pigs	Draft	Riding	Waggons	Carts
Eastbourne	130	142	159	192	7175	1	356	154	32	37	104
Willingdon	42	88	68	130	2848	-	154	33	12	15	22
Eastdean	28	8	16	37	3140	-	70	26	5	8	15
Friston	24	14	27	74	1716	-	73	15	3	6	10
Jevington	40	13	19	58	2966	-	86	21	4	11	19
Westdean	42	26	4	2	3776	-	115	24	5	12	17
Denton	18	5	8	13	1427	-	66	19	1	7	12
Bishopstone	36	64	20	46	3031	-	90	24	10	12	19
Bletchington	16	18	-	10	700	-	33	21	3	5	10
Hayton	6	-	6	2	1331	-	31	15	1	7	11
Tarring	27	-	10	7	1580	-	65	7	2	6	8
Alciston	22	-	19	20	1529	-	116	31	4	13	18
Alfriston	24	-	10	1	3725	-	269	45	14	19	27
Berwick	56	59	29	61	2688	-	130	28	6	8	12
Selmeston	56	101	67	53	1791	-	106	28	8	15	21
Wilmington	30	48	59	89	1706	-	122	31	11	14	11
Lullington	10	-	5	13	1170	-	30	7	1	3	4
Folkington	24	18	30	-	1424	-	69	12	5	7	9
Littlington	14	9	2	-	1300	-	58	13	7	5	9
Southmalling	61	27	43	28	3513	-	188	40	15	19	24
Ringmer	153	51	122	240	4364	-	418	116	28	57	72
Cliffe	-	-	10	3	12	-	36	11	8	2	5
Glynd	30	4	48	112	1793	-	111	14	7	8	23
Hailsham	50	100	136	104	2114	1	212	64	27	29	51
Hellingly	8	2	46	30	487	-	154	46	6	15	26
Arlington	96	141	86	238	3335	-	230	74	11	32	6
Stanmer	-	-	15	-	2000	-	40	16	10	5	6
Laughton	144	130	171	219	2345	-	305	97	9	33	42
Chalvington	18	9	53	49	447	-	78	25	4	12	16
Ripe	20	29	56	77	281	-	154	32	6	13	20
Beddingham	64	-	36	56	3085	-	129	36	8	17	27
Westfirle	58	128	57	113	2789	-	276	71	29	26	40
[Totals]	1217	1300	1437	2077	71686	2	4370	1196	302	468	721
[NB multiple errors; correct totals below]											
[Totals]	1347	1234	1437	2077	71588	2	4370	1196	302	478	716

Pevensey Rape Schedule No 2 [Southern Division]

Parishes	No of Persons appointed for the removal of horses and waggons conveying such Persons as are unable to remove themselves	No of the Overseers appointed to Superintend this Service	No of Persons appointed for the Removal of Cattle	No of Overseers for the same	No of Persons appointed for the Removal of Sheep and other Live Stock	No of Overseers for the same
Eastbourne	26	5	37	3	21	3
Willingdon	14	2	17	2	12	2
Eastdean	8	1	16	1	10	1
Friston	6	1	6	1	6	1
Jevington	7	1	6	2	9	1
Westdean	13	1	4	1	11	1
Denton	4	1	2	1	2	1
Bishopston	8	2	12	1	11	2
Bletchington	12	3	5	1	3	1
Hayton	6	1	4	1	6	1
Tarring	4	1	2	1	3	1
Alciston	7	3	5	2	2	2
Alfriston	6	3	3	3	3	3
Berwick	11	1	9	1	7	1
Selmeston	7	3	8	1	7	1
Wilmington	8	2	9	3	7	3
Lullington	2	-	2	-	2	-
Folkington	7	1	6	1	5	1
Littlington	7	1	7	1	6	1
Southmalling	16	1	16	1	15	1
Ringmer	12	3	16	3	16	3
Cliffe	7	6	4	4	4	4
Glynd	10	1	4	1	3	1
Hailsham	11	2	12	2	13	2
Hellingly	12	3	18	3	14	3
Arlington	14	2	8	3	4	2
Stanmer	4	1	2	1	2	1

[Pevensey Rape Schedule No 2 [Southern Division] continued]

Parishes	No of Persons appointed for the removal of horses and waggons conveying such Persons as are unable to remove themselves	No of Overseers appointed to Superintend this Service	No of Persons appointed for the Removal of Cattle	No of Overseers for the same	No of Persons appointed for the Removal of Sheep and other Live Stock	No of Overseers for the same
Chalvington	9	1	4	1	4	1
Laughton	16	3	6	2	4	2
Ripe	12	4	8	3	6	3
Beddingham	10	1	7	2	7	2
Westfirle	6	2	7	2	7	2
[Totals]	302	63	272	55	232	54

Pevensey Rape Schedule No 3 [Southern Division]

Parishes	No of persons	On Horseback	On Foot	Cavalry Swords	Cavalry Pistols	Infantry Firelocks	Infantry Pitchforks	Persons to be provided with arms at the place of General Assembly	Remarks
Eastbourne	66	3	63	4	3	62	55	-	
Willingdon	9	-	9	-	-	9	-	-	
Eastdean	4	-	4	-	-	4	-	3	
Friston									
Jevington									
Westdean									
Denton									
Bishopston	12	-	11	-	-	11	-	-	
Bletchington									
Hayton									
Tarring									
Alciston	4	-	-	-	-	4	-	-	
Alfriston									
Berwick	1	-	-	-	-	-	-	-	
Selmeston	12	-	11	-	-	11	1	-	
Wilmington	7	1	6	1	1	1	2	3	
Lullington									
Folkington									
Littlington									
Southmalling	14	-	14	2	-	12	-	-	
Ringmer	23	12	11	-	-	16	-	-	
Cliffe	88	7	71	8	7	72	2	-	
Glynd	20	-	20	-	-	-	20	-	
Hailsham									
Hellingly	60	4	47	-	3	13	32	13	
Arlington	8	-	8	-	-	8	-	-	
Stanmer	19								

[Pevensey Rape Schedule No 3 [Southern Division] continued]

Parishes	No of persons	On Horseback	On Foot	Swords (Cavalry)	Pistols (Cavalry)	Firelocks (Infantry)	Pitchforks (Infantry)	Persons to be provided with arms at the place of General Assembly	Remarks
Laughton	30	3	27	-	-	13	-	-	
Chalvington									
Ripe	16	-	16	-	-	16	-	-	
Beddingham	5	-	-	-	-	5	-	-	
Westfirle	35	1	22	-	-	-	-	-	
[Totals	423*	43†	380‡	15	14	252**	112	19	

* error: should read 433

† error: should read 31

‡ error: should read 340

** error: should read 257

Pevensey Rape Schedule No 4 [Southern Division]

Parishes	No of Persons	Felling Axes	Pick Axes	Spades	Shovels	Bill Hooks	Saws	For any other instrument the Pioneers may engage to bring
Eastbourne	104	21	24	24	9	-	28	
Willingdon	12	4	10	4	7	-	19	
Eastdean	-	-	-	-	-	-	-	
Friston	-	-	-	-	-	-	-	
Jevington	7	4	1	1	-	1	1	
Westdean	-	-	-	-	-	-	-	
Denton	-	-	-	-	-	-	-	
Bishopston	-	-	-	-	-	-	-	
Bletchington	-	-	-	-	-	-	-	
Hayton	-	-	-	-	-	-	-	
Tarring	8	-	1	2	2	2	1	
Alciston	7	-	2	2	2	-	1	
Alfriston	-	-	-	-	-	-	-	
Berwick	4	-	2	2	-	-	-	
Selmeston	2	2	-	-	-	-	-	
Wilmington	10	8	6	-	2	-	-	
Lullington	-	-	-	-	-	-	-	
Folkington	8	-	-	-	-	-	-	
Littlington	2	-	-	-	-	-	-	
Southmalling	22	9	-	9	1	-	1	
Ringmer	73	7	4	18	8	-	7	
Cliffe	56	-	-	20	10	-	12	
Glynd	3	2	1	2	-	1	1	
Hailsham	-	-	-	-	-	-	-	
Hellingly	32	17	9	5	-	-	4	
Arlington	26	9	5	8	5	2	4	
Stanmer	-	-	-	-	-	-	-	
Laughton	4	3	1	1	-	-	3	
Chalvington	8	5	-	2	2	-	-	
Ripe	16	8	4	10	7	-	6	
Beddingham	8	-	-	3	4	-	1	
Westfirle	12	9	4	-	2	-	-	
[Totals]	412	100	68	113	59	6	90	

[NB multiple errors; correct totals below]

| | 424 | 108 | 74 | 113 | 61 | 6 | 89 | |

Pevensey Rape Schedule No 6 [Southern Division]

Parishes	No of Persons willing to supply waggins	Number of Waggons with tilts and — Four Horses or more	Three Horses	Number of Carts with tilts and — Three Horses or more	2 Horses	No of Persons appointed to act as Servants with Teams	Conductors for the same in proportion of 1 to every 10 Waggons	Names of General Agents
1 District								
Eastbourne	5	No Tilt 5				10	1	James Smith
Willingdon	3	No Tilt 3				6		John Denman
Eastdean								
Friston								
Jevington								
Westdean								
2nd District								
Denton								
Bishopston								
Bletchington	3	No Tilt 4	1		10	6		William Washer
Hayton								
Tarring								
3rd District								
Alciston								
Alfriston								
Berwick	3	No Tilt 3				5	1	William Gouldsmith
Selmeston								
4th District								
Wilmington	2	No Tilt 3				6		John King
Lullington								
Folkington	2	No Tilt 1	1			2		John King
Littlington	1		2			2		James Gill
5th District								
Southmalling	6	No Tilt 8		No Tilt 3		21	2	John Farncombe
Ringmer	8	No Tilt 8	5	No Tilt 4	N T 3	8		
Cliffe								
Glynd	2	No Tilt 2			4			

[Pevensey Rape Schedule No 6 [Southern Division] continued]

Parishes	No of Persons willing to supply waggins	Number of Waggons with tilts and Four Horses or more	Number of Waggons with tilts and Three Horses	Number of Carts with tilts and Three Horses or more	Number of Carts with tilts and 2 Horses	No of Persons appointed to act as Servants with Teams	Conductors for the same in proportion of 1 to every 10 Waggons	Names of General Agents
6th District								
Hailsham	14	No Tilt 8	5	No Tilt 4	N T 3	28	2	William Long
Hellingly	1	No Tilt 1		No Tilt 1		2	1	John Akehurst
Arlington	1	No Tilt 1				1		
7th District								
Stanmer	1	No Tilt 5	7	No Tilt 6		4	1	Hugh Poole
8th District								
Laughton								
Chalvington								
Ripe								
9th District								
Beddingham	2		4					Sir Thomas Carr
West Firle	12	No Tilt 9	4		N T 2	25	1	Thomas Mackett
[Totals]	75	61	24	14	15	130	8	
[NB multiple errors; correct totals below]								
	66	61	29	18	22	126	9	

Pevensey Rape Schedule No 7 [Southern Division]

Parishes	Subscribers Names	Names and situations of Water Mills	Names and situations of Wind Mills
1st District			
Eastbourne	William Bignall William Baker Henry Hurst Elizabeth Mortimer		Bignall Mill Parsonage Mill Chapel Mill Round Mill
Willingdon			
Eastdean	John Ashby		Friston Mill
Friston			
Jevington	Nicholas Chapman		
Westdean			
2nd District			
Denton			
Bishopstone	Edward & William Catt	Tide Mill	
Bletchington	William Chambers		Bletchington Mill
Hayton			
Tarring			
3rd District			
Alciston			
Alfriston	Walter & William Woodhams		Berwick Mill
Berwick			
Selmeston			
4th District			
Wilmington			
Lullington			
Folkington			
Littlington			

No of Sacks of Flour of 280 lbs net each to be furnished by each Miller every 24 Hours	Whether such Subscribers will provide Wheat or not	Remarks
one Sack two Sacks two Sacks two Sacks	Yes Yes Yes Yes	The several proprietors of Mills have not the Cloths and are willing only to deliver the Meal Flour etc at the Mill
two Sacks	Yes	at the Mill no Cloth
six Sacks	No	at the Mill no Cloth
seven Sacks		will engage to provide Wheat the first 10 Days only after called on
three Sacks	No	
Six	Yes	

[Pevensey Rape Schedule No 7 [Southern Division] continued]

Parishes	Subscribers Names	Names and situations of Water Mills	Names and situations of Wind Mills
5th District			
Southmalling	Thomas Hill		Malling Mill
Ringmer	Ferdinand Martin Thomas Hill		Ringmer Mill Broyle Mill
Cliffe			
Glynd			
6th District			
Hailsham	James Ellis		Hailsham Mill
Hellingly	James Goldsmith Stephen Kennard & Co William Butler	Horsebridge Mill Hellingly Mill	North Street
7th District			
Stanmer			
8th District			
Laughton			
Chalvington			
Ripe	Matthew Mannington		Ripe Mill
9th District			
Beddingham	Sir Thomas Carr		Beddingham
West Firle			

No of Sacks of Flour of 280 lbs net each to be furnished by each Miller every 24 Hours	Whether such Subscribers will provide Wheat or not	Remarks
Six	Yes	at the Mill no Cloth
five	No	at the Mill no Cloth
three	Yes	at the Mill no Cloth
Four	Yes	at the Mill no Cloth
eight	Yes	
eight	Yes	
four	Yes	at the Mill no Cloth
two	Yes	at the Mill no Cloth
two	Yes	

Pevensey Rape Schedule No 8 [Southern Division]

Parishes	Subscribers names	For a constancy	On an Emergency	By the help of an additional Journeymen for a constancy	No of addl Journeymen required
1st District					
Eastbourne	Samuel Coleman	600	800	1200	2
	Thomas Grace	400	500	800	2
	Joseph Wilkins	100	120	170	1
	Mrs Ann Townsett	200	250	350	1
	Mrs S Young	50	60	200	1
Willingdon					
Eastdean					
Friston					
Jevington					
Westdean					
2nd District					
Denton					
Bishopston					
Bletchington		460	700	1200	6
Hayton					
Tarring					
3rd District					
Alciston					
Alfriston	Cornelius Gibson	320	480		
Berwick					
Selmeston					
4th District					
Wilmington					
Lullington					
Folkington					
Litlington					
5th District					
Southmalling	Thomas Hill	3600	7200	7200	4
Ringmer					

Column headers: No of Loaves of 3 lbs to be furnished by each subscriber every 24 Hours — By their usual number of Hands (For a constancy / On an Emergency)

For what kind of fuel the Ovens are Calculated	What Quantity is required every 24 Hours to keep each oven continuously at work supposing 6 batches to be baked	Whether. Fuel is abundant or not Answer Yes or no	Remarks
Wood or Furze	100 Furze Faggotts	No	
Wood or Furze	80 Furze Faggotts	No	
Wood or Furze	50 Do	No	
Wood or Coal		No	
Wood or Coal	50 Do Faggotts	No	
Wood	20 Faggotts	No	
Wood & Heath	9 Faggotts	No	
Wood	30 Faggotts	Yes	

[Pevensey Rape Schedule No 8 [Southern Division] continued]

Parishes	Subscribers names	For a constancy	On an Emergency	By the help of an additional Journeymen for a constancy	No of addl Journeymen required
5th District [cont]					
Cliffe	William Hammond	500	1000		1
	Jeremiah Steele	1000	2000		-
	William Hammond	1000	2000		1
	Edward Green	1000	2000		1
Glynd					
6th District					
Hailsham	Edward Jones	65	100		
	George Inskip	96	144		
Hellingly					
7th District					
Stanmer					
8th District					
Laughton					
Chalvington					
Ripe					
9th District					
Beddingham					
West Firle					
[Totals]		9391	17364*	10720†	20

Column header: No of Loaves of 3 lbs to be furnished by each subscriber every 24 Hours — By their usual number of Hands

* error: should read 17354
† error: should read 11120

For what kind of fuel the Ovens are Calculated	What Quantity is required every 24 Hours to keep each overn continuously at work supposing 6 batches to be baked	Whether. Fuel is abundant or not Answer Yes or no	Remarks
Wood	15 Faggotts	Yes	
Wood	15 Faggotts	Yes	
Wood	15 Faggotts	Yes	
Wood	15 Faggotts	Yes	
Wood	12 Faggotts	Yes	The oven too small to bake any more
Wood	12 Faggotts	Yes	
	403*		

* error: should read 423

Pevensey Rape Schedule No 9 [Southern Division]

	Name of the Proprietor	Proprietors Residence	Name of the Master	Masters Residence	Parish District or Hundred to which the craft belongs
1st District					
Eastbourne					
Willingdon					
Eastdean					
Friston					
Jevington					
Westdean					
2nd District					
Denton					
Bishopston					
Bletchington					
Hayton					
Tarring					
3rd District					
Alciston					
Alfriston	William Stevens Sarah Lower	Berwick Alfriston	Charles Lower Thomas Lower	Alfriston Alfriston	Alfriston Alfriston
Berwick					
Selmeston					
4th District					
Wilmington					
Lullington					
Folkington					
Litlington					
5th District					
Southmalling	Richard Hillman Robert Hillman John Hillman John Hillman Henry Hillman Henry Hillman Thomas Hillman Charles Hillman James Hillman	Southmalling Do Do Do Do Do Do Do Do			Southmalling Do Do Do Do Do Do Do Do
Ringmer					

In what county	Number or name of the craft	Tonnage	Whether decked or not	River or canal on which employed	Place to which the craft usually trades
Sussex	The Adventure	14	not	Cuckmere	Alfriston
Sussex	The Good Will	7	not	Cuckmere	Alfriston
Sussex	Nelson	40	Decked	River Ouse	Newhaven
Sussex	Wilkes	18	Decked	Do	Do
Sussex	Nancy	35	Decked	Do	Lindfield
Sussex	Cliffe	16	Decked	Do	Do
Sussex	Traveller	24	Decked	Do	Do
Sussex	Chargeable	14	Decked	Do	Do
Sussex	Wilkes	18	Decked	Do	Do
Sussex	Hope	20	not	Do	Do
Sussex	May	16	Decked	Do	Do

[Pevensey Rape Schedule No 9 [Southern Division] continued]

	Name of the Proprietor	Proprietors Residence	Name of the Master	Masters Residence	Parish District or Hundred to which the craft belongs
5th District [cont]					
Cliffe	Sarah Gasson	Cliffe			Cliffe
	Sarah Gasson	do			Cliffe
	Sarah Gasson	do			do
	Sarah Gasson	do			do
	Sarah Gasson	do			do
	Prince Hillman	do			do
	John Gasson	do			do
	William Robinson	do			do
	William Robinson	do			do
	William Robinson	do			do
	William Robinson	do			do
	William Robinson	do			do
	William Robinson	do			do
	William Robinson	do			do
	William Robinson	do			do
	William Robinson	do			do
	Samuel Hillman	do			do
	Samuel Hillman	do			do
	James Alderton	do			do
Glynd					
6th District					
Hailsham					
Hellingly					
7th District					
Stanmer					
8th District					
Laughton					
Chalvington					
Ripe					
9th District					
Beddingham					
West Firle					

In what county	Number or name of the craft	Tonnage	Whether decked or not	River or canal on which employed	Place to which the craft usually trades
Sussex	Good Intent	27	not Decked	River Ouse	Newhaven
Do	Pledger	24	Do	Do	do
Do	Sampson	22	Do	do	do
Do	William	20	Do	do	do
Do	Adventure	18	Do	do	do
Do	Swift Cutter	15	Do	do	do
Do	Tarter	15	Decked	do	do
Do	Mary	35	Do	do	do
Do	Sally	35	Do	do	do
Do	Woodlark	25	not Decked	do	do
Do	Randall	20	Decked	do	do
Do	George	16	Do	do	do
Do	Newhaven	15	Do	do	do
Do	Cliffe	15	Do	do	do
Do	Endeavour	14	not Decked	do	do
Do	Snipe	14	Do	do	do
Do	Susannah	20	Decked	do	do
Do	Longsplice	18	not Decked	do	do
Do	Goodwill	16	not Decked	do	do

Hastings Rape Schedule No 1

Parishes divided into Districts	Draught oxen	Fatting oxen	Cows	Young cattle and Colts	Sheep	Goats	Hogs & Pigs	Draft	Ridings	Waggons	Carts	Remarks
1st												
Salehurst	101	14	219	350	2509	-	392	174	45	73	134	
Ticehurst	102	50	214	206	2689	-	452	154	41	73	151	
Burwash	128	40	228	371	2483	1	472	126	36	52	109	
Etchingham	46	74	122	236	1211	-	146	67	15	29	52	
2nd												
Heathfield	118	9	199	344	1081	-	388	142	20	55	88	
Warbleton	114	25	177	226	1973	-	176	74	17	40	56	
Dallington	32	1	57	109	294	-	129	38	7	22	37	
3rd												
Peasmarsh	24	76	80	168	9301	-	250	79	16	28	42	*
Iden	52	59	59	216	8435	-	104	41	7	15	44	
Playden	8	2	27	26	2919	-	50	18	7	4	2	
Eastguildford	-	69	13	330	12216	-	18	8	5	-	-	
4th												
Brede	68	11	96	188	1057	-	99	81	9	34	44	
Udimore	78	17	133	176	3387	-	95	53	9	29	49	
Guestling	48	85	105	289	1486	-	196	81	15	29	6	
Icklesham	91	74	102	549	10888	-	167	57	23	30	45	
Pett	28	61	28	136	1410	-	102	19	5	6	-	†
5th												
Wartling	126	76	211	262	3017	-	379	93	23	40	69	
Herstmonceux	136	201	87	312	2602	-	233	58	30	38	68	
Ashburnham	101	41	78	172	1934	-	234	64	24	2	-	
Ninfield	40	26	127	147	1367	-	194	54	14	29	41	
Hove	66	112	69	176	1417	-	147	44	25	24	40	

* [Remark] John Offen jun has delivered no Return
† [Remark] Not half the Stock entered but returned in other Parishes where the Occupiers reside

[Hastings Rape Schedule No 1 continued]

Parishes divided into Districts	Draught oxen	Fatting oxen	Cows	Young cattle and Colts	Sheep	Goats	Hogs & Pigs	Draft	Ridings	Waggons	Carts	Remarks
6th												
Fairlight	63	11	54	151	3195	-	167	62	10	26	24	
Ore	14	8	42	46	1008	-	100	29	4	9	3	
Crowhurst	27	5	47	137	1780	-	80	54	10	24	34	
Westfield	88	7	140	309	4002	-	80	86	11	46	80	
Castle	22	-	30	30	207	-	44	16	2	5	10	
St Leonards	30	-	25	50	1200	-	30	16	3	6	7	
Hollington	12	10	33	49	160	-	45	27	3	12	17	
7th												
Beckley	48	59	132	263	2187	-	160	112	19	48	79	
Northiam	66	34	112	168	1890	-	219	77	21	32	70	
Bodiam	46	9	51	166	1199	-	103	29	7	14	6	
Ewhurst	40	14	99	189	2174	-	184	96	18	34	16	*
8th												
Mountfield	114	14	116	270	2261	-	250	68	14	34	65	
Sedlescomb	60	8	53	19	730	1	168	35	15	19	31	
Penhurst	24	8	14	42	330	-	41	13	4	7	9	
Brightling	52	7	76	130	1896	-	165	40	8	8	7	
9th												
Battle	148	29	149	274	1774	-	518	188	53	64	114	
Whatlington	16	-	37	54	272	-	93	40	9	15	22	
Catsfield	40	54	83	156	1989	-	87	53	14	17	28	
Bexhill	118	20	179	256	2428	-	206	83	13	10	5	†
[Totals]	2535	1520	3903	7748	204358‡	2	7199	2652	631	1102	1704	

[NB multiple errors; correct totals below]

| | 2535 | 1420 | 3903 | 7748 | 104358 | 2 | 7163 | 2649 | 631 | 1082 | 1704 | |

* [Remark] Ewhurst Mr Hyland & Mr Reed made no return
† [Remark] Bexhill William Drake Thomas Magglestone William Russell James Fuggles & Thomas Cruttenden refused to make a return of their stock
‡ [pencil annotation: 104358]

signed J Tilden Sampson
subd[ivision] clerk

Hastings Rape Schedule No 2

Parishes Divided into Districts	No of the names of Persons appointed for the removal of horses and waggons conveying such Persons as are unable to remove themselves	No of names of Overseers appointed to Superintend the Service	No of names of Persons appointed for the Removal of Cattle	No of names of Overseers for the same	No of names of Persons appointed for the Removal of Sheep and other Live Stock	No of names of Overseers for the same
[1st]						
Salehurst	22	3	21	2	12	2
Ticehurst	18	7	13	6	7	6
Burwash	27	8	18	11	3	-
Etchingham	28	2	25	2	20	2
[2nd]						
Heathfield	14	2	11	2	10	2
Warbleton	4	1	12	1	7	1
Dallington	15	2	9	1	11	1
[3rd]						
Peasmarsh	4	1	17	6	20	5
Iden	12	2	15	2	17	3
Playden	6	2	9	2	15	2
Eastguildford	1	1	5	1	7	2
[4th]						
Breede	13	4	22	6	33	5
Udimore	28	2	16	2	15	2
Guestling	24	4	30	4	30	4
Icklesham	28	3	25	4	26	5
Pett	8	2	8	2	10	2
[5th]						
Wartling	23	4	19	3	16	4
Herstmonceux	14	3	7	3	5	1
Ashburnham	1	1	6	1	7	1
Ninfield	4	4	18	4	20	2
Hove	28	4	14	4	14	4

[Hastings Rape Schedule No 2 continued]

Parishes Divided into Districts	No of the names of Persons appointed for the removal of horses and waggons conveying such Persons as are unable to remove themselves	No of names of Overseers appointed to Superintend the Service	No of names of Persons appointed for the Removal of Cattle	No of names of Overseers for the same	No of names of Persons appointed for the Removal of Sheep and other Live Stock	No of names of Overseers for the same
[6th]						
Fairlight	24	4	19	3	12	3
Ore	6	1	10	2	7	1
Crowhurst	4	2	3	2	2	1
Westfield	21	15	26	13	27	10
Castle	8	-	8	1	4	1
St Leonards	5	1	3	1	3	2
Hollington	4	1	3	1	8	1
[7th]						
Beckley	13	7	11	3	14	3
Northiam	8	5	12	3	46	3
Bodiam	22	2	13	2	10	1
Ewhurst	10	3	17	2	8	3
[8th]						
Mountfield	13	2	19	2	2	-
Sedlescomb	16	2	11	3	13	2
Penhurst	7	1	7	-	-	-
Brightling	14	1	13	2	12	2
[9th]						
Battle	35	6	13	5	14	5
Whatlington	9	2	5	2	8	2
Catsfield	20	3	8	2	7	2
Bexhill	18	3	53	4	50	3
[Totals]	579	123	574	122	542*	103†

* error: should read 552
† error: should read 101

Hastings Rape Schedule No 3

Parishes Divided into Districts	No of persons	On Horseback	On Foot	Swords (Cavalry)	Pistols (Cavalry)	Firelocks (Infantry)	Pitchforks (Infantry)	Persons to be provided with arms at the place of General Assembly
[1st]								
Salehurst	41	22	12	20	21	21	3	154
Ticehurst	6	-	6	-	-	6	-	-
Burwash	4	-	4	-	6	-	-	-
Etchingham	2	2	-	-	-	-	-	-
[2nd]								
Heathfield	20	-	1	3	4	15	-	1
Warbleton	1	-	1	-	-	-	1	-
Dallington	10	-	-	-	-	-	-	-
[3rd]								
Peasmarsh	6	6	-	-	6			
Iden	-	-	-	-	-	-	-	-
Playden	1	1	-	-	1	-	-	-
Eastguildford	-	-	-	-	-	-	-	-
[4th]								
Breede	-	-	-	-	-	-	-	-
Udimore	-	-	-	-	-	-	-	-
Guestling	-	-	-	-	-	-	-	-
Icklesham	1	1	-	1	-	-	-	-
Pett	-	-	-	-	-	-	-	-
[5th]								
Wartling	21	3	18	2	2	14	4	-
Herstmonceux	38	10	18	6	6	26	11	-
Ashburnham	3	-	3	-	-	3	-	-
Ninfield	2	1	1	1	1	1	-	1
Hove	-	-	-	-	-	-	-	-

Remarks
Want of time Occasioned so few Names At a Vestry held Sunday Evening 63 Gentlemen and Inhabitants have signed a paper declaring themselves ready to give their Assistance at the Alarming Crisis
John Noakes Farmer has made no return to any of the Schedules
From the Quantity of Cattle and Sheep in the Parish and no great Number of Inhabitants they have offered themselves in the other Schedules
Thomas Pelham and John Corman have not yet offered their Services
All employed in Driving Cattle and Sheep and in removing aged and infirm persons
But few Inhabitants in Consequence there are no more Names as the Men of the above Ages will be wanted and have offered in Schedule No 2
No more Men than have offered in Schedule No 2
William Whiting has not made any Offer

[Hastings Rape Schedule No 3 continued]

Parishes	No of persons	On Horseback	On Foot	Swords (Cavalry)	Pistols (Cavalry)	Firelocks (Infantry)	Pitchforks (Infantry)	Persons to be provided with arms at the place of General Assembly
[6th]								
Fairlight	2	2	2	2	-	-	-	-
Ore	-	-	-	-	-	-	-	-
Crowhurst	-	-	-	-	-	-	-	-
Westfield	-	-	-	-	-	-	-	-
Castle	-	-	-	-	-	-	-	-
St Leonards	-	-	-	-	-	-	-	-
Hollington	-	-	-	-	-	-	-	-
[7th]								
Beckley	-	-	-	-	-	-	-	-
Northiam	6	-	6	-	-	6		
Bodiam	-	-	-	-	-	-	-	-
Ewhurst	-	-	-	-	-	-	-	-
[8th]								
Mountfield	-	-	-	-	-	-	-	-
Sedlescomb	41	9	31	9	9	25	6	1
Penhurst	-	-	-	-	-	-	-	-
Brightling	13	-	13	1	-	7	6	-
[9th]								
Battle	154	24	129	18	17	39	23	69
Whatlington	-	-	-	-	-	-	-	-
Catsfield	42	4	38	4	4	21	13	4
Bexhill	-	-	-	-	-	-	-	-
[Totals]	414	78*	288†	67	72‡	191**	67	230

* error: should read 85
† error: should read 283
‡ error: should read 77
** error: should read 184

Remarks
James Phillips has made no return either of Service or of Stock
All the Men in the Parish between the Ages of 15 and 60 are employed. See Schedule No 2
All offered in Schedule No 2 & 4

Hastings Rape Schedule No 4

Parishes Divided into Districts	No of Names	Felling Axes	Pick Axes	Spades	Shovels	Bill Hooks	Saws	[Other implements]	Remarks
[1st]									
Salehurst	67	30	23	65	30	32	17		
Ticehurst	11	2	4	2	1	2	-		*
Burwash	58	47	22	41	24	50	37		
Etchingham	22	13	11	15	8	6	5		
[2nd]									
Heathfield	65	18	20	14	9	3	1		
Warbleton	5	2	4	2	-	-	1		
Dallington	6	6	4	7	2	8	-		
[3rd]									
Peasmarsh	27	10	8	15	5	5	5		
Iden	15	7	13	15	14	3	6		
Playden	6	4	-	2	-	-	-		
Eastguildford	-	-	-	-	-	-	-		None for reasons specified in Schedule No 2 & 3
[4th]									
Breede	34	17	8	19	12	7	15		
Udimore	6	3	1	2	-	-	-		
Guestling	18	11	2	11	2	7	2		
Icklesham	1	-	-	-	-	-	-		The same Remark as in Number 3
Pett	-	-	-	-	-	-	-		
[5th]									
Wartling	82	26	18	16	13	10	18		
Herstmonceux	88	23	33	29	16	8	13		
Ashburnham	5	-	-	2	1	-	-		One person without any implement or instrument whatsoever
Ninfield	6	5	-	-	-	-	1		
Hove	57								No implement or other instrument is returned. It is not certain that all will attend, as many of them have not been seen

* [Remark] From having so short a notice we have not been able to see a great Number of persons in this Parish the rest we are well assured will come forward in the most Loyal way in defence of their King and Country

[Hastings Rape Schedule No 4 continued]

Parishes Divided into Districts	No of Names	Felling Axes	Pick Axes	Spades	Shovels	Bill Hooks	Saws	[Other implements]	Remarks
[6th]									
Fairlight	19	5	2	6	3	-	3		
Ore	6	4	-	-	1	1	-		Wish not to be put in Companies
Crowhurst	30	13	4	9	1	3	-		
Westfield	29	23	18	16	14	9	13		
Castle	-	-	-	-	-	-	-		
St Leonards	3	2	-	2	-	1	1		Willing to act as Labourers in Case of an Invasion
Hollington	21	3	5	3	2	3	5		
[7th]									
Beckley	50	11	5	16	7	5	6		
Northiam	23	7	6	12	-	-	5		
Bodiam	-	-	-	-	-	-	-		The same Remark as in Schedule No 3
Ewhurst	11	7	2	8	4	3	2		
[8th]									
Mountfield	59	8	1	25	22	5	4		
Sedlescomb	28	13	7	13	3	2	12		
Penhurst	10	9	7	8	8	5	1		
Brightling	16	19	7	11	8	16	10	8 Wedges 1 Hoe	
[9th]									
Battle	46	27	22	36	18	8	25		
Whatlington	46	27	22	28	19	10	8		
Catsfield	23	5	5	6	3	2	3		
Bexhill	7	2							
[Totals]	1006	400*	284	456	251†	214	214‡		

* error: should read 409
† error: should read 250
‡ error: should read 219

Hastings Rape Schedule No 6

Parishes Divided into Districts	No of Subscribers	Number of Waggons with tilts and Four Horses or more	Number of Waggons with tilts and Three Horses	Number of Carts with tilts and Three Horses or more	Number of Carts with tilts and Two Horses	No of Persons appointed to act as Servants with Teams	Conductors for the same in proportion of 1 to every 10 Waggons	Names of General Agents
[1st]								
Salehurst		20 no T	7 with T / 1 no T	2 with T		44	7	
Ticehurst	23							The Revd Thomas Causton
Burwash	5	3 no T	2 no T					
Etchingham								
[2nd]								
Heathfield								
Warbleton	13	6 no T	9 no T	1 T	6 no T	34	6	
Dallington								
[3rd]								
Peasmarsh						30	4	J Lettice Vicar of Peasmarsh
Iden	4	4 with T			1 no T	6		Christopher Dive
Playden	6	3 no T	1 no T		2 no T	6		Thomas Haddock
Eastguildford								
[4th]								
Brede	6	5 no T	1 no T			6		John Richardson Constable
Udimore								
Guestling	2		2 no T			3		Moses Cloke
Icklesham	Not having a sufficient Number of Men to Man the Waggons in Case of an Invasion tis not in the power of the Inhabitants to assist Government with any but request the Assistance of Government							
Pett								
[5th]								
Wartling	1	2 no T				3	1	
Herstmonceux								
Ashburnham	2	2 no T				2		
Ninfield	15	12 no T	1 no T		2 no T	18	4	John King
Hove								

[Hastings Rape Schedule No 6 continued]

Parishes Divided into Districts	No of Subscribers	Number of Waggons with tilts and Four Horses or more	Number of Waggons with tilts and Three Horses	Number of Carts with tilts and Three Horses or more	Number of Carts with tilts and Two Horses	No of Persons appointed to act as Servants with Teams	Conductors for the same in proportion of 1 to every 10 Waggons	Names of General Agents
[6th]								
Fairlight	2	2 no T				2		
Ore	5	9 no T				6		
Crowhurst	10	8 no T	1 no T	1 T	2 no T	15		William Cheal
Westfield								
Castle								
St Leonards								
Hollington								
[7th]								
Beckley	5	5				12	2	Samuel Reeves*
Northiam	9	2 with T 5 without	2 no T			18	1	Edward Jeremiah Curteis Esq*
Bodiam								
Ewhurst		There are hardly sufficient no of Waggons Carts and Teams to remove the Infirm Children and our Victuals						
[8th]								
Mountfield								
Sedlescomb								
Penhurst								
Brightling	14	2 with T 6 no T		2 no T	1 with T 4 without	14	2	
[9th]								
Battle	1	1	1	1		4		
Whatlington								
Catsfield	11	13 with T 1 without		20 no T	6 with T	22		
Bexhill								
[Totals]	134	13 86 no T†	7 19 no T‡	5 22 no T	7 17 no T	245	27	

* [Remark] They are willing to serve Government with Corn Hay and Straw as far as in their power when called on so to do

† error: should read 27 84 no T

‡ error: should read 8 20 no T

Hastings Rape Schedule No 7

Parishes Divided into Districts	No of Subscribers Names	Names and situations of Water Mills	Names and situations of Wind Mills	No of Sacks of Flour of 280 lbs net each to be furnished by each Miller every 24 Hours	Whether such Subscribers will provide Wheat or not
[1st]					
Salehurst	3	2 Roberts-bridge	1 Salehurst	11	Yes
Ticehurst	2	1 Withernden 1 Dunster	1 near Ticehurst Town Cannot Furnish Customers	2 Sacks Dunsters Mill	Dunsters Yes
Burwash	1	I cannot engage for no certain Quantity but am willing to do the Utmost of my Power if called on Signed Edward Hildar			
Etchingham					
[2nd]					
Heathfield	3	willing to do what they can			
Warbleton	2	Rushlake & Crawl		Bucksteep Mill the Miller will not say without being obliged to it	No
Dallington					
[3rd]					
Peasmarsh	1		1		
Iden					
Playden	2 no Cloth		2	6	Yes
Eastguildford					
[4th]					
Brede					
Udimore	1		1	6 if wind at the Mill	No
Guestling	1 no Cloth	1		1	Yes
Icklesham					
Pett					
[5th]					
Wartling	1		2	20	Yes
Herstmonceux	1 no Cloth		1	20	No
Ashburnham					
Ninfield					
Hove					

[Hastings Rape Schedule No 7 continued]

Parishes Divided into Districts	No of Subscribers Names	Names and situations of Water Mills	Names and situations of Wind Mills	No of Sacks of Flour of 280 lbs net each to be furnished by each Miller every 24 Hours	Whether such Subscribers will provide Wheat or not
[6th]					
Fairlight	1		Fairlight Down	10	Yes
Ore					
Crowhurst					
Westfield	1		Westfield		Yes
Castle					
St Leonards					
Hollington					
[7th]					
Beckley	2	2 Beckley & Consters	1 Wind Mill	3	Yes
Northiam			2	Nothing certain can be said but they are willing to do anything they possibly can	
Bodiam			only a small Water Mill what can't Grind sufficient Grist for the Inhabitants		
Ewhurst		1 Flour at the Mill no Cloth	2	No	
[8th]					
Mountfield					
Sedlescomb					
Penhurst					
Brightling		1 at the Mill no Cloth	1	Uncertain	No
[9th]					
Battle	The Millers are now and probably will continue to supply the Bakers for the Troops at Silver Hill Barracks and in ths Parish				
Whatlington	1 at the Mill no Cloth	1	1 Sedlescomb	3	No
Catsfield	1 at the Mill no Cloth	1	1		Yes
Bexhill	2 no Cloth at the Mill		2	willing to deliver as much Flour as thay can over and above the Wants of their Customers	No

Hastings Rape Schedule No 8

Parishes Divided into Districts	Subscribers names	\multicolumn{4}{c	}{No of Loaves of 3 lbs to be furnished by each subscriber every 24 Hours}	No of addl Journeymen required
		For a constancy	On an Emergency	By the help of an additional Journeymen for a constancy		
[1st]						
Salehurst						
Ticehurst						
Burwash						
Etchingham						
[2nd]						
Heathfield						
Warbleton						
Dallington						
[3rd]						
Peasmarsh						
Iden						
Playden						
Eastguildford						
[4th]						
Brede						
Udimore						
Guestling						
Icklesham						
Pett						
[5th]						
Wartling	John Fuller	120			
	Thomas Chapman	80			
	Thomas Soper	60	120		2
Herstmonceux					
Ashburnham					
Ninfield	Benjamin Moore	three sacks	and 4 sacks	and no more	
	Daniel Hawthorn	2 Sacks	and 4 sacks	and no more	
Hove					

For what kind of fuel the Ovens are Calculated	What Quantity is required every 24 Hours to keep each overn continuously at work supposing 6 batches to be baked	Whether. Fuel is abundant or not Answer Yes or no	Remarks
Wood Wood Faggotts	12	No	
Wood Wood	4 2	Yes No	

[Hastings Rape Schedule No 8 continued]

Parishes Divided into Districts	Subscribers names	For a constancy	On an Emergency	By the help of an additional Journeymen for a constancy	No of addl Journeymen required
[6th]					
Fairlight					
Ore					
Crowhurst					
Westfield					
Castle					
St Leonards					
Hollington					
[7th]					
Beckley					
Northiam	None but private ovens				
Bodiam	No public Baker in the Parish				
Ewhurst					
[8th]					
Mountfield					
Sedlescomb					
Penhurst					
Brightling	Sarah Cruttenden Mary Veness	60	80		
[9th]					
Battle	1 Vacant Oven		780	Supposing four Batches only to be baked	
Whatlington					
Catsfield	60 private Ovens supposed to Bake in 24 Hours 360 Bushells of Flour and all				
Bexhill					

Column header: No of Loaves of 3 lbs to be furnished by each subscriber every 24 Hours — By their usual number of Hands

For what kind of fuel the Ovens are Calculated	What Quantity is required every 24 Hours to keep each overn continuously at work supposing 6 batches to be baked	Whether. Fuel is abundant or not Answer Yes or no	Remarks
Wood	6	No	
		Yes	
calculated to burn Wood			

Hastings Rape Schedule No 9

Parishes	Name of the Proprietor	Proprietors Residence	Names of the Masters	Masters Residence	Parish District or Hundred to which the craft belongs
[1st]					
Salehurst					
Ticehurst					
Burwash					
Etchingham					
[2nd]					
Heathfield					
Warbleton					
Dallington	Samuel Selmes & Co	Beckley	Edward Butler	Peasmarsh	Goldspur
[3rd]					
Peasmarsh					
Iden	James Turner	Iden	James Turner	Iden	Iden
Playden	John Reeves Do	Playden Do	Thomas Nichol William Pulford	Rye Do	Playden Do
Eastguildford	Thomas Gosley Do Do	Eastguildford Do Do	James Rhodes Benjamin Foster William Gosley	Rye Do Do	Eastguildford Do Do

[Note: all other Districts and Parishes in this Schedule are blank and omitted here}

In what county	Number or names of the craft	Tonnage	Whether decked or not	River or canal on which employed	Place to which the craft usually trades
Sussex	Constant Trader	22	No	Rother	from Rye to Peasmarsh by Playden & Iden
Sussex	The Thomas	15	No	Rother	Iden Playden Peasmarsh
Sussex	Plough	22	No	Rother	Newenden
Do	Two Brothers	12	No	Do	Do
Sussex	Ocean	21	No	Rother	Rye
Do	Traveller	16	No	Do	Do
Do	Otter	16	No	Do	Do

Signed J Tilden Sampson
Subdivision Clerk

[1 August 1803 continued]

Resolved

>That this meeting do not recommend the appointment of Officers under the General Defence Act considering the Amended Act to have done it away and therefore leave it to His Grace the Duke of Richmond to act as he pleases.
>
>In consequence of the time necessary for the Clerk of the General Meetings to prepare proper orders to be signed by the Lieutenant and Deputy Lieutenants they have adjourned this meeting to Wednesday the 10th day of August to be held at the Star Inn at Lewes at 10 of the Clock in the forenoon precisely and all the Subdivision Meetings are to be held before that Day fortnight

W Ellis Clerk

[10 August 1803]

Sussex (To wit)

At a Meeting of the Lieutenancy of the said County held at the Star Inn at Lewes on Wednesday the 10th day of August 1803 for carrying the Army en Masse and other Acts into execution

Present

His Grace the Duke of Richmond in the Chair
John Lord Sheffield
Henry Lord Viscount Gage
Lord St Asaph
John Fuller Esq Rosehill
George O Brien Earl of Egremont
William Newton Esq
Sir Thomas Carr Knight
George Shiffner Esq
Henry Thurloe Shadwell Esq
John Trayton Fuller Esq
Thomas Davis Lamb Esq
Thomas Cecil Grainger Esq
Thomas Kemp Esq
Francis Newberry Esq
Harry Bridger Esq
William Sewell Esq
Charles Gilbert Esq
Francis Hare Naylor Esq

Whereas it has appeared at this Meeting that there are several Places where the lower Orders of the People are ready and willing to form Volunteer Corps or to learn the use of Arms, but are in want of Gentlemen or Substantial Yeomen for Officers,

It is Resolved

by the Lieutenancy that great as the Merit is in such Gentlemen or Yeomen who have undertaken to serve as Privates in any Corps of this County, they would far better assist the present Exertions that are making for the General Defence of the Country if such of them as can be useful as officers would offer themselves for such Situations amongst their Neighbours and thereby greatly assist the present Levies that this Resolution be communicated to the Commanding Officers of Yeomanry and Volunteers and that they be desired to induce such Gentlemen who are Privates in their Troops & could be of more use as officers to offer themselves for such Service

that the same be advertized twice in Lewes Journal and once in Chichester Paper

Rape of Hastings

Lord St Asaph recommends Mr Gilmore Hervey of Battle to be Captain and he recommends Mr Lawrence and Mr Woodward to be Lieutenant and Ensigns of a Volunteer Company called the Battle Company consisting of not less than 100 Privates & a proportion of Non Commissioned Officers upon the Terms offered in Lord Hobart's Letter of the 3rd August

Offers were received of 122 men from Ashburnham Penhurst Ninfield & Catsfield but they wait for officers

Francis Hare Naylor Esq offers to be a Captain and recommends Mr Eardley Michel for his Lieutenant (Ensigns vacant) and 100 Privates, Herstmonceux Company. Francis Hare Naylor Esq also offers for William Pigou Esq of Windmill Hill in the Parish of Wartling as Captain of a Company of 100 Men, Wartling Company. He is not yet prepared for other officers

Mr Fuller recommends Mr Edward J Curties of Northiam as Captain of Pioneers in that Rape

South Pevensey

Lord Gage and the Gentlemen of this Division wish for a short time to prepare a plan for a Legion under his Lordship

North Pevensey

Lord Sheffield has it in Contemplation to propose an addition to his Legion which he will deliver in a Short Time

South Division of Lewes

Captain Shiffner recommends Thomas Kemp Esq's offer of being Captain of two Companies called Lewes Companies each to consist of 120 privates Officers and non Commissioned Officers in proportion, and will recommend his Officers in a short time

Colonel William Newton
G E Graham Esq
Thomas Partington Esq
John Martin Crips Esq
George Newnham Esq
Elijah Impey Esq
James Ingram of Rottingdean

each offers to raise a Company from 60 to 120 each but will give in further Particulars in a short Time

An offer is also made by Messrs Attree & Scutt of a Company at Brighton of 100 Men to cloth themselves but the Captain is not yet proposed

North Lewes

Captain William Sewell of Ivyford Lodge near East Grinstead recommends Parham[116] Nairne Esq of Burks Place Westhoathly and William Ward Lieutenant and John Reynolds Lieutenant, William Seaton of Worth to be Captain, the Subalturn [sic] to be hereafter proposed each Company from 60 to 120 Men

South Bramber

Mr Goring recommends Mr Richard Barnard Comber of Steyning to raise a Company of 120 Men called the Steyning Company

Harry Bridger Esq to raise a Company of 120 Men called the Shoreham Company

William Margisson Esq to raise a Company of Men to be called[117] Subalterns to be named in a short Time

At this Meeting the Deputy Lieutenants above mentioned issued out their precepts to the several & respective Constables of the City Borough and Hundreds within the said County requiring them to issue out their Warrants to the Churchwardens and Overseers of the Poor of the several Parishes and Places within their respective Jurisdictions according to the form therewith transmitted unto them

---

[116] This forename is corrected to Fasham in a later and different hand
[117] The name is left blank

And the said Deputy Lieutenants appointed the first Subdivision Meeting to be held for each Rape in the said County as follows

For the Rape of Chichester at the Swan Inn in Chichester on Saturday the 20th day of August Instant

For the Rape of Arundell at the Swann Inn in Petworth the same day

For the Lower Division of the Rape of Bramber at the Kings head Inn in Horsham, same day

For the Rape of Lewes at the Star Inn in Lewes on Monday the 22nd

For the Lower Division of the Rape of Pevensey at the Sheffield Arms Inn in Fletching the same day

For the Upper Division of the said Rape of Bramber at the Chequer Inn in Steyning on Wednesday the 24th

For the Rape of Hastings at the George Inn in Battle the same day

For the Upper Division of the Rape of Bramber at the Chequer Inn in Steyning on Wednesday the 24th day of the same month[118]

This Meeting requests that all Volunteers Corps will forthwith send to Mr William Ellis, Horsham, Clerk of the General Meetings a Return of the Names and Places of abode of Effective Men & Establishment of their Corps in order to their being transmitted to the General Commanding in the District

All offers of Service are desired to be made thro the Lieutenant of the Division of the Rape to the Lord Lieutenant

This Meeting requests that Mr Tredcroft Sir George Thomas & Mr Peachey will immediately transmit all offers of Service made to them to the Duke of Richmond

This Meeting is adjourned to the Castle Inn in Brighton to Monday the 22nd day of August Instant
        W Ellis Cl[er]k

---

[118] see above: note the repetition of the entry for Bramber Upper

[22 August 1803]

At a Meeting of the Lieutenancy held at the Castle Inn in Brighton in and for the Count of Sussex on Monday the 22nd August 1803 for carrying the several Acts relative to the General Defence of the Country into Execution

Present

His Grace the Duke of Richmond His Majesty's Lieutenant
George Obrien Earl of Egremont
Henry Lord Viscount Gage
Lord St Asaph
Lieutenant General Sir James Pulteney
Major General Charles Lennox
Major General White
Honorable John Thomas Capel
John Fuller Esq of Rosehill
William Stephen Poyntz Esq
Nathaniel Tredcroft Esq
Charles Goring Esq
Thomas Kemp Esq
Henry Shelley jun Esq
Charles Foster Goring Esq
William Newton Esq
Harry Bridger Esq
John Peachy Esq
Timothy Shelley Esq
Henry Thurloe Shadwell Esq
George Shiffner Esq

Resolved Unanimously

That it is the Opinion of this Meeting that the Letter of Lord Hobart of the eighteenth Instant expressing that the Yeomanry is to be included in the Number of 4818 Volunteers that are to be authorized to be raised in this Country [sic] refers only to such Yeomanry as are of any Expence to Government, or receive or require Arms from the Public Stores. But that Corps of Yeomanry or Volunteers that exist or offer their Services free of Expences whatever to Government and require no Arms to be supplied to them, may be received over and above the Number of 4818 specified for this County

That as all the Yeomanry or Volunteers in this County have confirmed their Offers of Service to the Southern Military District pursuant to the Act of 22nd of June 1802 it is presumed that they are not to be included in the Volunteers under the Act of the 11th of August instant which requires their service to be extended to any part of Great Britain

That the proportion of Men who will be admitted as Volunteers will be nearly six times the Quota that each Parish furnishes for the Militia and that the Commanding Officers be desired to take their Men from the several parishes nearly in that proportion, but making any small variations that circumstances may require

The Earl of Egremont, Colonel of the Sussex Yeomanry reports that the number of effective Yeomen that do receive aid from Government is nearly 370 Men

Resolved

That the whole Number of Volunteers to be raised being 4328 to be taken from the Six Rapes in the same proportions as they supply the militia which will be as follows

For the Rape of Chichester	772
For the Rape of Arundell	540
For the Rape of Bramber	561
For the Rape of Lewes	804
For the Rape of Pevensey	910
For the Rape of Hastings	661
Total	4248 [sic]

That it be represented to Government that it appears from the offers of Volunteers that have been made in this County that they amount to more than double the Number of 4818 to be authorized

That if these offers are reduced to the proposed Number, many have declared that they will withdraw their offer, particularly the younger Men who will be most usefull but who are fearful if the Farmers & Elderly Men are excepted they may be turned over or made to join the Regular Forces

But if the whole or nearly the whole are admitted they will be ready to be trained

Under these Circumstances and considering how small a force 4818 Volunteers is, for the extensive Coasts of this County, it is submitted to His Majesty's Ministers whether it would be too much to allow that Number to be doubled, which it is conceived would obviate the beforementioned difficulties and prevent the General Spirit now existing for Volunteering from experiencing any Check in this County

Resolved unanimously

That the offers for Volunteers must be under the Act of the 11th August 1803

By the Act of the 27th July last all Men (except such as are therein excepted) between the ages of 17 and 55 are to be Ballotted and classed and may be drawn out and embodied in Case of actual Invasion, or on the appearance of the Enemy in force upon the Coast and may be placed in such of the existing Regiments, Battalions or Corps whether Regulars, Militia or Fencibles as may from time to time be appointed to serve in Great Britain, and may be led into any part of Great Britain for the repelling and Prevention of such Invasion or for the suppression of any Rebellion or Insurrection within Great Britain, arising or existing at the Time of any such Invasion

But as Volunteers although they are liable to be called out and march in the same Manner as if Balloted, yet are not liable to be placed in any Regiment Battalion or Corps of Regulars Militia or Fencibles, but are to serve with their own officers only, under General Officers like the Militia

They are to be called out to exercise on every Sunday from the 25th of March to the 25 of December, or if they have any religious scruples of being exercised on a Sunday another day is to be fixed on by their Commanding Officer for that purpose

For such Sunday or other Day no allowance is to be made to them

Besides such Sunday or other Day they are to be exercised one more day in each Week not more than Twenty Days during the above mentioned period, and for such second Day they are to receive one Shilling, provided they have been exercised on the Previous Sunday or any other Day in lieu thereof

Twenty Shillings for each Man is allowed by Government towards Cloathing for Three Years

They are to take the oath of allegiance when enrolled to be under Military Law when embodied and to be deemed and punished as Deserters if they do not March when ordered

Two Guineas is to be given to each Man to provide him with Necessaries when he Marches and one Guinea when he returns

Each Volunteers family when he Marches is to be provided for like Militia Men

The Places and Times of Exercise to be appointed will be as Convenient as Circumstances will admit

The Meeting then proceeded to receive the offers of Service and begun with the

Rape of Hastings

When there appeared from the Report of John Fuller Esq Lieutenant of this Rape that

	Men
William Gilmore Harvey Esq as Captain proposed to raise one Company of	130
That if a proper officer could be found for Captain another Company might be raised of	134
Sir William Ashburnham Bart 1 Do	120
Francis Hare Naylor Esq each 1 Captain making	217
William Henry Pigou Esq together	
William Shadwell Esq 1 Do	120
Robert Miles Esq 1 Do	120
Robert Hawes Esq 1 Do	122
John Micklethwaite Esq Infantry & Cavalry	200
By his two Letters of the 12th August Instant *Ordered* to be sent to the Secretary of State	
John Fuller Esq of Rosehill on the same terms for	121

For the Southern Division of the Rape of Pevensey

a Proposal was delivered by Lord Viscount Gage Lieutenant of the Southern Division of the Rape of Pevensey *Ordered* to be laid before the Secretary of State by which it appeared that the following Gentlemen as Captains propose to raise

Edward Auger Gentleman	one Company of 120
Sir Thomas Law Knight	one Do of 120
William Stephens Gent	one Do of 120
John Bean Esq	one Do of 120
William Wheeler Gent	one Do of 120
William Longs Esq	one Do of 120
If a proper Captain can be found another Company may be raised of	of 120
	840

Lord Gage was proposed as Colonel Inigo Freeman Thomas Esq as Major Sir John Riggs Miller delivered in a proposal for Raising a Troop of Yeomanry and to equip and furnish themselves with Horses, Cloathes, Arms and Accoutrements at their own Expence to act within the Southern Division and subject to the same terms and Conditions with respect to the existing Yeomanry under the Command of the Earl of Egremont, to consist of 44 Yeoman besides 3 officers

Ordered to be laid before the Secretary of State Captain Mowatt has a Company of Volunteers Artillery at East Bourne which has been approved by Government

For the Northern Division of the Rape of Pevensey

Lord Sheffield the Lieutenant did not attend or send in any Proposals, probably considering his Legion that has been accepted by Government as superseding the necessity of such offers
Ordered that it be submitted to His Majesty's Secretary of State how far Lord Sheffield's Corps of Volunteers whose services are limited as expressed in this offer, are to be considered part of the Volunteer Corps, to be raised under the Act of 27th July 1803 whose services are required to extend to any part of England

A Letter from J H Challen Esq from Blatchington Place, August 9th offering to raise a Company of Coast Artillery 43 Men
To be laid before the Secretaries of State, not recommended by the Lieutenant of the said Rape

For the Southern Division of Lewes Rape

Captain Shiffner, Lieutenant of this Division, delivered in a Paper that is *Ordered* to be laid before the Secretary of State by which it appears that the following Gentlemen offer to raise Companies as follows

Lieutenant Colonel Newton	1 Company	110
Thomas Partington Esq	1 Do	100
George Edward Graham Esq	1 Do	170
Elijah Impey Esq	1 Do	51
John Martin Cripps Esq	1 Do	137
James Ingram Gent	1 Do	75
John Lewis Newnham Esq	1 Do	100
John Pelham Roberts Esq	1 Do	120
William Franklin Hick Esq	1 Do	132
		995

Lieutenant Colonel Newton was proposed as Lieutenant Colonel George Edward Graham Esq as Major

From the Town of Brighton

Colonel Moore's Company of Volunteer Artillery has been accepted by Government and consists of   100

a Letter from Mr Scutt dated the 18th of August with an offer of a Company of   100

Ordered to be laid before the Secretary of State

Northern Division of Lewes Rape

a Letter from Captain Sewell Lieutenant of this Division was Read
As also one from Francis Sergison Esq *Ordered* to be laid before the Secretary of State

Southern Division of the Rape of Bramber

Charles Goring Esq Lieutenant of this Division presented a Letter dated 13th of August
Ordered to be laid before the Secretary of State
The farther consideration of offers in this Division to be deferred till the next meeting

Northern Division of the Rape of Bramber

Nathaniel Tredcroft Esq Lieutenant of this Division presented offers from Lieutenant Colonel Bellis from the Town and Neighbourhood of Horsham for Infantry including Officers   138
and one from John Watling Esq including Officers for Cavalry   41
These offers to be laid before the Secretary of State
as to the rest of the Division, Mr Tredcroft wished to have the offers postponed till the next Meeting
The Lower Division of Bramber Rape not yet being ready with their offers of service
Ordered that it be postponed till the next General Meeting
The Upper Division of the said Rape being in the same predicament, to be postponed as above

For the Southern Division of the Rape of Arundel

Sir George Thomas Bart the Lieutenant of this Division did not attend but transmitted an offer he recommended from Edward Carleton Esq dated 16th of August offering to raise in and about Arundel 3 Companies under

Edward Carleton Esq
Charles Ibbetson Esq   250 may be increased to 300
John Busby Esq

Ordered to be laid before the Secretary of State

General White offered to raise Volunteers who had offered to the number of 461, but the officers to be recommended not being settled, This offer was postponed till the next Meeting

Northern Division of Arundel Rape

The Earl of Egremont Lieutenant of this Rape attended His Lordship thought that the Explanation to the Volunteers of the Terms on which they had to serve had best be first read to them and that the offers from this Division should be postponed till the next Meeting

Southern Division of Chichester Rape

John Peachey Esq the Lieutenant of this Division attended and produced an offer from the City of Chichester
Ordered to be laid before the Secretary of State, by which it appears that the Service offered is limited, but that under John Gage Esq as Colonel and John Quantock Esq as Major and five Captains viz

William Johnson
John Marsh
William Fowler   it is proposed to raise
John Murray and   including Officers 684 Men
Joseph Godman

Also a Letter from several Gentlemen and others included in the above Number dated 21 of August offering to form a Company of Rifle Men to Cloth themselves
Ordered to be laid before the Secretary of State

W Ellis Cl[er]k

[29 August 1803]

Sussex (to wit)

At a General Meeting of the Lieutenancy of the said County held at the Castle Inn in Brighton in the said County on Monday the 29th day of August 1803 for carrying the before mentioned Acts into further Execution

Present

His Grace the Duke of Richmond His Majesty's Lieutenant
George Obrien Earl of Egremont
Henry Lord Viscount Gage
John Lord Sheffield
Lord St Asaph
Lieutenant General Charles Lennox
Sir Charles Merrick Burrell Bart
George Shiffner Esquire
William Newton Esquire
Henry Shelley Junior Esquire
Henry Thurloe Shadwell Esquire

That

as the County will by the Act of Parliament be liable for a Fine of ten Pounds for every Man who shall be returned to the next Michaelmas Quarter Sessions deficient in either the old or Supplementary Militia. It is by this General Meeting of the Lieutenancy recommended to the Deputy Lieutenants and Justices of the Peace in the several Subdivision Meetings of this County to cause immediate Ballots to be had for those Parishes where such deficiencies arise and where such deficiencies have arisen from persons who have paid the penalties either of ten or fifteen Pounds to offer those penalties of ten or fifteen Pounds respectively which has been paid into the Hands of the Deputy Lieutenants on former Ballots to the Man that will now be ballotted in aid of the Seven Pounds ten shillings being the halfprice of a Volunteer which he will receive on serving himself or producing a proper substitute. And in case such Man so drawn shall not serve by himself or produce a substitute. It is recommended to the Deputy Lieutenants and Justices of the Peace at such Subdivision Meetings immediately to proceed to a second Ballot and to offer to the Man so chosen the first penalty which has been so received and likewise ten pounds of the second Penalty making together twenty five pounds twenty or (as the case may be) besides the Seven Pounds ten shillings the half price of a Volunteer which he will receive from the Parish if he serves or provides a Substitute, reserving the remaining five pounds of the second Penalty for the regimental Stock. And immediately to proceed in like manner to a third Ballot in case a Man is not found and soon offering all the preceeding penalties except the Reserve of five pounds before mentioned from the second Penalty for the regimental Stock until a Man is found

Resolved

That it is the Opinion of this Meeting That Seven Pounds ten shillings should be paid as half the current price of a Volunteer to a person who serves himself or provides a Substitute agreably to the Militia Act from the Date of the King's Proclamation ordering out the Supplementary Militia (26th May 1803) and ten pounds under the Army of Reserve Act from the time of the first Ballot, and do recommend the Deputy Lieutenants and Justices of the Peace for the several Subdivisions of the said County to adopt the same accordingly

Ordered

That the future Ballots for Militia Men be taken from the amended Lists returned for raising the Army of Reserve

It is the Opinion of this Meeting that seven days Notice ought to be given previous to any Ballot for the Militia and do recommend it to the several Subdivisions to adopt it accordingly

Ordered

That all the Subdivision Clerks do attend all future General Meetings

Ordered

That a Copy of the above be sent each Subdivision Clerk

Adjourned sine die subject to His Grace the Duke of Richmond's call on giving three Days Notice in the Lewes Journal

        [signed]   Wm Ellis
                         Clerk to the General Meeting of Lieutenancy

[17 September 1803]

Sussex (to wit)

At a General Meeting of the Lieutenancy held at the Castle Inn in Brighthelmstone in and for the said County on Saturday the 17th Day of September 1803 for carrying the before mentioned Acts into further Execution

Present

His Grace the Duke of Richmond His Majesty's Lieutenant
Henry Lord Viscount Gage
George Obrien Earl of Egremont
George Shiffner Esquire
Charles Goring Esquire
James Martin Lloyd Esquire
Inigo Freeman Thomas Esquire
John Fuller Esquire of Rosehill
Nathaniel Tredcroft Esquire
Timothy Shelley Esquire
John Peachey Esquire
Francis Hare Naylor Esquire
Thomas Cecil Grainger Esquire
Thomas Davis Lamb Esquire
William Newton Esquire
Charles Gilbert Esquire
Henry Thurloe Shadwell Esquire
William Stephen Poyntz Esquire
Henry Shelley Junior Esquire
Thomas Kemp Esquire
Major General Charles Lennox
Charles Foster Goring Esquire
Harry Bridger Esquire
Sir Thomas Carr Knight
Lieutenant General Sir James Pulteney
Colonel Carnegie Central Commissary
Thomas Partington Esquire
Sir Cecil Bysshopp Baronet

Read A Circular Letter from the War Office dated 8th July last notifying the places appointed for assembling Army of Reserve Men
Another Do from the War Office dated 31st August last respecting Arms
Another Do from the War Office dated 1st September Instant respecting Aliens

Another Letter from the War Office dated the 3rd respecting the Offers of Volunteers

Another Do from the War Office dated the 7th for arraying the Volunteers of the County

Another Do from the War Office dated the 12th September Instant for allowing an additional number of Volunteers

Another Do from the War Office dated the 16th for exempting a limited number of Volunteers from the Ballot for the Militia and Army of Reserve strictly conforming with the General Defence Acts

Read the Attorney and Solicitor Generals Opinion respecting the above Exemptions

Resolved

that the following Explanation of the nature of Service required from Volunteers, and the Exemptions and Advantages they will be entitled to under the late Acts of Parliament be printed and Copies sent to the several Gentlemen commanding the same

First

That they are to be trained and exercised and in case of actual Invasion, or the appearance of an Enemy in force upon the Coast, to march to any part of Great Britain for the Defence thereof, or for the suppression of any Rebellion, or Insurrection arising or existing during such Invasion, whenever they shall be summoned by the Lieutenant of the County, or in consequence of General Signal of Alarm, ordered for that purpose

Second

That when so ordered out in consequence of Invasion, or appearance of an Enemy in force upon the Coast, they are to be under Military Law, but to remain under their own Officers, and are not to be placed in any Regiment, Battalion, or Corps of Regulars Militia or Fencibles

Third

That they are liable to be called out to exercise on every Sunday from the 25th of March to the 25th of September or if they have any religious Scruples concerning being exercised on a Sunday, then they are to be exercised on some other Day, to be fixed upon by their Commanding Officer, but are not to receive any allowance for such Sunday, or other Day's exercise, and that they are to be exercised at least one other Day in each Week to the amount of twenty Days at the least, and for such additional Days not being more than twenty in a year, they are to be allowed one shilling per Day, provided they have been exercised on the previous Sunday, or other Day in lieu thereof

Fourth
That they are to be allowed by Government towards Cloathing for 3 Years the sum of twenty shillings to be disposed of by their Commanding Officer for that purpose

Fifth
That they are to take the Oath of Allegiance on their Inrollment

Sixth
That two Guineas are to be allowed to provide them necessaries by their Captain when called upon to march upon actual Service and one Guinea when they return

Seventh
That their families are to be provided for like those of the Militia Men, while they are engaged in actual Service

Eighth
That after having attended properly armed and accoutred, and equipped at the Muster and Exercise twenty four Days at the least between the 1st of January and last Day of December in each year (unless prevented by Sickness certified by a Medical Practitioner to the Commanding Officer and admitted by him) and having been so returned by their commanding Officer in his Muster Rolls, which are to be made every first of January, first of May, and first of September, they are to be exempt from all Ballot either in the Militia, or Army of Reserve, and remain so until struck out of the Muster Roll, for non attendance or default

Resolved
That the following Agreement and Oath be printed on parchment and signed and taken by the several Volunteers of this County and two Copies thereof sent to the Captain of each Company for the purpose of enrolling their Names on namely

We whose Names are hereunto subscribed do agree to serve in the Company to be commanded by .... in the .... to be commanded by .... in the .... Division of the Rape of .... upon the Terms required in respect to Volunteers by the several Acts of Parliament lately passed for the Defence of the Realm. And we do severally promise and swear that we will be faithful and bear true allegiance to His Majesty King George

Resolved

That one Uniform be adopted for the said Volunteers of which a specimen is left with General Lennox at Brighton

Scheme for Distribution of the Volunteers to be raised for the County of Sussex

	Regiment	Battalion	Corps	Companies	Total	Col	Lt Col	Major
Hastings		1		4 of 110	440		1	1
South Pevensey	1			8 of 120	960	1	1	2
North Lewes			1	3 of 60	180			1
South Lewes	1			8 of 120	960	1	1	2
North Bramber			1	3 of 100	300			1
South Bramber		1		4 of 110	440		1	1
North Arundel			1	3 of 60	180			1
South Arundel		1		4 of 80	320		1	1
Arundel Town			1	3 of 80	240			1
North Chichester			1	3 of 70	210			1
South Chichester	1			4 of 120	480	1	1	1
City of Chichester		1		5 of 60	300		1	1
				52	5010			

Resolved

That this Meeting be dissolved and that all future Orders of Service of Volunteers be transmitted through the Lieutenant of the Division to His Grace the Duke of Richmond the Lord Lieutenant of the County

[signed] Wm Ellis Clerk
to the Lieutenancy

[4 October 1803]

Sussex (to wit)

At a General Meeting of His Majesty's Lieutenant and Deputy Lieutenants acting in and for the said County held at the Half Moon in Petworth in and for the said County on Tuesday the 4th Day of October 1803 for carrying the Laws relating to the Army in Mass Act into Execution

Present

His Grace the Duke of Richmond His Majesty's Lieutenant
George Obrien Earl of Egremont
Sir George Thomas Baronet
John Sargent Esquire
John Peachey Esquire
William Battine Esquire
William Stephen Poyntz Esquire
Nathaniel Tredcroft Esquire

This being the first annual General Meeting approved by the Act for issuing Precepts to return fresh Lists and appoint Subdivision Meetings and the Returns under the Militia Law being ordered It was not thought necessary to proceed any further on this Act

[signed] Wm Ellis
Clerk to the Lieutenancy

[24 October 1803]

Sussex (to wit)

At a General Meeting of His Majesty's Deptenant [sic],[119] Deputy Lieutenants and Justices acting in and for the said County held at the Castle Inn in Brighton in and for the said County the 24th Day of October 1803 for carrying the several Acts relative to the General Defence of the Country into Execution

Present

His Grace the Duke of Richmond His Majesty's Lieutenant
Right Honourable Thomas Lord Pelham
Francis Newbery Esquire
George Shiffner Esquire
Honourable John Thomas Capel
Sir Charles Merrick Burrell Bart
John Leach Esquire
John Newbery Esquire
Walter Burrell Esquire &
Thomas Henry Harben Esquire

It appearing to this Meeting that the following Gentlemen had already raised the undermentioned Volunteer Troops and Corps Namely

Lord St Asaph	Battle	Cavalry
Capt Mowatt	Eastbourne	Artillery Volunteers
Capt Sewell	Twyford Lodge	Cavalry
Capt Shiffner	Combeplace	Do
Col Moore	Brighton	Infantry
Capt Campion	Danny	Cavalry
Sir Cecil Bysshopp Bart	Parham	Do
Lord Egremont	Petworth	Do
Capt Bale	Littlehampton	Volunteer Artillery
Duke of Richmond	Goodwood	Light Horse Artillery
Capt Lion	Chichester	Cavalry
Capt Poyntz	Midhurst	Do

Ordered

That the undermentioned Corps of Volunteers be raised at the following places in addition to the above namely

---

[119] Ellis's hand becomes shakier as time passes, and mistakes creep in

Hastings Rape	4 Companies
South Pevensey	8
North Lewes	3
South Lewes	8
North Bramber	3
South Bramber	4
North Arundel	3
South Arundel	4
Arundel Town	3
North Chichester	3
South Chichester	4
City of Chichester	<u>5</u>
	<u>52</u> Companies

[signed] Wm Ellis
Clerk

[12 November 1803]

    Sussex

    At a General Meeting of His Majesty's Lieutenant and Deputy Lieutenants and Captains of Volunteer Corps held at the Castle Inn in Brighthelmstone in and for the said County on Saturday the 12th Day of November 1803 for carrying the beforementioned Acts into Execution

Present

    His Grace the Duke of Richmond His Majesty's Lieutenant
    Henry Lord Viscount Gage
    Lord Saint Asaph
    George Obrien Earl of Egremont
    Right Honourable Thomas Lord Pelham
    Lieut Genl Sir James Pulteney
    Major Genl Charles Lennox
    Sir Cecil Bysshopp Baronet
    Sir George Thomas Baronet
    John Fuller Esquire, Rosehill
    Henry Thurloe Shadwell Esquire
    Charles Goring Esquire
    James Martin Lloyd Esquire
    Thomas Kemp Esquire
    Walter Smyth Esquire
    William Stephen Poyntz Esquire
    Charles Gilbert Esquire
    John Trayton Fuller Esquire
    George Shiffner Esquire
    Honourable John Thomas Capel
    William Frankland Esquire
    Henry Shelly Jun Esquire
    Harry Bridger Esquire
    Thomas Partington Esquire
    John Martin Cripps Esquire
    William Margesson Esquire

    Read A Letter from the Right Honourable Charles Yorke to the Duke of Richmond Dated the 9th of November 1803

    Read A confidential Letter from Do to Do 31st October 1803
        Copy of a Letter from the Duke of Richmond to Mr Yorke 3rd November 1803

A Letter from Mr Yorke to the Duke of Richmond 7th November 1803
A Note from Do to Do of same Date namely 7th November 1803
A Letter from Do to Do 1st November 1803 respecting Adjutants for Volunteers
A Letter from Do to Do respecting special Constables Dated the 8th of November 1803
A Letter from same to same Dated 10th November 1803 respecting Volunteers with the Inclosures in the last two Letters

Ordered

That the same be printed in the Lewes Journal and Hants Chronicle

Ordered

That for the supply of 50 Waggons for each of the three places named by Sir James Pulteney namely Cuckfield Maresfield and Cross in Hand. The Deputy Lieutenants shall order those Waggons which are to supply Wood and are to come empty shall be supplied from the Parishes North of the Said Places; and that the Waggons to supply Hay and Straw shall be supplied from the Parishes South of the said places, but not from the Division

That the Superintendants and Overseers of Parishes shall immediately fix upon the particular Farmer's Teams in each Parish that shall be appointed for this Service and send into the Commissary Mr Drury at Eastbourne a List of their Names and those of their Drivers
Two Drivers for each Team

Waggons with four good Horses and two Drivers for the use of the Regiments

Hailsham	4	
Pevensey	4	Pevensey Rape
Eastbourne	6	
Seaford	6	
Brighthelmstone	18	Lewes Rape
Lewes	16	
Shoreham	6	Bramber Rape
Worthing	4	
Arundel	8	Arundel Rape

Ordered

That the Deputy Lieutenants should fix upon the particular Farmers in the Neighbourhood of the above places who shall furnish these several Teams to be kept in readiness to repair to the several Places above mentioned on receiving the order so to do from the Inspectors or Superintendants or in case of General Harm and that a List of the Farmers Names and of the several Drivers be sent immediately to Major Bunbury at Eastbourne

The undermentioned Distribution will I am inclined to think be a preferable one and I shall submit accordingly for the approbation of Sir James Pulteney[120]

	Hay	Straw	Wood	Empty	Total
1st Division at Cuckfield	20	10	10	10	50
2nd Do at Maresfield	20	10	10	10	50
3rd Do Cross in Hand	20	10	10	10	50
	60	30	30	30	150

---

[120] This is the only time when Mr Ellis intrudes his personal opinion into the record of proceedings

County of									1803	
Return of			Commanded by							
Cavalry			Infantry			Artillery				
Number of Troops	Establishment per Troop	Total	Number of Companies	Establishment per Company	Total	Number of Companies	Establishment per Company	Total	Field Officers	Captains

This Return is to be filled up dated and signed by the Commandant, who will at the same time add his Residence[121]

No alteration can be made in the Establishment when fixed, unless regularly authorized by the Secretary of State through the Lord Lieutenant of the County

Wm Ellis
Clerk

---

[121] This Schedule appears not to have been circulated or completed

Return of	County of								1803	
						Commanded by		Allowances required and granted		
Subalterns	Staff Officer	Serjeants	Corporals	Drummers	Effective Rank and File	Date of acceptance	Terms of Service	Pay	Cloathing	Contingencies

Return of Arms		
No provided by Divisional	No provided by Government	No wanted from Government

[18 February 1804]

Sussex (to wit)

At a General Meeting of His Majesty's Lieutenant and Justices acting in and for the said County held at the White Hart Inn in Lewes in and for the said County on Saturday the 18th day of February 1804 for carrying the before mentioned Acts into Execution

Present

George Shiffner Esquire
Henry Thurloe Shadwell Esquire
Charles Gilbert Esquire
Thomas Kemp Esquire
Charles Lamb Esquire
John Marten Cripps Esquire

This Meeting was adjourned to the same place to be there held on Saturday the 10th Day of March next. His Grace the Duke of Richmond not attending

Wm Ellis
Clerk

[10 March 1804]

Sussex (to wit)

At a Meeting of the Lieutenancy held at the White Hart Inn in Lewes in and for the said County on Saturday the 10th Day of March 1804 for carrying the before mentioned Acts into Execution

Present

The Right Honourable Thomas Lord Pelham
The Right Honourable John Lord Sheffield
The Right Honourable Henry Lord Viscount Gage
Sir John Bridger Knight
Henry Thurloe Shadwell Esquire
George Shiffner Esquire
Inigo Freeman Thomas Esquire
Thomas Kemp Esquire

At this Meeting Mr William Ellis Clerk of the said General Meetings and Clerk of the Subdivision of Bramber Rape produced his Bills amounting to the sums following namely General Meeting Bill Three Hundred and thirty pounds and Eight pence Army of Reserve Subdivision Bill Thirty six pounds and Eight pence and General Bill Seventy Seven pounds six shillings and four pence

Ordered

That the same be now allowed
NB The Army in Masse Bill was not allowed Mr Tredcroft having refused to allow it previous to this Meeting, on which account the Deputy Lieutenants conceived they were obliged to reject it

Also at this Meeting Mr John Tilden Sampson Clerk of the Subdivision Meetings for the Rape of Hastings in the said County produced his Bills amounting to the Sums following namely General Defence Bill and Army in Masse One Hundred and Forty pounds three shillings and ten pence and Army of Reserve Bill Thirty four pounds two shillings and Eight pence

Ordered

That the same be now allowed

Also at this Meeting Mr William Baulcomb Langridge Clerk to the Subdivision Meetings for the Rape of Lewes produced his Bills amounting to the sums following namely General Defence Bill One Hundred and thirty eight pounds nineteen shillings Army in Masse seventy three pounds fourteen Shillings and sixpence and Army of Reserve Forty eight pounds and ten shillings

Ordered

that the same be now allowed

Also at this Meeting Mr Samuel Gwynne Clerk to the Subdivision Meetings for the Rape of Lewes produce his Bills amounting to the sums following namely General Defence Bill One Hundred and fifty pounds and ten Shillings Army in Masse Sixty nine pounds four shillings and ten pence and Army of Reserve Eighty three pounds Six Shillings and four pence

Ordered

that the same be now allowed

[signed] Wm Ellis
Clerk to the Lieutenancy

[20 February 1806]

Sussex (S)

At a Meeting of Lieutenancy held in pursuance of a special ~~Summons~~[122] by His Majesty's Lieutenant for the said County at the White Hart Inn in Lewes in the said County on Thursday the 20th of February 1806 for carrying the before mentioned Acts into further Execution

Present

Henry Thurloe Shadwell	
William Sewell	Esquires
Thomas Partington	Deputy Lieutenants
Thomas Kemp	

Return of the Waggons for the Conveyance of the Volunteer Force of the Western Division of the Sussex District Inspected in November and December 1805

---

[122] The word appears to have been scrubbed out

[Return of Waggons etc 1805]

Group	Proprietors Names	Do Residences	Distance from the Place of Inspection Miles	Waggons seats	Men	No of Horses
Northlands near Chichester	John Cosens	Hunston	1	6	18	4
	E Sadler	Midlavant	3½	6	18	4
	Thomas Millyard	EastHampnett	3	6	18	4
	Elizabeth Wares	Strettington	3	6	18	4
	Alexander Fogden	Strettington	3	6	18	4
	John Andrews	Boxgrove	3½	6	18	4
	John Harvey	Halnaker	3½	6	18	4
	John Elliott	Chichester	1½	6	18	4
South Chichester Battalion Commanded by Brigadier General Crosbie	Charles Cooper	Chichester	1½	6	18	4
	John Boniface	Oving	3½	6	18	4
	William Hasley Esq	Bramber	4	6	18	4
	John Grove	Oving	4½	6	18	4
	John Dyer Esq	Crockerhill	7	6	18	4
	Edward Woods Esq	Shopwick	3	6	18	4
	Thomas Trew Esq	Rawmere	4	6	18	4
	George Sayers	Chichester	1½	6	18	4
	Thomas Osborne	Tangmere	5	6	18	4
	John Osborn	Tangmere	5	6	18	4
	Richard Fogden	Halnaker	3½	6	18	4
	Thomas White	Halnaker	3½	6	18	4
	Mary Long	Woodhorne	5	6	18	4
	William & Thomas Collins	Aldingbourne	7	6	18	4
	Thomas Smith	Boxgrove	6	6	18	4
	Stephen Wooldridge	Chichester	1½	6	18	4
	James Cosens	Hunston	1	6	18	4
	Richard Cosens	Hunston	1	6	18	4
	William Dearling	Donnington	1			
	Total	26 Waggons	1 Cart	156	468	103*

* error: should read 104

Carts Seats	Men	No of Horses	Carts for Baggage	No of Horses	Drivers Names	Money adjudged by the Lieutenancy for the Loss of that Days Labour £ s d	Remarks on Roads etc
-	-	-	-	-	Edmund Cosens	- 16 -	Present Effectives 421 Rank & File Wanting to Complete 83
-	-	-	-	-	James Dance John Hunt Boy	- 16 -	
-	-	-	-	-	Henry Barber	- 16 -	
-	-	-	-	-	George Wills	- 16 -	
-	-	-	-	-	John Fogden Edward Millyard Boy	- 16 -	
-	-	-	-	-	Samuel Aylet Joseph Bonned Boy	- 16 -	
-	-	-	-	-	William Targett	- 16 -	Only 2 Horses kept on this Farm
-	-	-	-	-	Richard Powell	- 16 -	
-	-	-	-	-	William Hackman William Rogers Boy	- 16 -	
-	-	-	-	-	Edward Burchall	- 16 -	
-	-	-	-	-	Thomas Tyler	- 16 -	
-	-	-	-	-	Al Kemp[123]	- 16 -	
-	-	-	-	-	John White	- 17 -	
-	-	-	-	-	Richard Coote	- 16 -	
-	-	-	-	-	John Smith	- 16 -	
-	-	-	-	-	George Viney	- 16 -	
-	-	-	-	-	Richard Pannell	- 16 -	
-	-	-	-	-	" "	- 16 -	
-	-	-	-	-	James Fogden	- 16 -	
-	-	-	-	-	Thomas White	- 16 -	
-	-	-	-	-	John Bayley	- 16 -	
-	-	-	-	-	Richard Parker	- 17 -	
-	-	-	-	-	Thomas Smith	- 16 -	
-	-	-	-	-	Charles Farndell	- 16 -	
-	-	-	-	-	" "	- 16 -	
-	-	-	-	-	George Lamberth	- 16 -	
-	-	-	-	-	William Copas	- 7 -	

[123] Forename unclear

[Return of Waggons etc 1805] continued

	Proprietors Names	Do Residences	Distance from the Place of Inspection Miles	Waggons seats	Men	No of Horses
Southover near Lewes	John Geer	Hurstpierpoint	2	6	18	4
	John Cheesman	Cooksbridge	4	6	18	4
	Mrs Coomber	Offham	5	6	18	4
	Henry Webb	Southease	5	6	18	4
	George Shiffner Esq	Hamsey	2	6	18	4
	Thomas Hodson	Street	2	7	21	4
	Thomas Bull	Barcomb	8	7	21	4
South Lewes Battalion Commanded by Colonel Newtown	William Hamshar	Westminston	5	7	21	4
	John Broomfield	Clayton	6	6	18	4
	John Marten Cripps Esq	Chiltington	3	6	18	4
	Sarah Pannett	Chailey	8	7	21	4
	Revd Sir H J Poole	The Hook	8	7	21	4
	Robert Kenward	Newick	11	7	21	4
	Sir Elijah Impey	Newick Park	11	7	21	4
	Thomas Saxby	Northease	9	6	18	4
	Peter Rowland	Ditcheling	4	6	18	4
	John Coppard	Wivelsfield	8	7	21	4
	T & J Weston	Newick	11	-	-	-

Proceedings and Schedules

Carts Seats	Men	No of Horses	Carts for Baggage	No of Horses	Drivers Names	Money adjudged by the Lieutenancy for the Loss of that Days Labour £ s d	Remarks on Roads etc
-	-	-	-	-	John Hards Henry Marshal Boy	- 16 -	Present Effectives Rank & File 480 Wanting to complete 530
-	-	-	-	-	John Holland William Lord Boy	- 16 -	
-	-	-	-	-	Henry Elliott H J Elliot jun Boy	- 16 -	
-	-	-	-	-	John Snee John Shelley Boy	- 16 -	
-	-	-	-	-	Henry Nye George Linfield Boy	- 16 -	Ye roads in General Good but most of this Corps is in the Wild and the communication there But indifferent
-	-	-	-	-	Charles Baker James Edwards	- 16 -	
-	-	-	-	-	Thomas Setford William Jenner	- 18 -	
-	-	-	-	-	Daniel Ordur William Denman	- 16 -	
-	-	-	-	-	William Cook James Cook Boy	- 16 -	
-	-	-	-	-	John King Henry Huggott	- 16 -	
-	-	-	-	-	Thomas Pannett John Pannett	- 18 -	
-	-	-	-	-	Henry Hugget William Strudwick	- 18 -	
-	-	-	-	-	Robert Kenward[124] Benjamin Gurr Boy	1 - 1 -	
-	-	-	-	-	No Man Robert Ford Boy	1 - 1 -	
-	-	-	-	-	Samuel Evans Edward Green Boy	- 19 -	
-	-	-	-	-	John Johnson William Johnson	- 16 -	
-	-	-	-	-	Henry Bristow William Newman Boy	- 18 -	
-	-	-	1	2	Michal Turner	- 10 -6	

---

[124] The erroneous entry Robert Rinware has been corrected to Robert Kenward under Proprietors Name but remains uncorrected here

[Return of Waggons etc 1805] continued

	Proprietors Names	Do Residences	Distance from the Place of Inspection Miles	Waggons seats	Men	No of Horses
South Lewes Battalion Commanded by Colonel Newtown [cont]	John Marshall	Hurstpierpoint	8	-	-	-
	Thomas Coomber	Chailey Parish	10	-	-	-
	John Martin Cripps Esq	Chiltington	3	-	-	-
	Peter Rowland	Ditcheling	4	-	-	-
	John Wright	Rottingdene	7	-	-	-
	John Sicklemore	Lewes	5	-	-	-
	17 Waggons	5 Carts		113*	346†	79‡
North Lewes Corps Commanded by Major Smith Butlers Green near Cuckfield	Isaac Sayers	Cuckfield	1	6	18	4
	William Coppard	Cuckfield	1	6	18	4
	Thomas Packham	Cuckfield Parish	3	6	18	4
	Richard Ewins	Cuckfield Parish	3	6	18	4
	Thomas Cooke	Keymer	1	6	18	4
	John Coppard	Cuckfield Parish	½	6	18	4
	William Clutton	Cuckfield	1½	6	18	4
	Major Smith	Butlers Green	¼			
	Revd Henry Chatfield	Balcomb	5			
	Timothy Brown	Ardingly	4			
				42	126	31**

* error: should read 110
† error: should read 330
‡ error: should read 68
** error: should read 28

Proceedings and Schedules

Carts Seats	Men	No of Horses	Carts for Baggage	No of Horses	Drivers Names	Money adjudged by the Lieutenancy for the Loss of that Days Labour £ s d	Remarks on Roads etc
-	-	-	1	1	William Marshall	- 8 -	
-	-	-	1	1	Thomas Coomber	- 9 -	
2	8	2	-	-	David Goddard	- 8 -	
			1	2	Thomas Himenesley*	- 8 -	
2	8	1	-	-	Henry Hide	- 7 -	
-	-	-	1	2	John Sicklemore Thomas Sennock	- 8 -	
-	-	-	5	8			
-	-	-	-	-	James Smith Anthony Upton	- 16 -	Present Effectives Rank & File 122 Wanting to complete 67
-	-	-	-	-	William Knight James Burtenshaw	- 16 -	The Roads and Communication in the space of Residence of this Corps at particular seasons almost Impassible
-	-	-	-	-	Henry Packham David White Boy	- 16 -	
-	-	-	-	-	Charles Stone Richard Chasemore	- 16 -	
-	-	-	-	-	Edward Michel James Miles Boy	- 16 -	
-	-	-	-	-	William Coppard William Knowles Boy	- 16 -	4 More Waggons were ordered but not produced
-	-	-	-	-	Anthony Upton Charles Upton Boy	- 16 -	
-	-	-	1	1	Edward Badcock	- 7 -	
-	-	-	1	1	Thomas Breeding	- 7 -	
-	-	-	1	1	William Batten	- 7 -	
-	-	-	3	3			

* Surname unclear

[Return of Waggons etc 1805] continued

	Proprietors Names	Do Residences	Distance from the Place of Inspection Miles	Waggons seats	Men	No of Horses
North Chichester Corps Commanded by Major Poggott Fitzhall near Midhurst	William Damer	Ambersham	1	6	18	4
	James Lucas	Farnhurst	1	6	18	4
	Robert Tribe	Farnhurst	1	6	18	4
	A Capron	Linchmere	3	6	18	4
	Amos Hewick	Farnhurst	2½	-	-	4
	William Newman	Iping	4	6	18	4
	Joseph Good	Chidhurst	4	6	18	4
	John Restall	Trotton	4	6	18	4
	Samuel Twyford	Trotton	4	6	18	4
	Henry Foard	Eastbourne*	1	6	18	4
	Robert Shotter	Eastbourne*	1	6	18	4
	Robert Shotter	Eastbourne*	1	6	18	4
	J Timms	Copyhold	4			
	12 Waggons	3 Carts	Total	66	198	54†

* = Easebourne

† error: should read 48

Carts Seats	Men	No of Horses	Carts for Baggage	No of Horses	Drivers Names	Money adjudged by the Lieutenancy for the Loss of that Days Labour £ s d	Remarks on Roads etc
-	-	-	-	-	John Saunders Joseph Saunder	- 16 -	Present Effectives Rank & File 203 Wanting to complete 10
-	-	-	-	-	William Milton Thomas Milton Boy	- 16 -	
-	-	-	-	-	Robert Tribe John Coles Boy	- 16 -	
-	-	-	-	-	Robert Birch James Birch Boy	- 16 -	
-	-	-	-	-	John Boxall William Gale Boy	- 16 -	For Baggage
-	-	-	-	-	John Michenor William Furlonger Boy	- 16 -	
-	-	-	-	-	Henry Good William Burt Boy	- 16 -	The Communication good but the Roads in General Heavy and Sandy
-	-	-	-	-	William Blunden Thomas Blunden	- 16 -	
-	-	-	-	-	John Simmonds John Symmonds Boy	- 16 -	
-	-	-	-	-	Thomas Blake Charles Hurlick	- 16 -	
-	-	-	-	-	William Osgood	- 16 -	
-	-	-	-	-	Thomas Goddard Thomas Goddard Boy	- 16 -	
-	-	-	-	-	Thomas Timms	- 8 -	

[Return of Waggons etc 1805] continued

	Proprietors Names	Do Residences	Distance from the Place of Inspection Miles	Waggons seats	Men	No of Horses
South Bramber Corps Commanded by Major Margesson Offington Place near Broadwater	Mr Gregory	Henfield	in the Village	6	18	4
	Thomas Hewett	Henfield	Do	6	18	4
	Richard Pattenden	Henfield	Do	6	18	4
	Thomas Falkenor	Henfield	Do	6	18	4
	Mr Crofts	Shoreham	6	6	24	4
	Richard Brown	Shoreham	6	6	24	4
	Edward Brown	Steyning	6	6	24	4
	John Newland	Broadwater	6	6	24	4
	Major Margesson	Offington Place	5	6	24	4
	Captain Henty	West Tarring	6	6	24	4
	Richard Penfold	Broadwater	6	6	24	4
	Major Margesson	Offington Place	5			
		11 Waggons 1 Cart	Total	66	234*	45†
Arundel Corps Commanded by Major Carleton Arundel	Thomas Duke	Leominster	3	6	18	4
	John Faulkner	Todington		6	18	4
	John Boniface	Ford	7	6	18	4
	Benjamin Staker	Yapton	5	6	18	4
	William Halsted	Walberton	4	6	18	4
	T & E Collins	Walberton	4	6	18	4
	Charles Billinghurst	Yapton	5	6	18	4
	Charles Billinghurst	Yapton	5	6	18	4
	John Pullen	Arundel		6	18	4
	John Boniface	Yapton	5	6	18	4
		10 Waggons		60	180	40

* error: should read 240
† error: should read 44

Proceedings and Schedules 345

Carts Seats	Men	No of Horses	Carts for Baggage	No of Horses	Drivers Names	Money adjudged by the Lieutenancy for the Loss of that Days Labour £ s d	Remarks on Roads etc
-	-	-	-	-	John Hamesley James Mansell Boy	- 16 -	Present Effectives Rank & File 263 Wanting to Complete 73
-	-	-	-	-	Benjamin Hogsflesh G Batchelor Boy	- 16 -	
-	-	-	-	-	James Glazebrook John Glazebrook Boy	- 16 -	
-	-	-	-	-	Peter Graig Stephen Steyning	- 16 -	
-	-	-	-	-	Richard Brown	- 16 -	Roads good
-	-	-	-	-	Richard Stevens	- 16 -	Communication Easy
-	-	-	-	-	Thomas Bishopp Thomas Witton Boy	- 16 -	
-	-	-	-	-	Edward Longley Samuel Longley	- 16 -	
-	-	-	-	-	William Knowles	- 16 -	
-	-	-	-	-	Richard David	- 16 -	
-	-	-	-	-	Edward Hard	- 16 -	
-	-	-	-	-	John Paskins	- 7 -	
-	-	-	-	-	John Knowles	- 16 -	Present Effectives Rank & File 209 Wanting to Complete 31
-	-	-	-	-	James Danteer Edward Bewley	- 16 -	
-	-	-	-	-	George White	- 17 -	
-	-	-	-	-	Isher Standy	- 16 -	
-	-	-	-	-	Michael Secter	- 16 -	
-	-	-	-	-	John Mills	- 16 -	Roads good
-	-	-	-	-	Thomas Mathews James Miles	- 16 -	Communication
-	-	-	-	-	Richard Till Richard Andrews Boy	- 16 -	Easy
-	-	-	-	-	Charles Gray	- 16 -	
-	-	-	-	-	William Ealing Thomas Miller	- 16 -	

[Return of Waggons etc 1805] continued

Company	Proprietors Names	Do Residences	Distance from the Place of Inspection Miles	Waggons seats	Men	No of Horses
North Bramber of Horsham Company Captain Backoll Horsham	Ralph Joanes	Warnham	2	6	18	4
	Thomas Lloyd	Horsham		6	18	4
	Mr Tredcroft	Horsham		6	18	4
	Mr Tredcroft	Horsham		6	18	4
	Samuel Rowland	Horsham Parish	1½	6	18	4
		5 Waggons	Total	30	90	20
Angmering Company Captain Holmwood Angmering	John Peters	Rustington	1¼	6	18	4
	G S Jupp	Rustington	1¼	6	18	4
	Edward Harwood	Rustington	4	6	18	4
	Richard Marshall	Littlehampton	4	6	18	4
	William Kitchenor	Littlehampton	4	6	18	4
	Abraham Hobbs	Rustington	4	6	18	4
	William Moore	Angmering	2			
		6 Waggons		36	108	25*
North Arundel Corps Commanded by Major Biddulph Burton Park	Francis Bennett	Storrington	1½	6	18	4
	M T Trigg	Storrington	1½	6	18	4
	Honourable G King	Storrington	1½	6	18	4
	William Mitford Esq	Tillington	2	6	18	4
	John Sargent	Woollavington	5	6	18	4
	Charles Ibbetson	Burton	4	6	18	4
	Michael Ford	Horsham	1½	7	25	4
	James Ford	Frog Farm	½	7	25	4
	John Puttick	Tillington	2	7	25	4
	John Colebrook	Tillington	2	7	25	4

* error: should read 24

4

Carts Seats	Men	No of Horses	Carts for Baggage	No of Horses	Drivers Names	Money adjudged by the Lieutenancy for the Loss of that Days Labour £ s d	Remarks on Roads etc
-	-	-	-	-	Richard Peters John Gale	- 16 -	Present Effectives Rank & File 86 Wanting to Complete 84
-	-	-	-	-	William Burrage Jacob Burrage	- 16 -	
-	-	-	-	-	Daniel Muggridge	- 16 -	Waggons not properly fitted Ordered like the other Rapes
-	-	-	-	-	John Pratt	- 16 -	Roads good
-	-	-	-	-	Thomas Woolven John Napper	- 16 -	Communication easy
-	-	-	-	-			
-	-	-	-	-	Charles Haynes	- 16 -	Present Effective Rank & File 107 Wanting to Complete 7
	-	-	-	-	John Rinchet John Hazlegrove Boy	- 16 -	
-	-	-	-	-	James Humphrey James Hill	- 16 -	Roads good
-	-	-	-	-	James Balchman	- 16 -	Communication
-	-	-	-	-	James Boys Boy	- 16 -	Easy
-	-	-	-	-	William Page	- 16 -	
-	-	-	-	-	William Amore	- 7 -	
-	-	-	-	-	John Gumbrell	- 16 -	Present Effectives Rank & File 209 Wanting to complete 43
-	-	-	-	-	M Trigg John Bennett	- 16 -	
-	-	-	-	-	William Bennett P Bennett Boy	- 16 -	
-	-	-	-	-	Henry Henshott G King Boy	- 16 -	
-	-	-	-	-	William Barnes Moses Hilton Boy	- 16 -	
-	-	-	-	-	Joseph Havesay Reuben Riddle	- 16 -	
-	-	-	-	-	William Smith	- 16 -	
-	-	-	-	-	Richard Sops	- 16 -	
-	-	-	-	-	George Chandler	- 16 -	Roads good
-	-	-	-	-	James Pullen	- 16 -	Communication easy

[Return of Waggons etc 1805] continued

Proprietors Names	Do Residences	Distance from the Place of Inspection Miles	Waggons seats	Men	No of Horses
William King	Tillington	2	7	25	4
William Elliott	Petworth		7	25	4
Major Biddulph	Burton Park	3	7	25	4
Richard M Dixon	Sullington	1	-	-	-
Richard M Dixon	Sullington	1	-	-	1
Samuel Heather	Storrington Parish	2	6	18	4
Major Biddulph	Burton Park	3	-	-	-
James Snelling	Petworth	-	-	-	-
Mrs Steers	Petworth	-	-	-	1
Captain Ellis	Petworth	-	-	-	1
	14 Waggons Total		91	126*	64†

(North Arundel Coprs [cont])

* error: should read 301
† error: should read 59

	Total‡	
Seats	Men	Horses
660	1876	461

George Lyon Lt Col
Inspector Yeomanry Volunteers in Sussex

At a General Meeting of Lieutenancy held at the White Hart inn in Lewes in and for the County of Sussex on Thursday the 26th Day of February 1806.

We three of His Majesty's Deputy Lieutenants for the said County adjudge and allow the Sums above mentioned

[signed] W Sewell
H T Shadwell
Thos Partington

Wm Ellis Clerk to the General Meetings

‡ correct totals: Seats: 657 Men: 2041 Horses: 435

Carts Seats	Men	No of Horses	Carts for Baggage	No of Horses	Drdivers Names	Money adjudged by the Lieutenancy for the Loss of that Days Labour £ s d	Remarks on Roads etc
-	-	-	-	-	Richard Snelling	- 16 -	
-	-	-	-	-	Shadrack Michell	- 16 -	
-	-	-	-	-	William Simmons	- 16 -	
-	-	-	-	-	Stephen Humbleton	- 7 -	
Bat Horse[125] Complete						- 5 -	
-	-	-	-	-	John Hayller	- 16 -	
-	-	-	-	-	Samuel Burrell	- 8 -	
-	-	-	-	-	James Snelling	- 8 -	
Bat Horse Complete						- 5 -	
Bat Horse Complete						- 5 -	

[125] 'bat-horse: a sumpter-beast, a horse which carries the baggage of military officers during a campaign' (OED)

APPENDIX 1: BIBLIOGRAPHICAL ANALYSIS OF THE SOURCES

There are two principal sources for the contents of this volume:
- Proceedings under the Defence Acts: volume 2 or D ESRO L/C/G/3/1
- Proceedings under the Defence Acts: volume 3 or E ESRO L/C/G/3/2

They form part of a longer series of County Lieutenancy papers, viz:
>L/C : LIEUTENANCY - COUNTY
>L/C/D : Deputy Lieutenancy
>L/C/C : Commissions
>L/C/G : General Meetings
>L/C/G/1 : 'Militia'. 'General Meeting's Minutes' (1778 - 1805)
>L/C/G/2 : Supplementary Militia (1796 - 1799)
>L/C/G/3 : Proceedings under the Defence Acts (1801-1806)
>**L/C/G/3/1 : Proceedings under the Defence Acts: volume 2 or D (1801-1803)**
>**L/C/G/3/2 : Proceedings under the Defence Acts: volume 3 or E (1803-1806)**
>L/C/G/4 : 'Army of Reserve, 1804' (1804-1805)
>L/C/G/5 : 'General Meetings Lieutenancy Minutes' (1806 - 1822)
>L/C/G/6 : 'Sussex Lieutenancy General Meetings' (1823-1862)
>L/C/G/7 : Other papers

Details of the ESRO Catalogue entries for these volumes follow.

ESRO Catalogue entry for L/C/G/3

'Both volumes are inscribed 'Sussex. Proceedings of Meetings of Deputy Lieutenancy for the internal Defence of the Country. 1801'. They are numbered respectively '2' and '3' and lettered 'D' and 'E'. The numbering possibly refers back to 'On Lieutenancy. General Defence No 1' (L/C/V/1/2), and the lettering to the first minute book (L/C/G/1) and List of men enrolled (L/C/L/1). No volume marked 'C' of this series, which are all bound, in uniform vellum bindings, is extant. However, 'Army of Reserve' minute book (L/C/G/4) may in fact be the missing volume.

[This is not the case. L/C/G/4 is titled Army of Reserve 1804, and responds to an Act 'for establishing a permanent additional force for the defence of the Realm ... and the gradual reduction of the militia'. It postdates L/G/C/3/2]

'Alternatively there may have been a volume of proceedings dating from the 1798 Defence Act.

'The volumes record minutes of meetings held to execute the Defence Acts of 38 George III, c27 (1798), and 43 George III, cc55 and 96 (1803). These are entered in some detail giving useful information of measures taken by the county in danger of invasion. The Acts made provision for comprehensive returns, gave wide powers for evacuation of the population, stocks and stores, or the destruction of anything deemed of use to the enemy. The male population up to the age of 60 might be conscripted, and volunteer companies of pioneers or infantry were encouraged to be formed.

'A valuable set of returns for the years 1801 and 1803 has been entered which give figures for each parish of the population classified by fitness for service or for evacuation, of live stock, vehicles, barges, cornmills, baking ovens, weapons and implements available. There is also a return of waggons for conveying the Western Division's Volunteer Force, 1805.'

Bibliographic analysis

L/C/G/3/1 : Proceedings under the Defence Acts: volume 2 or D (1801-1803)

This is a bound ledger or minute book, approximately foolscap size. It contains approx 91 folios, 182 pages numbered recto-verso in pencil at the foot of each page.

Contents:

Proceedings of a meeting 13 August 1801. pp. 1-15
Proceedings of a meeting 14 September 1801. pp. 17-25
Proceedings of a meeting 8 October 1801. p. 27
Schedules by rape, hundred and parish:
Chichester Rape:
- Schedule 1 (men and boys capable of fighting etc.). pp. 28-33
- Schedule 2 (oxen, cows etc.) pp. 34-39
- Schedule 3 (men willing to serve, how armed etc.) pp. 40-45

Lewes Rape (Schedules as above)
- Sch 1 pp. 46-49
- Sch 2 pp. 50-53
- Sch 3 pp. 54-57

Pevensey Rape (Schedules as above)
- Sch 1 pp. 58-61
- Sch 2 pp. 62-65
- Sch 3 pp. 66-69

Hastings Rape (Schedules as above)
- Sch 1 pp. 70-73
- Sch 2 pp. 74-77
- Sch 3 pp. 78-81

Additional schedules by parish (??) (Schedules as above)
- Sch 1 pp. 82-85
- Sch 2 pp. 86-89
- Sch 3 pp. 90-93

Bramber Rape (Schedules as above)
- Sch 1 pp. 94-97
- Sch 2 pp. 98-101
- Sch 3 pp. 102-105

Proceedings of a meeting 16 January 1802 pp. 106-107
Proceedings of a meeting 7-8 July 1803 pp. 108-120
(including appointments of Deputy Lieutenants)
Proceedings of a meeting 21 July 1803 pp. 121-22
Schedule of parish superintendants appointed pp. 123-37
Proceedings of a meeting 1 August 1803 pp. 138-42
Schedules from Churchwardens pp. 143-82

L/C/G/3/2 : Proceedings under the Defence Acts: volume 3 or E (1803-1806)

This is a bound ledger or minute book, approximately foolscap size. It contains approx 91 folios, 182 pages (uncounted). Pages were specially numbered.for this edition. Approximately 95 pages are used; the remaining folios are blank. It is labelled Proceedings of the General Meetings continued

Contents:

Schedules 59 pp. following the meeting 1 August 1803 in the previous volume
- Livestock etc.
- Individuals with carts etc. able to transport goods
- Many namesProceedings of a meeting 10 August 1803 5 pp.

Proceedings of a meeting 22 August 1803 (raising volunteers) 8 pp.
Proceedings of a meeting 29 August 1803 6 pp.
Proceedings of a meeting 4 October 1803 3 pp.
Proceedings of a meeting 12 November 1803 4 pp.
Proceedings of a meeting 10 March 1804 1 p.
Schedules 9 pp.

APPENDIX 2: A NATION UNDER ARMS: SELECTED ACTS OF PARLIAMENT 1798-1806

Between 1798 and 1806, the Parliament of Great Britain, and then that of the United Kingdom, passed some 170 separate Acts (depending on the precise definition) related to the prosecution of the war, the armed forces, the militia, the yeomanry etc.; this illustrates the extent to which militarisation of society proceeded, but also the constant struggle of the establishment to control and direct it. These Acts are listed chronologically below.

Many Acts were known informally by a number of different names; for example, the Additional Force Acts 1803 were better known as the Army of Reserve Acts. Where relevant, the titles below are those specified by the Short Titles Act 1896.

1798 38 Geo. 3

Militia Act 1798 c. 17
Supplementary Militia Act 1798 c. 18
Supplementary Militia Act 1798 c. 19
Mutiny Act 1798 c. 23
Defence of the Realm Act 1798 c. 27
Quartering of Soldiers Act 1798 c. 32
Kent, Devon Fortifications Act 1798 c. 34
Habeas Corpus Suspension Act 1798 c. 36
Militia Act 1798 c. 44
Manning of the Navy Act 1798 c. 46
Yeomanry Cavalry Act 1798 c. 51
Militia Act 1798 c. 55
Militia Pay Act 1798 c. 64
Militia Act 1798 c. 66
Militia Allowances Act 1798 c. 70
Regiment of Cornwall and Devon Miners Act 1798 c. 74
Residence in France During the War Act 1798 c. 79
Provisional Cavalry Act 1798 c. 94

1798 39 Geo. 3

Army and Navy Act 1798 c. 4
Militia Act 1798 c. 5

1799 39 Geo. 3

Supplementary Militia Act 1799 c. 14

Habeas Corpus Suspension Act 1799 c. 15
Marine Mutiny Act 1799 c. 19
Mutiny Act 1799 c. 20
Provisional Cavalry Act 1799 c. 23
Militia Act 1799 c. 35
Quartering of Soldiers Act 1799 c. 36
Habeas Corpus Suspension Act 1799 c. 44
Militia Act 1799 c. 62
Militia of City of London Act 1799 c. 82
Militia Act 1799 c. 90
Militia Pay Act 1799 c. 97
Militia Allowances Act 1799 c. 103
Augmentation of 60th Regiment Act 1799 c. 104
Militia Act 1799 c. 106

1799 39 & 40 Geo. 3

Militia Act 1799 c. 1

1800 39 & 40 Geo. 3

Militia Act 1800 c. 15
Army and Navy Act 1800 c. 16
Habeas Corpus Suspension Act 1800 c. 20
Marine Mutiny Act 1800 c. 24
Mutiny Act 1800 c. 27
Militia Pay Act 1800 c. 37
Saltpetre Act 1800 c. 38
Quartering of Soldiers Act 1800 c. 39
Militia Allowances Act 1800 c. 44
Militia Allowances Act 1800 c. 75
Army and Navy Act 1800 c. 100

1800 41 Geo. 3

Army and Navy Act 1800 c. 29
Habeas Corpus Suspension Act 1800 c. 32

1801 41 Geo. 3

Militia (Ireland) Act 1801 c. 6
Mutiny Act 1801 c. 11
Habeas Corpus Suspension (Ireland) Act 1801 c. 15
Marine Mutiny Act 1801 c. 18

Habeas Corpus Suspension Act 1801 c. 26
Quartering of Soldiers Act 1801 c. 35
Militia Pay (England) Act 1801 c. 43
Militia Allowances Act 1801 c. 55
Militia Allowances Act 1801 c. 56
Militia (Scotland) Act 1801 c. 67
Customs Act 1801 c. 89
Militia Pay (Ireland) Act 1801 c. 98

1801 42 Geo 3

Militia Quotas Act 1801 c. 12

1802 42 Geo.3

Mutiny Act 1802 c. 25
Marine Mutiny Act 1802 c. 26
Restriction on Cash Payments Act 1802 c. 45
Militia Pay (England) Act 1802 c. 49
Mutiny Act 1802 c. 50
Marine Mutiny Act 1802 c. 51
Militia Allowances Act 1802 c. 55
Militia Allowances Act 1802 c. 64
Militia Allowances Act 1802 c. 65
Yeomanry and Volunteers Act 1802 c. 66
Yeomanry (Ireland) Act 1802 c. 68
Militia (Stannaries) Act 1802 c. 72
Mutiny Act 1802 c. 88
Militia Act 1802 c. 90
Militia (Scotland) Act 1802 c. 91
Quartering of Soldiers Act 1802 c. 108
Militia (Ireland) Act 1802 c. 109
Marine Mutiny Act 1802 c. 115
Militia (Ireland) Act 1802 c. 118

1802 43 Geo.3

Militia (Ireland) Act 1802 c. 2
Militia Pay (Ireland) Act 1802 c. 9
Militia (Exemption of Religious Teachers) Act 1802 c. 10

1803 43 Geo.3

Militia Act 1803 c. 19

Mutiny Act 1803 c. 20
Marine Mutiny Act 1803 c. 27
Militia (Ireland) Act 1803 c. 33
Militia (Great Britain) Act 1803 c. 38
Quartering of Soldiers Act 1803 c. 41
Relief of Families of Militiamen Act 1803 c. 47
Militia Act 1803 c. 50
Defence of the Realm Act 1803 c. 55
Militia (Great Britain) Act 1803 c. 62
Supply of Seamen Act 1803 c. 64
Militia (Great Britain) Act 1803 c. 71
Militia Allowances Act 1803 c. 72
Militia (Ireland) Act 1803 c. 76
Indemnity (Ireland) Act 1803 c. 77
Additional Force Act (England) Act 1803 c. 82
    (better known as the Army of Reserve Act)
Additional Force Act (Scotland) Act 1803 c. 83
Additional Force Act (Ireland) Act 1803 c. 85
Militia Pay (Ireland) Act 1803 c. 88
Militia (Scotland) Act 1803 c. 89
Militia Pay and Allowances Act 1803 c. 94
Militia Pay and Allowances Act 1803 c. 95
Levy en Masse Act 1803 c. 96
Militia (Scotland) (No. 2) Act 1803 c. 100
Defence of the Realm, London Act 1803 c. 101
Habeas Corpus Suspension (Ireland) Act 1803 c. 116
Levy en Masse Amendment Act 1803 c. 120
Yeomanry and Volunteer Cavalry Act 1803 c. 121
Defence of the Realm (England) Act 1803 c. 123
Defence of the Realm (Scotland) Act 1803 c. 124
Levy en Masse (London) Act 1803 c. 125
Habeas Corpus Act 1803 c. 140
Militia (Ireland) Act 1803 c. 142

1803 44 Geo.3

Habeas Corpus Suspension (Ireland) Act 1803 c. 8
Navy Act 1803 c. 13
Volunteers and Yeomanry (Great Britain) Act 1803 c. 18

1804 44 Geo.3

Mutiny Act 1804 c. 19

Marine Mutiny Act 1804 c. 20
Militia (Ireland) Act 1804 c. 32
Militia (Ireland) Act 1804 c. 33
Militia (Ireland) Act 1804 c. 34
Quartering of Soldiers Act 1804 c. 38
Militia Pay (Great Britain) Act 1804 c. 39
Militia Allowances Act 1804 c. 40
Militia Pay (Ireland) Act 1804 c. 41
Militia Act 1804 c. 50
Militia Act 1804 c. 51
Yeomanry Act 1804 c. 54
Defence of the Realm, etc. Act 1804 c. 56
Defence of the Realm, etc. Act 1804 c. 66
Defence of the Realm, etc. Act 1804 c. 74
Yeomanry (Accounts) Act 1804 c. 94
Defence of the Realm Act 1804 c. 95
Defence of the Realm, London Act 1804 c. 96
Habeas Corpus Act 1804 c. 102

1805 44 Geo 3

Habeas Corpus Suspension (Ireland) Act 1805 c. 4
Mutiny Act 1805 c. 16
Marine Mutiny Act 1805 c. 17
Militia (Great Britain) Act 1805 c. 31
Quartering of Soldiers Act 1805 c. 37
Irish Militia Act 1805 c. 38
Militia Allowances Act 1805 c. 60
Militia Allowances Act 1805 c. 61
Militia Pay (Great Britain) Act 1805 c. 62
Militia Pay (Ireland) Act 1805 c. 63
Manning of the Navy Act 1805 c. 72
Militia Act 1805 c. 90

1806 46 Geo 3

Marine Mutiny Act 1806 c. 8
Mutiny Act 1806 c. 15
Militia Pay (Great Britain) Act 1806 c. 19
Militia Allowances Act 1806 c. 20
Militia Allowances Act 1806 c. 21
Militia Pay (Ireland) Act 1806 c. 22
Enlistment of Foreigners Act 1806 c. 23

Militia (Ireland) Act 1806 c. 31
Mutiny Act 1806 c. 48
Defence of the Realm Act 1806 c. 51
Defence of the Realm (Ireland) Act 1806 c. 63
Mutiny Act 1806 c. 66
Pensions, to Soldiers Act 1806 c. 69
Defence of the Realm Act 1806 c. 90
Militia Act 1806 c. 91
Irish Militia Act 1806 c. 124
Yeomanry, etc. Act 1806 c. 125
Quartering of Soldiers Act 1806 c. 126
Navy Act 1806 c. 127
Militia Act 1806 c. 140
Defence of the Realm, London Act 1806 c. 144

APPENDIX 3:
38 GEORGE III CAP XXVII 5 APRIL 1798
[THE DEFENCE ACT 1798]

An Act to enable His Majesty more effectually to provide for the Defence and Security of the Realm, during the present War; and for indemnifying Persons who may suffer in their Property by such Measures as may be necessary for that Purpose.

Whereas it is expedient that His Majesty should be enabled to exercise, in the most effectual Manner, the Powers by Law vested in him for preventing and repelling an Invasion of this Kingdom by His Majesty's Enemies; and that, for such Purpose, Provision should be made to enforce prompt Obedience to such Orders as His Majesty shall think fit to issue for procuring the Information necessary to the effectual Exercise of such Powers upon any Emergency; and for applying, in the most expeditious Manner, and with the greatest Effect, the voluntary Services of His Loyal Subjects for the Defence of the Kingdom; and also to enable His Majesty to procure Ground which may be wanting for erecting Batteries, Beacons, and other Works, which may be deemed necessary for the Publick Service; and also to provide for the Indemnity (in certain Cases) of Persons who may suffer in their Property by Measures which may be taken for the Defence and Security of the Country, and Annoyance of the Enemy;

Be it enacted by the King's most Excellent Majesty, by and with the Advice and Consent of the Lords Spiritual and Temporal, and Commons, in this present Parliament assembled, and by the Authority of the same, That the Lieutenants of the several Counties, Ridings and Places within that part of *Great Britain* called *England*, and of the several Counties, Stewartries, Cities and Places in that Part of *Great Britain* called *Scotland*, and their Deputy Lieutenants, or such of them as His Majesty shall direct, and the Deputy Lieutenants acting as Lieutenants under the Laws now in Force, shall, respectively, in Obedience and Conformity to such Orders as His Majesty shall think fit to issue for such Purpose, procure Returns of the Numbers of Men residing within the several Counties, Ridings, Stewartries, Cities and Places aforesaid, who shall be of the Age of Fifteen years and under the Age of Sixty Years; distinguishing which of them are by Reason of Infirmity, incapable of active Service, and which of them are engaged in any Volunteer Corps, and which of them are willing to engage themselves to be armed, arrayed, trained and exercised for the Defence of the Kingdom, and upon what Terms; and which of them are willing to engage in Cases of Emergency, either gratuitously or for Hire, as Boatmen or Bargemen, or as Drivers of Carriages or Horses, or Drivers of Waggons, Carts, or Cattle, or as Pioneers, or other Labourers for any Works or Labour which may be necessary for the Publick Service; and also distinguishing all Aliens and Quakers, with such other Particulars as His Majesty shall think fit to require; and also to procure Returns of the Numbers of the Males and Females residing within the several Counties, Ridings, Stewartries, Cities, and Places aforesaid, who by Reason of Infancy, Age, or Infirmity, or for other Cause, may probably be incapable of removing themselves in case of Danger; and also for procuring Returns of all Boats, Barges, Waggons, Carts, Horses and other Cattle and Sheep, and of all Hay, Straw, Corn, Meal, Flour, and other Provisions, and of all Mills and Ovens, and all other Matters and Things which may be useful to an Enemy, or applicable to the Publick Service within the said Counties, Ridings, Stewartries, Cities and Places respectively; and which of such Boats, Barges, Waggons, Cars, and Horses, the owners thereof are willing to furnish, in case of Emergency, for the Publick Service, either gratuitously or for Hire, and with what Number of Boatmen, Bargemen, Drivers and other necessary Attendance, and upon what Terms and Conditions, and of all such other Particulars as His Majesty shall require, for the Purpose of enabling His Majesty, and the Persons acting under His Majesty's Authority, to give such Orders as may be necessary for the Removal, in case of Danger, of such Persons as shall be incapable of removing themselves; and for the Removal of all Boats, Barges, Waggons, Carts, Horses, Cattle, Sheep, Hay, Straw, Corn, Meal, Flour, and other Provisions, Matters and Things aforesaid, or for the Employment thereof in His Majesty's Service or otherwise, as the Exigency of the Case shall require; and generally to give such Directions touching such Matters respectively, as may be deemed most likely to defeat the Views of the Enemy, and most advantageous for the Publick Service.

II. And be it further enacted, That it shall be lawful for His Majesty, by and with the Advice of his Privy Council, to order and require, from Time to Time, as His Majesty shall see Occasion, the Lieutenants or Deputy Lieutenants acting as Lieutenants as aforesaid, to appoint proper Officers to be ready for arraying, training, exercising, and commanding such Men as shall be willing to engage themselves to be armed, trained, and exercised as aforesaid; and also proper Persons to be in like Manner ready, in case of Need, for superintending and directing the Execution of the several other Duties which may be necessary to be done, for the several Purposes herein-before mentioned; such Officers and other Persons to be appointed in such Numbers, and under such Regulations and Restrictions as His Majesty shall think fit to order and direct, such Lieutenants or Deputy Lieutenants acting as Lieutenants as aforesaid, first signifying to His Majesty the Names and Ranks of all Officers so to be appointed, and the Purposes for which they are so to be appointed, and appointing such Officers only as His Majesty shall approve; Provided always, that if the said Lieutenants, or Deputy Lieutenants acting as Lieutenants as aforesaid, shall not, within the Time which may be specified in the Orders which shall be given for such Purpose, signify to His Majesty the Names of a sufficient Number of Officers, whom His Majesty shall approve for the Command of such Men as aforesaid, and appoint such other Persons as shall be necessary for the Purposes aforesaid, it shall be lawful for His Majesty to appoint so many Officers and other Persons as shall be necessary for such Purposes.

III. And be it further enacted, That it shall be lawful for His Majesty, by Order under his Sign Manual, to authorize and require the several Lieutenants and Deputy Lieutenants aforesaid, to hold such General and Subdivision Meetings, within their respective Counties, Ridings, Stewartries, Cities, and Places, as His Majesty, or such Lord Lieutenant or other Chief Governor or Governors as aforesaid, shall think fit, and as shall be necessary for the Execution of this Act, and to require, for such Purposes, the Attendance of the Clerks of the several General Meetings and Subdivision Meetings of Lieutenancy, within their respective Counties, Ridings, Stewartries, Cities, and Places, and of all other Persons whose Assistance shall be necessary for carrying into Execution this Act, in such and the same Manner, and with the same Powers and Authorities, as by the several Acts now in Force, concerning the Militia Forces of this Kingdom, is provided with respect to such Militia Forces, so far as the Provisions in such Acts respectively are applicable to the Purposes of this Act.

IV. And be it further enacted, That the said Lieutenants, and their Deputy Lieutenants, and the Deputy Lieutenants acting as Lieutenants as aforesaid, and all Justices of the Peace, Constables, Tythingmen, Headboroughs, and other Officers, shall, for the Purposes of this Act, have the like Powers and Authorities to do, within their respective Counties, Ridings, Stewartries, Cities, and Places, respectively, all such Acts, Matters and Things, as shall be required by His Majesty to be done by them respectively in the Execution of this Act, as they respectively have to do the several Acts, Matters, and Things by Law required to be done by them respectively, by any Act now in Force concerning the Militia Forces of this Kingdom.

V. And be it further enacted, That all Lieutenants, Deputy Lieutenants, Governors, Deputy Governors, Justices of the Peace, Constables, and other Officers, and all other Persons, shall obey such Orders as they shall respectively receive under the Authority of this Act, and the several Provisions herein contained.

VI. And be it further enacted, That the Lieutenants or Deputy Lieutenants of the several Counties, Ridings, Stewartries, Cities, and Places aforesaid, within such Time as they shall be required by His Majesty so to do, shall issue Warrants to the several Constables, Tythingmen, Headboroughs, or other Officers of every Parish or Place, within the several Counties, Ridings, Stewartries, Cities, and Places aforesaid, to cause Returns to be prepared and made, touching the several Purposes aforesaid, or any of them, as His Majesty shall direct, for their respective Parishes and Places; and such Constables, Tythingmen, Headboroughs, and other Officers, shall make such Returns severally and respectively to the said Deputy Lieutenants at their respective Subdivision Meetings, according to the Warrants which shall be issued for such Purposes, and shall verify the same, upon Oath, before such Deputy Lieutenants.

VII. And be it further enacted, That it shall be lawful for His Majesty, in case of actual Invasion of this Kingdom, or if His Majesty shall see special Cause to apprehend that such Invasion will be actually attempted by the Enemy, to authorize and empower, by Order under His Sign Manual, the said Lieutenants and Deputy Lieutenants, or any of them, on any Emergency, and on the Requisition of the Officer commanding within the District, respectively, or of such other Persons as His Majesty shall specially empower to make such Requisition, to give all such Orders as shall be necessary for the Removal of any Boats, Barges, Waggons, Carts, or other Carriages, Horses, Cattle, Sheep, Hay, Straw, Corn, Meal, Flour, or Provisions of any kind, or any other Things which may be of Advantage to an Enemy, or useful for the Publick Service, and to take the same, if necessary, for the Publick Service; and also to give such Orders as shall be necessary for the Removal of the Inhabitants of any House, Hamlet, District or Place, or any of them, and especially such as by reason of Infancy, Age, or Infirmity, or other Cause, shall be incapable of removing themselves in case of Danger; and also, in case of Necessity, to destroy any Boats, Barges, Waggons, Carts, or other Carriages, Horses, Cattle, Sheep, Hay, Straw, Corn, Meal, Flour, or Provisions of any Kind, or any Thing which may be of Advantage to an Enemy; and to remove, destroy, or render useless any House, Mill, Bridge, or other Building, or any Matter or Thing whatsoever, and generally to do and act in the Premises as the Publick Service and the Exigencies of particular Cases shall require.

VIII. And be it further enacted, That any Persons who may enrol themselves in any Volunteer Corps of Infantry or Cavalry, subsequent to the Date of this Act, shall not be liable to be called out and placed under the Command of any General Officer commanding within the District in which such Corps may be formed, except in case of actual Invasion, or of the actual Appearance of the Enemy on the Coast, or of the Danger of Invasion being deemed so imminent as to make it adviseable for the Lieutenants or Deputy Lieutenants, or any of them, to give Orders for the Removal of Cattle, Corn, or any other Articles which may be of Advantage to the Enemy, or useful to the Publick Service, in the Manner herein-before mentioned.

IX. And be it further enacted, That if the Commanding Officer of any Corps or Company of Volunteers, who shall be appointed under the Authority of this Act, or who has been or shall be appointed under the Authority of an Act of the Thirty-fourth Year of His Majesty's Reign, intituled, *An Act for encouraging and disciplining such Corps or Companies of Men as shall voluntarily enrol themselves for the Defence of their Counties, Towns, or Coasts, or for the general Defence of the Kingdom, during the present War*, shall make any false Return of such Corps or Company, with Intent to defraud His Majesty, every such Officer shall forfeit and lose the Sum of Two Hundred Pounds.

X. And be it further enacted, That it shall be lawful for His Majesty to authorize any General Officer or Officers, or other Person or Persons commissioned for such Purpose, to survey and mark out any Piece of Ground wanted for the Publick Service, and to treat and agree with the Owner or Owners thereof, or any Person or Persons having any Interest therein, for the Possession or Use thereof, during such Time as the Exigence of the Service shall require; and in case the Owner or Owners of any such Ground, or any Person or Persons having any Interest therein, shall refuse or decline to enter into such Contract touching the same, as shall be satisfactory to such Officer or Officers, or other Person or Persons commissioned as aforesaid, or shall be unable to do so by reason of Infancy, Coverture or other Disability, it shall be lawful for the Person or Persons so authorized by His Majesty to require Two or more Justices of the Peace, or Deputy Lieutenants for the County, Riding, Stewartry, City, or Place where such Piece of Ground shall be, to put His Majesty's Officers into immediate Possession of such Piece of Ground, which such Justices, or Deputy Lieutenants shall accordingly do, and shall for that Purpose issue their Warrant, under their Hands and Seals, commanding Possession to be so delivered, and shall also issue their Warrants to the Sheriff of the County, Riding, Stewartry, City, or Place, wherein such Piece of Ground shall be situate, to summon a Jury to appear, and be on a Day and at a Place in such Warrant to be mentioned, to enquire of and ascertain the Compensation which ought to be made for the Possession or Use of such Piece of Ground, during the Time for which the same shall be required for the Publick Service, to the several Persons interested therein, and to whom the same ought to be paid, the Verdict of which Jury shall be certified by such Justices or Deputy Lieutenants to the Receiver General of the Land Tax of the County, Riding, Stewartry, City, or Place, where such Lands shall lie; which Receiver General shall, out of any Money in his Hands, pay such Compensation to such Person or Persons, in such Manner, and for such Purposes, as by such Verdict shall be directed: Provided always, that no such Piece of Ground shall be so taken for the Publick Service, without the Consent of the Owner or Owners thereof, unless the Necessity for the same shall be first certified by the Lord Lieutenant, or Two of the Deputy Lieutenants of the County, Riding, Stewartry, City, or Place in which such Land shall lie, or unless the Enemy shall have actually invaded the Kingdom at the Time when such Piece of Ground shall be so taken.

XI. And be it further enacted, That when it shall have been found necessary to take for the Publick Service, remove, or destroy any Waggons, Carts, or other Carriages, Horses, Cattle, Sheep, Hay, Straw, Corn, Meal, Flour or other Provisions, or any other Articles whatsoever, or to destroy or injure any House, Mill, Bridge, or other Building, or any Matter or Thing of Value, under the Directions aforesaid, the Commissioners of His Majesty's Treasury shall appoint Persons to enquire into and ascertain the Value of such Articles, and the Compensation which ought to be made for the same, by way of Purchase or Hire, or Recompence for Damage, or otherwise, according to the Nature of the Case; and if the Owner or Owners, or Person or Persons interested, shall be willing to accept the Compensation which shall be so ascertained, the same shall be paid by the Commissioners of His Majesty's Treasury or such Person or Persons as shall be appointed by them for that Purpose, in pursuance of a Certificate under the Hands of the Persons so employed to ascertain the same; and if the Owner or Owners, or Person or Persons interested shall not be willing to accept such Compensation, it shall be lawful for His Majesty to order Two Justices of the Peace of the County, Riding, Stewartry, City, or Place to settle and ascertain the Compensation which ought to be made to such Owner or Owners, or Persons interested; which Justices shall settle and ascertain the same accordingly, and shall grant a Certificate thereof to the Commissioners of His Majesty's Treasury, who shall order the same to be paid to the Person or Persons entitled thereto, out of any Money granted for the Supply of the Year.

XII. And be it further enacted, That the Warden of the Stannaries, and all other Officers of the Stannaries, shall, respectively, in Obedience to His Majesty's Orders, to be issued for that Purpose, procure like Returns to be made, and all other Matters to be done touching the Tinners of the Counties of *Devon* and *Cornwall*, according to the Customs of the Stannaries and Privileges of the Working Tinners, as are hereby required to be done by the Lieutenants and Deputy Lieutenants aforesaid, touching other Persons residing in the said Counties of *Devon* and *Cornwall*, not entitled to the Benefit of such Privileges; and such Warden and other Officers of the Stannaries shall have such and the like Powers and Authorities to do and execute all and every the Matters and Things which shall be so required to be done as aforesaid, as the said

Lieutenants and Deputy Lieutenants of the several Counties, Ridings, Stewartries, Cities, and Places aforesaid, have for doing the several Matters and Things hereby required to be done by them respectively.

XIII. And be it further enacted, That His Majesty's Commissioners of Lieutenancy for the City of *London*, the Lord Mayor of the said City, and the Aldermen, Deputies, and Common Councilmen of the several wards of the said City and Liberties thereof, and the Constables, Beadles, and other Ward Officers of the same, the Constable of the Tower of *London*, Lieutenants of the Tower Hamlets, and the Deputy Lieutenants of the said Hamlets, and their several Officers; the Justices of the Peace for the Tower Liberties, the Constables, and other Peace Officers within the same, the Warden of the Cinque Ports, Two ancient Towns, and their Members, his Lieutenant or Lieutenants, and his or their Officers, and the Mayors, Jurats, Justices of the Peace, Constables, and other Peace Officers for the Liberties of the Cinque Ports Two ancient Towns and their Members, and all other Justices of the Peace, Constables and other Peace Officers, within their respective Districts, and all other Persons having Authority within the same, shall put in Execution all and every the Powers and Provisions contained in this Act, in like Manner as they are respectively authorized to put in Execution the several Laws respecting the Militia Forces of this Kingdom, or any of them, within their respective Districts.

XIV. And be it further enacted, That the Form of Conviction by one of His Majesty's Justices of the Peace, in pursuance of this Act, set forth and expressed in the Schedule hereto annexed, may be used, with such Additions and Variations only as may be necessary to adapt the same to the particular Exigencies of the Case; and that no Objection shall be made, or Advantage taken, for Want of Form in any such Conviction, by any Person or Persons whatsoever.

XV. And be it further enacted, That the Acceptance of any Commission under the Authority of this Act, shall not vacate the Seat of any Member returned to serve in Parliament.

XVI. And be it further enacted, That the respective Clerks of the General and Subdivision Meetings of Lieutenancy, Constables, and other Officers, required to execute this Act, and who shall respectively execute the same to the Satisfaction of the Deputy Lieutenants assembled at their respective Subdivision Meetings, shall have and receive such Compensation for their Care, Trouble, and Expences, in and about the executing of this Act, as the said Deputy Lieutenants shall judge them respectively to have deserved for the same; and the said Deputy Lieutenants shall direct such Compensation to be paid by the Receiver General of the County, Riding, or Place, in *England*, or Receiver General in *Scotland*, as the Case shall require, out of any Money in his Hands, and such Receiver General shall pay the same accordingly, in case such Order as shall be made by such Deputy Lieutenants at such Subdivision Meetings shall be confirmed at a General Meeting, but not otherwise.

XVII. And be it further enacted, That in case any Constable, Headborough, Tythingman, or other inferior Officer, or other Person, shall disobey any Orders which shall be issued in pursuance of this Act, or shall obstruct or hinder the Execution thereof, every such Person, upon Conviction of such Offence, before any Justice of the Peace, of the County, Riding, Stewartry, City, or Place, where the Offence shall be committed, shall forfeit and pay a Sum not less than Five Pounds and not exceeding One hundred Pounds, at the Discretion of such Justice, to be levied by Distress and Sale in the Manner herein before directed with respect to the Penalty herein-before imposed; and for Want of sufficient Distress, then such Justice is hereby required to commit such Offender to the Common Gaol of the County, Riding, Stewartry, City, or Place, where the Offence shall be committed, for any Time not exceeding Three Months, and the Monies arising by such Penalty shall be paid to the Treasurer of the County, Riding, Stewartry, City or Place, where the Offence shall be committed, to be applied as Part of the Stock of such County, Riding, Stewartry, City or Place.

XVIII. And be it further enacted, That no Order or Conviction made in pursuance of this Act, by any Lieutenant, Deputy Lieutenant, or Justice of the Peace, shall be removed by *Certiorari*, Advocation, or Suspension, out of the County, Riding, or Place, wherein such Order or Conviction shall be made, into any Court whatever; and that no Writ of *Certiorari*, Advocation, or Suspension, shall supersede Execution or other Proceedings upon any such Order or Conviction, but that Execution and other Proceedings shall be had thereupon, any such Writ or Writs, or Allowance thereof notwithstanding.

XIX. And be it further enacted, That it shall be lawful for His Majesty to authorize any three Deputy Lieutenants of any County, Riding, Stewartry, City, or Place, in the Absence from such County, Riding, Stewartry, City, or Place, of the Lieutenant thereof, to do all Acts, Matters, and Things, in the Execution of this Act, which might lawfully be done by such Lieutenant, and the same shall be good and valid in the Law, as if done by such Lieutenants.

XX. And be it further enacted, That all Penalties by this Act imposed, for Recovery whereof no other Means are hereby provided, shall be recovered by

Action of Debt, Bill, Plaint, or Information, in any of His Majesty's Courts of Record at *Westminster*, or the Courts of Great Session in the Principality of *Wales*, or the Courts of the Counties Palatine of *Chester*, *Lancaster* or *Durham*, or in the Court of Session, or Court of Exchequer, in *Scotland*, as the Case shall require, wherein no Essoign, Privilege, Protection, Wager of Law, or more than One Imparlance shall be allowed.

XXI. And be it further enacted, That if any Action shall be brought against any Person or Persons for any Thing done in pursuance of this Act, such Action shall be commenced within Three Months next after the Fact committed, and not afterwards, and shall be laid in the County or Place where the Cause of Complaint shall arise, and not elsewhere; and the Defendant or Defendants in such Action or Suit may plead the General Issue, and give this Act and the special Matter in Evidence at any Trial to be had thereupon; and if the Jury shall find for the Defendant or Defendants in such Action or Suit, or if the Plaintiff or Plaintiffs shall be nonsuited, or discontinue his, her, or their Action or Suit, after the Defendant or Defendants shall have appeared, or if upon Demurrer Judgement shall be given against the Plaintiff or Plaintiffs, the Defendant or Defendants shall have Treble Costs, and have the like Remedy for the same as any Defendant hath in other Cases to recover Costs.

XXII. And be it further enacted, That this Act shall have Continuance during the present War with *France*.

XXIII. Provided always, That this Act, or any of the Provisions herein contained, may be altered, varied, or repealed, by any Act or Acts to be passed in this present Session of Parliament.

APPENDIX 4:
43 GEORGE III CAP LV 11TH JUNE 1803
[THE DEFENCE ACT 1803]

An Act to enable his Majesty more effectually to provide for the Defence and Security of the Realm, during the present War; and for indemnifying Persons who may suffer in their Property by such Measures as may be necessary for that Purpose.

Whereas it is expedient that his Majesty should be enabled to exercise, in the most effectual Manner, the Powers by Law vested in him, for preventing and repelling an Invasion of the United Kingdom of *Great Britain* and *Ireland*, by his Majesty's Enemies, and that for such Purpose Provision should be made to enforce prompt Obedience to such Orders, as his Majesty, or the Lord Lieutenant or other Chief Governor or Governors of *Ireland*, for the Time being, shall think fit to issue for procuring the Information necessary to the effectual Exercise of such Powers upon any Emergency, and for applying in the most expeditious Manner, and with the greatest Effect, the voluntary Services of his Majesty's loyal Subjects for the Defence of the said United Kingdom; and also to enable his Majesty, and the Lord Lieutenant or other Chief Governor or Governors of *Ireland*, for the Time being, to procure Ground which may be wanting for encamping his Majesty's Armies, and for erecting Batteries, Beacons, and other Works which may be deemed necessary for the publick Service; and also to provide for the Indemnity (in certain Cases) of Persons who may suffer in their Property by Measures which may be taken for the Defence and Security of the Country, and Annoyance of the Enemy;

be it enacted by the King's most Excellent Majesty, by and with the Advice and Consent of the Lords Spiritual and Temporal, and Commons, in this present Parliament assembled, and by the Authority of the same, That the Lieutenants of the several Counties, Ridings and Places within that part of the United Kingdom called *England*, and of the several Counties, Stewartries, Cities and Places in that Part of the United Kingdom called *Scotland*, and their Deputy Lieutenants, or such of them as his Majesty shall direct, and the Deputy Lieutenants acting as Lieutenants under the Laws now in force, shall respectively, in Obedience and Conformity to such Orders as his Majesty shall think fit to issue for such Purpose, and the Governors of Counties and Places in *Ireland*, and their Deputy Governors, or such of them as the Lord Lieutenant, or other Chief Governor or Governors of *Ireland*, for the Time being, shall direct, shall, in Obedience and Conformity to the Orders of such Lord Lieutenant, or other Chief Governor or Governors, procure Returns of the Numbers of Men residing within the several Counties, Ridings, Stewartries, Baronies, Cities and

Places within and throughout the said United Kingdome, who shall be of the Age of fifteen years and under the Age of Sixty years, distinguishing which of them are by reason of Infirmity incapable of active Service, And which of them are engaged in any Volunteer Corps, or in any Troops or Companies of Yeomanry, and what Corps, Troops, or Companies, and which of them are willing to engage themselves to be armed, arrayed, trained and exercised for the Defence of the United Kingdom, and upon what Terms; and which of them are willing to engage in Cases of Emergency, either gratuitously or for hire, as Boatmen or Bargemen, or as Drivers of Carriages or Horses, or Drivers of Waggons, Carts, Cars, or Cattle, or as Pioneers or other Labourers, for any Works or Labour which may be necessary for the publick Service; and also distinguishing all Aliens and Quakers, with such other Particulars as his Majesty, or such Lord Lieutenant or other Chief Governor of Governors of *Ireland*, shall think fit to require; and also to procure Returns of the Numbers of the Males and Females residing within the several Counties, Ridings, Stewartries, Baronies, Cities, and Places aforesaid, who by reason of Infancy, Age or Infirmity, or for other Cause, may probably be incapable of removing themselves in case of Danger; and also for procuring Returns of all Boats, Barges, Waggons, Carts, Cars, Horses and other Cattle and Sheep, and of all Hay, Straw, Corn, Meal, Flour, and other Provisions, and of all Mills and Ovens, and all other Matters and Things which may be useful to an enemy, or applicable to the publick Service within the said Counties, ridings, Stewartries, Baronies, Cities and Places respectively; and which of such Boats, Barges, Waggons, Carts, Cars, and horses, the owners thereof are willing to furnish, in case of Emergency, for the publick Service, either gratuitously or for Hire, and with what Number of Boatmen, Bargemen, Drivers and other necessary Attendants, and upon what Terms and Conditions; and of all such other Particulars as his Majesty, or such Lord Lieutenant or Chief Governor or Governors aforesaid shall require, for the Purpose of enabling his Majesty, and the Persons acting under his Majesty's Authority, or the said Lord Lieutenant or Chief Governor or Governors, and the Persons acting under his or their Authority, to give such Orders as may be necessary for the Removal, in case of Danger, of such Persons as shall be incapable of removing themselves; and for the Removal of all Boats, Barges, Waggons, Carts, Cars, Horses, Cattle, Sheep, Hay, Straw, Corn, Meal, Flour, and other Provisions, Matters and Things aforesaid, or for the Employment thereof in his Majesty's Service or otherwise, as the Exigency of the Case shall require; and generally to give such Directions touching such Matters respectively, as may be deemed most likely to defeat the Views of the Enemy, and most advantageous for the publick Service.

II. And be it further enacted, That it shall be lawful for his Majesty, by and with the Advice of his Privy Council, and for the Lord Lieutenant, or other Chief

Governor or Governors of *Ireland*, for the Time being, by and with the advice of his Majesty's Privy Council of *Ireland*, to order and require, from Time to Time, as his Majesty or such Lord Lieutenant or other Chief Governor or Governors as aforesaid, shall see Occasion, the Lieutenants or Deputy Lieutenants acting as Lieutenants as aforesaid, or the Governors or Deputy Governors of Counties in *Ireland* respectively, to appoint proper Officers to be ready for arraying, training, exercising, and commanding such Men as shall be willing to engage themselves to be armed, trained, and exercised as aforesaid, and also proper Persons to be in like Manner ready, in case of Need, for superintending and directing the Execution of the several other Duties which may be necessary to be done, for the several Purposes herein-before mentioned; such Officers and other Persons to be appointed in such Numbers, and under such Regulations and Restrictions as his Majesty, or such Lord Lieutenant or other Chief Governor or Governors in *Ireland*, shall think fit to order and direct; such Lieutenants or Deputy Lieutenants, acting as Lieutenants as aforesaid, or such Governors or Deputy Governors, first signifying to his Majesty, or to such Lord Lieutenant or other Chief Governor or Governors, the Names and Ranks of all Officers so to be appointed, and the Purposes for which they are so to be appointed, and appointing such Officers only as his Majesty, or such Lord Lieutenant or other Chief Governor or Governors in *Ireland* shall approve; Provided always, that if the said Lieutenants, or Deputy Lieutenants, acting as Lieutenants as aforesaid, or such Governors or Deputy Governors shall not, within the Time which may be specified in the Orders which shall be given for such Purpose, signify to his Majesty, or to such Lord Lieutenant or other Chief Governor or Governors aforesaid, the Names of a sufficient Number of Officers, whom his Majesty or such Lord Lieutenant or other Chief Governor or Governors, in *Ireland*, shall approve for the Command of such Men as aforesaid, and appoint such other Persons as shall be necessary for the Purposes aforesaid, it shall be lawful for his Majesty, or for such Lord Lieutenant or other Chief Governor or Governors as aforesaid, in *Ireland*, to appoint so many Officers and other Persons as shall be necessary for such Purposes.

III. And be it further enacted, That it shall be lawful for his Majesty, by Order under his Sign Manual, or for such Lord Lieutenant or other Chief Governor or Governors aforesaid, by Order in Writing, under his or their Hand or Hands, to authorize and require the several Lieutenants and Deputy Lieutenants aforesaid, and the several Governors or Deputy Governors of Counties in *Ireland*, to hold such General and Subdivision Meetings, within their respective Counties, Ridings, Stewartries, Cities, and Places as his Majesty, or such Lord Lieutenant or other Chief Governor or Governors as aforesaid, shall think fit, and as shall be necessary for the Execution of this Act; and to require for such

Purposes the Attendance of the Clerks of the several General Meetings and Subdivision Meetings within their respective Counties, Ridings, Stewartries, Cities, and Places, and of all other Persons whose Assistance shall be necessary for carrying into Execution this Act, in such and the same Manner, and with the same Powers and Authorities as by the several Acts now in Force concerning the Militia Forces of *Great Britain* and *Ireland* respectively, is provided with respect to such Militia Forces, so far as the Provisions in such Acts respectively are applicable to the Purposes of this Act.

IV. And be it further enacted, That the said Lieutenants and their Deputy Lieutenants and the Deputy Lieutenants acting as Lieutenants as aforesaid, and such Governors or Deputy Governors of Counties in *Ireland*, and all Justices of the Peace, Constables, Tything Men, Headboroughs, and other Officers, shall, for the Purposes of this Act, have the like Powers and Authorities to do within their respective Counties, Ridings, Stewartries, Baronies, Cities, and Places respectively, all such Acts, Matters and Things as shall be required by his Majesty, or by such Lord Lieutenant or other Chief Governor or Governors as aforesaid, to be done by them respectively in the Execution of this Act, as they respectively have to do the several Acts, Matters, and Things by Law required to be done by them respectively by any Act or Acts now in Force, concerning the Militia Forces of *Great Britain* and *Ireland* respectively.

V. And be it further enacted, That all Lieutenants, Deputy Lieutenants, Governors, Deputy Governors, Justices of the Peace, Constables, and other Officers, and all other Persons, shall obey such Orders as they shall respectively receive under the Authority of this Act, and the several Provisions herein contained.

VI. And be it further enacted, That the Lieutenants or Deputy Lieutenants, and the Governors or Deputy Governors of the several Counties, Ridings, Stewartries, Cities, and Places aforesaid, within such Time as they shall be required by his Majesty, or by such Lord Lieutenant or other Chief Governor or Governors as aforesaid, so to do, shall issue Warrants to the several Constables, Tything Men, Headboroughs, or other Officers of every Parish or Place within the several Counties, Ridings, Stewartries, Baronies, Cities, and Places aforesaid, to cause Returns to be prepared and made, touching the several Purposes aforesaid, or any of them, as his Majesty, or such Lord Lieutenant, or other Chief Governor or Governors, shall direct for their respective Parishes and Places; and such Constables, Tything Men, Headboroughs, and other Officers shall make such Returns severally and respectively to the said Deputy Lieutenants, or to the said Deputy Governors at their respective Subdivision Meetings, according to the Warrants which shall be issued for such Purposes, and shall verify the same upon Oath before such Deputy Lieutenants or Deputy Governors.

VII. And be it further enacted, That it shall be lawful for his Majesty, in case of actual Invasion of the said United Kingdom, and for the Lord Lieutenant, or other Chief Governor or Governors of *Ireland* for the Time being, in case of actual Invasion of *Ireland*, or if his Majesty, or such Lord Lieutenant or other Chief Governor or Governors as aforesaid, shall see Cause to apprehend that such Invasion will be actually attempted by the Enemy, to authorize and empower, by Order under his majesty's Sign Manual, or by Order in Writing under the Hand or hands of such Lord Lieutenant or other Chief Governor or Governors, the said Lieutenant and Deputy Lieutenants, governors or Deputy Governors, or any of them, on any Emergency, and on the Requisition of the Officer commanding within the District, respectively, or of such other Persons as his Majesty, or such Lord Lieutenant or other Chief Governor or Governors as aforesaid, shall specially empower to make such Requisition, to give all such Orders as shall be necessary for the Removal of any Boats, Barges, Waggons, Carts, cars, or other Carriages, Horses, Cattle, Sheep, Hay, Straw, Corn, Meal, Flour, or Provisions of any kind, or any other Things which may be of Advantage to an Enemy, or useful for the publick Service, and to take the same, if necessary, for the publick Service; and also to give such Orders as shall be necessary for the Removal of the Inhabitants of any House, Hamlet, Village, District or Place, or any of them, and especially such as by reason of Infancy, Age, or Infirmity, or other Cause, shall be incapable of removing themselves in case of Danger; and also, in case of Necessity, to destroy any Boats, Barges, Waggons, Carts, Cars, or other Carriages, Horses, Cattle, Sheep, Hay, Straw, Corn, Meal, Flour, or Provisions of any Kind, or any Thing which may be of Advantage to an Enemy, and to remove, destroy, or render useless and House, Mill, Bridge, or other Building, or any Matter or Thing whatsoever, and generally to do and act in the Premises as the publick Service and the Exigencies of particular Cases shall require.

VIII. And be it further enacted, That any Persons who may enrol themselves in any Volunteer Corps of Infantry or Cavalry subsequent to the Date of this Act, shall not be liable to be called out and placed under the Command of any General Officer commanding within the District in which such Corps maybe formed, except in Conformity to the Terms of their original Offers of Service, and except in case of actual Invasion, Or of the actual Appearance of the Enemy on the Coast, or of the Danger of Invasion being deemed so imminent as to make it adviseable for the Lieutenants or Deputy lieutenants, in *Great Britain*, or for the Governors or Deputy Governors in *Ireland*, or any of them, to give Orders for the Removal of Cattle, Corn, or any other Articles which may be of Advantage to the Enemy, or useful to the publick Service, in Manner herein-before mentioned.

IX. And be it further enacted, that if the Commanding Officer of any Corps or Company of Volunteers in *Great Britain*, who shall be appointed under the Authority of this Act, or who has been or shall be appointed under the Authority of an Act, passed in the forty-second Year of the Reign of his present Majesty, intituled, *An Act to enable his Majesty to avail himself of the Officers of certain Yeomanry and Volunteer Corps to continue their Services*, shall make any false return of such Corps or Company, with Intent to defraud his Majesty, or if the Commanding Officer of any Troop or Company of Yeomanry in *Ireland*, shall make or give any false Return or Certificate, every such Officer shall forfeit and lose the Sum of two hundred Pounds.

X. And be it further enacted, That it shall be lawful for his Majesty, or for the Lord Lieutenant or other Chief Governor or Governors of *Ireland* for the Time being, to authorize any General Officer or Officers, or other Person or Persons commissioned for such Purpose, to survey and mark out any Piece of Ground wanted for the publick Service, and to treat and agree with the Owner or Owners thereof, or any Person or Persons having any Interest therein, for the Possession or Use thereof during such Time as the Exigence of the Service shall require; and in case the Owner or Owners of any such Ground, or any Person or Persons having any Interest therein, shall refuse or decline to enter into such Contract touching the same as shall be satisfactory to such Officer or Officers, or other Person or Persons commissioned as aforesaid, or shall be unable to do so by reason of Infancy, Coverture or other Disability, it shall be lawful for the Person or Persons so authorized by his Majesty, or by such Lord Lieutenant, or other Chief Governor or Governors as aforesaid, to require two or more Justices of the Peace, or Deputy Lieutenants, or Deputy Governors for the County, Riding, Stewartry, City, or Place where such Piece of Ground shall be, to put his Majesty's Officers into immediate Possession of such Piece of Ground, which such Justices, or Deputy Lieutenants, or Deputy Governors shall accordingly do, and shall for that Purpose issue their Warrant, under their Hands and Seals, commanding Possession to be so delivered; and shall also issue their Warrants to the Sheriff of the County, Riding, Stewartry, City, or Place wherein such Piece of Ground shall be situate, to summon a Jury, to appear and be on a Day and at a Place in such Warrant to be mentioned, to enquire of and ascertain the Compensation which ought to be made for the Possession or Use of such Piece of Ground, during the Time for which the same shall be required for the publick Service, to the several Persons interested therein, and to whom the same ought to be paid; the Verdict of which Jury shall be certified by such Justices or Deputy Lieutenants to the Receiver

General of the Land Tax of the County, Riding, City, or Place in *England*, or to the Collector of the Land Tax of the County, Stewartry, City or Place in *Scotland*, or to the Collector of his Majesty's Revenues for Districts in *Ireland*, where such Lands shall lie; which Receiver General or Collector shall, out of any money in his hands, pay such Compensation to such Person or Persons, in such Manner and for such Purposes and by such Verdict shall be directed: Provided always, that no such Piece of Ground shall be so taken for the publick Service without the Consent of the Owner or Owners therefor, unless the Necessity for the same shall be first certified by the Lord Lieutenant, or two of the Deputy Lieutenants, or by one Governor, or two Deputy Governors of the County, Riding, Stewartry, City, or Place in which such Lands shall lie, or unless the Enemy shall have actually invaded the United Kingdom at the Time when such Piece of Ground shall be so taken.

XI. And be it further enacted, That when it shall have been found necessary to take for the publick Service, remove, or destroy any Waggons, Carts, Cars or other Carriages, Horses, Cattle, Sheep, Hay, Straw, Corn, Meal, Flour or other Provisions, or any other Articles whatsoever, or to destroy or injure any House, Mill, Bridge, or other Building, or any Matter or Thing of Value, under the Directions aforesaid, the Commissioners of his Majesty's Treasury in *Great Britain*, or the Lord Lieutenant or other Chief Governor or Governors of *Ireland* for the Time being, shall appoint Persons to enquire into and ascertain the Value of such Articles, and the Compensation which ought to be made for the same by way of Purchase or Hire, or Recompence for Damage or otherwise, according to the Nature of the Case; and if the Owner or Owners, or Person or Persons interested, shall be willing to accept the Compensation which shall be so ascertained, the same shall be paid by the Commissioners of his Majesty's Treasury in *Great Britain* and *Ireland* respectively, or by such Person or Persons as shall be appointed by them for that Purpose, in pursuance of a Certificate under the Hands of the Persons so employed to ascertain the same; and if the Owner or Owners, or Person or Persons interested shall not be willing to accept such Compensation, it shall be lawful for his Majesty, or such Lord Lieutenant or other Chief Governor or Governors of *Ireland* as aforesaid, to order two Justices of the Peace of the County, Riding, Stewartry, City, or Place to settle and ascertain the Compensation which ought to be made to such Owner or Owners, or Persons interested; which Justices shall settle and ascertain the same accordingly, and shall grant a certificate thereof to the Commissioners of his Majesty's Treasury in *Great Britain* and *Ireland* respectively, who shall order the same to be paid to the Person or Persons entitled thereto out of any Money granted for the Supply of the Year.

XII. And be it further enacted, That the Warden of the Stannaries, and all other Officers of the Stannaries in *Great Britain*, shall respectively, in Obedience to his Majesty's Orders to be issued for that Purpose, procure like Returns to be made, and all other Matters to be done touching the Tinners of the Counties of *Devon* and *Cornwall*, according to the Customs of the Stannaries and Privileges of the working Tinners, as are hereby required to be done by the Lieutenants and Deputy Lieutenants aforesaid, touching other Persons residing in the said Counties of *Devon* and *Cornwall*, not entitled to the Benefit of such Privileges; and such Warden and other Officers of the Stannaries shall have such and the like Powers and Authorities to do and execute all and every the Matters and Things which shall be so required to be done as aforesaid, as the said Lieutenants and Deputy Lieutenants of the several Counties, Ridings, Stewartries, Cities, and Places aforesaid, have for doing the several Matters and Things hereby required to be done by them respectively.

XIII. And be it further enacted, That his Majesty's Commissioners of Lieutenancy for the City of *London*, the Lord Mayor of the said City, and the Aldermen, Deputies, and Common Councilmen of the several wards of the said City and Liberties thereof, and the Constables, Beadles, and other Ward Officers of the same; the Constable of the Tower of *London*, Lieutenants of the *Tower* Hamlets, and the Deputy Lieutenants of the said Hamlets, and their several Officers; the Justices of the Peace for the Tower Liberties, the Constables, and other Peace Officers within the same; the Warden of the Cinque Ports, two ancient Towns, and their Members, his Lieutenant or Lieutenants, and his or their Officers, and the Mayors, Jurats, Justices of the Peace, Constables, and other Peace Officers for the Liberties of the Cinque Ports, two ancient Towns, and their Members; and all other Justices of the Peace, and all Persons whosoever exercising the Powers of Justices of the Peace in any Part of the said United Kingdom; and all Constables and Peace Officers within their respective Districts; and all other Persons having Authority within the same, shall put in Execution all and every the Powers and Provisions contained in this Act, in like Manner as they are respectively authorized to put in Execution the several Laws respecting the Militia Forces of the said Kingdom, or any of them respectively, within their respective Districts.

XIV. And be it further enacted, That the Form of Conviction, by one of his Majesty's Justices of the Peace, in pursuance of this Act, set forth and expressed in the Schedule hereunto annexed, may be used with such Additions and Variations only, as may be necessary to adapt the same to the particular Exigencies of the Case, and that no Objection shall be made, or Advantage taken, for want of Form in any such Conviction, by any Person or Persons whatsoever.

XV. And be it further enacted, That the Acceptance of any Commission under the Authority of this Act, shall not vacate the Seat of any Member returned to serve in Parliament.

XVI. And be it further enacted, That the respective Clerks of the General and Subdivision Meetings in *Great Britain* and *Ireland*, respectively, Constables, and other Officers required to execute this Act, and who shall respectively execute the same, to the Satisfaction of the Deputy Lieutenants or Deputy Governors assembled, at their respective Subdivision Meetings, shall have and receive such Compensation for the Care, Trouble, and Expences, in and about the executing of this Act, as the said Deputy Lieutenants or Deputy Governors shall judge them respectively to have deserved for the same; and the said Deputy Lieutenants, or Deputy Governors shall direct such Compensation to be paid by the Receiver General of the County, Riding, or Place, in *England*, or the Collector of the Land Tax of the County, Stewartry, City, or Place, in *Scotland*, or by the Collector of his Majesty's Revenue, for the District in *Ireland*, as the Case shall require, out of any Money in his Hands; and such Receiver General or Collector, respectively, shall pay the same accordingly, in case such Order as shall be made by such Deputy Lieutenants, at such Subdivision Meetings, shall be confirmed at a General Meeting in *Great Britain*; and in case such Orders as shall be made by such Deputy Governors, in *Ireland*, shall be confirmed by the Governor or Governors of the County, City, or Place, but not otherwise.

XVII. And be it further enacted, That in case any Constable, Headborough, Tythingman, or other inferior Officer or other Person, shall disobey any Orders which shall be issued in pursuance of this Act, or shall obstruct or hinder the Execution thereof, every such Person, upon Conviction of such Offence, before any Justice of the Peace, of the County, Riding, Stewartry, City, or Place, where the Offence shall be committed, shall forfeit and pay a Sum not less than five Pounds and not exceeding one hundred Pounds, at the Discretion of such Justice; and in Default of immediate Payment thereof, then such Justice is hereby required to commit such Offender to the Common Gaol of the County, Riding, Stewartry, City, or Place, where the Offence shall be committed, for any Time not exceeding three Months; and the Monies arising by such Penalty shall be paid to the Treasurer of the County, Riding, Stewartry, City or Place, where the Offence shall be committed, to be applied as Part of the Stock of such County, Riding, Stewartry, City or Place.

XVIII. And be it further enacted, That no Order or Conviction made, in pursuance of this Act, by any Lieutenant, Deputy Lieutenant, Governor, Deputy Governor or Justice of the Peace, shall be removed by *Certiorari*,

Advocation, or Suspension, out of the County, Riding, Stewartry, City, or place wherein such Order or Conviction shall be made, into any Court whatever; and that no writ of *Certiorari*, Advocation, or Suspension, shall supersede Execution or other Proceedings upon any such Order or Conviction, but that Execution and other Proceedings shall be had thereupon, any such Writ or Writs, or Allowance thereof notwithstanding.

XIX. And be it further enacted, That it shall be lawful for his Majesty, and for the Lord Lieutenant, or other Chief Governor or Governors of *Ireland* for the Time being, in *Ireland*, to authorize any three Deputy Lieutenants, or three Deputy Governors, of any County, Riding, Stewartry, City, or Place, in the Absence from such County, Riding, Stewartry, City, or Place of the Lieutenant or Governors thereof, to do all Acts, Matter, and Things in the Execution of this Act, which might lawfully be done by such Lieutenant or Governors; and the same shall be good and valid in the Law as if done by such Lieutenants or Governors.

XX. And be it further enacted, That all Penalties by this Act imposed, for Recovery whereof no other Means are hereby provided, shall be recovered by Action of Debt, Bill, Plaint, or Information in any of his Majesty's Courts of Record at *Westminster*, or in *Dublin*, or the Courts of Great Session in the Principality of *Wales*, or the Courts of the Counties Palatine of *Chester*, *Lancaster* or *Durham*, or in the Court of Session or Court of Exchequer in *Scotland*, as the Case shall require, wherein no Essoign, Privilege, Protection, Wager of Law, or more than one Imparlance shall be allowed.

APPENDIX 5: EXTRACTS FROM CORRESPONDENCE BETWEEN THE DUKE OF RICHMOND, WILLIAM ELLIS AND LT COL N POWLETT, INSPECTING FIELD OFFICER

[In the first three months of 1806, there was a bit of a spat between the Duke of Richmond, William Ellis, Clerk to the General Meetings and Lt. Col. N. Powlett, the Inspecting Field Officer, who reported to the Inspector General in London. The story is contained in correspondence reprinted in Papers Presented to the House of Lords.[126]]

23 February 1806, Powlett to Richmond

I am sorry to be thus troublesome to your Grace, but I have been called upon to know why I have not made the Circuit of the County of Sussex ... I wrote to the Clerk of General Meetings ... but hitherto without success ...

27 February 1806, Powlett to Ellis

... You are now, Sir, earnestly requested to comply with the Contents of my Letter to you

27 February 1806, Ellis to Richmond:

... inclosed send you a copy of both Colonel Powlett's letters to me, from which I trust your Grace will perceive that I could not interfere in the Business till I had had your Grace's Commands, which the Moment I received I transmitted to every Subdivision Clerk ...

2 March 1806, Richmond to Powlett:

I had the honour of receiving your Letter of the 23 February last, and immediately transmitted a Copy of it to Mr William Ellis, Clerk of the Peace at Horsham, desiring him to inform me what steps had been taken in consequence of my former Direction ... and inclosed I have the Honour to send you a Copy of his Answer ...

4 March 1806, Powlett to Richmond:

... I wrote a Letter, of which the following is a Copy, to Mr Ellis, the Clerk of General Meetings, earnestly requesting him, under your Grace's Authority, to comply with the Wishes of Government ... I still impatiently wait to have the Honour of complying with my Part of the Duty ...

---

[126] Further Papers, Presented to the House of Lords, Relating to the Army and Volunteer Corps, Pursuant to Addresses of the 31st March 1806, 21 April 1806 pp. 61-68

4 March 1806, Powlett to Ellis:

...In order still to facilitate what is required from the County, I most earnestly recommend your complying with the Instructions contained in Lord Hawkesbury's Letter ... It does not become me to fix the Subdivision Meetings, even if I knew how to address the Subdivision Clerks; it is your duty to do this under the Direction of the Lord Lieutenant ...

4 March 1806, Powlett to the Inspector General

The letters I have this day received, through the Hands of the Duke of Richmond, leave me no other Alternative for my own Justification than laying before you my Correspondence with the County of Sussex ... I trust it will appear to you that I have left nothing undone on my Part that could induce the County of Sussex to comply with the Wishes of Government in assembling its Parish Officers ... I fear little effectual will be done without your Interference ...

11 March 1806 Powlett to Richmond

Mr Ellis has this Day inclosed me a List of the Subdivision Clerks, and places of Subdivision Meetings, requesting me to write to the Subdivision Clerks, when they would in consequence assemble their Parish Officers at the Times most convenient to me; but this Order you must be aware can only properly be done through the Authority of your Grace as Lord Lieutenant of the County ...

13 March 1806, Richmond to Powlett [in full]

Sir
I this day received your Letter of the 10th Instant [sic], informing me that Mr Ellis had sent you a list of the Subdivision Clerks and Places of their Residence, requesting you would write to them, when they would in consequence assemble their Parish Officers at the Time most convenient to you.

I do not conceive upon what Ground it is that Mr Ellis has troubled you with this Request, as from one of the Subdivision Clerks he has received a Letter, signifying to him that the Deputy Lieutenant of that Rape, to whom he has communicated the Secretary of State's Letter, had not given him any Orders or Directions in consequence thereof. Mr Ellis further informed me, that at a late Adjournment of the Quarter Sessions of the Peace relative to this Act, he had laid Lord Hawkesbury's Letter before them, and that they had been of Opinion that they did not feel themselves called upon to take any Steps in consequence; and I have not heard that any of the other Subdivision Clerks have signified a different Opinion.

Your Letter seems to think that I, as Lord Lieutenant, should give the necessary Orders; but this I confess I know not how to set about. I do not conceive that a Lord Lieutenant has any Authority over Parish Officers but such as the Law may direct in particular Cases; and I am not aware of any Part of the Act that authorizes him, after the first Instructions have been given to them by the Deputy Lieutenant, to call upon them to assemble again to receive further Instructions from Persons not authorized by the Act. Indeed, as Lord Lieutenant, I have no List of the Parish Officers, and who continually change at Easter, transmitted to me, so that I do not know the Persons to whom I should address any Order for such Meeting, if I had the Power to give it.

None of the Duties imposed by the Acts of Parliament are executed immediately by the Lord Lieutenant, but through the Medium of the Deputy Lieutenants with the Parish Officers; and I have transmitted to them Lord Hawkesbury's Letter, and requested them, as far as it is in their Power, to comply with it. They, you see, decline to interfere; and as they are not authorized by Law to request this Attendance, which would be attended by considerable Inconvenience and Expence to many of them, I really do not see how the Deputy Lieutenants would be justified in ordering it, or that the Parish Officers would be bound to obey it.

I have further to mention, that in my Answer to Lord Hawkesbury's Letter I informed his Lordship that, as far as concerned me, the Statement is not correct that the Lord Lieutenant had represented the Deficiencies to arise in a great Measure from the Ignorance of the Parish Officers in understanding the Law, as I had informed his Lordship that I was satisfied they had the fullest Instructions thereupon from the Deputy Lieutenants; and that their not finding Men in this County, where there are no Manufactures, was entirely owing to the Impossibility of getting them at the limited Price.

I have the Honour to be, Sir,
Your most obedient humble Servant,
Richmond

16 March 1806, Powlett to Richmond

... I now consider my Efforts at an End; but I cannot help regretting that your Grace did not, in the first Instance, do me the Honour to tell me it never was your Intention to comply in this Case with the Wishes of Government.

17 March 1806, Powlett to the Inspector General

> ... I have the Honour of communicating my last and unsuccessful Endeavours to induce the Lord Lieutenant of the County of Sussex to comply ... I have thought it my Duty to write to the Lord Lieutenant on the Occasion of declining any further Efforts on my Part, conceiving them, as I do, to be entirely useless.

APPENDIX 6: EXTRACT FROM A LETTER FROM THE DUKE OF RICHMOND TO LORD HOBART, SECRETARY OF STATE FOR WAR AND THE COLONIES, 14 AUGUST 1801[127]

Inclosed I have the Honor of transmitting to Your Lordship a Copy of the Proceedings of the Meeting held Yesterday, in which Lieutenant General Hulse, the General commanding the District, and Major General Whyte, commanding in Sussex under him, who were both present, appeared fully to concur. The Impracticability of removing the Dead Stock appearing so evident, it was suggested that a number of County Gentlemen, Clergy or principal Farmers might be found, each undertaking for the Removal of Live Stock from such Parish or Parishes as his influence might extend to, and that a number of these might be formed into larger Lots, such as Hundreds or otherwise, as might be found convenient, under the Direction of some Deputy Lieutenant, to whom the General, being made acquainted with the Extent of these Lots, might, whenever he thought proper, make the necessary application for the Removal of the Live Stock from such Portions of the County as he might wish to have cleared more or less, according to circumstances; and that this operation, if well arranged, could be performed, with help from the Corps of Guides to shew them the Roads they were to take, better, perhaps, by such Persons under the Civil Power, authorized by the Act of Parliament, than by the Military Yeomanry Corps. All the Gentlemen present, who are not engaged in Provincial Military Corps, readily offered themselves for this Service, and many others were suggested to whom Application should be made, and it was conceived, that if the Lord Bishop of this Diocese was desired to exhort the Clergy under him to take an active Part in this Business, much assistance might be derived from their Exertions.

Lord Egremont, as Colonel of the Yeomanry Cavalry, expressed the Readiness of his Corps to act in any Capacity His Majesty's Government might think most usefull; but the far greater Gratification the Zeal of so many Gentlemen who had exerted themselves in bringing these Troops to some sort of Perfection would feel, if by the Arrangement now proposed they could be employed in the first moment of a Landing directly against the Enemy, rather than in retiring from him with the Cattle. In these Sentiments all the Officers of Yeomanry Corps present hartily agreed, & Lieutenant General Hulse, who seemed to approve of the Idea, expressed the Satisfaction he should have in the Accession of so useful a Force for immediately opposing the Enemy.

---

[127] Hampshire Record Office, 11M49/231

If this plan should meet with the Approbation of His Royal Highness the Commander in Chief, and of His Majesy's Ministers, I shall immediately proceed to appoint the Subdivision Meetings for getting the Returns, & take the necessary Measures for compleating the Detail and carrying it into Execution.

APPENDIX 7: LETTER FROM THE DUKE OF RICHMOND TO LORD BOLTON, LORD LIEUTENANT OF HAMPSHIRE, 29 AUGUST 1801[128]

The Meeting of the Lieutenancy, held at Lewes, on the 13th Instant, having found that it would be impracticable, in case of Invasion, to remove the Dead Stock & Inhabitants, from any considerable Part of this County, and being of opinion that it would be more adviseable to direct the Attention of the County in the first Instance to the Removal, on such Event, of the Live Stock, particularly Draft Cattle and Carriages, which might be most useful to the Enemy, and which if undertaken by such Gentlemen as are not engaged in the Military, Yeomanry or Volunteer Corps, and who have Influence in their Neighbourhood, might by proper Arrangements, be to a considerable Degree carried into Execution; several Gentlemen there present offered themselves for this Service. And the Proceedings of the Lieutenancy now having received the Approbation of Government, I am to request the Favor of You to inform me whether you would lend Your Assistance on this Public Occasion, and the Parishes You would undertake for

It is intended by the Lieutenancy, first to require (as by the Act of the 38th of Geo. 3rd C: 27 they are authorized to do) Returns from each Parish of the Number of Horses, Draft Oxen, Waggons and Carts, that there are at the Time within the Parish, and also of the Carters and Drivers who will engage to attend such Team or Cart specifying their Names ... And likewise the Names of such Gentlemen, Clergy or Principal Farmers, who are willing to undertake the Management of the Removal of such Live Stock from such Parish, under the Direction of some Gentleman who would superintend the Removals from the Hundred, or such other larger District, in which it might be found adviseable to class a Number of Parishes for this Purpose.

The Orders for Removal would be signified to the superintending Gentlemen for the whole, or such Parts as occasion might require, by such Deputy Lieutenant as would be appointed for the Rape or Division in which such Districts would be situated. And the Places to which each Removal is to be made, and the Roads they are to take, would be previously fixed upon. Under Agents would also be appointed in each Parish to assist the Gentleman, Clergy or Principal Farmer, who will undertake the Removals. Those who would undertake for a Parish, would be denominated Parish Directors of Removals. Those for larger Districts, Superintendants of Removals.

[128] Hampshire Record Office, 11M49/231

I have thought it right to trouble you so far with the Detail of the proposed Plan, that you might form some idea how the Business was to be conducted.

The Favor of your Answer, transmitted to me, so that I may receive it before the 13th of next Month is requested, as another General Meeting of the Lieutenancy will be held at Lewes, on 14th September, when it will be necessary to know what Gentlemen will lend their Aid on this occasion, & for what number of Parishes.

APPENDIX 8: CIRCULAR LETTER FROM LORD HAWKESBURY TO LORDS LIEUTENANT 31 DECEMBER 1805

My Lord,[129]

Upon a careful Inspection of the Number of Men raised by the respective Counties under the Additional Forces Act, it appears that out of the Ninety-one Counties and Places considered as Counties under the Militia Laws, of which Great Britain is composed, Three-fifths of the whole Number of Men raised by Parish Officers, or their Heritors or their Agents, have been furnished by Ten Counties, and those on an Average not particularly favourable to the levy of Men for Military Service; that above Five-Sixths of the Whole have been supplied by Twenty counties; and that of the remaining Seventy-One Counties, Twenty-five have not found a Single Man by their Parish Officers or their Heritors or their Agents.

It also appears, from the Reports lately received from the Lieutenants of the several Counties, in which they were called on to state the Causes that had hitherto obstructed the Execution of the Act within their respective Counties, that, in Addition to certain Impediments which it will require the Intervention of the Legislature to remove, the Failure was chiefly to be attributed to the Supineness and Inactivity of the Parish Officers and the Heritors, and their Agents, resulting principally, as they conceived, from their Ignorance of the Provisions of the Act, of the Mode of executing their Duty, and of the Advantages resulting both to themselves and their Parishes from their carrying the Law into Effect.

In order to afford to the Parish Officers, the Heritors, and their Agents, all the necessary Information for the Direction of their Conduct, to relieve the Deputy Lieutenants from the troublesome Detail of instructing Men in their Duty, and to facilitate to the Parishes the transfer of their Recruits to the receiving Parties, so soon as raised, His Majesty's Government have thought it expedient that an intelligent Officer should be directed to make a Circuit through each County, for the Purpose of meeting the Parish Officers, the Heritors and their Agents, in the Manner least inconvenient to them, and of giving them such Information and Assistance upon the Spot as they may require.

It is hoped by an Inspection of this Nature, repeated at stated Intervals, until the full Quota has been supplied, assisted by intermediate Reference to the

---

[129] Papers, Presented to the House of Lords, Relating to the Army and Volunteer Corps, Pursuant to Addresses of the 31st March 1806, 16 April 1806 pp. 121-22

Officer charged with this Duty, in case of any Thing particular occurring, that the Service may be materially assisted; and I have received the King's Commands most earnestly to request your Lordship to make an immediate Arrangement within your County for the Assembly of the [Parish Officers] on successive Days, within a convenient Distance of their own Homes, notifying the Dates and Places of Assembly to the Officer, who is directed to report himself to your Lordship, and to the Clerk of the General Meetings of the Lieutenancy, as charged with the above Duty; and I am further to request that your Lordship will cause some Civil Officer, fully informed of the Proceedings already taken under the Act within the County, and to whom a suitable Allowance will be made for his Trouble and Loss of Time on the Occasion, to accompany the Officer in the Circuit he is directed to make.

I have the honour to inclose to your Lordship a Copy of the Instructions which have been addressed by the Inspector General of the Recruiting Service, under His Royal Highness the Commander in Chief's Orders, with a View to the above Object.

His Majesty has charged me to recommend the carrying the above Measure into Effect, to your Lordship's particular and early Attention.

I am, etc
Hawkesbury

INDEX: PERSONS RECORDED IN THE PROCEEDINGS AND SCHEDULES

Note: as far as possible, variant spellings and abbreviations of names have been assimilated to entries for the same individual. Titles and ranks are given where they are normally included and, in the case of variation, in the form most common or complete.

Acton, A William 203
Acton, Francis 233
Adams, George 116
Adams, John 220
Adams, Thomas 228
Ades, Thomas 123
Agate, John 119
Agate, Michael 120
Agate, Thomas 234
Agate, William 234
Akehurst, John 273
Akehurst, Samuel 222
Akehurst, Thomas 122
Alcorn, William 254
Alderton, James 284
Alexander, Hugh 182
Alexander, William 214
Alfry, Henry 234
Allfrey, William 238
Amoore, John 120
Amoore, William 118, 347
Andrews, James 120, 204
Andrews, John 336
Andrews, Nicholas 117
Andrews, Richard 345
Anscombe, Allen 232, 234
Anscombe, James 238, 248
Anscombe, John 236
Apted, Richard 234
Arkwell, William 232
Arnold, William 222
Asbridge, Jonathan 119
Ashburnham, George, 3rd Earl of
    Ashburnham, formerly Lord St
    Asaph 105, 111, 114, 124, 127, 307,
    308, 311, 318, 325, 327
Ashburnham, Sir William 123, 314
Ashby, James 258
Ashby, John 258, 274
Ashby, Thomas 260
Ashcroft, James 226
Ashdown, John 213
Ashfield, Stephen 242
Ashfold, John 210

Ashford, John 236
Ashley, Richard 202
Atheroll, Henry 256
Atterton, Charles 233
Attlee, Richard 204
Attree 309
Attree, James 234
Attree, Richard 122
Auger, Edward 122, 314
Austen, Revd 123
Axford, James 241
Ayers, Charles 235
Aylet, Samuel 337
Ayling, Richard 117
Backshall, John 233
Badcock, Edward 341
Bailey, Joseph 116
Baker, Charles 339
Baker, Revd John 120, 121, 122
Baker, William 274
Balchman, James 347
Balcombe, Lucy 202
Balcombe, Samuel 232
Bale, Capt 325
Bale, Revd 123
Ball, Thomas A 204
Bandfield, John 236
Bannister, John 233
Bannister, William 240, 241
Barber 129
Barber, Henry 337
Barber, John 123, 237, 242, 246
Barber, Samuel 205
Barber, Thomas 213
Barker, Edward 120
Barnes, William 347
Barnett, John 235
Bartley, Charles 235
Bartley, John 210
Bartley, Richard 236
Bashford, John 236
Batchelor, G 345
Batchelor, John 121, 237, 243
Batchelor, William 237

Bathurst, Revd Charles 120
Batten, John 208
Batten, William 341
Battine, William 324
Bayley, John 337
Bayton, George 117
Beal, Benjamin 204, 205
Beal, Richard 235
Beal, William 235
Bean, John 314
Beard, Nathaniel 214
Beard, Thomas 214, 218
Beard, Thomas Rook 206, 207, 216
Bechely, Nathaniel 235
Bechely, William 235, 242
Beckett, John 120
Beeching, Henry 237, 244
Beeching, John 236
Bellis, Col 316
Bennett, Francis 118, 346
Bennett, John 236
Bennett, P 347
Bennett, William 235, 347
Berry, Abraham 238
Berry, Mrs 204
Berry, Philip 207
Berry, Thomas 122
Bethune, Mrs 240
Bethune, Revd Charles 238
Betts, John 235
Betts, Richard 235
Betts, Thomas 236
Bewley, Edward 345
Biddulph, Maj 348
Bignall, William 274
Billinghurst, Charles 344
Bine, Stephen 208, 209
Bingham, Revd R 121
Bingham, William 232
Birch, James 343
Birch, Robert 343
Bishop, George 208, 218
Bishop, Henry 232
Bishopp, Thomas 345
Blackman, Ben 123
Blackman, Thomas 120, 207
Blair, Dr Thomas 197
Blake, Thomas 343
Blaker, William 121, 242, 243
Blower, Richard 235

Blunden, James 119
Blunden, Stephen 118
Blunden, Thomas 343
Blunden, William 343
Boara, John 254
Body, John 122
Boniface, John 118, 336, 244
Bonned, Joseph 337
Booker, James 237
Booker, John 237, 240, 246
Booker, Richard 232
Booker, William 234
Boom, Joseph 116
Boorn, John Pilgrim 129
Borer, John 208
Borer, William 121, 208
Bostock, Revd 123
Botten, James 216
Botting, Greenfield 236
Botting, Henry 236
Botting, John 214, 244, 245
Bourne, John 233
Box, John 232
Boxall, John 343
Boxall, Richard 119
Boyd, William 122
Boys, James 347
Braizer, Edward 234
Braizer, James 234
Braizer, Samuel 235, 241, 242
Bray, Richard 237
Bray, William 236, 242
Breeding, Thomas 341
Brereton, William 14
Bridger, Harry 111, 114, 120, 307, 309, 311, 320, 327
Bridger, Sir John 105, 333
Brisco, Wastel 123
Bristow, Henry 339
Broad, James 236
Broad, John 236
Broad, William 244
Broadbridge, William 119
Brook 202, 226
Brook, James 258
Brook, Stephen 124
Brook, Thomas P 204
Brooker, Herbert 210
Brooker, James 241
Brooker, Thomas 234, 242

Brooker, William 234
Brookes, James 240
Broomfield, John 210, 211, 338
Broomfield, William 210
Brown, Edward 344
Brown, Isaac 233
Brown, John 119, 212
Brown, Richard 344, 345
Brown, Thomas 215, 260
Brown, Timothy 340
Brown, William 215, 226
Browne, John 232
Browne, Joseph 232, 233
Browne, Revd T 240
Browne, Thomas 232
Bryan, William 262
Bryant, John 205
Buckman, Simeon 233
Buckwell, Thomas 222
Budd, Henry 119
Budgen, James 232
Budgen, Obadiah 232
Budgen, Thomas 232
Bull, John 121, 208, 210, 211
Bull, Thomas 338
Burchall, Edward 337
Burchell, William 119
Burrage, Jacob 347
Burrage, William 347
Burrell, John 118
Burrell, Samuel 349
Burrell, Sir Charles Merrik 105, 114, 318, 325
Burrell, Walter 325
Burt, John 238
Burt, William 242, 343
Burtenshaw, Henry 211, 234
Burtenshaw, James 210, 234, 341
Burtenshaw, John 240, 242
Burtenshaw, John 242
Busby, John 317
Bushby, George 118
Buss, James 124
Bussby, William 204
Busson, John 210
Butler, Edward 304
Butler, James 116
Butler, William 276
Bysshopp, Sir Cecil 105, 114, 320, 325, 327

Caffyn 208
Caffyn, Jacob 246
Caffyn, John 121, 242, 243
Caffyn, Thomas 238
Cameron, D J 123
Camp, James William 202, 220
Campion, Capt 325
Campion, H S 208
Campion, William John 10
Cane, Edward 122
Capel, Hon John Thomas 105, 111, 127, 311, 325, 327
Capper, Revd James 122
Capron, A 342
Carey, Revd I H S 118
Carleton, Edward 114, 118, 317
Carnegie, Col 129, 320
Carr, Sir Thomas 105, 114, 122, 273, 276, 307, 320
Carter, James 202, 222,
Catt, Edmund 122
Catt, Edward 274
Catt, William 274
Causton, Revd Thomas 123, 296
Challen, J H 315
Challen, Napper 129
Challen, Richard 118
Challen, William 116
Chambers, James 237
Chambers, William 122, 274
Chandler, George 347
Chandler, William 205
Chapman, Henry 119
Chapman, Nicholas 274
Chapman, Thomas 300
Charlwood, Sarah 262
Charman, Henry 183
Charman, William 119
Chart, William 234
Chase, Richard 114, 122
Chasemore, Philip 119
Chasemore, Richard 341
Chatfield, John 119, 120
Chatfield, Revd Henry 121, 240, 340
Chatfield, Richard 236
Chatfield, Robert 208
Chatfield, Thomas 118
Cheal, Henry 234
Cheal, William 297
Cheesman, John 204, 338

Child, William 122
Childs, Francis 238
Childs, Philip 232
Chitty, Christopher 202, 203
Christmas, Richard 121, 218
Churcher, Emery 129
Clark, Dive 123
Clear, Henry 236
Clifford, Mrs Har[?] 240
Clifford, Thomas 232, 233
Cloke, Moses 296
Clutton, Isaac 121, 238
Clutton, Revd Henry 121
Clutton, William 242, 340
Coak, Thomas 232
Colebrook, John 117, 119, 346
Coleman, Samuel 278
Coles, John 343
Collett, Revd J Smith 123
Collins, E 344
Collins, Thomas 118, 336, 344
Collins, William 336
Colman, James 258
Comber, John 232, 233, 237, 240
Comber, Richard 119, 240, 241, 309
Comber, Stephen 236
Comber, Thomas 232, 241
Comber, William 237
Combes, Robert 202
Comerell, John William 114, 119
Constable, Richard 119
Constable, William 123
Cook, James 339
Cook, Richard 119, 240
Cook, Thomas 240
Cook, William 339
Cooke, James 243
Cooke, Thomas 235, 242, 340
Coomber, Mrs 338
Coomber, Thomas 340, 341
Cooper, Charles 336
Cooper, Edmund 122
Cooper, Robert 202
Cooper, Thomas 123
Cooper, William 119
Coote, Richard 337
Copas, William 337
Coppard, James 204, 205
Coppard, John 123, 234, 338, 340
Coppard, Nathaniel 264

Coppard, William 340, 341
Corman, John 291
Cornford, Edward 222
Cosens, Edmund 337
Cosens, James 336
Cosens, John 336
Cosens, Richard 116, 336
Cottrell, Stephen 11
Coulstock, John 210
Courthope, George 114, 123
Cox, Richard 205
Cranston, Edmund 1
Cranston, Edward 14, 15, 105, 111, 123
Crawford, Gibbs 123
Crawley, Revd 123, 255
Creasey, Richard 233
Cremer, George 236
Cripps, John Martin 129, 206, 309, 315, 327, 332, 338, 340
Croft, Revd P G 120
Crofts 344
Croskey, Stephen 208
Crosskey, John 236
Croucher, John 242
Crowhurst, Nicholas 262
Cruttenden, Sarah 302
Cruttenden, Thomas 122, 220, 287
Cuckney, Thomas 235
Curteis, Edward Jeremiah 123, 297, 308
Cutler, John 120
Cutler, William 119
Cutress, Charles 213
Dadsell, Ed O 254
Dadswell, Nicholas 258
Dalrymple, John Apsely 123
Dalton, John 232
Damer, William 342
Dance, James 337
Dancy, John 234, 242
Dancy, Joseph 235
Dancy, Michael 236
Dancy, Richard 236
Danteer, James 345
Davey, Edmund 205, 237, 244
Davey, Henry 210
David, Richard 345
Davidson, James 212
Day, James 228
Day, Thomas 228
Dean, Edward 202

Dearling, William 117, 336
Delves, Revd William 123
Dench, Edward 232
Dench, James 234
Dench, Thomas 240
Dendy, Charles 129
Denman, John 122, 272
Denman, Samuel 208
Denman, William 339
Dennett, John 202, 210
Dewdney, Arthur 121, 232
Dickins, Charles Scrase 105, 111
Dive, Christopher 296
Dixon, Richard M 348
Dodson, Revd John 121, 208
Dowlan, Edward 215, 236
D'Oyley, Revd Matthias 122
Drake, William 287
Drury 328
Duke, Thomas 344
Dumbrell, Richard 214
Dundas, Gen Sir David 3, 6, 105
Duplock, John 202
Duplock, William 203
Durrant, William 260
Dyer, John 336
Dyer, R S 212
Eager, John 218
Ealing, William 345
Ede, Anthony 208
Ede, John 234
Ede, Jonathan 218
Ede, Mary 248
Ede, Richard 235
Ede, William 210, 236
Edwards, James 203, 339
Edwards, Thomas 237
Elles, Thomas 119
Elliott, H J 339
Elliott, Henry 339
Elliott, John 234, 336
Elliott, William 348
Ellis 332
Ellis, Capt 348
Ellis, James 124, 276
Ellis, John 238
Ellis, Thomas 204
Ellis, William 9, 14, 101, 103, 104, 113, 119, 126, 129, 306, 310, 317, 319, 323, 324, 326, 329, 330, 333, 334, 348

Ellman, John 120, 122, 127
Ellman, Thomas 120
Ellsey, John 236
Ellyot, Francis 237
Ellyott, John 237
Elmes, Sarah 204
Elphick, Charles 234
Elphick, Edward 258
Elphick, George 120, 202, 203
Elsey, William 233
English, William 210
Etheridge, James 236
Ethridge, Daniel 236
Evans, Samuel 339
Everest, Peter 260
Ewen, Charles 116
Ewins, Richard 340
Falkenor, Thomas 344
Farncombe, Henry 123
Farncombe, John 272
Farndell, Charles 337
Faulconer, T 204
Faulconer, William 120
Faulkner, John 344
Fearon, Revd Joseph Francis 121, 238
Feldwick, William 232
Field, James 234, 236
Fielder, Moses 122
Fiest, John 237
Fiest, Thomas 234
Flint, Benjamin 234
Flint, Richard 244
Float, Mary 218
Foakes, William 238
Foard, Henry 342
Fogden, Alexander 336
Fogden, James 337
Fogden, John 337
Fogden, Richard 336
Follett, Robert 129
Foord, Charles 205
Foord, Thomas 218
Ford, James 346
Ford, Michael 346
Ford, Robert 339
Forster, Joseph 118
Foster 208
Foster, Benjamin 304
Fowler, William 317
Francis, J 240

Francis, John 240
Francis, W 240
Francis, William 232
Frankland, William 327
Franks, John 235
Freeman, Joseph 234
Friend, Daniel 205
Friend, John 256
Fry, Robert 254
Fuggles, James 287
Fuller, John 1, 14, 15, 103, 105, 110, 111, 114, 124, 127, 300, 307, 308, 311, 314, 320, 327
Fuller, John Trayton 1, 10, 105, 111, 123, 307, 327
Fuller, Joseph 202
Fuller, Revd Thomas 123
Fuller, Robert 119
Fuller, T 73
Fuller, Thomas 119, 122
Furlonger, William 343
Gabbitas, Revd William 120
Gadd, Henry 117
Gage, Henry Viscount 105, 111, 127, 307, 308, 311, 314, 315, 318, 320, 327, 33
Gage, John 317
Gale, John 347
Gale, William 343
Gallup, Robert 121, 208
Gardener, George 236
Garland, Rebecca 262
Garrett, William 256
Gasson, John 284
Gasson, Sarah 284
Gates, Isaac 232
Gatford, John 234, 236, 248
Gearon, Richard 236
Geer, John 218, 338
Geere, Charles 226
Geere, John 210
Geere, Thomas 214
Gell, Francis 119
Gibbs, Thomas 116, 233
Gibson, Cornelius 278
Gilbert, Charles 14, 106, 111, 114, 122, 127, 307, 320, 327, 332
Giles, Thomas 222
Gill, James 272
Glazebrook, James 345
Glazebrook, John 120, 216, 345

Goble, James Holmes 106, 111, 114
Goddard, David 341
Goddard, James 235
Goddard, Thomas 343
Goddard, William 121, 210
Godfrey, Henry 214
Godley, John 210, 218
Godman, Joseph 317
Godsmark, John 235
Godsmark, Michael 234
Godsmark, William 236
Golds, John 120
Golds, Thomas 120
Goldsmith, James 276
Goldsmith, Joseph 216
Goldsmith, William 122
Goley, John 264
Good, Henry 343
Good, Joseph 342
Goring, Charles 10, 14, 105, 106, 111, 114, 120, 127, 309, 311, 316, 320, 327
Goring, Charles Foster 111, 114, 120, 311, 320
Goring, William 232
Gorringe, Thomas 205
Gorringe, William 120
Gosley, Thomas 304
Gosley, William 304
Gouldsmith, William 272
Grace, Thomas 278
Graham, George Edward 121, 129, 309, 315, 316
Graig, Peter 345
Grainger, Thomas Cecil 105, 111, 114, 121, 127, 129, 237, 238, 242, 248, 249, 307, 320
Gray, Charles 345
Greatherd, John 226
Gree, John 212
Green, Edward 280, 339
Green, Revd John Cheal 118
Green, William 1, 10, 14
Greenfield, Richard 237
Gregory 344
Gregory, James 212
Gregory, William 213
Grenville, John 212
Grey, Gen Sir Charles 2, 4, 7
Groome, Revd William 118
Grove, Henry Hart 262

Grove, John 336
Grover, James 264
Grover, Thomas 264
Gumbrell, John 347
Gurr, Benjamin 339
Gurr, Isaac 258
Guy, William 258
Gwynne, Samuel 103, 127, 334
Hackman, William 337
Haddock, Thomas 296
Hall, Nathaniel 120
Halstead, Henry 116
Halsted, William 344
Hamesley, John 345
Hammond, William 280
Hampton, Francis 119
Hamshar, John 121, 212
Hamshar, Richard 121, 206, 208, 214, 236, 244, 245
Hamshar, William 338
Harben, Thomas Henry 114, 325
Hard, Edward 345
Hardcan, James 214
Harding, John 238
Harding, Richard 238
Hards, John 339
Hards, Richard 240
Hardwick, John 121
Hardy, Revd Robert 118
Hargrave 212
Harland, Anthony 260
Harland, Edward 210
Harland, James 207
Harland, John 246
Harland, William 211
Harman, Thomas 205
Harmer, Henry 206
Harmer, James 210, 211
Harmer, Michal 244
Harrison, John 120
Hart, Richard 214
Harvey, Edward 10
Harvey, John 336
Harvey, William Gilmore 314
Harwood, Edward 346
Hasley, William 336
Havesay, Joseph 347
Hawes, Robert 123, 314
Hawkins, John 117
Hawthorn, Daniel 300

Hayller, John 349
Haylor, Nathaniel 234
Haynes, Charles 347
Haynes, George 123, 262
Hazlegrove, John 347
Heasman, Charles 240
Heasman, Christopher 121
Heasman, Henry 119, 236
Heasman, William 237
Heath, Revd Nicholas 121
Heather, Richard 260
Heather, Samuel 348
Heaver, Benjamin 258
Heaver, Edward 260
Heaver, William 237, 242, 246
Helford, Nathaniel 210
Hemsley, Richard 205
Hemsley, William 236, 242
Henderson, Edward 119
Henley, Robert 214
Hennard, John 216
Henshott, Henry 347
Henty, Capt 344
Henty, George 118
Henty, John 236
Herriott, Thomas 208
Hersee, Charles 118
Hervey, Gilmore 308
Hewett, Thomas 344
Hewick, Amos 342
Hick, William Franklin 120, 315
Hide, Henry 341
Hider, Henry 210
Hildar, Edward 298
Hilder, Thomas 124
Hill, James 347
Hill, Thomas 220, 264, 276, 278
Hillier 129
Hillman, Charles 282
Hillman, Henry 282
Hillman, Humphrey 205
Hillman, James 282
Hillman, John 282
Hillman, Prince 284
Hillman, Richard 282
Hillman, Samuel 284
Hillman, Thomas 282
Hills, James 235
Hills, John 236
Hilton, John 222

Hilton, Moses 347
Himenesley, Thomas 341
Hipkins, William 117
Hoad, Christopher 123
Hoadley, James 205
Hoath, Martin 232
Hobart, Lord 1, 2, 3, 8, 12, 13, 106, 110, 308, 311
Hobbs, Abraham 346
Hobbs, Henry 117
Hobbs, James 206
Hobbs, John 117
Hobbs, William 213, 264
Hobden, Henry 218
Hobden, John 234
Hobden, Richard 204
Hobdin, Henry 212
Hobger, Thomas 129
Hodson, Thomas 338
Hodson, William 121
Hogben, Thomas 116
Hogsflesh, Benjamin 345
Holand, Francis 123
Holden, William 118, 235
Holder, Edward 205
Holland, John 339
Holland, Richard 119
Hollands, James 237
Hollands, John 205, 236, 240, 246
Hollands, Philip 234
Hollands, Thomas 211
Holman, Charles 207
Holman, John 232
Holman, William 232
Holmes, Thomas 119
Homewood, Francis 216, 217
Homewood, George 235
Homewood, John 234
Hooker, Revd T R 121
Hooper, Leonard 256
Hooper, Revd T Poole 120
Howell, John 204, 205
Hubarne, Walter 242
Hubbard, Henry 209
Hudson, Revd Thomas 121
Hugget, Henry 339
Huggott, Henry 339
Hughes, John 119
Hulse, Lt Gen 1, 2, 4
Humbleton, Stephen 349

Humphrey, James 234, 347
Humphrey, Michael 233
Humphrey, William 235
Hunt, John 337
Hurbarne, Walter 237
Hurley, Richard 120
Hurlick, Charles 343
Hurst, Henry 274
Hurst, Walter 240, 241, 246
Hutchins, Revd James 120
Hyland 287
Ibbetson, Charles 317, 346
Ide, James 119
Impey, Sir Elijah 129, 309, 315, 318
Ingram, James 214, 215, 309, 315
Ingram, John 206
Ings, Thomas 243 244
Inskip, George 280
Ireland, John 119
Islip, Revd Walter 117
Isted, Edward 232
Isted, Thomas 236
Izard, Joseph 236
Jarden, William 232
Jeal, John 238
Jeffery, Benjamin 232
Jeffery, Henry 246
Jeffery, Thomas 232
Jeffery, William 232
Jenner, Edward 234, 248
Jenner, James 234
Jenner, John 122
Jenner, Thomas 206, 207
Jenner, William 208, 209, 339
Jennings, John 234
Jennings, William 234
Joanes, Ralph 346
Johnson 213
Johnson, James 235
Johnson, John 339
Johnson, Thomas 206
Johnson, William 103, 317, 339
Jones, Edward 280
Jones, Richard 260
Judge, Thomas 216
Juniper, John 234
Jupp, G S 346
Jupp, John 118
Jupp, Thomas 236
Kell, Christopher 45, 49, 103

Kemp, Al 337
Kemp, Henry 262
Kemp, Nathaniel 121
Kemp, Thomas 1, 10, 15, 105, 111, 114, 121, 127, 307, 308, 311, 320, 327, 332, 333, 335
Kennard, John 234, 264
Kennard, Stephen 276
Kennard, William 220
Kennett, Henry 222
Kensell, William 236
Kent, James 204
Kent, Thomas 222
Kenward, Robert 338, 339
Kenward, Thomas 220
Kenward, William 204, 254
Killick, Thomas 119
Kimber, Richard 232
Kine, Thomas Swaine 122
King, G 347
King, Hon G 346
King, James 237
King, John 122, 123, 207, 272, 296, 339
King, Richard 264
King, Thomas 210, 236
King, William 348
Kinleside, Revd William 118
Kinsett, William 243
Kitchener, Thomas 210
Kitchenor, William 346
Knight, George 235
Knight, John 232, 235, 236, 240
Knight, Mary 242
Knight, Richard 204, 205
Knight, William 341
Knowles, James 242, 243
Knowles, John 345
Knowles, William 341, 345
Laker, William 118
Lamb, Charles 332
Lamb, Thomas Davis 106, 127, 307, 320,
Lamb, Thomas Phillips 10, 15, 73, 105, 111
Lamberth, George 337
Lane, George 116
Langdale, Revd Edward 122
Langford, John 123
Langridge, Richard 233
Langridge, William 264, 333
Langridge, William Balcombe 45, 49, 103

Larkin, Nicholas 123
Lashmar 212
Lashmar, John 222, 258
Latter, Henry 260
Law, Sir Thomas 314
Lawrence 308
Leach, John 325
Lee, John 234
Lee, William 216
Legg, John 234
Leney, Isaac 235
Lennox, Charles, 3rd Duke of Richmond 1, 10, 12, 105, 114, 306, 307, 311, 318, 320, 324, 325, 327, 328, 332
Lennox, Maj Gen Charles 105, 114, 127, 311, 318, 320, 323, 327
Leopard, William 232, 243, 244
Leppard, Henry 236
Lettice, Revd J 296
Lewis, Revd Thomas 123
Lickfold, John 119
Lidbetter 255
Lidbetter, Thomas 119, 120
Lindfield, James 237
Lindfield, John 236
Lindfield, William 208
Linfield, George 339
Linfield, Thomas 208
Lintott, Charles 237
Lion, Capt 325
Lloyd, J M 1
Lloyd, James Martin 106, 127, 320, 327
Lloyd, Thomas 346
Loase, Robert 218
Lock, John 246
Lock, William 232
Long, Mary 336
Long, William 122, 273
Longhurst, John 236
Longhurst, William 237
Longley, Edward 345
Longley, Samuel 345
Longs, William 314
Lord, William 339
Lower, Charles 282
Lower, Henry 224
Lower, Sarah 282
Lower, Thomas 214, 282
Loxley, Henry 236
Lucas, James 342

Luxford, John 10, 123
Lyon, Lt Col George 348
Mackett, Thomas 273
Magglestone, Thomas 287
Mannington, Matthew 276
Mansbridge, James 237
Mansell, James 345
Marchant, John 208, 209
Marchant, Thomas 213
Marchant, William 235
Margesson, Maj 344
Margesson, William 309, 327
Markwick, John 206
Markwick, William 14, 124
Marsh, John 317
Marshal, Henry 339
Marshall, John 216, 340
Marshall, Revd John 120
Marshall, Richard 118, 346
Marshall, William 210, 244, 341
Martin 238
Martin, Ferdinand 276
Martin, John 116, 204
Martin, Joseph 122
Martin, Nicholas 254
Martin, Revd Richard Lomax 119
Martin, Stephen 208
Martin, Thomas 233, 240
Mason, John 238
Mason, Walter 124
Mathews, Thomas 345
May, Edward 206
Maynard, Thomas 234, 241, 242
McCabe, Miles 242
McGeorge, John 234
McPherson, Sir John 123
Meads, Francis 262
Mellersh, John 117
Merricks, Richard 116
Mial, Richard 232
Michel, Edward 341
Michell, Eardley W 123, 308
Michell, Edward 234
Michell, Henry 242, 243
Michell, James 232
Michell, John 234, 236
Michell, Shadrack 349
Michenor, John 343
Micklethwaite, John 314
Miles, James 119, 341, 345

Miles, Robert 314
Miles, William 254
Miller, Sir John Riggs 127, 315
Miller, Thomas 345
Mills, John 345
Millyard, Edward 337
Millyard, Thomas 336
Milton, Thomas 343
Milton, William 343
Milward, Edward 123
Mitchell, Henry 237
Mitchell, John 208, 209, 235
Mitchell, Matthew 236
Mitchell, Richard 237
Mitchell, Samuel 235
Mitchell, Thomas 237
Mitchell, William 120
Mitford, William 105, 111, 119, 346
Molinieux, Samuel 234
Moon, John 254
Moore, Benjamin 300
Moore, Col 316, 325
Moore, William 346
Moorey, Richard 214
Morfew, William 238
Morley, John 204, 205, 232
Morris, Susan 206
Morris, William 123
Mortimer, Elizabeth 274
Moseley, John 123
Mowatt, Capt 315, 325
Muddle, Edmund 233
Muggridge, Daniel 347
Mullins, George 118
Murray, John 317
Murrell, Joseph 118
Nairne, Fasham 238, 240, 309
Napper, John 106, 347
Nash, Richard 256
Naylor, Francis Hare 123, 127, 307, 308, 214, 320
Neal, John 119
Neve, Robert 256
Newbery, Francis 1, 105, 114, 123, 307, 325
Newbery, John 325
Newding, George 222
Newland, John 344
Newland, William 118, 339, 342
Newnham, George 309

Newnham, John 106, 122, 129
Newnham, John Lewis 315
Newnham, Richard 264
Newton, Lt Col William 1, 10, 15, 40, 44,
    48, 103, 105, 111, 114, 121, 127, 129,
    202, 233, 258, 307, 309, 311, 315, 316,
    318, 320
Nichol, Thomas 304
Nicholas, Benjamin 232
Nicholas, Henry 233
Noakes, John 291
Noakes, William 120
Norman, George 233
Norman, John 232
Norris, Thomas 234
Nott, Revd 122
Nye, Henry 205, 339
Nye, William 207
Ockenden, James 235
Ockenden, William 210
Offen, John 286
Olive, Thomas 217
Olive, William 216
Oliver, George 118
Ordur, Daniel 339
Orton, George 237
Osborn, John 336
Osborn, William 234
Osborne, George 116
Osborne, John 208, 209
Osborne, Thomas 336
Osgood, William 343
Ovington, John 129
Pace, John 235, 246
Packham, Charles 234
Packham, Edward 121
Packham, George 234
Packham, Harry 234
Packham, Henry 234, 341
Packham, James 234
Packham, John 234, 236
Packham, Thomas 234, 340
Packham, William 234, 235
Pagden, James 122
Pagden, Peter 123
Page, Thomas 254
Page, William 347
Pain, Thomas 233, 260
Paine, Cornelius 121
Paine, John 121

Paine, Richard 237
Palmer, Robert Rice 119
Palmer, Thomas 118
Pankhurst, John 122
Pannell, Richard 337
Pannett, John 240, 339
Pannett, Sarah 338
Pannett, Thomas 339
Parker, Joseph 232
Parker, Richard 337
Parker, Thomas 232, 234
Parker, William 232
Parlett, Thomas 118
Parlett, William 118
Parsons, Daniel 222
Parsons, William 234
Partington, Thomas 120, 129, 309, 315,
    320, 327, 335, 348
Paskins, John 345
Pattenden, Richard 344
Peachey, John 111, 129, 310, 311, 317,
    320, 324,
Peckham, John 258
Peckham, William 122
Pelham, Henry Cresset 14
Pelham, Rt Hon Lord Thomas, Earl of
    Chichester 1, 105, 214, 291, 325, 327,
    333
Pelland, Edward 232
Penfold, Hugh 119
Penfold, John 183, 234
Penfold, Richard 344
Penfold, William 220
Percival, Spencer 127
Pescot, George 216
Peskett, William 218
Peters, John 118, 346
Peters, Richard 347
Peters, Stephen 235
Pettitt, William 202
Philcox, James 123
Phillips, Henry 205
Phillips, James 293
Philpott, Richard 117
Picknell, Edward 234
Picknell, Samuel 235
Pierce, Caleb 258
Pierrepoint, Revd William 119
Piggott, James 117
Pigou, William Henry 308, 314

Pink, James 236
Pinnix, Edward 117
Pix, Thomas 123
Playsted, Henry 123
Pocock, Thomas 212
Pollard, John 212
Pollard, Thomas 210
Pollington, John 254
Poole, Hugh 122, 214, 273
Poole, Revd Sir Henry J 121, 206, 338
Postlethwaite, Henry 116
Potter, James 232, 240, 241
Potter, John 232
Powell, Richard 337
Poynton, Admiral 240
Poyntz, Walter Stephen 1, 106, 111, 114, 118, 127, 311, 320, 324, 325, 327
Pratt, John 210, 347
Pratt, Thomas 122, 210
Privatt, Thomas 240
Privilly, Thomas 208
Pulford, William 304
Pullen, John 344, 347
Pulteney, Lt Gen Sir James 105, 311, 320, 327, 328, 329
Puttick, John 346
Quantock, John 105, 111, 317
Randall, James 214
Randall, William 236
Rason, Thomas 122
Rason, Walter 122
Raynes, Revd Edward R 120
Read, John 232
Reddish, Revd Thomas 118
Reed 287
Reed, Thomas 204
Reed, William 205
Reeves, John 123, 304
Reeves, Samuel 123, 297
Renville, Jane 242
Restall, John 342
Reynard, William 256
Reynolds, John Clifford 238, 309
Rhodes, James 304
Rice, William 232, 242
Richardson, John 296
Richardson, Thomas 120
Rickman 216
Rickman, Thomas 204, 216
Riddle, Reuben 347

Rideout, Revd John 120
Rideoutt, Revd Richard 124
Rider, Revd Rab Carr 122
Ridge, Ben 122
Ridge, Benjamin 206
Ridge, William 122
Ridley, Thomas 235
Rinchet, John 347
Riste, John 232
Roberts, Clement 119
Roberts, John Pelham 210, 315
Robinson, William 284
Rogers, Thomas 120
Rogers, William 337
Rose, James 232
Rose, Revd 122
Roser, William 204
Roswell, Thomas 204, 205
Roves, Edward 205
Row, Miles 116
Rowland, Mary 224
Rowland, Peter 208, 338, 340
Rowland, Samuel 346
Rowland, William 237
Russell, John 232
Russell, Richard 212
Russell, Thomas 123
Russell, William 117, 234, 240, 287
Sadler, E 336
Sampson, John Tilden 103, 124, 287, 333
Sanders, Thomas 236
Sargent, John 324, 326
Saunder, Joseph 343
Saunders, John 236, 258, 343
Sawyers, William 210
Saxby, Thomas 338
Sayers, Edward 212, 213, 234
Sayers, George 336
Sayers, Henry 242
Sayers, Isaac 242, 340
Sayers, John 118, 119
Sayers, Maurice 118
Scrase, William 120, 205
Scutt 309, 316
Seaton, William 238, 246, 309
Secter, Michael 345
Selmes, Samuel 304
Sennock, Thomas 341
Sergison, Francis 316
Setford, Thomas 339

Seward, Thomas 119
Sewell, Capt William 111, 114, 121, 127, 129, 237, 240, 248, 249, 307, 309, 316, 325, 335, 348
Sewell, Capt William 309
Sewell, Capt William 316
Sewell, Capt William 325
Shackleford, Thomas 222
Shadwell, Henry Thurloe 1, 10, 15, 103, 105, 114, 112, 307, 311, 318, 320, 327, 332, 333, 335, 348
Shadwell, Thomas Lucas 122, 204
Shadwell, William 314
Sharp, Richard 122
Sharpe, William 222
Shaw, Abraham 264
Shaw, John 236
Sheffield, John Lord 14, 15, 105, 111, 123, 307, 308, 315, 318, 333
Shelley, B 119
Shelley, Henry 1, 10, 14, 40, 44, 48, 114, 127, 311, 318, 320, 327,
Shelley, John 202, 203, 206, 339
Shelley, Timothy 106, 111, 114, 119, 311, 320
Sherlock, John 233
Shiffner, Capt George 1, 10, 15, 103, 106, 111, 114, 121, 127, 129, 204, 228, 307, 308, 311, 315, 318, 320, 325, 327, 332, 333, 338
Shirley, John 256
Shirley, William 232, 236
Shirt, William 206
Short, John 235
Shotter, Robert 342
Shotter, William 117
Sicklemore, James 222
Sicklemore, John 216, 340, 341
Sicklemore, William 222
Simmonds, Daniel 120
Simmonds, John 254, 343
Simmonds, William 203, 349
Skinner, John 232
Skinner, Mary 204
Skinner, Richard 119
Smart, William 220
Smith, Albert 208
Smith, Allen 233
Smith, James 272, 341
Smith, John 205, 258, 337

Smith, Joseph 204
Smith, Maj 340
Smith, Robert 121, 212
Smith, Sarah 220
Smith, Thomas 124, 264, 336, 337,
Smith, William 226, 234, 347
Smyth, Walter 14, 106, 111, 327
Snashall, John 206
Snee, John 339
Snelling 349
Snelling, James 234, 348
Snelling, Richard 349
Snelling, William 235
Soper, Thomas 300
Sops, Richard 347
Sowell, William 105
Sparkes, Henry 116
Sparkes, Robert 118
Sparkes, Thomas 117
Spencer, Lord Robert 111
Spratley, Francis 212
Staker, Benjamin 344
Staker, Bernard 118
Staker, John Brown 118
Stammer, John 235
Standen, John 210, 258
Standen, William 236
Standy, Isher 345
Stanford, James 234
Stanford, Stephen 237
Stanford, William 119, 121
Stapeley, John 121
Staples, Richard 216
Stapley, Thomas 254
Steadman, John 237, 262
Steadman, Thomas 240
Steadman, William 237
Stedman, Richard 233
Steele, James Nutley 220
Steele, Jeremiah 280
Steer, Stephen 220
Steere, James 234
Steers, Mrs 348
Stenning, James 234
Stephens, Joseph 226
Stephens, William 314
Stepney, John 232
Stevens, John 122, 256, 260
Stevens, Richard 345
Stevens, William 282

Stewart, Revd John F 119
Steyning, Stephen 345
Stoffell, Stephen 244
Stone, Charles 341
Stone, James 234
Stone, Richard Owen 123
Stone, Thomas 246
Stoner, John 234
Stoner, Robert 236
Stoner, Thomas 235
Stonham, John 123
Stoveld, William 236
Streater, John 235
Streatfield, John 232, 233
Streatfield, Richard 122, 233, 254, 264
Streatfield, William 232
Street, Richard 120
Streeter, Edward 222
Streeter, John 218
Streeter, Richard 222
Strudwick, William 339
Stubbington, John 116
Sturt, John 213
Sumner, William 236
Sutton, Thomas M 127
Symmonds, John 343
Taley, Thomas 210
Tanner, Anthony 208, 209
Tanner, William 121
Targett, William 337
Tate, William 120
Taylor, Elizabeth 224
Taylor, John 237
Taylor, Thomas 119
Taylor, William 236
Terry, Edward 258
Tester, Edward 232, 240, 241, 264
Tester, George 233
Tester, James 232
Tester, Richard 232, 240
Tester, Thomas 242
Tester, William 232, 242
Thomas, George White 111
Thomas, Inigo Freeman 1, 10, 15, 105, 111, 114, 127, 315, 320, 333
Thomas, Sir George 14, 105, 111, 310, 317, 324, 327
Thomset, Joseph 202, 236, 242
Thomson, Samuel 258
Thornton, John 234

Thorpe, Christopher 123
Thorpe, John 123
Thwaites, Revd 117
Tidy, William 240, 246
Till, Richard 345
Tillston, B 212
Tilt, Revd William 208
Timms, J 342
Timms, Thomas 343
Tingley, Joseph 232
Tinley, Henry 214
Tomsett, James 120
Totty, Revd Hugh 123
Tourle, Thomas 202, 256
Tourle, William Knight 204
Tourney, Robert 123
Towers, Revd Johnson 121, 240
Towler, John 116
Townsett, Ann 278
Towse, James 232
Towse, John 118
Tredcroft, Nathaniel 14, 106, 111, 119, 127, 310, 311, 316, 320, 324, 333, 346
Tredcroft, Revd Edward 118
Trew, Thomas 336
Tribe, Robert 342, 343
Trigg, Lucy 220
Trigg, M T 346, 347
Trill, John 121
Tullett, Charles 235
Tullett, Thomas 237
Tulley, John 232, 236
Tulley, Michael 236, 244
Tulley, Mrs 210
Tulley, Philip 236
Turner, James 304
Turner, Jethro 264
Turner, John 117, 119, 256
Turner, Michal 339
Turner, Revd 123
Turner, Thomas 218, 233
Turner, William 233
Twyford, Samuel 4, 105, 111, 342
Tyler, Thomas 337
Upton 116
Upton, Anthony 341
Upton, Charles 234, 341
Upton, James 234
Upton, William 234
Uwins, Richard 234

Uwins, Thomas 236
Vallance, John 121, 212, 213
Vaughans, William 235
Veness, Mary 302
Verrall, George 204
Verrall, John 202, 204
Verrall, Richard 206, 214
Verrall, William 120, 202, 203
Vine 202, 226
Viney, George 337
Virgoe, John 234
Wadey, Thomas 210
Waillard Nicholas 122
Wakelin, Joseph 206
Walder, James 235
Walder, John 240, 242
Walder, Thomas 232
Wales, George 238
Waller, Thomas 232
Walls, Benjamin Kemp 206
Ward, William 238, 309
Wares, Elizabeth 336
Warner, Thomas 222
Warnham, Samuel 236
Warren, Revd Henry 120
Washer, William 122, 272
Waterman, Jonton 205
Waters, Isaac 232
Waters, Michael 232
Waters, William 226
Watling, John 316
Watson, Brooke 114, 129
Watson, George 232
Webb, Henry 120, 204, 205, 338
Webber, George 211
Webber, John 208
Webber, Revd Charles 116
Webber, Samuel 233
Weeden, John 237
Weller, Edward 202, 203, 220
Weller, William 262
Wells, Noah 237
Wells, William 237
Welsh, John 237
Welsh, Nathaniel 242
Wenham, James 204
West, John 236
West, Revd Henry 120
Weston 197
Weston, Henry 258

Weston, J 338
Weston, T 338
Whapham, Samuel 237
Wheeler, Benjamin 233
Wheeler, William 314
Whistler, Revd W 121
Whitcomb, Revd Francis 121
Whitcomb, Thomas 208
White, Charles 119
White, David 341
White, George 345
White, Thomas 336, 337
Whitehurst, John 235
Whiteman, John 216
Whiteman, Thomas Dominick 121
Whiting, William 236, 291
Whitter, William 117
Whyte, Maj Gen John 1, 2, 105, 311, 317, 337
Wickens, Ann 258
Wickens, Samuel 254
Wickens, Thomas 204, 205
Wicker, William 121, 206
Wickham, Henry 208
Wickham, Thomas 210
Wigney, William 212, 213
Wilds, A 200
Wileman, John 242
Wileman, Thomas 238
Wilkins, Jospeh 278
Williams, Revd Charles 117
Wills, George 337
Wilmot, R 37
Wing, John 232
Winton, Francis 204, 205
Wisdom, William 122
Wise, Stephen 118
Witton, Thomas 345
Wood, Henry 237
Wood, James 121, 232, 237, 244
Wood, John 120, 208, 209, 244
Wood, Mary 244
Wood, Peter 236
Wood, Revd Peter 120
Wood, Robert 256
Wood, William 233,
Woodhams, Walter 274
Woodhams, William 122, 123, 274
Woodland, George 129
Woodman, James 232

Woodman, William 232
Woods, Edward 336
Woods, James 117
Woodward 308
Woodward, John 122
Woodward, Revd George 122
Woodward, Revd W P 122
Woodyer, James 235
Wooldridge, Stephen 336
Woolven, Thomas 347
Woolver, Henry 182
Woolver, William 182
Wright, John 340
Wyatt, George 120
Wyatt, Richard 118
Wymark, John 222
Wyndham, George O'Brien, Earl of
    Egremont 1, 10, 105, 111, 114, 119,
    307, 311, 312, 315, 317, 318, 320, 324,
    325, 327
Yaldwin, Richard 118
Yorke, Charles Philip 327, 328
Young, Mrs S 278
Young, Thomas 242

INDEX: PARISHES AND PLACE NAMES

Names have been rationalised to aid searching and, where appropriate, are presented in their modern form (Balcombe, not Balcomb; East Dean not Eastdean; Fernhurst, not Farnhurst; Selsey not Selsea etc). Brighthelmstone is indexed as Brighton, despite the former being more common in the text. Occasional historic references have been retained (e.g. 'Meeching als Newhaven').

Albourne 92, 96, 100, 120, 177, 179, 181, 183, 185, 187, 189, 191
Alciston 50, 54, 58, 122, 266, 267, 269, 271, 272, 274, 278, 282
Aldingbourne 18, 24, 32, 116, 130, 134, 138, 141, 144, 147, 150, 154, 336
Alfriston 52, 56, 58, 122, 266, 267, 269, 271, 272, 274, 278, 282
All Saints Lewes 38, 42, 46, 120, 192, 194, 196, 200, 202, 216, 220, 226
Amberley 80, 84, 88, 118, 161, 163, 165, 167, 169, 171, 173, 175
Ambersham 342
Angmering 78, 82, 86, 118, 160, 162, 164, 166, 168, 170, 172, 174, 346
Appledram 18, 24, 32, 116, 130, 134, 138, 141, 144, 147, 150, 154
Ardingly 40, 44, 48, 121, 230, 232, 238, 239, 240, 246, 248, 340
Arlington 50, 54, 58, 122, 266, 267, 269, 271, 273
Arundel 14, 78, 82, 86, 103, 111, 118, 160, 162, 164, 166, 168, 170, 172, 174, 310, 312, 317, 323, 326, 328, 344
Ashburnham 62, 68, 74, 123, 286, 288, 290, 294, 296, 298, 300, 308
Ashington 92, 96, 100, 120, 177, 179, 181, 183, 185, 187, 189, 191
Ashurst 92, 96, 100, 119, 177, 179, 181, 183, 185, 187, 189, 191
Balcombe 40, 44, 48, 121, 230, 232, 238, 239, 240, 246, 248, 340
Barcombe 38, 42, 46, 120, 192, 194, 196, 200, 204, 216, 220, 228, 338
Barlavington 78, 82, 86, 119, 160, 162, 164, 166, 168, 170, 172, 174
Barnham 78, 82, 86, 118, 160, 162, 164, 166, 168, 170, 172, 174
Battle 14, 66, 72, 76, 124, 287, 289, 292, 295, 297, 299, 302, 308, 325
Beckley 62, 68, 74, 123, 287, 289, 292, 295, 297, 299, 302

Beddingham 52, 56, 58, 122, 266, 268, 270, 271, 273, 276, 280, 284
Beeding Lower 90, 94, 98, 176, 178, 180, 182, 184, 186, 188, 190
Beeding North 119
Beeding South 120
Beeding Upper 90, 94, 98, 176, 178, 180, 182, 184, 186, 188, 190
Bepton 20, 28, 36, 117, 132, 136, 140, 143, 146, 149, 152, 158
Berwick 50, 54, 58, 122, 266, 267, 269, 271, 272, 274, 278, 282
Bexhill 66, 72, 76, 124, 287, 289, 292, 295, 297, 299, 302
Bignor 80, 84, 88, 119, 161, 163, 165, 167, 169, 171, 173, 175
Billingshurst 80, 84, 88, 118, 161, 163, 165, 167, 169, 171, 173, 175
Binderton 20, 26, 34, 117, 131, 136, 139, 142, 145, 148, 151, 156
Binsted 78, 82, 86, 118, 160, 162, 164, 166, 168, 170, 172, 174
Birdham 16, 24, 32, 116, 130, 134, 138, 141, 144, 147, 150, 154
Bishopstone 50, 54, 58, 122, 266, 267, 269, 271, 272, 274, 278, 282
Bletchington 50, 54, 58, 122, 266, 267, 269, 271, 272, 274, 278, 282
Bodiam 64, 70, 76, 123, 287, 289, 292, 295, 297, 299, 302
Bolney 40, 44, 48, 121, 230, 236, 238, 239, 242, 246, 248
Bosham 16, 24, 32, 116, 131, 135, 138, 141, 144, 147, 150, 154
Boxgrove 18, 24, 32, 116, 131, 135, 139, 142, 145, 148, 151, 156, 336, 336
Bramber (North) 323
Bramber (South) 323
Bramber 14, 92, 96, 100, 104, 111, 119, 119, 177, 179, 181, 183, 185, 187, 189, 191, 310, 312, 316, 326, 333, 336

Brede 62, 68, 74, 123, 286, 288, 290, 294, 296, 298, 300
Brightling 64, 70, 76, 124, 287, 289, 292, 295, 297, 299, 302
Brighton 38, 42, 46, 121, 193, 195, 198, 201, 212, 218, 222, 228, 309, 316, 325, 328
Broadwater 90, 94, 98, 120, 176, 178, 180, 182, 184, 186, 188, 190, 344, 344
Burpham 78, 82, 86, 118, 160, 162, 164, 166, 168, 170, 172, 174
Burton 80, 84, 88, 119, 161, 163, 165, 167, 169, 171, 173, 175, 346
Burton Park 348, 348
Burwash 62, 68, 74, 123, 286, 288, 290, 294, 296, 298, 300, 304
Bury 80, 84, 88, 119, 161, 163, 165, 167, 169, 171, 173, 175
Butlers Green 340
Buttolphs 90, 96, 98, 119, 176, 178, 180, 182, 184, 186, 188, 190
Buxted 52, 56, 60, 122, 250, 251, 252, 253, 254, 258, 262, 264
Castle 66, 72, 76, 123, 287, 289, 292, 295, 297, 299, 302
Catsfield 66, 70, 76, 124, 287, 289, 292, 295, 297, 299, 302, 308
Chailey 40, 44, 48, 121, 192, 194, 196, 200, 206, 216, 220, 228, 338, 340
Chalvington 52, 56, 60, 122, 266, 268, 270, 271, 273, 276, 280, 284
Chichester (North) 323
Chichester (South) 323
Chichester 14, 111, 116, 117, 132, 136, 139, 142, 145, 148, 151, 156, 310, 312, 317, 323, 325, 326, 336, 336, 336, 336
Chichester St Andrew 18, 26, 34
Chichester St Bartholomew 18, 26, 34, 117, 132, 136, 139, 142, 145, 148, 151, 156
Chichester St Martin 18, 26, 34
Chichester St Olave 18, 26, 34
Chichester St Pancras & St James 18, 26, 34, 117, 117, 132, 132, 136, 136, 139, 139, 142, 142, 145, 145, 148, 148, 151, 156, 156
Chichester St Peter the Less 18, 26, 34
Chichester Subdeanery 18, 26, 34
Chichester The Close 18, 26, 34, 117, 132, 136, 139, 142, 145, 148, 151, 156

Chichester The Pallant 18, 26, 34
Chiddingly 52, 56, 60, 123, 250, 251, 252, 253, 254, 258, 262, 264
Chidham 16, 24, 32, 116, 131, 135, 138, 141, 144, 147, 150, 154
Chiltington 40, 44, 48, 120, 192, 194, 196, 200, 206, 216, 220, 228, 338, 340
Chithurst 22, 30, 36, 117, 132, 137, 140, 143, 146, 149, 152, 158, 342
Clapham 90, 94, 98, 120, 176, 178, 180, 182, 184, 186, 188, 190
Clayton 40, 44, 46, 121, 193, 195, 198, 201, 210, 218, 222, 228, 338
Cliffe 50, 54, 58, 266, 267, 269, 271, 272, 276, 280, 284
Climping 78, 82, 86, 118, 160, 162, 164, 166, 168, 170, 172, 174
Coates 80, 84, 88, 119, 161, 163, 165, 167, 169, 171, 173, 175
Cocking 20, 28, 36, 117, 132, 136, 140, 143, 146, 149, 152, 158
Coldwaltham 80, 84, 88, 119, 161, 163, 165, 167, 169, 171, 173, 175
Combe 90, 96, 98, 119, 177, 179, 181, 183, 185, 187, 189, 191
Combe Place 325
Compton 20, 26, 34, 117, 131, 135, 139, 142, 145, 148, 151, 156
Cooksbridge 338
Cowfold 92, 96, 100, 119, 177, 179, 181, 183, 185, 187, 189, 191
Crawley 40, 44, 48, 121, 230, 234, 238, 239, 242, 246, 248
Crockerhill 336
Cross in Hand 328, 329
Crowhurst 66, 72, 76, 123, 287, 289, 292, 295, 297, 299, 302
Cuckfield 40, 44, 48, 121, 230, 234, 238, 239, 242, 246, 248, 328, 329, 340
Dallington 64, 70, 76, 123, 286, 288, 290, 294, 296, 298, 300, 304
Danny 325
Denton 50, 54, 58, 122, 266, 267, 269, 271, 272, 274, 278, 282
Didling 22, 30, 36, 117, 132, 136, 140, 143, 146, 149, 152, 158
Ditchling 40, 44, 48, 121, 192, 194, 196, 201, 208, 218, 222, 228, 338, 340
Donnington 18, 24, 32, 116, 130, 134, 138, 141, 144, 147, 150, 154, 336

Duncton 80, 84, 88, 119, 161, 163, 165, 167, 169, 171, 173, 175
Durrington 90, 94, 98, 120, 176, 178, 180, 182, 184, 186, 188, 190
Earnley 16, 24, 32, 116, 130, 134, 138, 141, 144, 147, 150, 154
Eartham 18, 26, 32, 116, 131, 135, 139, 142, 145, 148, 151, 156
Easebourne 20, 28, 36, 117, 132, 136, 140, 143, 146, 149, 152, 158
East Aldrington 40, 44, 46
East Dean 20, 26, 34, 50, 54, 58, 117, 122, 131, 136, 139, 142, 145, 148, 151, 156, 266, 267, 269, 271, 272, 274, 278, 282
East Grinstead 52, 56, 60, 123, 250, 251, 252, 253, 256, 260, 262, 264, 309
East Guldeford 62, 68, 74, 123, 286, 288, 290, 294, 296, 298, 300, 304
East Hoathly 52, 56, 60, 122, 250, 251, 252, 253, 254, 258, 262, 264
East Lavant 16, 24, 32, 116, 131, 135, 139, 142, 145, 148, 151, 156
East Marden 20, 28, 30, 34, 117, 131, 135, 139, 142, 145, 148, 151, 156
East Wittering 16, 24, 32, 116, 130, 134, 138, 141, 144, 147, 150, 154
Eastbourne 50, 54, 58, 122, 266, 267, 269, 271, 272, 274, 278, 282, 315, 325, 328, 342
Eastergate 78, 82, 86, 118, 160, 162, 164, 166, 168, 170, 172, 174
Easthampnett 336
Edburton 90, 94, 98, 120, 176, 178, 180, 182, 184, 186, 188, 190
Egdean 80, 84, 88, 119, 161, 163, 165, 167, 169, 171, 173, 175
Elsted 22, 30, 36, 117, 132, 136, 140, 143, 146, 149, 152, 158
Etchingham 64, 70, 76, 123, 286, 288, 290, 294, 296, 298, 300, 304
Ewhurst 64, 70, 76, 123, 287, 289, 292, 295, 297, 299, 302
Fairlight 64, 70, 74, 123, 287, 289, 292, 295, 297, 299, 302
Falmer 40, 44, 48, 121, 193, 195, 198, 201, 214, 218, 224, 228
Felpham 78, 82, 86, 118, 160, 162, 164, 166, 168, 170, 172, 174
Fernhurst 20, 28, 36, 118, 133, 137, 140, 143, 146, 149, 152, 158, 342

Ferring 78, 82, 86, 118, 160, 162, 164, 166, 168, 170, 172, 174
Findon 90, 94, 98, 120, 176, 178, 180, 182, 184, 186, 188, 190
Fittleworth 80, 84, 88, 119, 161, 163, 165, 167, 169, 171, 173, 175
Fletching 14, 52, 56, 60, 122, 250, 251, 252, 253, 254, 258, 262, 264
Folkington 50, 54, 58, 122, 266, 267, 269, 271, 272, 274, 278, 282
Ford 78, 82, 86, 118, 160, 162, 164, 166, 168, 170, 172, 174, 344
Framfield 52, 56, 60, 122, 250, 251, 252, 253, 254, 258, 262, 264
Frant 52, 56, 60, 123, 250, 251, 252, 253, 260, 262, 264
Friston 50, 54, 58, 122, 266, 267, 269, 271, 272, 274, 278, 282
Frog Farm 346
Fulking 38, 42, 46, 121, 192, 195, 198, 201, 208, 218, 222, 228
Funtington 16, 24, 32, 116, 131, 135, 139, 142, 145, 148, 151, 156
Glynd 50, 54, 58, 122, 266, 267, 269, 271, 272, 276, 280, 284
Goodwood 325
Goring 78, 82, 86, 118, 160, 162, 164, 166, 168, 170, 172, 174
Graffham 20, 28, 36, 117, 132, 136, 140, 143, 146, 149, 152, 158
Gritham 80, 84, 88, 118, 161, 163, 165, 167, 169, 171, 173, 175
Guestling 64, 70, 76, 123, 286, 288, 290, 294, 296, 298, 300
Hailsham 52, 56, 60, 122, 266, 267, 269, 271, 273, 276, 280, 284, 328
Halnaker 336
Hamsey 38, 42, 46, 120, 192, 194, 196, 200, 204, 216, 220, 228, 338
Hangleton 38, 44, 46, 121, 193, 195, 198, 201, 212, 218, 222, 228
Hanmer 193, 195, 198, 201, 218
Hardham 80, 84, 88, 118, 161, 163, 165, 167, 169, 171, 173, 175
Hartfield 52, 56, 60, 123, 250, 251, 252, 253, 256, 260, 262, 264
Harting 22, 30, 36, 117, 132, 136, 140, 143, 146, 149, 152, 158
Hastings 14, 103, 111, 123, 128, 308, 310, 312, 314, 323, 326, 333

Hayton 122, 266, 267, 269, 271, 272, 274, 278, 282
Heathfield 62, 68, 74, 123, 286, 288, 290, 294, 296, 298, 300, 304
Heene 90, 94, 98, 120, 176, 178, 180, 182, 184, 186, 188, 190
Heighton 50, 54, 58
Hellingly 52, 56, 60, 122, 266, 267, 269, 271, 273, 276, 280, 284
Henfield 92, 96, 100, 120, 177, 179, 181, 183, 185, 187, 189, 191, 344
Herstmonceux 123, 286, 288, 290, 294, 296, 298, 300, 308
Heyshott 20, 28, 36, 117, 132, 136, 140, 143, 146, 149, 152, 158
Hollington 66, 72, 76, 123, 287, 289, 292, 295, 297, 299, 302
Horsham 92, 96, 100, 119, 177, 179, 181, 183, 185, 187, 189, 191, 346, 346
Horsted Keynes 52, 56, 60, 123, 250, 251, 252, 253, 256, 260, 264
Houghton 80, 84, 88, 119, 161, 163, 165, 167, 169, 171, 173, 175
Hove 40, 44, 48, 66, 70, 76, 121, 123, 193, 195, 198, 201, 212, 218, 222, 228, 286, 288, 290, 294, 296, 298, 300
Hunston 18, 26, 32, 116, 130, 134, 138, 141, 144, 147, 150, 154, 336, 336, 336
Hurstmonceux 62, 68, 74
Hurstpierpoint 40, 44, 46, 121, 192, 195, 198, 201, 208, 210, 218, 222, 228, 338, 340
Icklesham 64, 70, 76, 123, 286, 288, 290, 294, 296, 298, 300
Iden 62, 68, 74, 123, 286, 288, 290, 294, 296, 298, 300, 304
Ifield 90, 94, 98, 119, 176, 178, 180, 182, 184, 186, 188, 190
Iford 38, 42, 46, 120, 128, 192, 194, 196, 200, 202, 216, 220, 226
Iping 20, 28, 36, 117, 132, 137, 140, 143, 146, 149, 152, 158, 342
Isfield 52, 56, 60, 122, 250, 251, 252, 253, 254, 258, 262, 264
Itchenor 16, 24, 32
Itchingfield 90, 94, 98, 119, 176, 178, 180, 182, 184, 186, 188, 190
Jevington 50, 54, 58, 122, 266, 267, 269, 271, 272, 274, 278, 282

Keymer 40, 44, 46, 121, 192, 195, 198, 201, 208, 218, 222, 228, 340
Kingston 38, 42, 46, 78, 82, 86, 118, 120, 128, 160, 162, 164, 166, 168, 170, 172, 174, 192, 194, 196, 200, 202, 216, 220, 226
Kingston by Sea 90, 94, 98, 120, 176, 178, 180, 182, 184, 186, 188, 190
Kirdford 80, 84, 88, 119, 161, 163, 165, 167, 169, 171, 173, 175
Lancing 90, 94, 98, 120, 176, 178, 180, 182, 184, 186, 188, 190
Laughton 52, 56, 60, 122, 266, 268, 270, 271, 273, 276, 280, 284
Leominster 78, 82, 86, 118, 160, 162, 164, 166, 168, 170, 172, 174, 344
Lewes (North) 323
Lewes (South) 323
Lewes 14, 103, 111, 120, 121, 129, 308, 310, 312, 315, 316, 326, 328, 333, 340
Lewes St John 120, 196, 200, 216, 220, 226
Lewes St Michael 38, 42, 46, 120, 192, 194, 196, 200, 202, 216, 220, 226
Lewes St Peter & St Mary Westout 38, 42, 46, 120, 192, 194, 196, 200, 202, 216, 220, 226
Linch 20, 28, 36, 117
Linchmere 22, 30, 36, 342
Lindfield 52, 56, 60, 123, 250, 251, 252, 253, 256, 260, 264
Little Horsted 52, 56, 60, 122, 250, 251, 252, 253, 254, 258, 262, 264
Littlehampton 78, 82, 86, 118, 160, 162, 164, 166, 168, 170, 172, 174, 325, 346
Littlington 50, 54, 58, 122, 266, 267, 269, 271, 272, 274, 278, 282
Lodsworth 22, 30, 36, 118, 133, 137, 140, 143, 146, 149, 152, 158
Lullington 50, 56, 58, 122, 266, 267, 269, 271, 272, 274, 278, 282
Lurgashall 80, 84, 88, 119, 161, 163, 165, 167, 169, 171, 173, 175
Lynch 132, 136, 140, 143, 146, 149, 152, 158
Lynchmere 118, 133, 137, 140, 143, 146, 149, 152, 158
Madehurst 78, 82, 86, 118, 160, 162, 164, 166, 168, 170, 172, 174
Maresfield 52, 56, 60, 122, 250, 251, 252, 253, 254, 258, 262, 264, 328, 329

Mayfield 52, 56, 60, 123, 250, 251, 252, 253, 254, 258, 262, 264
Meeching als Newhaven 38, 42, 46
Merston 18, 26, 34, 116, 130, 134, 138, 141, 144, 147, 150, 154
Mid Lavant 20, 28, 34, 116, 131, 135, 139, 142, 145, 148, 151, 156, 336
Middleton 78, 82, 86, 118, 160, 162, 164, 166, 168, 170, 172, 174
Midhurst & St John's 20, 28, 36, 117, 117, 132, 136, 140, 143, 146, 149, 152, 158, 325
Mountfield 64, 70, 76, 124, 287, 289, 292, 295, 297, 299, 302
Mouscombe 191
New Fishbourne 18, 26, 34, 116, 131, 135, 138, 141, 144, 147, 150, 154
New Shoreham 92, 96, 100, 120, 177, 179, 181, 183, 185, 187, 189, 191
Newhaven 120, 128, 192, 194, 196, 200, 202, 216, 220, 226
Newick 38, 42, 46, 121, 192, 194, 196, 200, 206, 216, 220, 228, 338, 338
Newick Park 338
Newtimber 38, 42, 46, 121, 192, 195, 198, 201, 208, 218, 222, 228
Ninfield 66, 70, 76, 123, 286, 288, 290, 294, 296, 298, 300, 308
North Marden 20, 28, 34, 117, 131, 135, 139, 142, 145, 148, 151, 156
North Mundham 18, 26, 34, 116, 130, 134, 138, 141, 144, 147, 150, 154
North Stoke 78, 82, 86, 118, 160, 162, 164, 166, 168, 170, 172, 174
Northchapel 80, 84, 88, 119, 161, 163, 165, 167, 169, 171, 173, 175
Northease 338
Northiam 64, 70, 76, 123, 287, 289, 292, 295, 297, 299, 302, 308
Nuthurst 90, 94, 98, 119, 176, 178, 180, 182, 184, 186, 188, 190
Offham 338
Offington Place 344
Old Shoreham 90, 94, 98, 120, 176, 178, 180, 182, 184, 186, 188, 190
Ore 66, 72, 76, 123, 287, 289, 292, 295, 297, 299, 302
Oving 18, 26, 34, 116, 130, 134, 138, 141, 144, 147, 150, 154, 336, 336

Ovingdean 40, 44, 48, 121, 193, 195, 198, 201, 214, 218, 224, 228
Pagham 16, 24, 32, 116, 130, 134, 138, 141, 144, 147, 150, 154
Parham 80, 84, 88, 118, 161, 163, 165, 167, 169, 171, 173, 175, 325
Patcham 38, 42, 46, 121, 193, 195, 198, 201, 212, 218, 222, 228
Patching 92, 96, 100, 120, 177, 179, 181, 183, 185, 187, 189, 191
Peasmarsh 62, 68, 74, 123, 286, 288, 290, 294, 296, 298, 300, 304
Penhurst 64, 70, 76, 124, 287, 289, 292, 295, 297, 299, 302, 308
Pett 64, 70, 76, 123, 286, 288, 290, 294, 296, 298, 300
Petworth 14, 78, 82, 86, 119, 160, 162, 164, 166, 168, 170, 172, 174, 325, 348
Pevensey 14, 103, 111, 122, 308, 310, 312, 314, 315, 326, 328
Piddinghoe 38, 42, 46, 120, 128, 192, 194, 196, 200, 204, 216, 220, 228
Piecomb 38, 42, 46, 121, 193, 195, 198, 201, 210, 218, 222, 228
Playden 62, 68, 74, 123, 286, 288, 290, 294, 296, 298, 300, 304
Plumpton 40, 44, 48, 120, 192, 194, 196, 200, 206, 216, 220, 228
Poling 78, 82, 86, 118, 160, 162, 164, 166, 168, 170, 172, 174
Portslade 38, 42, 46, 121, 193, 195, 198, 201, 212, 218, 222, 228
Poynings 38, 42, 46, 121, 192, 195, 198, 201, 208, 218, 222, 228
Preston 40, 44, 48, 78, 82, 86, 118, 121, 160, 162, 164, 166, 168, 170, 172, 174, 193, 195, 198, 201, 212, 218, 222, 228
Pulborough 80, 84, 88, 118, 161, 163, 165, 167, 169, 171, 173, 175
Racton 20, 28, 34, 117, 131, 135, 139, 142, 145, 148, 151, 156
Rawmere 336
Ringmer 50, 54, 58, 122, 266, 267, 269, 271, 272, 276, 278, 282
Ripe 52, 56, 60, 122, 266, 268, 270, 271, 273, 276, 280, 284
Rodmell 38, 42, 46, 120, 128, 192, 194, 196, 200, 202, 216, 220, 226
Rogate 22, 30, 36, 117, 132, 137, 140, 143, 146, 149, 152, 158

Rotherfield 52, 56, 60, 123, 250, 251, 252, 253, 254, 258, 262, 264
Rottingdean 40, 44, 48, 121, 193, 195, 198, 201, 214, 218, 224, 228, 340
Rudgwick 92, 96, 100, 119, 177, 179, 181, 183, 185, 187, 189, 191
Rumboldsweek 18, 26, 34, 116, 130, 134, 138, 141, 144, 147, 150, 154
Rusper 90, 94, 98, 119, 176, 178, 180, 182, 184, 186, 188, 190
Rustington 78, 82, 86, 118, 160, 162, 164, 166, 168, 170, 172, 174, 346
Salehurst 64, 70, 76, 123, 286, 288, 290, 294, 296, 298, 300, 304
Seaford 328
Sedlescombe 64, 70, 76, 124, 287, 289, 292, 295, 297, 299, 302
Selham 22, 30, 36, 117, 132, 136, 140, 143, 146, 149, 152, 158
Selmeston 50, 54, 58, 122, 266, 267, 269, 271, 272, 274, 278, 282
Selsey 16, 24, 32, 116, 130, 134, 138, 141, 144, 147, 150, 154
Shermanbury 92, 96, 100, 119, 177, 179, 181, 183, 185, 187, 189, 191
Shipley 92, 96, 100, 119, 177, 179, 181, 183, 185, 187, 189, 191
Shopwick 336
Shoreham 191, 309, 328, 344
Sidlesham 16, 24, 32, 116, 129, 130, 134, 138, 141, 144, 147, 150, 154
Singleton 20, 28, 34, 117, 131, 136, 139, 142, 145, 148, 151, 156
Slaugham 40, 44, 48, 121, 230, 236, 238, 239, 242, 246, 248
Slindon 16, 24, 32, 116, 131, 135, 139, 142, 145, 148, 151, 156
Slinfold 92, 96, 100, 119, 177, 179, 181, 183, 185, 187, 189, 191
Sompting 90, 94, 98, 120, 176, 178, 180, 182, 184, 186, 188, 190
South Bersted 16, 24, 32, 116, 130, 134, 138, 141, 144, 147, 150, 154
South Malling 50, 54, 58, 122, 266, 267, 269, 271, 272, 276, 278, 282
South Pevensey 323
South Stoke 78, 82, 86, 118, 160, 162, 164, 166, 168, 170, 172, 174
Southease 38, 42, 46, 120, 128, 192, 194, 196, 200, 204, 216, 220, 226, 228, 338
Southover 120, 128, 192, 194, 196, 200, 202, 216, 220
Southwick 90, 94, 98, 120, 176, 178, 180, 182, 184, 186, 188, 190
St John the Baptist Southover 38, 42, 46
St John under the Castle Lewes 38, 42, 46, 192, 194
St Leonards 66, 72, 76, 123, 287, 289, 292, 295, 297, 299, 302
St Thomas in the Cliffe 122
Stanmer 50, 54, 58, 121, 122, 214, 224, 228, 266, 267, 269, 271, 273, 276, 280, 284
Stedham 22, 30, 36, 117, 132, 137, 140, 143, 146, 149, 152, 158
Steyning 14, 92, 96, 100, 119, 177, 179, 181, 183, 185, 187, 189, 191, 309, 344
Stopham 80, 84, 88, 119, 161, 163, 165, 167, 169, 171, 173, 175
Storrington 80, 84, 88, 118, 161, 163, 165, 167, 169, 171, 173, 175, 346, 348
Stoughton 20, 28, 34, 117, 131, 135, 139, 142, 145, 148, 151, 156
Street 40, 44, 48, 121, 192, 194, 196, 201, 206, 218, 220, 228, 338
Strettington 336, 336
Sullington 90, 94, 98, 176, 178, 180, 182, 184, 186, 188, 190, 348
Sullington North 119
Sullington South 120
Sutton 80, 84, 88, 119, 161, 163, 165, 167, 169, 171, 173, 175
Tangmere 16, 24, 32, 116, 130, 134, 138, 141, 144, 147, 150, 154, 336, 336
Tarring 50, 54, 58, 92, 96, 100, 120, 122, 177, 179, 181, 183, 185, 187, 189, 191, 266, 267, 269, 271, 272, 274, 278, 282
Telscombe 38, 42, 46, 120, 128, 192, 194, 196, 200, 204, 216, 220, 228
Terwick 22, 30, 36, 117, 132, 137, 140, 143, 146, 149, 152, 158
Thakeham 90, 94, 98, 119, 176, 178, 180, 182, 184, 186, 188, 190
The Hook 338
Ticehurst 62, 68, 74, 123, 286, 288, 290, 294, 296, 298, 300, 304
Tillington 78, 82, 86, 119, 160, 162, 164, 166, 168, 170, 172, 174, 346, 346, 348
Toddington 344

Tortington 78, 82, 86, 118, 160, 162, 164, 166, 168, 170, 172, 174
Treyford 22, 30, 36, 117, 132, 136, 140, 143, 146, 149, 152, 158
Trotton 22, 30, 36, 117, 132, 137, 140, 143, 146, 149, 152, 158, 342
Twineham 40, 44, 48, 121, 230, 236, 238, 239, 244, 246, 248
Twyford Lodge 325
Uckfield 52, 56, 60, 122, 250, 251, 252, 253, 254, 258, 262, 264
Udimore 62, 68, 74, 123, 286, 288, 290, 294, 296, 298, 300
Up Marden 20, 28, 34, 117, 131, 135, 139, 142, 145, 148, 151, 156
Upwaltham 18, 26, 34, 117, 131, 136, 139, 142, 145, 148, 151, 156
Wadhurst 52, 56, 60, 123, 250, 251, 252, 253, 254, 258, 262, 264
Walberton 78, 82, 86, 118, 160, 162, 164, 166, 168, 170, 172, 174, 344
Waldron 52, 56, 60, 123, 250, 251, 252, 253, 254, 258, 262, 264
Warbleton 62, 68, 74, 123, 286, 288, 290, 294, 296, 298, 300, 304
Warminghurst 90, 94, 98, 120, 176, 178, 180, 182, 184, 186, 188, 190
Warnham 90, 94, 98, 119, 176, 178, 180, 182, 184, 186, 188, 190, 346
Warningcamp 78, 82, 86, 118, 160, 162, 164, 166, 168, 170, 172, 174
Wartling 62, 68, 74, 123, 286, 288, 290, 294, 296, 298, 300, 308
Washington 90, 94, 98, 119, 176, 178, 180, 182, 184, 186, 188, 190
West Blatchington 38, 42, 46, 121, 193, 195, 198, 201, 212, 218, 222, 228
West Chiltington 80, 84, 88, 118, 161, 163, 165, 167, 169, 171, 173, 175
West Dean 20, 28, 36, 50, 54, 58, 117, 122, 131, 136, 139, 142, 145, 148, 151, 156, 266, 267, 269, 271, 272, 274, 278, 282
West Firle 52, 56, 58, 122, 266, 268, 270, 271, 273, 276, 280, 284
West Grinstead 92, 96, 100, 119, 177, 179, 181, 183, 185, 187, 189, 191
West Hoathly 40, 44, 48, 121, 230, 232, 238, 239, 240, 246, 248, 309

West Itchenor 116, 130, 134, 138, 141, 144, 147, 150, 154
West Lavant 16, 24, 32
West Stoke 16, 24, 32, 116, 131, 133, 135, 139, 142, 145, 148, 151, 156
West Tarring 344
West Thorney 16, 24, 32, 116, 131, 135, 138, 141, 144, 147, 150, 154
West Wittering 16, 24, 32, 116, 130, 134, 138, 141, 144, 147, 150, 154
Westbourne 20, 28, 34, 117, 131, 135, 139, 142, 145, 148, 151, 156
Westfield 66, 72, 76, 123, 287, 289, 292, 295, 297, 299, 302
Westhampnett 18, 26, 34, 116, 131, 135, 139, 142, 145, 148, 151, 156
Westmeston 40, 44, 48, 121, 192, 194, 196, 201, 206, 218, 220, 228, 338
Whatlington 66, 72, 76, 124, 287, 289, 292, 295, 297, 299, 302
Wiggenholt 80, 84, 88, 118, 161, 163, 165, 167, 169, 171, 173, 175
Willingdon 50, 54, 58, 122, 266, 267, 269, 271, 272, 274, 278, 282
Wilmington 50, 54, 58, 122, 266, 267, 269, 271, 272, 274, 278, 282
Wisborough Green 80, 84, 88, 119, 161, 163, 165, 167, 169, 171, 173, 175
Wiston 90, 94, 98, 120, 176, 178, 180, 182, 184, 186, 188, 190
Withyham 52, 56, 60, 123, 250, 251, 252, 253, 256, 260, 262, 264
Wivelsfield 40, 44, 48, 121, 192, 194, 196, 200, 206, 218, 220, 228, 338
Woodhorne 336
Woodmancote 92, 96, 100, 120, 177, 179, 181, 183, 185, 187, 189
Woolbeding 22, 30, 36, 117, 132, 137, 140, 143, 146, 149, 152, 158
Woollavington 80, 84, 88, 119, 161, 163, 165, 167, 169, 171, 173, 175, 346
Worth 40, 44, 48, 121, 230, 234, 238, 239, 240, 246, 248, 309
Worthing 328
Yapton 78, 82, 86, 118, 160, 162, 164, 166, 168, 170, 172, 174, 344